ARISTOTLE'S POLITICS

ARISTOTLE'S POLITICS

Living Well and Living Together

EUGENE GARVER

THE UNIVERSITY OF CHICAGO PRESS

CHICAGO AND LONDON

The University of Chicago Press, Chicago 60637
The University of Chicago Press, Ltd., London
© 2011 by The University of Chicago
All rights reserved. Published 2011.
Paperback edition 2014
Printed in the United States of America

20 19 18 17 16 15 14   2 3 4 5 6

ISBN-13: 978-0-226-28402-6 (cloth)
ISBN-13: 978-0-226-15498-5 (paper)
ISBN-13: 978-0-226-28404-0 (e-book)
10.7208/chicago/9780226284040.001.0001

Library of Congress Cataloging-in-Publication Data

Garver, Eugene.
    Aristotle's Politics: living well and living together / Eugene Garver.
        p. cm.
    "Completes a trilogy on Aristotle: Aristotle's Rhetoric: an art of character
(University of Chicago Press, 1994) and Confronting Aristotle's Ethics: ancient and
modern morality (University of Chicago Press, 2006) were the first two books in
the series"—Preliminaries.
    Includes bibliographical references and index.
    ISBN-13: 978-0-226-28402-6 (hardcover : alk. paper)
    ISBN-10: 0-226-28402-6 (hardcover : alk. paper)   1. Aristotle. Politics.
2. Aristotle—Political and social views. 3. Political science.   I. title.
    JC71.A7G37 2011
    320.01'1—dc22
                                                                    2011013137

CONTENTS

ACKNOWLEDGMENTS

I have been thinking about Aristotle for more than half my life. My first paper on the *Politics* was published over fifteen years ago. I fear that this means that it is very probable that there are people I should thank whom I have forgotten. Some of the deepest influences have been so completely incorporated into my own thinking that I can't even remember them as influences.

I can at least thank some conversation partners, including Lenn Goodman, Ed Halper, and David O'Connor. I'm glad that David Depew still has not published most of his work on the *Politics*; we have had so many productive discussions over so many years that I'm not sure I would have been able to produce this book if he had gotten there first. The Aristotle reading group at the University of Minnesota, especially Betty Belfiore, Norman Dahl, and Sandra Peterson, has been just the right kind of critical yet sympathetic audience for many inchoate ideas, forcing me to translate them from mentalese into something like English. Along with the other members of the Minnesota Conference on Ancient Philosophy, what Peterson calls the Minnestoa, they heard early versions of several of my chapters and forced me to clarify things further. David Keyt and Lenn Goodman were very helpful referees for the Press. Joan Spring acted as a conscientious copy editor.

My earlier thinking on Book I appeared as "Aristotle's Natural Slaves: Incomplete *Praxeis* and Incomplete Human Beings," *Journal of the History of Philosophy* 32 (1994): 1–22, and in "Aristotle and the Will to Power: Character and Reason in Slavery and Freedom," *Philosophy and the Contemporary World* 13 (2006): 74–83. My thoughts on Book III appeared as "*Politics* III and the Incompleteness of the Normative," *Ancient Philosophy* 18 (1998): 381–416. I prematurely offered part of what is now chapter 4 to a very lively group of scholars at Marquette University in 2008. I had the chance to reflect on Book V in three papers: "The Uses and Abuses of Philosophy: *Politics* V as an Example," *History of Political Thought* 26 (2005): 189–208, "Factions and the Paradox of Aristotelian Practical Science," *Polis* 22 (2005): 181–205, and "The Revolt of the Just," *Aristotle's Politics and Contemporary Politics*, ed. Lenn Goodman and Robert Tallesio, 93–108 (Albany: SUNY Press, 2007). Thanks to referees and editors of all those journals. Not too many traces of those papers appear, at least on the surface, in the present volume. Some of the material in chapter 6 appeared first in *Boston Area Colloquium on Ancient Philosophy* 26 (2009): 229–249. Thornton Lockwood, my commentator, and David Roochnik, my host at Boston University, offered very useful and stimulating comments.

Because I've been thinking and writing about the *Politics* for so long, there is little correspondence between the secondary works I have learned the most from and those I cite in the notes. My failure to cite something is no sign that I haven't read it or learned from it. I've always thought that Aristotle and I are personae enough and that nothing much is advanced by my also arguing with what others have had to say about him.

Also because this project has taken so long to complete, I have at different times looked at and used a variety of translations of the *Politics* alongside the Greek text. Different translators often bring to the foreground different aspects of Aristotle's ideas that I would miss by simply relying on the Greek, so I am grateful to all those who have gone before me.

This volume completes a trilogy that began with *Aristotle's Rhetoric: An Art of Character* and continued with *Confronting Aristotle's Ethics: Ancient and Modern Morality*, both published by the University of Chicago Press. I now hope to be finished with Aristotle. He's inhabited my mind for long enough.

It is with great sorrow that I dedicate this book to the memory of my wife, Jane Bennett.

Caelo	*On the Heavens [De Caelo]*
Cat.	*Categories*
de An.	*de Anima*
Gen. Corr.	*De Generatione et Corruptione*
EE	*Eudemian Ethics*
GA	*Generation of Animals*
HA	*History of Animals*
Met.	*Metaphysics*
NE	*Nicomachean Ethics*
PA.	*De Partibus Animalium*
Ph.	*Physics*
Poet	*Poetics*
Pol.	*Politics*
Rh.	*Rhetoric*
Top.	*Topics*

Aristotle's *Politics*:
Living Well and Living Together

"$\mathbf{M}$an is a political animal" (*politikon ho anthrōpos zōon*). The whole of the *Politics* thinks through the meaning and implication of the idea that human beings are political animals. Aristotle identifies the problems of political life, and offers solutions. My aims are more modest. I try to identify problems with Aristotle's text, and offer solutions. If Aristotle and I are any good, understanding Aristotle's argument will tell us something not only about Aristotle's thought but also about the problems of living together.[1]

To understand Aristotle's project we have to make sense of the relations among (1) political philosophy, (2) the practical wisdom of the statesman, and (3) political action. My book differs from others by drawing this picture explicitly, which lets me articulate the complex relations among those three activities. Noting similarities and differences between the *Politics* and the *Ethics* will occupy a large part of this book, but for now I simply assert that I will show that the relation among those three is quite different from the parallel relation between (1) ethical philosophy, (2) the practical wisdom of the virtuous person, and (3) practical action. Philosophy, that is, plays a different role in understanding how to live well together than it does in an individual's understanding of how to live well—not only, I will argue, a different role but a greater role.

My book has six chapters. Each chapter concerns a problem that animates a book of the *Politics*; each problem turns on the relations among political philosophy, the practical wisdom of the statesman, and political action, and on the varying connections between ethics and politics. Each raises a question of what it means for people to be political animals; each shows something more about how political philosophy can be practical. The *Politics* contains eight books. I treat Book VI as an appendix to Book V, and Book VIII as a continuation of Book VII. Book VI also remains for me the least philosophically exciting thing Aristotle ever wrote. No doubt it is my fault for failing to see its interest, but I await someone to show me what I'm missing. The other six books of the *Politics* are the focus of one chapter each. Instead of summarizing each of my chapters, I will very briefly note those six specific problems that I find at the center of Aristotle's argument in each book. Next, I will jump to a crucial passage in the middle of the *Politics* that systematically articulates the ambiguity in the idea of a best constitution. That leads, third, to a preliminary statement about the complex interrelations between ethics and politics. The introduction ends with my picture of how understanding the *Politics* can tell us something about politics itself.

I. SIX CHAPTERS TO LIVING WELL AND LIVING TOGETHER

Chapter 1. If man is a political animal, why do so few people live in poleis, and so few of them live as citizens? (Even worse, as we will see later, the better the polis, the fewer of its residents qualify as citizens.) By looking at Aristotle's two brief accounts of slavery, in Books I and VII, I argue that the real problem the statesman needs to worry about is not slavery but despotism or mastery. In *Politics* I, Aristotle affirms a principle he also endorses elsewhere, that different functions should be assigned to different people (I.2.1252b1–5). No one can be both a master and a slave, or a husband and wife, or a ruler and someone ruled. There is one conspicuous violation of this principle. Heads of households, who are masters of slaves, are also citizens. Some nineteenth-century abolitionists argued that the ethical cast of mind necessary for slavery and for citizenship are mutually exclusive, but Aristotle argues in Book VII that the same abilities lead to both mutuality and friendship and to domination. Book I sets the tone for the rest of the *Politics* by posing the relation between living and living well as the relation between economic and political institutions and desires. *The practical problem of politics is how to form a community that aims at a common good out of people with the capacity and so the permanent possibility of aiming at despotism instead.*

Chapter 2. Politics II differs from Aristotle's treatments of earlier thinkers in his other works. In the *Ethics* only virtuous people are worth listening to, but here his standards seem more open. The *Ethics* explores the best human life, which already exists, while in the *Politics* the best state will not necessarily have much resemblance to any existing state. Since there is agreement on what the best life is, only those who live it have anything worthwhile to say. Without agreement on the best constitution, Aristotle in the *Politics* will listen to anyone. *He listens to a variety of opinions and looks at a similar variety of constitutions, real and imagined, to address his central question for the ideal state: What do people need to have in common in order to live together in a political community?* Instead of pointing to shared values, common ancestry, a shared history, or even a common enemy, Aristotle narrows the question to a consideration of property, the ways it should be private and how it should be common. I want to find the strengths and weaknesses of this narrowing.

Chapter 3. While modern constitutional thought looks for a single correct framework that will let people pursue a variety of good lives, Aristotle's thought is just the reverse: there is a single best life, but a variety of correct constitutions. *Therefore the subject of my third chapter is: Why doesn't knowledge of the best life lead directly to a single best form of politics? The solution turns on the relation between political philosophy and the knowledge of the statesman.* All constitutions embody a conception of justice, and all of them, he says, fall short of true justice. "All men hold that justice is some kind of equality. . . . What we have to discover is equality and inequality for what sort of persons. That is difficult, and calls for political philosophy" (III.12.1282b18–23). The philosopher articulates the true nature of justice, but the statesman is always stuck with a partial idea of justice. That difference creates problems for seeing what the statesman is to do with the knowledge offered by the philosopher.

Chapter 4. Book IV begins with the claim that any complete science or art has to allow the practitioner four distinct orientations to the best—the best absolutely, the best in general, the best in particular circumstances, and the "best on a hypothesis." This programmatic statement organizes the rest of the *Politics*, Books IV–VIII, but in complicated ways that illuminate the nature of practical thinking about politics. Each part of the *Politics* devoted to one of the kinds of best will identify a best constitution, but none of these best constitutions is easy to trace back to the three correct constitutions listed in Book III.

I will look at his distinction of the four kinds of best in the next part of this introduction. In chapter 4 proper, I will examine Book IV's most impressive achievement as *Aristotle shows the statesman how to construct a constitution and a way of life ethically superior to the citizens who comprise the state.*

Chapter 5. Book V narrows the focus of the statesman to preserving whatever constitution exists. It is hard to see how such a constrained vision can generate anything other than an amoral project of erecting *raison d'état*

into an ultimate value. In such circumstances it is hard to see how political philosophy can be something other than either reason in the service of
partisan interests, or, even worse, some neutral arbiter that will usurp the
role of the practical politician. I approach that problem by focusing on an
anomaly in Aristotle's treatment of factions and stasis. Regardless of how
just or deviant a given constitution is, Aristotle writes as though preserving it is good and destroying it is bad. The programmatic statement at the
beginning of Book V presents preservation and destruction as alternatives,
with the former always to be pursued; improvement of the existing constitution is not listed as an alternative. The relation between preservation and
reform is the subject of my fifth chapter. Seeing how Aristotle advises the
statesman to deal with factions will lead to the surprising conclusion that
*only the statesman can be in a position to improve common life, and does
so by aiming at stability.*

Chapter 6. Books VII and VIII concern the ideal state. *They raise the
question of how life and virtue can be practical without being responsive
to undesirable conditions.* Without some evil to battle against, is anything
left of goodness? If we can imagine a world in which justice is not needed
because there are no injustices to correct, and generosity unnecessary because there is no one around in need of help, would there be any worthwhile
practical action left? It is easier and more common for people to be virtuous
in times of war than peace, in part because what virtue requires in times of
need is more obvious than what the good person does in times of leisure.
While Aristotle has no interest in Plato's philosopher-kings, it seems as
though the ideal state leaves no problems for the statesman except philosophical ones.[2]

II. BOOK IV.1–2: THE FOUR KINDS OF BEST AND ARISTOTLE'S FOUR CAUSES

How is the *Politics* at the same time philosophical and practical? More generally, how can reasoning be practical? The start of Book IV gives Aristotle's
answer. The first two chapters begin by announcing: "in all the arts and sciences which embrace the whole of any subject, and do not come into being
in a fragmentary way, it is the province of a single art or science to consider
all that appertains to a single subject" (IV.1.1288b1). Any such complete
art or science has to do four things, which Aristotle first enumerates for
gymnastics and then three times for politics (1288b13–20, 1288b21–34,
1288b37–39, 2.1289b13–26). These will be four different ways in which philosophy can be practical.

Unfortunately, as usual Aristotle's answer has to be teased out from what he gives us. While he says that gymnastics, medicine, shipbuilding, tailoring, and "every other art" have the same requirements in order to be complete, he gives no indication that he himself follows such a procedure in any other art or science. Nor does he tell us how the rest of the *Politics* will be organized around the four kinds of best.

I here collect the different descriptions of those four inquiries. Aristotle lists them four times, but he shuffles their order. I will list them in the order Aristotle uses the first time he presents them for politics. Within each of the four, the first will be Aristotle's description of the four orientations of gymnastics, and the other three will be his three political enumerations.

1. (a) that which is best (for the best is necessarily fitting for the body that is naturally the finest and the most finely equipped.
   (b) what the best regime (*politeia*) is, and what quality it should have to be what one would pray for above all, with external things providing no impediment
   (c) the best regime
   (d) [no description offered][3]

2. (a) what sort of training is advantageous for what sort of body
   (b) which regime is fitting for which cities—for it is perhaps impossible for many to obtain the best . . . the best that circumstances allow
   (c) the regime that is [the best] possible
   (d) which of the others [beside the best constitution] is choiceworthy for which [cities]—for perhaps democracy is more necessary for some than oligarchy, and for others the latter more than the former

3. (a) which is best—a single one for all—for most bodies
   (b) the regime that is most fitting for all cities
   (c) the regime that is easier and more attainable for all
   (d) the regime that is the most attainable and that is the most choice worthy after the best regime, and if there is some other that is aristocratic and finely constituted but fitting for most cities

4. (a) if someone should desire neither the disposition nor the knowledge befitting those connected with competitions
   (b) the regime based on a presupposition—for any given regime should be studied, both how it might arise initially and in what manner it might be preserved for the longest time once in existence (I am speaking of the case where a city happens neither to

be governed by the best regime—and is not equipped even with
the things necessary for it—nor to be governed by the regime that
is [the best] possible among existing ones, but one that is poorer

(c) [not described, unless it is the regime that is easier, as opposed to
more attainable for all]

(d) the sources of destruction and preservation for regimes both in
general and in the case of each separately, and the reasons for
which these things particularly come about in accordance with
the nature of the matter.

The four inquiries he outlines correspond to the four causes.[4] The first, "that
which is best in the abstract" (haplōs) (1288b26), orients politics around the
end of politics, that is, the best life. The second, the best relative to circumstances, starts with the material cause and organizes political inquiry
around the best that can be made out of given material. The third, the best
on a hypothesis, starts not from the true end of politics, but any posited end,
and so looks for means and devices that will preserve any given constitution. The final inquiry, the search for "the form of constitution which is
best suited to states in general," articulates a formal cause that can organize
almost any material, any kind of people. Each inquiry is oriented to a different value, to the best, the possible, the easy, and the common (ou gar
monon tēēn aristēēn dei theōrein, alla kai tēēn dynatēēn, homoiōs de kai
tēēn raōi kai koinoteran hapasais) (1288b37–38).[5]

In chapter 4, I will show how those four orientations organize Politics
IV–VIII. More pertinent for our purposes here is how these four inquiries
are practical in different ways. The best haplōs, which he also describes as
the best in our prayers (IV.1.1288b23, see too II.1.1260b29, II.6.1265a17–18,
IV.1295a29, IV.1325b36), presents the best polis as derived from its final
cause, virtue and happiness. This is the subject of Books VII and VIII. The
simply best state depends on conditions that cannot be the object of deliberation and planning. Therefore, one of the outstanding questions I will have
to address in my final chapter is how knowledge of the city of our prayers
can be practical, and why the statesman needs knowledge of such a thing.

The second most clearly practical use of political philosophy comes in
Books V and VI. To see how to constitute a state under some given conditions, the best on a hypothesis, Aristotle directs attention to the best application of efficient causes. The statesman here is like the gymnastics coach
whose client wants to be in the best possible shape after years of neglect,
and who is willing to do what it takes to get into good shape as long as it
doesn't take more than twenty minutes a day and doesn't involve stopping

smoking. If the challenge to the best absolutely was to see how such knowledge can have anything to do with action, the challenge here is for the statesman to do anything other than pander, giving the people what they want, which is the accusation Socrates levels against the rhetoricians as sham politicians in the *Gorgias*. Does the person of practical wisdom need to know the devices of cleverness as Gorgias's physician-brother is impotent without arts of persuasion? The statesman meets that challenge by aiming not at happiness but at stability and preservation of the given constitution in the face of factions and the threat of revolution. Books V and VI break down the distinction between preserving an existing constitution and improving it. The best state is the most stable one. Political philosophy gives the statesman a target, stability, and a set of resources for reaching it.

These are the two obvious ways of making philosophy practical: it identifies the end of action or organizes and collects the means someone can use toward any end. The other two kinds of best are less obvious kinds of practical projects, and just how they are practical will be one of my main concerns in chapter 4. These two are less obvious because they understand political life as neither natural nor artificial. The more natural a polis, the closer the four causes come to coinciding. That is the ideal of Books VII and VIII. If the state is natural, then there is no process of making that can bring it about, and so we have to pray for its enabling conditions. The more the polis seems an artifact, the more distinct its causes have to be, as the argument of Books V and VI displays. When the polis is a work of art, the statesman is a maker, standing apart from other citizens and treating them as material to be organized and, sometimes, manipulated. Book I shows how the state is natural but also shows some of the limitations of understanding the state as natural. Book II looks at the state as an artifact and shows the limitations of that mode of understanding. It is because the constitution is neither natural nor artificial that the four causes have the practical independence they do. The practical independence of the four causes makes necessary the four distinct kinds of best for a complete treatment of politics. Book IV presents practical philosophy based on the material and then the formal cause; it is here Aristotle discovers constitutions can be better than the citizens who make them up.

Each of the four kinds of best can be and has been singled out as *the* theory of politics. Most obvious are the utopian or Platonic best *haplōs* and the strategic or Machiavellian best on a hypothesis. But there is also the *Federalist* project of a stable constitution without reliance on virtuous politicians, and the approach exemplified by Montesquieu of arguing that different peoples are suited to different kinds of government. Part of the interest of the *Politics* is in seeing what becomes of each of these approaches when it is a part of a more complete understanding, rather than something that claims to be sufficient by itself.

III. ETHICS AND POLITICS

Nothing in the *Ethics*—or anywhere else in Aristotle's corpus—corresponds to the explicit distinction of the four kinds of best. That does not mean that the *Ethics* does not treat them. Aristotle never says that the four kinds of best must be treated separately. But the ambiguity Aristotle notes in the four meanings of "best" bar the smooth inference in the *Ethics* which is often called the "ergon argument." To find a "clearer statement of what the best good is" (I.7.1097b24), Aristotle proposes to look at the "function (*ergon*) of a human being" (b25).

> For just as the good, i.e., [doing] well, for a flautist, a sculptor, and every craftsman, and, in general, for whatever has a function and [characteristic] action, seems to depend on its function, the same seems to be true for a human being. (b25–29)

> We say that the function of a [kind of thing]—of a harpist, for instance—is the same in kind as the function of an excellent individual of the kind—of an excellent harpist, for instance. . . . The function of a harpist is to play the harp, and the function of a good harpist to play the harp well. (1098a8–12)

Thus Aristotle infers that the best life occurs when the human being is functioning well, that is, when he or she is acting virtuously. That pattern of reasoning can't work for the *Politics*. The function of the polis is to allow human beings to live well. But that doesn't tell us what a *good* polis is. The argument of the *Politics* then violates the ergon argument: the function of anything is supposed to be the same nature as the function of a good instance of that thing. Knowing what something is, is supposed to tell what a good thing of that kind is. Intervening and preventing an immediate inference is the fact that what is a constitution, the form of the polis, is not dictated by the end of the polis. There are plural constitutions, some correct, most not. Nothing in the *Ethics* corresponds to that plurality.

If there are several constitutions, it is natural to ask which form is best suited to the end of the polis, living well. But that question contains an ambiguity without counterpart in the *Ethics*. In Book III, there are three correct

constitutions—monarchy, aristocracy, and polity—and three corresponding
deviant constitutions—tyranny, oligarchy, and democracy—which are only
distinguished from each other by the number of rulers. But the bulk of Book
IV is spent distinguishing between better and worse democracies and oligarchies, and when in Book IV he turns to talking about aristocracy and
polity, they bear no resemblance to some correct counterparts of democracy
and oligarchy. The same holds in Book V. Books VII and VIII discuss what,
by the standards of Book III, would be called an aristocracy, but it is quite
different from the aristocracy of Books IV–VI. What counts as a correct constitution varies according to the four kinds of best. The relation between a
good constitution and a good life varies with the four kinds of best.

One way to sum up these complications is to say that the polis really
has two distinct ends. First, the function of the state is to allow the citizen
to live well. But we also learn that the function of the citizen is to preserve the state (III.4.1276b27). Any polis aims at self-preservation. A good
constitution makes it possible for its citizens to live well, and this end of
the state is subordinate to the end of the individual life, living well. But a
good constitution is also a stable constitution. Stability and making the
good life possible are both marks of a good constitution, but they are distinct. The four kinds of best differ in the relation between those two ends
(see IV.11.1295a35–12.1296b38.) Taken by itself, the good life as the end of
politics makes politics instrumental; taken by itself, stability as the end of
politics makes politics amoral. Politics needs both ends, but they are two
different ends. The *Politics* has to highlight stability or self-preservation as
a goal in a way the *Ethics* does not. The *Ethics* says that a virtuous person
"will choose . . . a year of living finely over many years of undistinguished
life; and a single fine action over many small actions" (IX.8.1169a23–26);
no statesman could make that choice. There is no greater good for which a
polis could die.

That people are political animals does not imply that it is easy for us to
get along. Living together is exactly as difficult as living well (II.5.1263a15).
While political communities differ from other associations by aiming at
living well rather than mere life, most actual constitutions aim only at the
lower end of life itself, and faction is such a great problem that the common
function of citizens is preserving the state.[6] Because good constitutions differ in the relation between the two ends of stability and living well, the
good citizen, unlike the good person, is defined relative to the constitution.
There is, he says, one good person and one good life, but as many kinds of
good citizens as there are constitutions. Some constitutions have lower, others higher, standards for being a good citizen. That is, the distance between

the good person and the good citizen varies from constitution to constitution. In my final chapter I will argue that it is only in Books VII and VIII that the good life, which is the aim of the polis, is the Aristotelian good life. Other constitutions have looser and lower standards and aim at good lives that fall short of Aristotle's own vision of the best life.

For the same reason, the relation between the individual good life and the constitution changes as relations between the twin ends of stability and the good life change. At one extreme, in Books V and VI, a constitution is good if it can be the necessary condition for a good life, affording enough freedom from factions that people do not have to worry about losing their property or their citizenship. At the other extreme, in Books VII and VIII, to live well is to live the political life. In between, Aristotle will find that some people make good citizens because they are too occupied with economic activities to participate much in political life. They have minimal virtues of courage, temperance, and justice, but there is no reason to think that people like that engage in virtuous actions for their own sake.

The *Politics* is better equipped than the *Ethics* to help us answer an all-important question that Aristotle himself never addresses explicitly: how good must a community or a constitution have to be for people to be able to live good—virtuous and happy—lives?[7] The *Ethics* gives a few hints about the political background conditions that its happy life needs.[8] The *Politics*, if anything, threatens to give us too many different answers. Sometimes it looks as though stable constitutions provide the conditions in which virtue and living well. But sometimes the relation between political institutions and the good life seems more intimate: the constitution is a way of life in which total immersion in political activity constitutes the good life. Constitutions such as those considered in Book V offer people the opportunity to lead lives that are ethically superior to the constitutions themselves, while in Book IV Aristotle shows ways in which constitutions can be ethically superior to the citizens who comprise them. Different configurations of the relation between ethics and politics dictate those different answers.

There is no single relation between ethics and politics, because each is in a sense authoritative over the other. On the one hand, politics is superior to ethics because achieving the good for the state is "a nobler and more divine" achievement than achieving the good for the individual (*NE* I.2.1094b7–10, see too *Pol.* III.12.1282b15). Viewed in another way, though, ethics is prior to politics; the ethical practices of living a good life set the terms for decisions about how to organize a common life. The purpose of politics is living well, but only individuals, not poleis, live well and happily. Political activity always has an end outside itself, namely, living well, while ethical activity is its own end. The state exists so that people can live well. Political *knowledge* is superior to ethical knowledge, but political *activity* exists for the sake of ethical activity. "Political science spends most of its pains on making citizens to be a certain character, that is, good and capable of noble acts" (I.1.1252a1–6, *NE* I.4.1095a15, 1099b29).

Ethics and politics are each authoritative over the other. And in both cases that authority can be abused. The end of politics, stability, can become detached from the good life, and then the state's authority makes individuals into means for maintaining the state. The end of ethics, the good life, can be detached from politics and from living together, and then the state provides the security that is a necessary condition for living a virtuous life.

Those diverging relations between ethics and politics come to a head when *Politics* III says that the good man and the good citizen are different, that they are only identical for rulers in the best state (III.4.1277b17–19). It seems to me of first importance in understanding both the *Ethics* and the *Politics* that Aristotle never draws the implication that there could be a *conflict* between the good man and the good citizen, between the demands of ethics and of politics. The good person never faces conflicting demands between what a virtuous person would do and what a good citizen would do. Virtue never dictates that he or she act in a way different from the demands of citizenship.

Ethics and politics share a common end, the best human life. Moreover, practical deliberation takes the same form in both: "On any important decision we deliberate together because we do not trust ourselves" (*NE* III.3.1112b10–11). There is nothing here parallel to the modern distinction between the rational and the reasonable: how we think about what to do is not different in kind from thinking about how to act with (or against) others. If people really are political animals, then the individualistic assumption of much of modern moral and political theory is unintelligible; politics is not a matter of coordination or building trust through iterated prisoners' dilemmas, but of people discovering how to fulfill their nature by living together and so living well. Aristotle explains what he means by saying that people are political animals:

> It is clear why a human being is more of a political animal than a bee or any other gregarious animal. . . . No animal has speech (*logos*) except a human being. A voice (*phonê*) is a signifier of what is pleasant or painful, which is why it is also possessed by the other animals. . . . But speech is for making clear what is beneficial or harmful, and hence also

what is just or unjust. For it is peculiar to human beings . . . that they alone have perception of what is good or bad, just or unjust, and the rest. And it is community in these that makes a household and a polis. (I.2.1253a8–18)[9]

Political thought is more comprehensive than the *Ethics*. Both the *Ethics* and *Politics* say that goodness comes from nature, habit or character (*ēthos*) and reason (*Pol.* VII.13.1332a39–40, VII.15.1334b7–8, b14–17, *NE* X.9.1179b20, *EE* I.1.1214a11–19). The *Ethics* concentrates on developing character, while the *Politics* looks at nature and reason as well. The priority of politics over ethics is signaled in these lines from the *Eudemian Ethics*: "The absolutely good is absolutely desirable but what is good for oneself is desirable for oneself; and the two ought to come into agreement. The purpose of politics is to bring about this agreement in cases where it does not yet exist" (*EE* VII.2.1236b38–1237a1). There are ethical problems that only politics can solve.

Because of its narrower focus, the *Ethics* contains no genealogy parallel to the genesis of the state in *Politics* I, no consideration of other views of the best life like that in *Politics* II, no worries parallel to questions about how to determine the identity of a state over time in Book III, no balancing of competing claims and factors as there is in *Politics* IV, no consideration of the best way to live in difficult and dangerous times such as we encounter in *Politics* V and VI, and no reflection on the circumstances needed for living the best life parallel to Books VII and VIII. These are different ways of bringing reason and nature to bear on practical problems alongside habit and character, and of making conflict and stability prominent. Habituation, becoming a certain sort of person by performing the actions that such a person would perform, leaves little room for philosophy, or indeed for practical wisdom, in the acquisition of the virtues. There is far greater room for philosophy in establishing good constitutions.

I need to make one more comment on the relation between the *Politics* and Aristotle's other works, especially the *Ethics*, to explain how my approach to the *Politics* differs from others. I don't see him using applying many conclusions from the *Ethics* to the *Politics*, or from his other works either. I do, however, see many structural similarities between the peculiar ways Aristotle thinks through political problems and his approach to other problems. I therefore turn to analogies between his problems and solutions in the *Politics* and problems and solutions in other works. Even if the *Politics* is a work that stands on its own, it is always a work of Aristotle's, embodying his unusual way of thinking. I also find helpful analogies between the *Politics* and Plato's *Republic*. However, all these analogies are useful only to people already familiar with the *Ethics*, the *Poetics*, or the *Republic*. Others can safely ignore them.

IV. WHAT CAN THE *POLITICS* TELL US ABOUT POLITICS?

In a way, the genesis of this book started when I was eighteen years old and attended a lecture by Mortimer Adler. Adler declared—with a certainty that made me want to deny whatever he asserted, whether I understood it or not—that while Aristotle's *Ethics* is about the timeless problems of how to live, and so is as true and useful today as it was when it was written, his *Politics* is too time- and placebound to be of any value to us. Surely Adler has a point. The modern state is not what Aristotle had in mind when he talked about the polis; the modern written constitution is not his *politeia*; the modern citizen is not his *politēs*.[10] The subject of ethics seems more constant, leaving no central terms untranslatable.

I knew almost nothing about Aristotle at the time, and my reaction was probably nothing more than an automatic adolescent response to an authoritarian personality, but I decided that Adler must be wrong. I wanted to find ways of arguing—if I ever should learn anything about Aristotle— that the *Ethics* was tied to the particular circumstances of Aristotle's moral world, while the *Politics* remains of timeless value. Out of such accidents is a career born. While it would be simply perverse to maintain the thesis I had hoped to be able to assert all those years ago, I do think that the *Ethics* is more bound to time and place, and the *Politics* less, than is generally as- sumed. In *Confronting Aristotle's Ethics* I stressed how alien and sometimes repugnant the *Ethics* is because I wanted to counter the widespread assump- tion that Aristotle is talking to and about us. Here in talking about the *Politics*, I find no such party to oppose, and so can talk more freely about the ways in which the *Politics* can help us think through our own problems. The distinction between eternal truths and those bound by circumstances is itself questioned in the *Politics*, and the *Politics* gives us resources to do better.

I think that this story of Adler's lecture, and the contrast between the *Ethics* and the *Politics*, lets me confront in a more productive way the natu- ral question about the relation between understanding an ancient author and understanding contemporary problems. Do Aristotle's claims about the existence of natural slaves, or his denial of the possibility of a vacuum, bar the utility of his works in thinking through our own problems?[11] Like anyone else, Aristotle expresses judgments consonant with the prejudices

of his time, place, and class, or of some time, place, and class with which
he associates himself. The prejudices we notice are the ones we don't share.
But what matters is what Aristotle does with them. It is easy to notice
and condemn his acceptance of slavery, but more useful and challenging to
take seriously his concerns about the contrast term, despotism, which has
a longer life and greater power than slavery. To take another example, from
chapter 3, justice in the *Politics* consists of the distribution of offices by the
constitution. It is not concerned with the distribution of goods and services
by the government to the people. Is this a prejudice of Aristotle's or of his
time, or is it a considered part of his analysis? (When, in Book IV, Aristotle
recommends strengthening the middle class, he never sees redistribution of
resources as a way of making the middle class more numerous or powerful.)
And for one final example: Aristotle rarely talks about the Athenian polis
and constitution in the *Politics*; indeed, he refers more to Sparta than to
any other polis. We have to decide for ourselves whether the weight of his
examples is simply a given of political discourse of his time and place, or
whether he thinks we can learn more about constitutions from the Spartan
than from the Athenian experience.

In fact, I think the *Politics* is more likely than the *Ethics* to help us
think through contemporary problems, just the opposite of what most people assume. The explicitly contextual nature of political inquiry removes
the temptation, so often felt in ethics, of thinking that Aristotle is speaking
to us. It would be ridiculous and unrealistic to propose to solve America's
current political problems by reinstating the polis, and equally pointless
to criticize Aristotle for failing to see a modern nation-state as the way to
address problems of fourth-century Greece. Ethics seems a more constant
subject matter than politics. Therefore people propose, and sometimes even
fruitfully produce, returns to Aristotelian virtues. That there is no corresponding movement in politics is to the advantage of politics.

We read *Politics*, then, to understand politics. Why not cut out the mid-
dleman and think directly about politics? One of the strangest things about
the contemporary practice of philosophy is that we generally try to grasp
truths about the world through thinking about texts, about what other philosophers have had to say. We take this practice so much for granted that
it is easy not to notice how odd such a practice is. I believe that we can do
better in thinking about politics through the *Politics* than we could without
the help of a great mind. I have tried to start by thinking *about* the *Politics*
and eventually be able to think *with* the *Politics*.

Using a great philosophical work to understand the phenomena it directs us toward is something like using early generations of computers. (I

was a not very good programmer in 1963.) You had to understand what was going on under the hood in order to use them. A well-designed computer today allows you to use it without needing any understanding of how it works. That is the technological ideal. A well-designed work of philosophy never works like a well-designed computer. The bulk of one's time and effort is spent understanding the organs, functions, and various systems that make the *Politics* come alive, but the eventual payoff consists in understanding politics. In this book I emphasize my efforts at following the argument of the *Politics*, and have less to say about its implications for politics in general and for political life today. From a common understanding of the *Politics*, different people can reasonably draw different consequences for politics itself. I can show why, for example, Aristotle thinks that ethical education is the most important job for the statesman; what relevance Aristotle's thought has for our contemporary situation seems much more indeterminate and debatable.

I've been claiming, and will argue in detail in what follows, that there is a greater role for philosophy in politics than in ethics. That greater role also means that just how the *Politics* is supposed to be practical is more complicated than how the *Ethics* is. "We are inquiring not in order to know what virtue is, but in order to become good, since otherwise our inquiry would have been of no use'" (*NE* II.1.1103b27–29). The *Ethics* insists that its audience consists of people who already have good habits and a love for the noble. The *Ethics* can help people who already act virtuously become fully virtuous by reflecting on their already good actions and good habits. The audience for the *Politics* must be broader, and so its practical purpose, less straightforward. It can't be written for people who already live in good poleis, since we do not even have ready means of identifying good poleis. If you have already to be good to profit from the *Ethics*, there is no parallel limitation for the *Politics*. Its practical purposes, whatever they are, will have to go beyond reflection to criticism and reform.

On the other hand, there are continuities between my inquiry and Aristotle's. Aristotle sees philosophy as a problem-solving enterprise. His works begin with statements of the difficulties and puzzles he finds in the phenomena and in the views of earlier thinkers on the same subjects. Philosophical inquiry ends when all the problems have been resolved. I look for apparent inconsistency, incoherence, or ambiguity in Aristotle's own text as clues that something important is going on, that Aristotle is thinking through difficult problems in his own way, not fully captured by some stable definition or conclusion, but best understood through following the argument itself.

This volume completes a trilogy that began with *Aristotle's Rhetoric: An Art of Character*, and continued with *Confronting Aristotle's Ethics: Ancient and Modern Morality*. With a treatment of Aristotle's *Politics* alongside his *Ethics* and *Rhetoric*, my exploration of Aristotle's practical philosophy is complete. I see Aristotle offering a unique vision and a unique way of thinking about human activity and human relations. Both his vision and his mode of thought offer rich challenges to contemporary understandings of human action, allowing us better to see ourselves by contrast.

CHAPTER ONE

Book I:
Slavery and the Will to Power

My exploration of the *Politics* begins by focusing on its most notorious feature, the endorsement of slavery. This might be thought a minor feature of the *Politics*, important only because it highlights the distance between Aristotle's moral world and ours. His discussion of slavery occupies only three chapters in Book I and part of another in Book VII. But the issues slavery raises cut deep into Aristotle's way of thinking and help us understand what he means by saying that people are political animals (I.2.1253a7–18, III.6.1278b15–30; *NE* VIII.12.1162a16–19, IX.9.1169b16–22; *EE* VII.10.1242a19–28).

Looking back, we reasonably see Aristotle's discussion of slavery as defending the indefensible. The justification of slavery, coupled as it is in Book I with an analogous denigration of women, is so easy to take as the occasion for outrage that it is hard to get past that feeling to examine the details of his arguments. He defends the naturalness of slavery in Book I and, to make things worse, in Book VII gives a racial interpretation to slavery as he locates those suited to be slaves in Asia, as opposed to Europeans too wild to be domesticated and to the Greeks whose ideal psyches make them natural masters. We can be appalled, or we can separate Aristotle the philosopher from Aristotle the Greek who was not able to overcome the prejudices of his time. Aristotle's defense of slavery is then a depressing example of a great mind unable to escape the prejudices of his times, and of philosophy enlisted as rationalization in the service of a hidden and distasteful political agenda.[1] If we temporarily suspend those reactions, though, and look at some of the details of Aristotle's discussions of slavery, I think we find a richness that makes both his moral vision and our own moral lives more complicated.

For starters, while contemporary discussions of Aristotle's treatment of slavery typically describe it as a "justification" for slavery, Aristotle himself would be surprised to learn that he was justifying or even defending slavery.[2] The discussions of slavery have a different purpose within his larger project. The *Politics* begins by criticizing those—such as Plato's *Statesman*—who do not see that statesman, king, household manager (*oikonimikon*), and master of slaves (*despotikon*) are different kinds of rulers (1.1.1252a7–8, I.3.1254a17–19). The discussion of slaves and masters in Book I is part of his larger project of showing how the polis emerges out of the household and therefore how the good life emerges out of aiming at life itself, without being reducible to it. His "defense" of slavery is more a matter of fencing slavery in, part of the project of cabining economic activity that occupies the first book of the *Politics* as it develops the autonomy of politics. Greece knew slaves who were not part of a household: there were the workers in the silver mines, and the Scythian archers who served as a police force in Athens, but Aristotle's vision is narrowed to household slaves.[3] The helots of Sparta don't fit his account either. He devotes more of Book I to economics—household management—than to ruling slaves, but it is the latter activity that has to be separated from the art of the statesman.

Citizens have political relations toward each other, not relations of mastery and slavery. Therefore, strictly speaking, slavery is not a political but rather a prepolitical problem. In consequence, Aristotle treats questions about slavery as fairly easy; they can be solved by philosophical analysis rather than political deliberation, in contrast to the difficult subjects about citizenship and justice that require the nuanced division of labor between philosopher and statesman. Yet Aristotle also recognizes ways in which slavery can expand beyond this restriction to the household, and so become a more serious political problem, of greater interest to people who live in a world that doesn't accept his separation of the economic from the political. We have succeeded in abolishing slavery for the most part, but at the price of making economic activity much more dominant in our lives than Aristotle would have wanted. Compared to the world as Aristotle described it, slavishness and the pursuit of wealth are no longer shameful. Slavishness and the desire to dominate others have not disappeared along with the abolition of slavery. Even if poleis aren't around anymore, the tension between Aristotle's claim that man is a political animal and his observation that relatively few people live politically is a problem that remains with us.[4]

I. SLAVERY: INCOMPLETE ACTIONS
AND INCOMPLETE SOULS

Slaves have incomplete souls; they are incomplete people. To make such claims intelligible, I have to appeal to more of Aristotle's technical language and ideas from other works than I will need to do for most of the book. Aristotle sees a substance, such as a soul, as incomplete if it is defined by an essence, a formula or logos, outside itself. Its completion consists in reference to something outside itself.

> The deliberative part of the soul is entirely missing from a slave, a woman has it but it lacks authority; a child has it but it is incompletely developed. (I.13.1260a12–14)

> Since a child is incompletely developed, it is clear that his virtue too does not belong to him in relation to himself but in relation to his end and his leader. The same holds of a slave in relation to his master. (1260a31–34)

The soul of a child is incomplete because it is not yet complete. One cannot understand a child except by seeing her as on the way to becoming an adult. The souls of earthworms and of domestic animals are not incomplete; they just cannot do a lot of the things my soul can do. Slaves, in contrast to children but like women, are permanently incomplete. Biology speaks about "maimed" individuals of a species—lacking a hand, or the capacity to digest peanuts without allergic reaction—but not incomplete ones, and certainly not whole large groups of incomplete individuals. The oddness of such people is signaled by the fact that in Book I Aristotle argues first for the necessity of slaves, and of the naturalness of the master/slave relation, and only then looks around to determine the existence of people who fit the bill. Thus chapter 4 ends: "It is clear from these considerations what the nature and capacity of a slave are. For anyone who, despite being human, is by nature not his own but someone else's is a natural slave" (1254a12–15). And chapter 5 starts: "But whether anyone is really like that by nature or not, we should investigate next" (1254a17–18). (To see how odd it is for Aristotle first to show that natural slaves are necessary, and then that they exist, imagine proceeding in the same way, first showing the necessity of the male/female relation, and then proving the existence of women.) Aristotle's ensuing investigation is less empirical than one might expect, since nature does not act powerfully enough for us to identify natural slaves by inspection (I.5.1254b26–1255a1). So the argument in I.5 shows that there have to be natural slaves, not what they look like. The account of what makes someone naturally suitable for slavery will have to wait until VII.7.

I understand the slave's incompleteness this way. The slave's actions are by their nature incomplete; his acts fit the definition of motion in the *Physics* as the actualization of the potential qua potential (III.1.201a 10–11, 27–29, b 4–5), an incomplete activity whose completion lies outside itself in the end aimed at. It is no defect for a making, a *poiēsis*, to be a motion, just as it is no defect in a cow not to be a human being. Motions and makings are supposed to be incomplete, because they are done for the sake of an end outside themselves. With respect to *poiēsis*, there is nothing wrong with what slaves do; their performance is completely adequate. Otherwise it would be a burden to keep them around. It is, though, a failing for action, praxis, to be incomplete. Slaves have incomplete souls because they cannot fully engage in action.[5] It is because slaves cannot engage in praxis and so, *a fortiori*, in the good life, that slaves are instruments (*organa*) with respect to praxis, not *poiēsis*. Slaves might be defined as instruments for action, but they themselves can only engage in making.

When Aristotle defines motion as the actualization of a potential qua potential, he goes on to say that motion is incomplete because "the subject of whose potentiality *kinesis* is the *energeia* is incomplete" (*Ph.* III.1. 201b31–33; see also *Met.* IX.6. 1048b23–35). So here: incomplete praxis is the praxis of an incomplete human being. All humans engage in productive actions. But slaves differ from complete human beings because their central, essential, characteristic activities are incomplete. They act for the sake of something outside the actions, namely, the master. Since their actions are essentially incomplete, or, what is the same thing, essentially instrumental, children, women, and slaves are all in different ways incomplete human beings: "The activity of imperfect things is imperfect" (*EE* II.1. 1219a37–38); "Nothing incomplete is happy because it is not a whole" (*EE* II.1.1219b7–8).[6]

It follows that slaves are by nature part of a master/slave relation. If their actions are incomplete, then those actions, and the slaves themselves, must be part of someone else. That argument doesn't apply to domestic animals. Their souls are not incomplete, and they are not part of the master. The master, in an important sense, *is* the household. The ruler of a polis, by contrast, is not the same as the polis itself. *L'état, c'est moi* is the definition of tyranny. A household comprises a master and a set of other people who are incomplete and so depend on the head of the household. A polis is a self-sufficient community of self-sufficient people (III.1.1275b20–21).

Aristotle does not write slaves out of humanity, though, because of their incompleteness. As we will see, slavishness, the psychological attitude manifested most obviously in slaves, is a truly human trait. Beasts and gods form the nonhuman boundaries around humanity: "Anyone who cannot form a community with others, or who does not need to because he is self-sufficient, is no part of a polis—he is either a beast (*thērion*) or a god" (I.2.1253a28–29; cf. *NE* VII.1.1145a20–28); this is very different from saying that without a polis people are either masters or slaves. It is wild beasts—not the domesticated animals with which he compares slaves—and gods, not despots, who can and must naturally live outside cities. Beasts and gods are perfect exemplars of their kinds, unlike masters and slaves, who are incomplete human beings. (We will later see the senses in which Aristotle does and does not follow Hegel in seeing masters as well as slaves as incomplete.) Any people who can fully live their lives without a polis are complete in some nonhuman way, as beasts and gods are, rather than incomplete or corrupt in some human way, like slaves and the unruly Europeans whom we will meet in VII.7. In contrast to beasts and gods, people are political animals.[7]

Both the slave and the person who makes mastery the center of his life fail to live politically; they do not successfully live some other way, as animals do. They are failed political animals. Slaves fail in a way that makes them incomplete. Mastery is more complex. The full human being and citizen is a master, but only of slaves. Someone who makes dominating others, especially free people, the organizing goal of his life is a failure in a more serious way that I will turn to in later sections of this chapter. Our human nature impels us to live as citizens in poleis, although not everyone can or does; not everyone wants to.

Not being able to engage in praxis makes someone an incomplete human being. Praxis is tied to human nature and the human function in ways making is not. There are no natural farmers or poets: "a slave is among the things that exist by nature, whereas no shoemaker is, nor any other sort of craftsman" (I.13.1260b1–2).[8] There are natural men and women, adults and children, and, according to Aristotle, free men and slaves. All these natural distinctions are connected to praxis. Praxeis are constitutive of the good life and the good community. Makings are essentially incomplete, and slaves are in no way inferior to freemen in the performance of *poiēsis*. But excellence in craft cannot qualify anyone for citizenship.[9]

II. SLAVERY AND SLAVISHNESS

I now want to look at slavery outside its literal application within the household to see its political significance, and then, in the next section, consider mastery and its expansion beyond the household. There is slavery and there is slavishness. Slavishness is not confined to the household but is more widely distributed. In I.13 Aristotle notes that "vulgar craftsmen have a kind of delimited slavery" (*ho banausos technitēs aphōrismenēn tina echei douleian*) (1260b1). "A slave shares his master's life, whereas a vulgar craftsman is at a greater remove" (1260a39–40), although which of these undesirable situations is ethically preferable, Aristotle does not say.[10] The metaphorical extensions of slavery to the craftsman who works for money in Book I is recalled in Book VIII, where he says that those who play music or practice other crafts to win attention or wealth aim at pleasure rather than what is good and so they too are banausic (VIII.6.1341a5–14). Slavishness as a psychic condition extends more widely than the institution of slavery itself. "It makes much difference what object one has in view in a pursuit or study; if one follows it for the sake of oneself or one's friends, or on moral grounds, it is not illiberal, but the man who follows the same pursuit because of other people would often appear to be acting in a menial and servile manner" (VIII.2.1337b17–21; see also see III.4.1277b3–7, VII.16.1335b5–11, *NE* IV.3.1124b31–1125a1, *Rh.* I.9.1367a–31). People engaged in trade and moneymaking try to please their customers, and so choose the pleasant over what is truly good.[11] Therefore they cannot be good citizens, and will not be citizens in a good state.

Slavishness is even more threatening today, since it is less shameful. Slavishness is in a sense a default position: if people are not brought up properly, they will choose life rather than a good life, and so lead vulgar and slavish lives. People who organize their lives around acquiring wealth are slavish, even if not slaves, because to aim at wealth is to aim at satisfying the ends of people other than oneself. The customer, rather than virtue, is always right. Being wealthy might protect someone in Greece against being sold into slavery, but it does not protect anyone from living a slavish life. (If part of slavishness is directing one's actions toward satisfying another, it does not follow that the opposite of slavishness is selfishness. It is choosing things that are their own end, things worth doing for their own sake.)

Slavish people cannot lead a civic life and cannot be happy, because they aim at life rather than living well: so much for the civil society Adam Smith sees emerging out of people's desires to please each other and satisfy their demands instead of through servile emotions. "It is not from the benevolence of the butcher, the brewer, or the baker, that we expect our dinner, but from their regard to their own self-interest. We address ourselves, not to their humanity but to their self-love, and never talk to them of our own necessities but of their advantages."[12] The trouble, for Smith, with relying on the benevolence of the butcher is that dependence puts us in a servile position; appealing instead to their self-love makes us equals. Smith turns Aristotle on his head. Aristotle would see people appealing to each other's self-interest as acting slavishly and asking others to do the same. The crux of the difference is that for Aristotle only self-sufficient people can constitute a self-sufficient community. "Political animals are those whose joint work (*ergon*) is one common thing" (*Hist. An.* I.1. 488a7–8). "There cannot be a polis of slaves any more than a city of animals" (III.9.1280a31–33). Slavish people allow economic life to dominate political life, and too many people of this kind would destroy political life. (One line of Smith's followers would see this as precisely the benefit of commerce.)

While economic self-sufficiency leads to political self-sufficiency, it is only a necessary condition for political self-sufficiency. If one thinks that all you need for political autonomy is economic autarchy, one is no longer in a position to criticize slavishness and the life of endless acquisition. Economic self-sufficiency does not seem difficult to achieve, while political life, being the most fulfilling kind of life, is also rare. Many readers of both the *Ethics* and the *Politics* have noted that human nature seems in these works differs from the conception of nature that Aristotle describes elsewhere as what happens always or for the most part. Few people achieve the living well and living together that Aristotle takes as the fulfillment of human nature. The simple reason that human nature behaves differently from nature in general is that human nature requires quite strict conditions for its full realization. Living well requires living under a good constitution. At the same time, a good constitution requires good citizens to maintain it. It looks like there is a vicious circle that is difficult to break out of.[13]

Aristotle supplies no evident argument that economic self-sufficiency is a necessary condition for the political and ethical self-sufficiency of living well. It is easy to assume that economic self-sufficiency generates leisure, which makes living well possible, but that is not Aristotle's argument. Does the fact that families are not economically self-sufficient make it obvious that they aren't ethically self-sufficient either, obvious that no one can live well within a family?[14]

I think the connection between economic and ethical self-sufficiency comes through equality. Equality is impossible within a family because it has to be structured to satisfy immediate needs. Poleis are associations of equal citizens. Political justice, he tells us in the *Ethics*, "exists only between men whose mutual relations are governed by laws," and those people "who have an equal share in ruling and being ruled are naturally subject to law" (V.6.1134a29–b14, see *Pol.* III.6.1279a10, III.17.1287a18). Once the natural genesis described in Book I arrives at an association of equals, the progression stops, because there lies the possibility of ethical self-sufficiency. There are no further associations beyond the polis in this story: federations, the Greeks taken as a whole, humanity itself might be communities in other ways, but they cannot figure in Aristotle's project here. The requisite kind of equality is possible only among people who are not naturally related. Not only is the family natural, but the relations within the family— father/children, husband/wife, master/slave—are natural, too, and therefore people related naturally to each other cannot also be connected by political equality. The polis is natural, but the relations within the state, relations of ruler to ruled, are not themselves natural. (As I will argue in chapter 3, from this comes the fact that there are several political constitutions but no similar variations among families.) We can lead good lives only in communities of equals.[15]

Organizing one's life around living rather than living well produces slavishness that goes deep enough to disqualify one from Aristotelian citizenship. To this extent, then, slavishness is a permanent practical problem, although it may not be a temptation felt by the audience of the *Ethics* and *Politics*. The irony of history is at work here. Slavery was finally abolished in part due to the triumph of slavishness; that is, lives of unlimited acquisition produced a new economic order that made slavery seem anachronistic, and made it possible for modern economies to flourish without slave labor. While most people have to be coerced into being slaves, no such compulsion is necessary for living slavishly. That is what makes it the default position. If a slavish life is one that neglects virtue in favor of pleasing others in order to bring wealth and pleasure to oneself, slavishness then consists in an inability to have one's life organized around true ends. One aims at pleasure and life instead. Capitalism abolished slavery by making slavishness universal, which in turn made it possible for other forms of economic and social organization, such as communism, to invent additional ways of making slavishness universal.

Aristotle could not conceive of capitalism and its transformation of vulgar craftsmen into an entire system of unlimited acquisition. Nor could he predict that a system of unlimited acquisition would lead to ever higher levels of prosperity. The virtues of commerce have made us all turn away from political participation and made modern citizens in Aristotle's eyes slavish. Technological progress has transformed the Aristotelian problems of slavery and slavishness. Whether it also transforms problems of despotism remains to be seen.

But before turning to that question, an analogy might help. Arguably, technological advances in warfare, the development of mass armies and asymmetrical warfare, have taken away most opportunities for the courage exhibited in facing an enemy, conquering fears of death in battle at the hands of an opponent faced with the same emotional predicament. The suicide bomber may have to conquer fears of death, but they aren't fears of death at the hands of the enemy. Nor is the B-52 pilot who drops bombs from an altitude above the range of antiaircraft artillery in a position that calls for courage. The current situation is neither better nor worse than older forms of war—one never has a choice between them—and the same holds for the differences between Aristotelian economics confined within the household and more developed economies. We live in a truly different world.

Aristotle's conclusion that there are natural slaves repels us because we think there are no such people. Aristotle, though, is arguing against *two* possibilities, that there are no natural slaves, that is, that anyone enslaved is enslaved against nature and merely by convention, and that *all* people are people who could potentially be slaves. Those two positions may not be all that different. Neither discriminates among people. Practically speaking, neither is much of a bar against enslavement. If there are no natural slaves, then it doesn't much matter whom I enslave. If everyone is, for example, a slave to his bodily desires, then enslavement by another doesn't make much difference, and so Christianity was able for almost two millennia to rationalize slavery by putting it in the context of sin or a condition indifferent to salvation. Finding that Asians make ideal slaves is a stronger protection against Greeks being enslaved than Solon's reforms.[16]

III. DESPOTISM

Like slavery, mastery expands beyond the boundaries of the household, but in an even more politically threatening way. (I will use "despot" and "master" interchangeably as translations of *despotēs*. At issue later in my argument will be the relation between being a slave master and being a ruler or *hegemon*.) Our moral attention is naturally on the slave part of the master/slave relation—since that helps us look down on Aristotle—but mastery is more politically and philosophically troublesome. The barbarians conflate women and slaves, and treat their sons as slaves, showing how uncivilized they are (*Pol.* I.2.1252b4, II.9.1271b20–24, *NE* VIII.10.1160b24–30). But there is one feature within the household that violates his general rule that nature makes a single thing for a single task (*ergon*).[17] Even in a proper household within a proper polis, the same person is master, father, husband, and citizen. Later abolitionists will argue that the experience of mastering slaves prevents people from possessing the virtues necessary for citizenship, but Aristotle is untroubled by the way the same man is both despot within the household and citizen in the polis.[18] He denies that citizenship and mastery are incompatible, while equally denying that mastery and civic participation are the same.

A single psychic capacity, *dynamis*, to be specified when we get to VII.7, has two distinct activities, *energeiai*, ruling slaves and participating in the polis. Owning slaves is a necessity, while political participation is worth doing for its own sake. The good man will own slaves, but will find nothing to be proud of in such mastery and will delegate the job to stewards if he can afford it. "Those who have the resources not to bother with [commanding slaves] have a steward do so, while they themselves engage in politics or philosophy" (I.7.1255b35–38; see VIII.4.1339a32–b10).[19]

As I mentioned, the *Politics* begins by criticizing those who don't see that statesman, king, household manager, and master of slaves exercise different kinds of rule (1.1.1252a7–8); masters rule primarily for themselves and only incidentally for their slaves, the political ruler does the opposite (III.6.1278b3–a3). Yet the same person exercises political and despotic rule, political rule in the polis and despotic rule in the household. He rules in his own interest when commanding his slaves and for the sake of the people ruled in the polis; he rules over people with whom he has nothing in common in slavery and over fellow citizens who, at the limit of friendship, have all things in common. Offhand, these two capacities to rule seems as unlikely to go together as the talents for running for office and those needed to govern. There is no reason to think that these two talents are both manifestations of the same psychic capacity, and every reason to think that being good at running for office makes one less capable of governing once elected. The same person is both master and citizen: the principal problems of politics, internal stasis and the temptations of conquest, come from that fact.

Solon solved the threat of free men becoming slaves by eliminating debt slavery. Aristotle thinks the problem of slavish vulgar craftsmen can be solved if the polis exists in fortunate enough circumstances that the constitution can deny citizenship to such people. That is why I ended the first section by saying that slavishness is not a very serious political problem in Aristotle's eyes. The problem of free men becoming despots won't be solved so easily and cannot be solved by a single political measure; it is a problem that has to be faced perennially. Just as someone can be slavish without being a slave, one can be free, in the sense of not being enslaved, without possessing the virtue of the *eleutherotēs*, which we translate, literally but probably forgetting its literal sense, as liberality. Without the proper moral education, men are likely to confuse mastery with political rule, think that ruling is desirable and being ruled only grudgingly acceptable, and think that for one's state to be free it has to dominate others, and that the more people one rules over, the better. It may be natural for some men, namely, Greeks, to both rule and be ruled. But few men see alternating between ruling and being ruled as its own end. This is not ethical blindness; ruling and being ruled can only be worth choosing for its own sake in the right circumstances.[20]

The permanent political problem of despotism permeates the *Politics*.[21] Aristotle, as usual, translates a Platonic problem into a more temperate variant. While the tyrant dominates the beginning and end of the *Republic*, the temptation of despotism never leaves the *Politics*. Aristotle has to argue for the existence of natural slaves, but he feels no need for a parallel argument about natural masters, even though, as we will see, natural masters as much as natural slaves need a psychic precondition that is not universal. To anticipate, in VII.7 Aristotle will locate in Asia a home for natural slaves, but there is no place, apart from Greece itself, in which natural despots can be found! Book III distinguishes correct and corrupt constitutions by whether rule is for the sake of the whole state or that of the rulers, so many political rulers do not accept Aristotle's distinction between the political ruler and the despot. Tyranny is, barely, a form of constitution, and he looks at how to preserve it in Books V and VI, but despotism as a way of life is considered only as part of his treatment of the best state and the best life in Book VII. "Some say that the kind of political system that involves being a master and tyrant (*despotikon kai tyranikon*) is the only one that is happy. And for some this is the defining purpose of the laws and the political system: to exercise a master's rule (*despozōsi*) over neighbors" (VII.2.1324b1–4).

This placement indicates something deeper than simply *corruptio optimi pessima est*. Rather, politics encounters despotism in the two parts of the *Politics* where politics most directly encounters nature, first in the nature that impels people to unite into families, villages, and ultimately political communities, and then the nature we find at the end of that process, when we are in a position to consider the ideal constitution, which requires the best natural material and equipment.

That only Greeks, who uniquely live in poleis, can live well and be happy is no cause for smugness because there is another uniquely Greek possibility, too—the capacity for domination. Aristotle's ethnocentric claim

that both of these are only found among the Greeks seems to me less important than the idea that both are realizations of the same cast of mind. That
cannot be dismissed as anachronistic prejudice.

IV. SLAVERY, DESPOTISM, AND HUMAN NATURE

To understand the relation between slavery and slavishness, between slave
mastery and domination more generally, I want to look in detail at Aristotle's arguments in VII.7 for the conclusion that only the Greeks, with their
well-blended intelligence and *thumos*, can be leaders, as well as the seemingly independent claim that "*thumos* is the capacity of the soul by which
we feel friendship" (1327b40).[22] Chapter 7 ends with Aristotle saying that
this brief discussion is enough to answer his question about the natural en-
dowment of citizens in the best state, and one should not expect the same
precision as comes through perception. While this is a remark that could,
and does, apply to the whole of his practical science of ethics and politics, it
is significant that he says it here. This chapter raises a very important question: what kind of nature should citizens of the best state have. His answer
seems to be: the same nature that enables people to be citizens of any state.
And his support for an answer is very thin. It consists in a quick moral geography, and an even quicker reference to the *Republic*. Such an important
question, one would think, deserves more. The connections between the
three activities that seem unique to the Greeks, and therefore are presumably all functions of the same combination of intelligence and *thumos*—political rule, mastery, and friendship—are not developed at all. And yet the
inseparability of ethics and politics for Aristotle means that the power to
live well and the power to live together as equals require each other.

When he says that some people can aim at the good life while others
are suited instead to being natural slaves, I do not think he is committed to
stipulating anything about those souls all the way down. His sense of capacity is not open to the modern thought-experiments of asking what would
happen if an infant of a certain sort were transplanted into specific conditions.[23] The later ethological interest in a common human nature evolves
from a moral interest in human beings as such. Without an obligation to
treat all humans morally rather than an essentially political morality in
which I have full moral relations only with fellow citizens, the modern idea
of human nature will not emerge.[24] Without such a universal obligation to
all human beings, Aristotle and his contemporaries would have no reason
to be moved by a counterfactual, "If this person were brought up right, he
would not have a slavish nature."[25] His moral psychology is then resolutely

superficial. Only in this way can the brevity of treatment of the question in VII.7 be appropriate. These ethnic generalizations report the way people present themselves, and nothing deeper.[26] Aristotle's excursions into moral ecology are always in the service of this project of framing the autonomy of politics, the way activities that aim at the good life emerge from but are not reducible to activities that aim at life. Lacking a modern conception of nature, Aristotle will not be able to use his own conception to participate in many modern arguments. As we will see, without a theory of universal human nature, there is no state of nature and so no original act of appropriation of property in Book II—indeed, there will be no narrative of the origin of property at all. Without a state of nature to which society reverts during a revolution, Books V and VI see no appeals to heaven or to natural rights in a revolution, only one partial conception of justice battling another. Our newer idea of human nature became necessary when ethics separated itself from politics.

Instead of a universal human nature acting as a principle for ethics and politics, Aristotle presents us with the puzzle that if man is a political animal, why do so few people live in poleis, and live in poleis as active citizens, finding fulfillment of their natures in political activity?[27] If nature were more potent, we would be able to tell natural masters and slaves apart by the respective excellence of their souls and bodies, but in fact we find freemen with slavish bodies and slaves with erect ones (I.5.1254b27–1255a3), and nature doesn't always breed true (I.6.1255a39–b3).

The inquiry into the best civic material in VII.7 begins with his saying that "one may pretty much grasp what these [natural] qualities are by looking at those Greek poleis that have a good reputation, and at the way the entire inhabited world is divided into nations" (1327b20–22). He does nothing with the first of these sources of data. There is no argument of the kind: everyone knows that Thebes is better than Corinth, so let's see the differences in the nature of their citizens. The contrasting civic characters of Athens and Sparta was a topos already in Thucydides, but Aristotle does not appeal to such differences. Nowhere is the difference among Greeks employed to account for different constitutions in Books III–VI, not even in IV.3.1289b27–1290a29, where he derives the diversity of constitutions from the diversity of citizens.

The chapter continues:

> The nations in cold locations, particularly in Europe, are filled with spiritedness, but relatively lacking in thought and art; hence they remain freer, but lack [political] governance and are incapable of ruling their

neighbors. Those in Asia, on the other hand, have souls endowed with
thought and art, but are lacking in spiritedness; hence they remain ruled
and enslaved. But the stock of the Greeks shares in both—just as it holds
the middle in terms of location. For it is both spirited and endowed with
thought, and hence both remains free and governs itself in the best manner and at the same time is capable of ruling all. (VII.7.1327b24–33)[28]

Asians make ideal slaves, he claims, because they have logos and *techne*.
They not only can follow orders like domestic animals but can engage in
the reasoning required for the crafts; otherwise they would be more trouble
than they are worth. At IV.15.1299a24, Aristotle goes so far as to speak
about slaves ordering slaves, which shows how intelligent slaves can be.
While slaves lack deliberative capacity, to *bouletikon* (I.13.1260a12), and
consequently, Aristotle says, lack full intellectual (*dianoetike*) as well as
moral virtue, their deficiency is not fundamentally a cognitive one. Since
many animals have *thumos* but not logos, it is easy to assume that slaves,
as intermediate between animals and people, must therefore be deficient in
logos, but that is not the case. Slaves fail to be complete human beings, but
not by reverting to some more animal nature; the slavish Asians who have
logos and craft also conveniently lack *thumos* and therefore are willing to
take orders. Praxis, doing as opposed to making, takes *thumos* as well as
intelligence. A good slave has to be both intelligent and docile.[29] Their intelligence does not lead to practical reason, to the ethical and political second
nature that allows some people to live by choice and aim at living well.
Intelligence by itself is not enough for living well.[30]

   The wild Europeans, by contrast, are useless on both counts: they have
no logos and so no skills worth exploiting, yet they have *thumos*, which
keeps them free and prevents them from being enslaved. Without logos, their
love of freedom does not develop into political rule and being ruled. To take
this psychology seriously puts us in a better position to understand some of
today's outstanding political problems, in which we see many instances of
people with a love of freedom that does not lead directly to a stable political
life. The desire for freedom is not necessarily accompanied by the friendliness necessary for civic life. As we will see repeatedly in the *Politics*, people
often accept formal reciprocity of ruling and being ruled because they know
they can't get away with permanently ruling themselves, but few people
take reciprocity as a virtue worth practicing for its own sake.

   If we can get past the repellent racism of Aristotle's picture and its convenient ecology that puts Greece not only at the center of the world but also
at the pinnacle of human possibility, his placement of the Greeks between

two undesirable alternative possibilities can prevent us from simply thinking of slavery or slavishness as the corruption of human nature, as what
happens to people when they are not given the right moral education or
put in the right social circumstances, what I earlier called the default position. We now see that there are two opposed natural failings, represented
by the Asian and European extremes. More seriously, we can uncover a
specifically Greek form of corruption, that of despotism as a way of life, and
not just something men do within the household. We have to uncover this
possibility because Aristotle does not give a specific geographic location for
the naturally despotic soul, as he does for the natural slaves: the natural
despot is a Greek.

Just as the ethical virtues are means between a pair of vices, so the ideal
Greek conditions seem to be a mean between two opposed degenerate ways
of living, the slavish and the despotic. When discussing the ethical virtues,
Aristotle will sometimes note that one extreme is a vice, while the other
a mistake for which one is not culpable (e.g., NE IV.3.1125a17–19). In this
case, to be despotic is to fail to realize one's potential for living politically,
while to be slavish is not to have that potential in the first place. But that
analogy only goes so far. First, while to be slavish is to fail in certain specific
ways that he locates in Asia; Europeans fail in a different way, one which
does not generate its own permanent possibility that we need to worry about.
There is, that is, no moral possibility that stands to the wild European freedom as slavishness stands to slavery. Instead, second, despotism is a corruption of the human qualities that can lead to the political life. A despotic way
of life fails to exploit the unique possibilities for living well that politics
offers.

Aristotle refutes both the slavish and the despotic lives. In both cases,
his refutation is through an ethical, rather than a purely logical, argument.
Demolishing the appeals of the slavish life is, he thinks, easier. All he has
to do is appeal to the sense of the noble and to shame in his listeners.[31] The
slavish life is vulgar and ignoble. No one—certainly no Greek—wants to
be a slave. To the extent that he can show that other habits and actions are
slavish, and so associate them with slavery, he will make those other habits
and actions unattractive. Despotism is harder to refute, and Aristotle will
return to it again and again in the Politics. Many people—think of Callicles
and Thrasymachus—believe that despotism is not shameful but is in fact
noble. They are partly right. The desire to rule permanently has the same
psychic source as the desire to rule and be ruled in turn.

Aristotle never calls despotism ignoble, let alone vulgar, because it is
rooted in thumos and even in a desire for the noble. "Men do not become

tyrants to avoid shivering" (II.5.1267a14). Despotism is for Aristotle a permanent political problem because it has the same psychological basis as citizenship and friendship.

Citizens are masters within their households. Citizens, then, are sometime despots, but they are never slavish. The citizen must pull off the difficult psychological feat of not acting on his existing active despotic powers while acting as a citizen. They cannot be kept distinct simply by keeping them in different realms, the household and the polis, in the way modern politics, for example, tries to make religion a private virtue but a public vice.

Instead, the citizen lives with both activities by regarding his despotic powers as powers to perform merely necessary acts, to be overshadowed and looked down on whenever possible by free, civic activities. Slave ownership is not a vice but it is merely necessary. "If every instrument (*organon*) could perform its function, whether by obeying another or by anticipating what to do . . . then a master-artist would need no servants and a master would need no slaves" (I.4. 1253b34–1254a1). There is no corresponding fantasy that would see the withering away of the desire for domination. Someone whose political desires cannot rule his despotic desires becomes a tyrant (II.7.1267a3–14). Being a despot may give these men a good reason to look down on women, the poor, and the barbarian, but, Aristotle teaches, mastery is nothing to be proud of. It's like being proud that one is superior to one's livestock. Citizenship, with its restraining reciprocity, is more noble than mastery. Mastery is merely necessary. Mastery is a legitimate activity. It is just not a respectable way of life.

V. NATURAL RULERS, POLITICAL AND DESPOTIC

The discussion of slavery in Book I affirms the naturalness of the master/slave relation and the natural suitability of some people to be slaves. Book VII makes Aristotle's analysis even more offensive to modern ears, since he locates natural slaves in certain non-Greek races or nations (*ethnoi*), and not in others. But Aristotle is strangely quiet and indirect in both places when it comes to the question of whether there are natural masters, people who naturally fit the dominant half to the master/slave relationship. As we've just seen, the argument of VII.7 seems to imply that there are, but Aristotle never explicitly says so. The sixth chapter of Book I ended the discussion of natural slaves by saying that "some people are slaves everywhere, whereas others are slaves nowhere" (1255a32), but the discussion then turns not to natural masters but to noble birth. "The same holds of noble birth. Nobles regard themselves as well-born wherever they are, not only when they are among their own people, but they regard non-Greeks as well born only when they are at home. They imply a distinction between a good birth and freedom that is unqualified and one that is not unqualified" (I.6.1255a33–35). The reader is left to draw the conclusion that there is a distinction between natural or "unqualified" (*haplōs*) masters and those who are masters merely by convention.[32]

The same absence of a direct statement about natural masters recurs in Book VII, and there the omission of an explicit discussion is more serious. As in Book I, here too there are natural slaves, but natural despots emerge only indirectly. The Europeans certainly are not natural despots, since they cannot "rule their neighbors." I infer—Aristotle again doesn't draw this inference—that only Greeks can be natural despots.[33]

Ruling seems to be an undifferentiated capacity variously exercised in living politically—which means ruling and being ruled in turn—as well as in domestic despotic rule and in hegemonic rule of one polis over others. The *Politics* begins by attacking those who think that statesman, king, household manager, and master of slaves are the same (I.1.1252a7–8, I.3.1254a17–19), and returns to that point throughout the *Politics*:

> It is not for this purpose that one must pay attention to military preparation—to enslave those who do not deserve it—but rather, first, to avoid one's own enslavement by others; secondly, to seek a position of leadership in order to benefit those who are ruled, but not to be master over all; thirdly, to be master over those who deserve to be slaves. (VII.14.1333b38–1337a1)

As I will show in my final chapter, the early chapters of Book VII, on the way to defining the ideal constitution, worry that those who think the best life is a political life interpret that life as a despotic one of conquest and hegemony. If only Greeks, with their political combination of *thumos* and intelligence, could be despots, then despotism is a serious political threat in a way slavishness is not. Slaves have the wrong nature, which prevents them from leading good lives. Despots have the *right* kind of nature, and yet still degenerate without a proper education and proper political circumstances. "A master is just his slave's master, not his simply, while a slave is not just his master's slave, he is entirely his" (I.4.1254a11–12).[34]

The fact that the same capacity is at work in political rule and in despotic rule is good reason for Aristotle not to affirm that there are natural rulers, or despots, even though there are natural slaves. Political rule, like virtue in the *Ethics*, must be neither natural nor contrary to nature (II.1.1103a25). There are no natural citizens. For the same reasons, there are no natural masters. Only people who have a particular natural capacity, which Aristotle specifies in VII.7, can develop into political beings. Only men with the capacity for political rule and therefore for despotism have the capacity for tyranny. For Aristotle, then, "oriental despotism" would be a contradiction in terms. Persian kings are not natural tyrants, only Greek tyrants are.

Mastery and slavery thus occupy very different places in the *Politics*. Book I is interested in the master/slave relation but only discusses whether there are natural slaves, not natural masters. Book VII looks to mastery more than slavery, but now it is mastery's political, rather than domestic, forms—conquest and leadership (*hegemonikon*). Since leadership and political rule are manifestations of the same power, Aristotle must show how leadership can avoid leading to despotism. The discussion of slavery in Book I occurs in the context of worrying about how economically necessary activities didn't take over one's life and lead to a life of unlimited acquisition. Book VII worries about how political activities can avoid being their own form of unlimited conquest. The economic life of unlimited acquisition consists in mastery over things, while the political life of domination consists in mastery over people.[35] The first, he argues, is irrational because it is unlimited, and means should be limited by their end. The second he has to take more seriously, since doing something for its own sake rightly has no limit, and the person who sees the best life as the active life of conquest aims at dominating others not in order to gain wealth but because it is, he thinks, the highest realization of his faculties.

Two more quick notes on the moral geography before moving on. As we've seen, the trouble with Europeans is that they don't have enough intelligence. The trouble with Asians is that they don't have enough *thumos*. Greeks have an adequate supply of both. But there is an odd, unmentioned consequence. *Politics* VII talks about Europeans and Asians in terms of their respective deficiencies, not in terms of excess. There are no nations with too much intelligence or *thumos*. One might think that intelligence is a virtue, and so cannot be possessed in excess. But even so, having an excess of *thumos* certainly seems possible. We meet people in *Ethics* VII whose *thumos* is so strong that while knowing the better they choose the worse.

Finally, Aristotle introduces us to people with insufficient understanding and others with inadequate *thumos*. The tripartite soul to which both he and Plato often appeal suggests a third possibility. But Aristotle's argument has no room for people whose souls are characterized by a dominance, or an absence, of *epithumia*. The *Republic* contains such people, lots of them, as Socrates says the workers of the ideal state have a dominant *epithumia*. Appetite, unlike the other two parts, may be a human constant, but at the same time it is nothing specifically human. It has no political significance. How different this all is from the passionate universal human nature that has dominated ethical and political thought since the Enlightenment.

VI. *THUMOS*: DOMINATION AND FRIENDSHIP

Politics VII.7 has two parts. The first is the moral geography, which locates the ideal mixture of intelligence and *thumos* in Greeks, producing the power that allows for ruling of all sorts, despotic and political. Aristotle then turns to the *Republic*, which separates people into three classes depending on whether their souls are dominated by appetite, *thumos*, or *nous*, intelligence. This would not seem to help Aristotle at all since he has already located people who live by *thumos* alone, not in auxiliaries, as in the *Republic*, but in the wild Europeans, and he finds people whose souls are dominated by intelligence in the slavish Asians, not in philosopher-kings. Aristotle's ideal citizens have the right combination of intelligence and *thumos*, while Socrates's ideal state separates people according to their dominant psychic power. While Aristotle maintains that the same right combination of intelligence and *thumos* makes both despotic and political rule possible, the argument in VII.7 up until here appears to be far too weak an argument to support such an important conclusion. And the *Republic* looks like the wrong place to turn for help.

Aristotle supplies what transition there is between the moral geography and the turn to the *Republic* with nothing but a *gar*, translated as "for": "For as to what some assert should be present in guardians, to be friendly to those they know and fierce to those they do not, and *thumos* is what makes them friendly" (1327b38–40).[36] With the intimate relation Aristotle sees between justice and friendship, it makes sense to ally the capacity for living politically with the capacity for friendship, but neither has anything obviously to do with mastery. To put Aristotle's interpretation of the *Republic* slightly differently, Socrates notes that *thumos* allows guardians to distinguish friends from enemies. He fails to note that *thumos* allows guardians, or anyone, to *have* friends and enemies. Guardians and auxiliaries might love their country, but none of the citizens of the *Republic* is a complete human being, and so none is capable of friendship.[37]

Here, then, is the connection between the moral geography and the treatment of the *Republic*, the connection that Aristotle does not himself draw. While the second part of VII.7 talks about friendship, the first part ends by talking about virtue. Although national differences are presented as differences in their capacities for ruling and being ruled, the conclusion Aristotle draws is not about these: "Both *thumos* and intelligence should be present in the natures of people if they are to be easily guided to *virtue* by the legislator." You need both *thumos* and intelligence to be guided to virtue. The conclusion, but nothing leading up to it, talks about virtue. They are connected through citizenship. Without *thumos* and intelligence, one cannot be political. Without being a political animal, one cannot be guided to virtue. And conversely, only people who can be guided to virtue are fully political animals. Friendship is confined to people capable of virtue and who therefore have both *thumos* and intelligence (e.g., *NE* VIII.5.1157b30–32, VIII.13.1163a22–24). While the best form of friendship can occur only when both people are virtuous, even the most minimal kind of friendship is possible only among political animals.[38]

Socrates says that guardians must be both friendly and fierce, and that both of those come from *thumos*, but he gives no reason why anger and friendship should be manifestations of a single faculty.[39] Fierceness may lead naturally to domination, and friendliness to political rule, but we still need an argument connecting them, and simply saying that they both come from *thumos* doesn't do it. Aristotle offers a slight argument for what Socrates merely asserts: "*thumos* is the psychic power by which we feel friendship. A sign of this is that our *thumos* is aroused" the most against an insult from a friend. An insult from a friend stimulates the *thumos* the most because it combines two features, *thumos* as the capacity for friendship and as the capacity for feeling insults, expressed in anger.

The discussion of the *Republic* advances the argument over the moral geography because friendship links the two kinds of rule, political and despotic. "A city is maintained by proportionate reciprocity. For people seek to return either evil for evil, since otherwise [their condition] seems to be slavery, or good for good, since otherwise there is no exchange" (*NE* V.5.1132b32–1133a2). Proportionate reciprocity here is purely responsive. But someone can do evil in anticipation of possible evil, and good in anticipation of possible good; the first is despotic, the second friendly and political.[40]

When *thumos* and intelligence are combined in a single person, each is transformed, making friendship and ruling possible. The *thumos* that allows distinctions between friends and enemies is not the *thumos* of the wild Europeans. The intelligence that makes ruling possible is not the intelligence of the slavish Asians. Just as *phronēsis* is not reducible to *technē*, so the *thumos* of political animals is not the *thumos* of other animals (*NE* III.3, VIII.4.1338b18–20, 29–30) or other human beings.[41] Reason and *thu-*

mos develop together into faculties that are powers for both thought and desire. Hence Aristotle can say that choice is indifferently deliberate desire or desiring deliberation (*NE* VI.2.1139b5, see III.3.1113a10–12).[42]

Not wanting to be ruled is not the same as wanting to rule others. Like an Asian slave who has calculative but not deliberative power, a purely rational economic man would not be "roused more against those with whom one is familiar and against friends than against those one does not know, when one takes oneself to be slighted" (1328a2–3). Such a rational person would only consider his own injuries, and not pay attention to the source of the injury. Cost-benefit analysis and instrumental reasoning will not get us from *techne* to *phronesis*, or from the desire not to be ruled to the desire to rule. One needs a sense of self—contributed by *thumos*—to differentiate between an injury and its source, so that it isn't just that my foot has been hurt by being stepped on, but that it is *my* foot, and therefore *your* heedlessness is more painful and harder to bear than the weight of your foot itself.[43] No economic calculator would want to be a despot, or a citizen. Being a free rider would be the ideal. For Aristotle, this would be proof of the slavishness of the life of economic rationality.[44]

Thumos is the natural capacity that makes possible the "power to command and the love of freedom." Friendliness and individual self-assertion both develop from this single natural power. It takes *thumos* to distinguish between mine and thine, to move from the natural condition of the family in which household members have everything in common, and so have no need for justice, to the ethical and political condition of citizens who share everything with their friends, and so have a kind of friendship that is the fulfillment of justice. Aristotle's arguments against Socrates in Book II warn against thinking that the political ideal is the family writ large: the sharing and caring for each other in the family may be natural, but the sharing and caring for fellow citizens is not, and takes moral education. Personal identity, which is a function of *thumos*, is the condition of relationships with others. "The defining features of friendship that are found in friendships to one's neighbors would seem to be derived from features of friendship towards oneself" (*NE* IX.4.1166a1–2). Slaves lack *thumos* and therefore cannot aim at their own good and so aim at, and are fulfilled by, the good of another. Plato's warriors may need *thumos*, but this is not a *thumos* that lets them distinguish between mine and thine—they have no private property—only between the polis and its enemies. If their *thumos* leads to friendliness, it certainly cannot lead to self-love, as Aristotelian friendship does. Aristotle differs from the *Republic* in thinking that the ruler's friendliness need not be selfless.

Thumos is the capacity for specifically human self-motion, the ability to make decisions and act on them. Although man is a rational animal, rationality by itself is not enough for ethical development, because we need something further to aim at the goods that can be chosen for their own sakes. "Logoi stimulate and encourage liberal youths. Given innate *ēthos* and true love of the noble (*philokalon*), they can be influenced by virtue" (*NE* X.9.1179b7–10). That innate love for the noble can have no source other than the *thumos*, and its absence makes some people slavish. Human self-motion differs from natural self-motion because this kind of self-motion and self-assertion are only possible with the recognition of other people qua other, and of self qua self. Just as self-assertion and friendship are the same basic and natural psychic capacity of *thumos*, so too are the ability to choose acts that are their own end and the ability to rule and be ruled politically two expressions of the same developed psychic capacity. The combination of logos and *thumos* generates a self with a personal identity lacking in Aristotle's Asiatics and Europeans, a self capable of attachments to objects and other people, rather than a self that views the world as nothing but objects of its desires and fears.

Similarly, ruling and being ruled in turn require more than modern passive citizenship; it involves the capacity for reciprocity and justice. Only rightly developed selves can have civic relations to others. "The society of the good (*suzēn tois agathois*) may supply a sort of training in goodness" (*NE* IX.9.1170a16). Aristotle's citizen-master has to be strong and smart enough to rule within the household for his own benefit, not the slave's. He has to be strong and smart enough to rule in the polis for the sake of the whole and not his own sake. The latter job obviously takes much more practical intelligence. The free rider might be rational by modern standards, but not Aristotle's, which integrates logos and *thumos*: the magnanimous citizen "is the sort of person who does good but is ashamed when he receives it; for doing good is proper to the superior person but receiving it is proper to the inferior" (IV.3.1124b9–10).

VII. ARISTOTLE'S SLAVERY AND CONTEMPORARY PROBLEMS

Why should any of this be of interest to us today? Now that we have finally removed slavery from the moral imagination, and no longer impute moral qualities to different races, does this part of Aristotle's political vision have anything to say to us? I believe it does.

We have seen Aristotle denying three properties of humanity that we think of as universal. He denies that everyone desires freedom, that the desire for ruling is universal, and that we all share the ability to engage in friendly relations. The Enlightenment brought a great deal of progress to mankind by insisting on the universality of these things in a common human nature. That vision led to the abolition of slavery, the triumph of democracy, and the growth of universal human rights. These are good reasons to be glad that Aristotle's moral geography, with its convenient rationale for slavery, has been discredited.

On the other hand, current attempts to spread democracy throughout the world may be foundering on the assumption that everyone wants freedom. We slide too easily from thinking that people do not want to be oppressed to the conclusion that they desire freedom in the stronger sense of wanting to rule themselves and be free political agents. Modern legal devices such as Bills of Rights protect people from being ruled in crucial ways by others, which has dampened the need to act politically in order to be free.[45] We also ignore the presence of slavishness in our own independent countries—it is invisible because it is so prevalent, as it takes the form of commerce—and think that the only necessary condition for freedom is the removal of oppression. As I said in the first section, slavishness is in a sense a default position: if people aren't brought up properly, they will choose life rather than a good life, and so lead vulgar and slavish lives. Far from being natural allies, capitalism and political freedom can be at odds. We do not profit by ignoring either the ethical or the political implications of this possibility.[46]

Book I traces the emergence of the polis out of the natural association of the family, and so prepares the way for the discussion of the polis in the rest of the *Politics*. But a great deal of the discussion in Book I remains within the realm of the household, the *oikos*, and of economics. There are two escapes from nature and its limitations on activity to the necessities of life. One is the unlimited acquisition condemned as irrational and ignoble in Book I, and the other is the political life, which overcomes nature as states come into existence for the sake of life but exist for the good life (I.2.1252b28–29, 1281a2, see *Post. An.* 94b34–37).[47] But the true rival of political life is the life of domination and rule over men, not the unlimited acquisition of things. While unlimited acquisition is irrational and ignoble, despotism unfortunately is neither of those. It even has a legitimate place in the good life, in managing household slaves.[48]

When Aristotle presents the development of the polis in Book I, he identifies two emergent phenomena. The polis develops out of the family and

village. And justice, which we encounter only when Aristotle turns to the
constitution proper in Book III, develops not out of the family but out of
reciprocal exchange not within but between economic units, households as
units of production and consumption. Mastery and the desire to rule emerge
within the household; friendship and equality emerge in the exchanges between them. Therefore, two great problems for the rest of the *Politics*—the relation between the mastery found within the household and the political rule
unique to the polis, and the relation between the reciprocal exchange found
between households and the justice unique to the polis. Book I sets the tone
for the rest of the *Politics* by posing the relation between living and living well
as the relation between economic and political institutions and desires.

The development of the polis is fragile and never irreversible. The story
of the genesis of the polis in Book I has no implications for the genesis of
any particular polis. While the polis is natural, no particular polis is. The
Republic starts out to define the origin of any city, but soon becomes more
narrowly concerned with the genesis of the best city. This is similar to the
elision sometimes found in social contract theories between explaining the
origins of sociability and justifying the obligations to obey a particular sovereign and live in a particular society. Aristotle separates these two tasks.
Book I is an account of the genesis of the polis, not of any particular polis.
Political rule is rule over and by equals. That rule is political has no implications for the form of government; democracy is only one way of ruling
over and by equals. The coming to be of the polis and of a particular polis
have completely different accounts, which makes practical science different
from theoretical science, a point we'll return to when facing the fact that
nothing in the genealogy of the polis accounts for the plurality of constitutional forms. Corrupt constitutions, factions, and the love of domination
are all permanent possible forms of regression. The activity of politics is a
permanent struggle against these possibilities.

The same reasons that make political life rare also make reasoning of
limited value in persuading people that the political life is the good life. The
limited value of argument forces a distinction, as I will show, between political philosophy and political wisdom and practice, between what I've elsewhere called logical and ethical argument.[49] Aristotle would not be moved
by a criticism that his arguments don't appeal to all rational agents. There
are *no* moral or political arguments that appeal to just anyone—here is a
great gulf between Aristotelian and modern thinking. Once more: "*Logoi*
stimulate and encourage liberal youths. Given innate *ēthos* and true love of
the noble (*philokalon*), they can be influenced by virtue" (*NE* X.9.1179b7–
10). The rest of us have to be compelled.

Where moderns take profit as a legitimating excuse for doing things that otherwise would be wrong, Aristotle sees money as corrupting acts that would otherwise be acceptable. Modern political thought reaches beneath what Aristotle thought as solid ground to supplant *thumos* with the milder motives of commerce.[50] Imagine what Aristotle would make of "anger management"! In Book VII he even offers an argument from shame against despotism and so turns *thumos* against itself: since it is ignoble for states to conquer and enslave other states, the same holds for individuals. Therefore, as we will see in Book II, ruling and being ruled in turn is both a given and a goal. Under circumstances of equality in which ruling and being ruled in turn is possible, Aristotle's ethical arguments show that it is also noble. Such demonstration is the function of political philosophy.

CHAPTER TWO

Book II:
Aristotle's State as a Work of Art

*P*olitics I is incomplete. While the ergon argument in the *Ethics* argues reasonably that identifying the nature of *x* will tell us what a good *x* is—how could knowing what a pianist is not at the same time show what a good pianist is?—I pointed out in the introduction that the definition of the polis does not tell us what a good polis is. This is not a failure of Book I but an indication of the peculiarity of political life and political knowledge. The genealogy of the polis in Book I does nothing to explain why most men don't live in poleis as citizens, and why poleis, unlike families, have a variety of forms of constitutions. Book I says nothing about what, if anything, people can do to affect the transition from being political animals to living in poleis. The fact that people by nature have logos and can talk about justice does not mean that justice, too, is natural, or that people want to act justly. "What counts as living together (*suzēn*) is sharing conversation and thought (*koinonein logon kai dianoias*) and not pasturing in the same place as in the case of grazing animals" (*NE* IX.9.1170b12–13). Book I leaves unexplained the transition from life to the good life.

To recall from my first chapter just one dimension of this incompleteness, the genealogy in Book I shows that the polis is the final step in the development of communities because it is economically self-sufficient. Missing is an account of the relation between economic self-sufficiency and the ethical self-sufficiency of the good life. I will argue that the fact that there is no single relation between the two leads to the variety of constitutions and the variety of relations between a good polis and a good life.

That such questions remain after Book I shows the limits of nature in political life. Nature will only get us so far. Ethics, too, had to worry about the fact that few people fully realize their nature and lead good lives,[1] but in politics things are harder still. The purpose of the polis, the good life, not only fails to tell us what a good polis looks like, but Aristotle tells us repeatedly in Books III–VIII that there are a variety of constitutions and, even worse, a variety of good constitutions. Function, that is, does not determine form. Chapter 3 will show how Aristotle constructs a specifically political relation between form and function, but first I want to see how *Politics* II moves from considering the polis as natural to the polis as the product of human artifice. "The desire (*hormē*) towards this kind of community [the polis] exists in all men by nature, but the first man to put it together is the cause of the greatest of goods" (I.2.1253a30).[2] Aristotle has exhausted the resources of the analogy between the polis and natural things in the first book, and so turns to the analogies between poleis and artifacts in Book II, to discover the limitations of that analogy as well. Book III will finally put us in a position to think about the state in terms of *phronēsis*, practical wisdom, and neither art nor nature.

I. THE IDEAL STATE AND ITS PROBLEMS

Politics II examines past attempts to describe an ideal state. Without explanation, Aristotle announces at the beginning the unifying theme of that examination: "We must make a beginning that which is a natural beginning for this investigation. It is necessary that all citizens be partners either in everything, or in nothing, or in some things but not in others" (II.1.1260b35–37). Citizens should share those things that make the polis into a unity, and a unity of a specific kind. "Political animals are those whose joint work (*ergon*) is one common thing" (*Hist. An.* I.1.488a7–8). There is some connection between being the best state and being a unified state, although, as we will see, it is not true that the more unified a state, the better. Aristotle represents Socrates's thought as committing the despotic or pleonectic fallacy of thinking that if something, here unity, is good, then the more we have of it, the better. Oddly, we will learn in Book II what sort of unity the polis can be, and we already know from Book I that the polis is natural, but we only discover what the polis *is* in Book III. If the polis is artificial, then it makes sense for its unity to be the subject of examination, since a unified object is the outcome of good art. Unity is not a metaphysical idea; a unified state is one that is not liable to faction.

Apart from saying that it is a "natural beginning," Aristotle gives no reason why an examination of the ideal state should focus on what citizens share. He gives no reason why he should interpret that question narrowly in terms of common property. This narrowing seems especially arbitrary since he starts by looking at Plato's *Republic* and the attention to property hardly seems to do justice to the *Republic*.³ *Politics* II starts with Socrates's proposal that children, women, and property should be communal (II.1.1261a6). Chapters 2 through 4 present Aristotle's criticism of the community of women and children in the *Republic*, and chapter 5 of holding all property in common. When chapter 6 turns to the *Laws*, he complains that "Socrates settled very few topics in the *Republic*: the way in which women and children should be shared in common; the system of property; and the organization of the constitution . . . Otherwise he has filled out his account with extraneous discussions, including those about the sort of education the guardians should receive" (II.6.1264b28–40). This last remark is especially odd, since Aristotle's own account of the ideal constitution in Books VII and VIII discusses education, not of the guardians, since there are none, but of all citizens.

As Book II leaves the *Republic* behind, it seems to lose focus. Chapter 6 looks at the *Laws*, and begins by complaining that "most of the *Laws* consist, in fact, of laws, and he has said little about the constitution" (1265a1–2). Much of Aristotle's discussion of the *Laws* has to do with its regulation of property and then chapter 7 moves on to "other constitutions proposed either by private individuals or by philosophers and statesmen" (1266a31). Phaleas's proposals, which occupy chapter 7, "hold that the most important thing is to have property well-organized," but Aristotle counters by saying "while equalizing property of citizens is among the things that helps prevent faction, it is certainly no big thing, so to speak" (1266a36–37, 1267a37–38). The criticisms of Hippodamus, which occupy chapter 8, attack his most unusual proposals, without any theme connecting those criticisms. The same happens in chapter 9 for the Spartan constitution, chapter 10 for the Cretan, 11 for the Carthaginian, and 12 for the Athenian and some others. Book II ends by criticizing the results of the practice of lawgiving. The figure of the lawgiver does not appear again in the *Politics*; it only makes sense when the state is a work of art.⁴

Starting with his criticism of the *Laws*, Aristotle increasingly sharpens his insistence that laws must be subordinate to the constitution (see too IV.1.1289a13–20). The apparent loss of focus in *Politics* II comes from the lack of subordination of laws to constitution in the proposals and states he looks at. That subordination might seem obvious today, since the constitution *means* the fundamental law, and it is almost always written. His singling out of individual laws seems both to confirm and to violate this insistence—hence the ambiguous relation of Book II to the criticism of the sophists in *Ethics* X.9 for "thinking it an easy task to assemble the laws with good reputations and then legislate. For they think they can select the best laws, as though the selection itself did not require comprehension" (1181a16–18)—contrast that remark with the opening sentence of *Politics* II.1, which seems to endorse that very practice: ". . . we must investigate other constitutions too, both some of those used in poleis that are said to be well-governed, and any others described by anyone that are held to be good, in order to see what is correct or useful in them" (1260b28–31). The issue of how much can be accomplished through the regulation of property is a paradigm for the subordination of laws to the constitution.

Aristotle's question in Book II is the following: What are the *means* by which people, specifically people capable of leading autonomous lives and therefore people who will enter the polis as equals, become a single community aiming at living well? This is one orientation to the fundamental question of the *Politics*, the orientation from the efficient cause. Man is a political animal. He leads a complete, self-sufficient, and happy life by being part of a complete and self-sufficient community, the polis. At every stage in Aristotle's inquiry, he will need to show us how to avoid the twin dangers of one side of self-sufficiency obliterating the other, either of the state merely providing the background conditions in which individuals can lead autonomous lives or of individuals sacrificing themselves for the good of the whole.

The simple answer, repeated in different ways in Book II and the rest of the *Politics*, is that property, whether common or private, is not the means to unity and community, as most people seem to think, but that education is that means. "The most important of all the things that have been mentioned for the endurance of constitutions, which all men now make light of, is to be educated in harmony with the constitutions" (V.9.1310a12–14). But Aristotle arrives at that conclusion only by examining the different proposals to create a good state through the distribution of property. He moves from a more superficial and self-defeating means of unity to a truly political and self-reinforcing one. Plato is central to Book II because, even though the *Republic* argues that education is the central factor that makes the ideal state, the *Republic* also bars rulers from owning private property in order to make them virtuous. By turning from property to education as the appropriate efficient cause of the good political community, Aristotle turns political philosophy and the activity of the statesman from making to doing, from *technē* to *phronēsis*. The state cannot be a work of art.

A polis consists of a multitude, as we said before, and should be unified and made into a community by means of education. It is strange, at any rate, that the one who aimed to bring in education, and who believed

that through it the polis would be excellent, should think to set it straight
by measures of this sort, and not by habits, philosophy, and laws—as in
Sparta and Crete, where the legislator aimed to make property communal by means of the messes. (II.5.1263b35–40)

There are two outstanding oddities in Book II. First is why Aristotle narrows the question of what citizens have to have in common to a question of
property.[5] Second, though, is a question that bears on the *Politics* as practical knowledge and its relation to political wisdom. Why should Aristotle
pay any attention at all to what private citizens and philosophers (*hai men
idiōtōnon hai de philosophōn*) (II.7.1266a31–32) have to say? This question
seems especially urgent when we compare his procedure in Book II to his
remark in *NE* VI that we should pay attention to the unarticulated sayings
of experienced men (VI.11.1143b11–13) and to the attack on the sophists at
the end of *NE* X.9. The sophists in their ignorance just pick good laws without thinking about constitutions:

> They think they can select the best laws, as though the selection itself
> did not require comprehension, and as though correct judgment were not
> the most important thing, as it is in music. [They are wrong;] for those
> with experience in each area judge the products correctly and compre-
> hend the ways and means of completing them. . . . Laws would seem to
> be the products of political science; how, then, could someone acquire
> legislative science, or judge which laws are best, from laws alone? For
> neither do we appear to become experts in medicine by reading text-
> books. (1181a18–1181b3)

What Aristotle ridicules there doesn't seem any different from what he himself does, especially in the last four chapters of Book II, which look at laws
held in good repute. There are many differences between the *Ethics* and the
Politics, but how he treats competing views is one of those crucial differences.[6] After this attack on the sophists, *NE* X.9 announces a program for
political study, and scholars have argued about whether the *Politics* follows
that program. That issue seems to me subordinate to this question of why
Plato, Phaleas, and Hippodamus are worth listening to in the first place if
the sophists are not. The *Ethics* limits its audience to people who already
have good ethical habits, and, with the exception of Plato in I.6, only pays
attention to the ethical opinions of the virtuous. He remarks of Hippodamus that "his love of honor caused him also to adopt a rather extraordinary general lifestyle. Some people thought he carried things too far, indeed,

with his long hair, expensive ornaments, and the same cheap warm clothing worn winter and summer. He . . . was the first person, not actually engaged in politics, to attempt to say something about the best constitution" (II.8.1267b22–28). I was reminded of Stesilaus in the *Laches* who taught the art of fighting in armor, but was ridiculous when "in the circumstances of actual warfare gave a much finer demonstration against his will" (183e), but Aristotle only criticizes what Hippodamus, Phaleas, and Plato had to say, not their right to say it. In the *Ethics*, Hippodamus's love of honor and its consequences would have led Aristotle to dismiss whatever he had to say.[7]

Paying attention to Hippodamus signals an important difference between the *Politics* and the *Ethics*. It changes the status of philosophy, including Aristotle's own authority, and it changes the audience for these works. In the *Ethics* Aristotle can comfortably address himself to other serious, right-thinking people who already act virtuously. For ethics, there is a "we," an audience whose values can be the basis of argument and persuasion. There is no such "we" in the *Politics*. The *Politics* faces a predicament more like the contemporary situation in which it feels as though everything is up for grabs. There are no exemplars to point to for a best constitution in the way Aristotle can point to Pericles as a paradigm of an individual leading a political life.

II. PROPERTY AND A UNIFIED POLIS

Here is the problem for Book II. If all communities aim at some good, and if the political community aims at the highest good (I.1.1252a1–7), then it seems to follow immediately that all members of a political community share in that highest good. "Communities should have one thing that is common and the same for all their members, whether they share in it equally or unequally" (VII.8.1328a27–29); that passage names the common thing as happiness. But that isn't the direction Aristotle goes here. Even if all citizens share in the highest good, Aristotle has to look for a *practical* answer to the question of what all citizens must have in common. The natural ties that bind a family together aren't available for poleis, and the statesman has to find an alternative. Family members live together, but they do not have a common life in the sense that Aristotle will develop for citizens.

Aristotle has to ask about unity in terms of efficient causes, and hence property, because the other three causes won't do here. First, the polis isn't natural enough for final causes to determine the unity of the polis. The first line of the *Politics* says that all communities, and not just political communities, are oriented toward a common end that all members share: "We see that every polis is a community of some sort, and that every community is established for the sake of some good" (1252a1–2). Common ends are not specifically political. One might think that the more a community is united by a common purpose, the more unity the community itself would have. But the existence of alliances shows that that inference is fallacious. Alliances have a clear common purpose in military victory, but alliances constitute a community in only the most minimal and least unified sense.

In addition, the states most generally praised, such as Sparta, Crete, and Carthage, are those with evident agreement about their ends, so that their laws are not a haphazard collection, but such a common end does not necessarily make those states better than others, just easier to study. "Even though most customs have been established pretty much at random in most cases, anywhere the laws have to some extent a single aim, it is domination. So in Sparta and Crete the educational system and most of the laws are set up for war" (VII.2.1324b5–9). Aristotle leaves open whether these poleis just happen to have two properties, that they organize their laws toward a single aim, and that that aim is domination, or whether states with a single goal must make that goal domination. In either case, happiness and virtue cannot be a "single aim" in the same sense as domination. The unity of the state will be different in the two cases.

Next, the formal cause of unity of the state is the constitution, the embodied idea of justice. But justice doesn't make its appearance in the *Politics* until midway through Book III. Aristotle has to see what unifies a polis here in Book II, then define what a polis is at the start of Book III, and only then discuss constitutions and finally be ready to talk about justice. Better understanding these arguments about property and the unity of the polis will be a start at making sense of this odd sequence.

Finally, there is good reason for Aristotle not to ask about the material cause of unity, either. He does not ask what prepolitical common nature people must have to be citizens of a single state, as he does at VII.4.1325b33–1326a5 for the ideal state, or what nature people have to have to be citizens of poleis at all, his question in VII.7, which we examined in chapter 1. Poleis are unique among associations because they are made of men different in kind (II.2.1261a24; see III.4.1276b20–1277a10, IV.3.1290a2–7), so a common material cause cannot be the source of the polis's unity. The unity of a polis, that is, does not come from the unity of the people who comprise it, *pace* the thinking of those who think political unity must come from the ethnic, linguistic, or historical unity of a nation. Alliances, by contrast, arise from people who are similar, and therefore their value and power are measured by quantity: the more, the stronger. Neither military alliances nor ethnic unity have anything political about them, because they are not based on people differing in kind. We are left with the efficient cause to uncover the unity of the polis.

What, then, is the means by which self-sufficient people differing in kind become parts of a self-sufficient polis? "Things which are to become one differ in kind" (II.2.1261a29–30). What, in more Aristotelian terms, is the power whose actuality is the best state? What, that is, best arrangement of prepolitical materials will lead to an ideal state? These are the questions the proposed constitutions in Book II confront and get wrong. Their error is in posing the wrong relation between virtue and law, and between virtue and external goods. All aim at a unified state; all, tacitly, agree that the way to unify the state is by making people virtuous. They differ on the means available to the statesman to create virtue.

If the goal is a common *energeia*, a common way of life, then common *property* Aristotle argues, is not the way to get it. Seeing what is wrong with making property the means of creating a political unity out of diversity, whether through making property common or equal, is the best way of seeing just how the political community is an ethical unity. Possessing in common does not lead to living in common.

As I've mentioned, the criterion he uses in Book II to distinguish the polis from other communities is that "the city is made up not only of a number of human beings, but also of human beings differing in kind. A city does not arise from persons who are similar" (II.2.1261a25–26). Later in the *Politics*, though, he will tell us that the "polis tends to consist as much as possible of people who are equal and similar, and this condition belongs especially to those in the middle" (IV.11.1295b25–26, see too VII.8.1328a35–41, in which the polis is a community of similar men). The *dynamis*—potentiality— for a political community is people differing in kind; its *energeia*—actuality— is people who are equal and similar because of their common political activity. The problem of the *Politics* overall, the problem of political animals, is how self-sufficient people can live in a self-sufficient community. The middle term making the necessary connection between self-sufficient people and a self-sufficient community is *equality*.

It is clearly better, where possible, for the same people always to rule. But among those where it is not possible, because all are naturally equal (*to tēn phusin isous*), and where it is at the same time just for all to share in the benefits or burdens (*eit' agathon eite phaulon*) of ruling, it is at least possible to approximate to this if those who are equal take turns and are similar when out of office. (II.2.1261a37–1261b2)[8]

It is a perennial political problem, represented throughout the *Politics*, to see how such equality can coexist with forms of inequality, or alternatively, what other forms of equality, especially economic equality, are required by political equality. While today this problem most often takes the form of the relation between political and economic justice, Aristotle's concern is with the relation between political and economic self-sufficiency. This, I think, is the philosophical reason for the emphasis in Book II on property.

Prior to political activity, I've just said, the *dynamis* of the polis is dissimilar people. Political activity transforms them into similar and equal citizens. The similarity among citizens will be their equal ethical self-sufficiency. Just as his accounts of nutrition and sensation in the *de Anima* show how the soul transforms unlike into like, so here the city must be made of people who are, as material, unlike, and the state transforms them into similars. If they are made one in potential or matter, they will be a unity but not a political community. Things made from heterogeneous parts are more natural, and have more significant unity, than those made from homogeneous parts (*PA* II.1.646a12–24, 646a35–b10, *Pol.* IV.4.1290b25–39). The city has more unity than an alliance, because it is made up of things with *less* unity than the alliance (II.2.1261a24–29): "What is more self-sufficient is more choiceworthy, what is less a unity is more choiceworthy than what is more so" (1261b14–15). Unity and self-sufficiency as aspects of community are at odds.

III. PRIVATE PROPERTY, ANCIENT AND MODERN

At this point, it is worth contrasting Aristotle's approach with modern understandings of the relation of property to the constitution. Justice is mostly absent from Book II. Aristotle's discussion of property differs from modern analyses because he sees no *right* to private property. The whole discussion of what we should share takes place in the absence of any assertion of rights.[9] We need private property for friendship, to help others, to repay debts, and to retaliate against injury. Private property promotes the ethical virtues of possession (care and temperance) and use (liberality). Temperance and liberality "are the only choiceworthy states that bear on the use of property. One cannot use property either mildly or courageously, for example, but one can use it temperately and generously" (II.6.1265a35–37). He doesn't mention justice here because justice includes the right use of other people's property, not one's own, and there is nothing unique about a political community in protecting people against acts of injustice. In this sense, justice is not the primary political virtue; liberality is. It turns out that the solution to the problem of political unity is not an arrangement of property but the virtue of liberality.

Without a right to private property, the connection between a citizen and his property is very thin. Property consists in the resources that a man happens to have, nothing like modern ideas that private property is tied up with personal identity. There is no labor theory that could justify who owns what. In fact, there is no justification at all.[10] There is no assertion that property is deserved or earned. On the contrary, *unearned* wealth is superior to wealth acquired through labor, since he argues later that working and aiming at wealth is vulgar and incompatible with virtue.[11] We justly acquire slaves through war, not commerce (I.8.1256b24–26). Productivity, whether farming or practicing a craft, is necessary, not noble. Therefore, in asking in Book II about whether things should be owned in common or privately, he asks about things that are necessary rather than intrinsically valuable. Our relations to those things are similarly merely necessary. And yet there are virtues consisting in the right way of acting toward these necessities, virtues that supply the transition from the economic and necessary to the political realm of acts worth choosing for their own sake. Any answer tying possession to merit or desert would backfire in a world in which it is better not to earn one's property.[12]

Aristotle is not adverse to heavy-handed political authority over property. When he presents his own ideal state he says that private property should be distributed so that each citizen owns land near the frontier and near the city (VII.10.1330a13–20), and notes that unequal wealth is one of the greatest sources of faction and instability (V.3.1303b15–17). He even talks about "the public service of having children" (VII.16.1335b28), so he doesn't object to the *Republic* on the grounds that its legislation about wives and children, or education, violates rights to privacy. There is private property in the *Politics*, but no idea of privacy and no public/private distinction. Aristotle objects to the property arrangements proposed by others not because the state has no business engaging in such distribution, and certainly not because such redistribution is unjust. Modern arguments about whether libertarianism or socialism is more conducive to democracy will find no help here. Aristotle's attention is on the transition from our non-political relations with things to the political relation with other people, and so his reasoning has a generality that makes it unsuited to generating particular political implications. Not only is the discussion of what citizens must share limited to property, but the discussion of property is limited to the issue of what citizens must share.[13]

Therefore, Aristotle's conclusions about property—private ownership

but public use; the laws should not legislate equal property—carry no implications about the best form of constitution; nor do they give any weight in
arguments for or against democracy or oligarchy. In Book IV he argues that
constitutions with a large middle class are more stable than the alternatives
and are more conducive to the development of virtue, but he never draws
the implication that therefore the state should redistribute wealth to build a
large middle class.[14] Indeed in V.9 he argues in the opposite direction when
he says that leveling property will destroy democracy and oligarchy, which
depend on the existence of the many and the rich (1309b38–1310a2), but
neither line of argument appears in Book II, which pays no attention to the
different kinds of constitutions, since it pays no attention to justice.

IV. PROPERTY VERSUS EDUCATION AS A UNIFYING FORCE

While Plato's common property was designed to eliminate faction
(II.7.1266a36–39), it in fact increases it (II.5.1263b22–25). (The women and
children held in common in the *Republic* become a source of faction, too.)
Aristotle contends that these disorders are not due to private property but
to vice (II.5.1263b17–22). Therefore, he infers, the common power that leads
to common ends and common action will be education (II.5.1263b28–38).
I take this to be the crucial inference in Book II. Education, not property,
is the efficient cause and the means by which heads of households become
part of a single political community, self-sufficient individuals as parts of a
self-sufficient community. Education here must mean habituation toward
the virtue of using property in common and for common purposes, and not
necessarily teaching and learning in the more intentional or specific sense
which is the subject of the final two books. Education drops out of consideration between Book II and Books VII and VIII because the intermediate
books are concerned with constitutional justice, with who should rule, and
not with what they should do once selected to rule, apart from not committing acts of injustice. In the best state, education and distributive justice are
connected. We become the sort of people who can equally rule and be ruled
by using in common our private property.

Throughout the *Politics* Aristotle repeatedly seems fallaciously to identify the virtuous and moderate with the mediocre: since the middle class
avoids the vices of the rich and the poor, it must be virtuous; if one's desires
are moderate, then one will be temperate and virtuous, etc. Discussing moderation in the context of property in Book II makes temperance something

more than the mediocrity and self-control that might be necessary conditions for good action but are not states of character good in themselves.
Temperance in the *Ethics* has nothing to do with property; it is moderation
and restraint with respect to the pleasures of food, drink, and sex, but here
in *Politics* II it is the virtue of preserving one's property. One could be temperate in preserving ones property without caring about other people, but
liberality in the use of property requires a concern for others. Temperance,
therefore, would not by itself unify a state; for that one needs liberality as
well. (True temperance, then, requires liberality too.) Their combination is
a modest form of the unity of the virtues appropriate to property.

Aristotle's vision of the best system of property requires ownership to
be private and its use common, and he says this will combine the good
of both, the virtues of care and temperance and the virtue of liberality
(II.5.1263a22–25). "It is the special business (*ergon idion*) of the legislator to create in men the disposition to use private property in common"
(1263a39–40). "Even if one prescribed a moderate amount of property for
everyone, it would be of no use. For one should level desires more than property, and that cannot happen unless people have been adequately educated
by the laws" (II.7.1266b28–30). Moderation of desires is necessary but not
sufficient; in addition, people need the virtue of liberality, which has to do
with using property to help others, not to restrain oneself. The *Republic*'s
abolition of private property might create temperance, but not liberality,
and liberality is the virtue of the use, as opposed to possession and preservation, of property.[15] One might think that if people had enough property,
they would be temperate, and it is only because of the threat of scarcity that
people become wasteful and gluttonous, but it is less plausible that a sufficient amount of property makes people act liberally. Temperance by itself
might not promote leisure and its proper use: "it is generally agreed that to
be well-governed a constitution should have leisure from necessary tasks.
But the way to achieve this is not easy to discover" (II.9.1269a34–35). Self-
sufficiency is redefined when we add liberality to temperance, transforming
it from economic to ethical and political self-sufficiency.

Politics II asks what people must share. It starts with three chapters that
treat the most radical kind of sharing, the *Republic*'s community of women
and children. Property (II.5.1262b37) is a more plausible instrument for creating unity than women and children. Property, unlike women and children, allows the distinction between possession and use (*ktēsis* and *chrēsis*).
In fact, while he never defines property or indicates its scope—apart from
criticizing Phaleas for equalizing only land and forgetting that there are

other kinds of property—one could define property as something for which we can distinguish possession from use.

What the *Ethics* calls justice is in the *Politics* divided into two distinct political problems, the first, the use of property, which appears in Book II not as a question of justice at all, and the second, the justice of awarding offices in proportion to merit, which narrows constitutional justice to distributions of office and honor, not property. In the *Ethics* justice concerns goods we can compete over. *Pleonexia* is about "not all goods, but only those involved in good and bad fortune, goods which are, [considered] without qualification, always good, but for this or that person not always good" (*NE* V.1.1129b3–4).[16] Special or particular justice "is found in the distribution of honors or wealth or anything else that can be divided among members of a community who share in a political system" (V.2.1130b30–32). But the scope of property in the *Politics* is narrower than that of justice, defined by the distinction between possession and use. I can't possess some honor but let you use it.

The distinction between possession and use accounts for the fact that while in Book I Aristotle listed five ways of life, nomadic, raiding, fishing, hunting, and farming (I.8.1256b1–2), in Book II and in the rest of the *Politics* he assumes that all poleis are based on farming, not the other ways of living. The other four ways of life are evolutionary dead ends that provide a community with economic self-sufficiency—these are "ways of life whose fruits are natural and do not provide food through exchange or commerce"—but neither the moral self-sufficiency of a virtuous life nor the political self-sufficiency of the polis. He offers no explanation for this assumption that all poleis are based on farming, but the argument of Book II provides one. Only agriculture allows for communities with a settled and permanent location. Only in farming can one distinguish between possession and use in the form of land and its produce. The virtue of liberality doesn't have to do with sharing land, but with sharing the food yielded by the land. There is no analogous potency/act distinction for the other ways of life. Land is the potential for food, while spears and nets are not the potential for fish.[17]

Given this shift from property to education, Aristotle need not explore here, as he does in Book VII, further ambiguities of what is common. At VII.10 he recommends that

> the territory must be divided into two parts, one of which is communal and another that belongs to private individuals. And each of these must again be divided in two: one part of the communal land should be used to support public services to the gods, the other to defray the cost of messes;

one part of the private land should be located near the frontiers, the other near the city-state, so that, with two allotments assigned to each citizen, all of them may share in both locations. (VII.10.1330a9–15)

In Book II, by contrast, all property is privately owned, and what is common is its liberal use. The common ownership in Book VII is common ownership of land; the common use in Book II is common consumption of food. For Book II the practical question is the means by which people will come to share what each has. Plato thought common use would be achieved through common ownership: if people held all goods in common, then no one would object to using them together. But Aristotle finds that if use is common, it doesn't matter whether ownership is common or not; all the advantages Plato saw in common ownership are achieved through common use, and there are good distinct reasons, connected to care and temperance, for keeping it private.

By relocating the question of the common from property to education, Aristotle excludes the distribution of ownership from the concern of the statesman of the ideal state. That is, he takes existing property arrangements for granted. Aristotle doesn't just reject the proposals about property made by the people he examines, he rejects the management of property altogether. The reason comes out in Book VII: "We need resources in order to live a good life, although we need fewer of them if we are in a better condition, more if we are in a worse one" (VII.13.1332a1–2, see too *NE* X.8.1179a3–6). Virtue and citizenship require some property, but it isn't worth trying to calculate how much: more important that legislators devote their attention to an education that will make people act, and in particular use their property, in common and for common ends. Under Aristotle's own ideal constitution, the state's power over property distributions will be greatest, although the dependence of living well on property will be at its least. Under inferior constitutions, inferior men rely more on property to live well, and so people are more attached to their property, and the role of the state in distribution will be less.

The constitutions examined in Book II.1–8 failed by concentrating on temperance rather than liberality, possession of property rather than use, and therefore even Plato neglected education. In the last four chapters Aristotle criticizes constitutions that were directed toward war and not peace, and therefore not toward the right uses of leisure. Leisure is not so much a matter of owning property as being free from concerning oneself with economic self-sufficiency. His argument therefore enacts, but does not discuss, the connection between liberality and leisure. Those who think we organize the constitution by managing property can only regard leisure as material surplus. The Spartan constitution formed for war can't handle peace and leisure (II.9.1271b1-6, see VII.2.1324b4-9, VII.14.1333b6-34, VII.15.1334a40-b4). It is easier to see how to organize a constitution for war than for peace.

Alongside Aristotle's moves from temperance to liberality, and from property to education, is a reconsideration of the statesman as efficient cause, shifting the statesman from craftsman to *phronimos*, the person with the virtue of practical wisdom. Temperance is a plausible object of an art of ruling. It is similarly reasonable to think of an *art* of war. But liberality cannot be an object of *technē* in the way temperance might be, and there are no arts of peace and leisure. (The activities that constitute the right use of leisure might include appreciating and participating in the arts of music, but that's a different story, which we will hear in Book VIII.) Therefore, the well-regarded constitutions of chapters 9-12 are partially successful. At least they are able to organize the state toward a goal. The goals they aim at, though, cannot be worth choosing for their own sakes.

Aristotle's predecessors picked the wrong kind of efficient cause to unite free and self-sufficient men into a self-sufficient community.[18] It is wrong to equalize property, and wrong to insure that all have equal and enough property. But in fact it is best if all do have equal and sufficient property (II.9.1270a34-b1) and for no one to have excessive wealth or poverty. It is wrong to demand that people care for each other by not letting them care about themselves, as the *Republic* does. Although for Aristotle the law compels virtue, and he doesn't see good action destroyed by being required, in these cases the laws regarding property are the wrong instrument for a good end.[19] The law commands just actions not through coercion but through habit and education. Laws equalizing property are the wrong means because they make the relation between ruler and ruled into a relation of form and matter, the relation between the craftsman and his material. Virtue in the *Ethics* is self-replicating: we become virtuous by performing virtuous actions. That circularity places constraints on the efficient causes the statesman can use to unify the polis by making citizens care about each other. However the constitution creates the conditions for becoming virtuous, it must not interfere with that self-replicating nature.

V. THE MODESTY AND AMBITION OF THE *POLITICS*

I began by asking why proposals for the ideal state provide the context for asking what people must share, which leads to the discussion of property. The answer is that the question of sharing is especially acute in the ideal state because such a state is the self-sufficient unity of self-sufficient people, a condition other poleis only approximate. On the one side happiness is virtuous activity, *energeia kat'aretēn*. Virtue depends on action being one's own; this is the self-sufficiency of virtue and happiness. But virtue at the same time is action that aims at and achieves a common good, the good of the self-sufficient political community. Making an action one's own threatens to make the action serve the individual only, as self-love can degenerate into selfishness. On the other hand, if good actions are those that serve the common good, it doesn't matter who does them. (The issue of mercenaries in war, which has such a long history, turns on exactly that idea.) Such a standard for action threatens to make good action into sacrifice. The same pair of problems faces property arrangements. Liberality insures that the individual's self-sufficiency doesn't mean isolation but participation in a self-sufficient community.

Just as in the *Ethics* friendship toward another depends on self-love, so here the friendly, and fierce, attachment to one's polis is possible only if one has something of one's own to hold dear. Instead of thinking that love for one's own is incompatible with love for the whole, as Socrates maintains in the *Republic*, Aristotle will make love for one's own the basis for loyalty to the whole, and love for the whole the basis of love for one's fellow citizens.[20]

While the ancient state, at least as Plato and Aristotle present it, seems more intrusive than the modern, with no recognition of privacy, here is a respect in which the tables are turned. The line of modern political thinkers from Rousseau through Rawls and Habermas look for commonality in shared opinion, a secular equivalent of articles of faith; more conservative thinkers try to find secular equivalents to rituals of confession of allegiance. Such visions of politics produce a divided self, an alienated self that keeps one side private and shows another face in public. (Or, as in Rousseau, they attempt to overcome that alienation.) Aristotle's strategy is more modest. Private ownership and common use avoid dividing the self into private comprehensive views or preferences and the common public reason of a neutral political framework. Civic participation never means casting aside and bracketing one's particularity. We never leave behind life in pursuit of the good life. There is no problem of selfishness and altruism. Aristotle's autonomous citizens do not have a divided self; the only character with a divided self we encounter in the *Politics* is Jason, tyrant of Pherae, who felt hungry only when he was not ruling (III.5.1277a23–25).

One of the reasons for the popularity of the idea of justice as redistributing property is because people today think that a state directing education

would be too coercive.[21] Aristotle doesn't worry whether state action is coercive or not, and he thinks education will solve problems of people acting well together that common ownership will not, because education as
a solution means the statesman acts so that citizens will act in the future,
while the common property solution has the statesman making arrangements that will make choices by the citizens unnecessary. Some sort of
property distribution may be the natural answer to the question of what
citizens must share, but it makes the activity of the legislator into an exercise of *techne*, instead of the harder and less obvious praxeis that constitute statesmanship and citizenship. Those who would equalize property or
eliminate private property, or who elevate private property, both then and
now, do away with liberality. Where the Spartans needed temperance but
not liberality to live for war, moderns need temperance but not liberality
to engage in commerce.

VI. POLITICS AS PRACTICAL, NOT PRODUCTIVE

There is a unity to Book II, and thus to Aristotle's criticisms of Plato, and
to the movement from the concern with property that dominates the treatment of Plato to the increasingly diffuse criticism of other thinkers and
well-regarded states. The unity consists in finding that all previous attempts
at visualizing an ideal state get the idea of constitution wrong—wrong because they conceive of politics as *techne*, not as praxis. They consequently
attempt to get property arrangements, the constitution, and laws to do a
job that only education and virtue can accomplish. Book II illuminates the
nature of political wisdom by showing how it cannot be reduced to *techne*.

Therefore, although Aristotle treats Plato much more seriously and in
greater detail (chapters 1–6) than he does Phaleas (chapter 7), those two
thinkers in fact present two extreme alternatives that together formulate
a critical political problem. In Plato the state is self-sufficient just because
the individual is not; in Phaleas the individual will be self-sufficient, and
the state therefore is not. Both Plato and Phaleas want to get rid of faction:
instead of the modern opposition of unity and diversity, Aristotle and his
predecessors saw the choices as community versus faction, friendship versus enmity. Plato's guardians have no loyalties except to the state, and so
there is no possibility of faction among them. "We regard friendship as the
greatest of goods for poleis, since in this condition people are least likely to
factionalize. . . . But in a polis this sort of community [of wives and children]
inevitably makes friendship watery" (II.4.1262b7–15). Phaleas's citizens

have equal property, and therefore nothing to fight over. Plato's guardians have friendship toward the whole, but not toward any particular individuals. Phaleas's citizens have no need for friendship because they are individually self-sufficient. Aristotle's education will develop virtue and friendship. Aristotle's criticisms resemble the remark in *Federalist* 10 that removing faction by removing its causes would eliminate liberty as well. Once Aristotle gets around to his own positive proposals, we have to see how his plan for education will create unity and eliminate faction without eliminating diversity.

As I mentioned at the start of this chapter, the first two books of the *Politics* respectively show how the polis is natural and then artificial, and the two show the limitations of what we can know about politics as either natural or artificial. While he said in Book I that the polis is natural (I.2.1252b30, 1253a1), we quickly see that it cannot be treated in the way Aristotle's theoretical sciences treat things that exist by nature. For just one reason I've already mentioned, the narrative of the development of the polis out of families and villages has no relation to the history of any particular polis. Therefore the polis is natural without qualifying as an Aristotelian substance. It exists by nature, and it has a nature, but it is not itself a substance but is instead, we will learn at the beginning of Book III, made of substances, its citizens. That composition is occluded by the genesis of the polis out of households, not of people. It comes to be out of households but it is made up of citizens. When he says that the polis comes into existence for the sake of life, but exists for the good life, he shows that process of generation does not account for its essence. The state never leaves its origins behind: it never aims at the good life to the exclusion of life, as Plato's property-less, family-less guardians do. The state then differs from natural substances because in nature, the final, efficient and formal causes are identical, while in politics, they are distinct. The polis is natural, but politics is not a matter of theoretical knowledge.

There are natural poleis, but no natural democracies or aristocracies. Thus each particular polis has both a constitutional form and an allied end that are not merely specifications of *the* end of *the* polis, living well. True, the end of each polis is its conception of the good life, and correct constitutions are distinguished from deviant constitutions by the fact that they aim at living well. But constitutions are not only structures of ruling and being ruled, a formula general enough that it could apply to the relation of form to matter in any natural substance (I.6.1254b14–16). A constitution is a structure of ruling and being ruled according to a conception of justice, and this

conception is held by citizens. The form of an animal is not evidently, and
certainly not consciously, held by all the parts. But constitutions are objects
of knowledge, and struggle, by citizens. Therefore, while natural, poleis are
also made.

By contrast, Book II looks at the artificial nature of the polis and shows
the limitations of that way of thinking. The move from the limitations of
seeing the polis as natural to seeing it as artificial is signaled by Aristotle's
remark that, although Book I told us that man is a political animal, "it is difficult to live together and to share in any human enterprise" (II.5.1263a15).
Recall too: "The desire (hormē) towards this kind of community [the polis]
exists in all men by nature, but the first man to put it together is the cause
of the greatest of goods" (I.2.1253a30). Living together is as difficult as living well.

Aristotle spends far more time refuting Plato in the *Politics* than in the
Ethics because the difference between *phronēsis* and *technē* is harder to
discern in politics than in ethics. Plato and the others misinterpret this productive dimension by taking politics to be a *technē*, themselves the craftsmen, and the people their material. Given this orientation, the emphasis
on property is inevitable. Compared to ethical activity, political activity is
productive. It aims at a good outside its own actions, namely, producing,
through education, virtue in its citizens (VII.9.1329a21, *NE* X.7.1177b4–15).
Consider this contrast between politics and *phronēsis*:

> Political science (*hē politikē*) and *phronēsis* are the same state, but their
> being is not the same. One type of *phronēsis* about the city is the rul-
> ing part; this is legislative science (*nomothetikē*). The type concerned
> with particulars [often] monopolizes the name "'political science'" that
> [properly] applies to both types in common. This type is concerned with
> action and deliberation, since [it is concerned with decrees and] the de-
> cree is to be acted on as the last thing [reached in deliberation]. (*NE*
> VI.8.1141b24–27)

Ethics has no counterpart to "legislative science" and so is restricted to the
deliberative part of *phronēsis*. Legislative science requires less experience
than deliberation and allows for independent judgment. Even if Plato gets
things wrong, philosophy has a greater role in politics than in ethics.[22]

This greater role for philosophy changes the relation between the *Politics*
and its audience; philosophy will be practical in the *Politics* in a way different from and greater than in the *Ethics*. It also changes Aristotle's attitude
toward his competition. "It is an impossible or difficult thing to become

excellent judges without participating in the works" (VIII.6.1340b23–25). Aristotle does not draw the natural implication that Plato, Phaleas, and Hippodamus aren't worth listening to, since they lack appropriate experience.

Many people today also think that philosophy, or at least expertise as distinct from practical wisdom, can have a greater role in politics than in ethics, but for very different reasons. If the function of politics was to solve coordination problems among people with diverse needs and desires that were themselves beyond rational consideration, then it would make sense for experts in an art of politics to devise solutions to political problems even if there are not experts qualified to give moral advice. This is the hope of liberal democracy, as I will show in the next chapter, but Aristotle doesn't see politics and ethics that way. It isn't that politics is rational while ethics is not, but that the rationality of politics has an independence from practical experience that the rationality of ethics lacks.

Aristotelian reflection therefore does not stand outside to criticize, or to ask how something is possible, but to move from the *hoti* to the *dioti*, the "what" to the "why," finding causal accounts that make life coherent. The *Ethics* finds causes by placing virtuous action in a larger whole, a life or a community, a unified life in a unified community. In the *Politics*, self-sufficiency tells us there is no whole larger than the polis. We can't understand political life by putting it in a larger whole. Instead, reflection uncovers relations between end and form, the good life and the constitution. Understanding the efficient cause in Book II is a necessary preliminary to understanding the relation of formal and final cause, which is the subject of political science starting in Book III.[23]

No one, according to the *Ethics*, can understand being virtuous and choose actions for their own sakes without actually being virtuous. This is the converse of the Socratic thesis that anyone who knows the nature of virtue will necessarily act virtuously. Only someone who acts virtuously can know the nature of virtue. Similarly, the only people who can see that political life is for the sake of living well are those who live in poleis that aim at living well. From the outside, doing things for their own sake and ruling and being ruled in turn are mysterious: they pose unanswerable challenges of what's in it for me: why not, if you can, get the result without the effort, which is desirable in art?

The entire challenge of the *Politics* is to break out of this potentially vicious circle, Aristotle affirmed, for example, when he says that "it is held to be impossible for a polis to be well governed if it is not governed aristocratically, but by bad people, and equally impossible for a polis that is not well governed to be governed aristocratically" (IV.8.1296b41–1294a2). If good constitutions were, as Plato thought, all and only those ruled by good men, then it would also be impossible for good constitutions to be known except by the good. The *Politics* shows that political knowledge does not depend on experience, because the excellence of constitutions is not simply a function of the excellence of the rulers. The rest of the *Politics* explores the slippage between good constitutions and good lives. The *Politics* is in this way a more philosophical work than the *Ethics*.

That politics is an art is a partial truth. It is true enough to allow Aristotle to take Plato and the others seriously here. They all go wrong by making the artful nature of politics exclude praxis. The statesman is productive in a way the ethical agent is not, but practical in a way the craftsman is not. True productive activities are imitations, while the statesman's activity is not mimetic. The trouble is that people are not inert like poetic materials, and the legislator must understand how limited his powers are. People talk back, and in particular, as political animals they talk back about justice. Socrates and the other inventors of imaginary cities act as though they were poets, creating an ideal state to be the object of contemplation from outside.

The Aristotelian legislator has a relation to his subjects that is setting in motion continuous creation, not a unique act that sets in motion a machine that will go of itself.[24] Aristotle had no concept of inertia, and so no thought that practical things could be settled in one act. For example, he says that Phaleas thought that equalizing property "was not difficult to do when poleis were just being founded, but that in those already in operation it would be more difficult" (II.7.1266a40–b2). The thinkers Aristotle studies in Book II all thought that constitutions were made by lawgivers who stood outside the constitution contemplating it as an object, while Aristotle's statesman will be a citizen. Founding a city is not a different activity from reforming or ruling existing ones (IV.1.1289a2–4).

Hippodamus wants to reward political innovators (II.8.1269a19–24); Aristotle sees such rewards as appropriate for technical innovations but not for politics, showing the limitations of politics as *technē*. Similarly, Book III argues for the superiority of the rule of law because, while we might prefer that doctors use their judgment rather than simply follow rules in treating us, the suspicion of rulers' self-interest makes such a preference inappropriate in politics (III.16.1287a33–41). The technical side of politics must be subordinate to praxis. Aristotle shows us how to effect such subordination.

It is one thing to say that consumers can judge the products of the crafts. I know whether the cobbler has done his work well by whether my feet get blisters. But Aristotle does not say that the patient can judge whether a physician has done her work well. "It might be held that the same person is able to judge whether or not someone has treated a patient correctly, and to treat patients and cure them of disease when it is present—namely, the doctor" (III.11.1281b39–41). Aristotle corrects this claim not by saying that the patient can judge whether he has been treated correctly, but by saying that "'doctor'" applies to the ordinary practitioner of the craft, to a master craftsman, and thirdly to someone with a general education in the craft. "For there are people of this third sort in (practically speaking) all the crafts. And we assign the task of judging to generally educated people no less than to experts" (1282a2–6).[25]

The person of general education lies between the consumer and the expert practitioner, more rational than the first and less knowledgeable than the second. The existence of general education has political implications for the relation of ruler and ruled. The generally educated person understands science because science presents a rational structure intelligible from the outside. Laws present such a structure, although in more embodied fashion than the sciences. Laws require ethical as well as rational abilities for their comprehension. Thus, the ruled citizens of Book III who differ from their rulers by possessing only right opinion rather than *phronēsis* have an attitude toward their laws and rulers that far exceeds in rationality the obedience of slaves to commands. To perceive a rational structure from the outside is, precisely, education. Therefore, education is the means by which the polity becomes a unity and men become citizens.

VII. FROM THE PREFACE TO POLITICS TO POLITICS ITSELF

Book II starts with a bang and ends with a fizzle. Aristotle leads us from Plato's audacious plans to dissolve the family in order to produce a truly unified state, and ends by mentioning Pittacus's proposal to punish drunken misbehavior more seriously than sober acts. While Socrates blithely tells Glaucon that the rulers of his ideal polis will be able to figure out for themselves any necessary legislation, Aristotle allows no such detached contempt for the detailed business of legislation. The deflation the reader feels as Aristotle leads us on this descent is itself a preparation for politics itself.[26]

The first three books of *Politics* constitute three prefaces to politics, and seeing the three together lets us understand the function of Book II. The three prefaces are respectively, a natural, an artificial, and a political treatment of politics. The main character in Book I is the head of the household,

as Aristotle shows the truth and the limitations of the natural relation of
citizen to polis. The main character of Book II is the legislator; here Aristotle shows the truth and the limitations of the polis as artifact. The main
character of Book III is the citizen. He is the same person as the head of the
household but is ruled and rules in turn by equals. The citizen is a potential
legislator. The polis is artificial enough that we can judge good laws without
ourselves being rulers, but political rather than artificial since we can only
become rulers by being ruled. Aristotle avoids committing the errors he accuses the sophists of committing in *Ethics* X.9 because, while there can be
external criticism of legislation, people still must become rulers only through
being ruled, as they become virtuous by performing virtuous actions.[27]

Each of these is a preface to politics because none is fully practical. In
particular, Book II's conclusions about property, education, and what is
uniquely common to the polis carry no implications about what is the best
constitution, or the relation between the best constitution and the best life.
Book II builds on the distinction Aristotle develops in Book I between acquisition and use, changing it into a distinction between possession and
use, as the origins of property become irrelevant. The function of the legislator is to educate the people so they will use their property liberally.
The virtue of the citizen is to use his property liberally, while in Book III
the function of the citizen is the security of the constitution. Those two
ideas are connected by the idea that "reciprocal equality preserves poleis."
"Things from which a unity must come differ in kind. This is why reciprocal equality preserves poleis, as we said earlier in the *Ethics*, since this must
exist even among people who are free and equal" (II.2.1261a28–31). "A city
is maintained by proportionate reciprocity. For people seek to return either
evil for evil, since otherwise [their condition] seems to be slavery, or good
for good, since otherwise there is no exchange" (*NE* V.5.1132b32–1133a2).
Books IV–VIII will construct complex relations between virtue and security
far more complicated than the straightforward relation of virtue and happiness in the *Ethics*.

Therefore, the conclusion of Book II is the opposite of the thesis from
the *Republic* with which the book begins. Socrates argues that one can only
have friendly feelings toward other citizens if one's primary loyalty and
commitment is to the state, and then indirectly and consequently toward
other people. Aristotle shows that the disposition to use one's property toward common purposes and mutual aid, liberality, is a precondition for exercising the function of citizen in Book III. We first have ethical relations
to other people and then are in a position to have an ethical relation to the
state. The function of the legislator is education, while the function of the

citizen is preserving the constitution. Being a potential and then an actual ruler is how self-sufficient citizens live in a self-sufficient community. This relation of individual and community places restrictions on what education and the laws can be, but these restrictions are not noted in Book II, which is concerned only with restrictions on the function of legislation. There is more to be done.

After Book II, the main sources of unity and conflict in the polis are in agreements and disputes about justice. Not only is there no justice in Book II, but there is no talk about justice, either, and no talk at all. To that extent, the men of Book II are, like the men of Book I, developing and not complete political animals. The prepolitical world of Books I and II is a happier picture than Protagoras's Prometheus myth, but they agree in distinguishing *technē*, which satisfies the needs of living, from justice, which is specifically about living well. Protagoras's craftsmen must talk, since they pass their skills on to their children, but such education is not an integral part of their crafts, while speech and education are an integral part of justice.

Finally, Book II has some implications for today. Plato is the main target in Book II, but in denying the role of philosopher-kings and the technicians of the other proposed ideal constitutions, Aristotle does not deny a role for the statesman. There is a fundamental difference between politics and economics. The reciprocal justice of economic exchange does not require a polis or a neutral judge. It can go on in the prepolitical circumstances of the household and village, and there are no fundamental differences marked between international and domestic trade. Political justice, though, requires a structure as well as the activities of individual agents. The wisdom of the market, of people satisfying their desires, cannot be a model for political wisdom, and economic reciprocity cannot be the model for political justice. Book III will have to display the differences between economic reciprocity and political justice.

CHAPTER THREE

The Justice of Book III and
the Incompleteness of the Normative

I. ARISTOTLE VERSUS LIBERALISM: THE RIGHT
AND THE GOOD

The *Politics* posits a relation between ethics and politics very different from what we find today. Currently we assume a plurality of ways of living well, with the function of politics to coordinate these differences by a modus vivendi, overlapping consensus, neutral framework, or public reason. In the *Ethics* Aristotle presents a single good practical life, while the *Politics* offers a diversity of possible ways communities can organize themselves to live well. We accept moral diversity as a given, Rawls's "fact of pluralism," and then try to find a single political structure in which these different ways of living can coexist.[1] Our emphasis on moral diversity has led to a search for political unanimity and neutrality. Aristotle's emphasis on a single best life leads him, on the contrary, to a greater openness to political diversity than we see today. His discussions of justice, we will see, never pretend to neutrality as the contemporary idea of justice as fairness does. We find ethics and the good life the place for diversity, and politics the place for uniformity, while for Aristotle it's the other way around.[2]

That difference between Aristotle's thinking and our own changes the nature of practical reason. Today, practical reason can supply methods of political decision making that all can accept and that can be applied neutrally, while practical reason has no such powerful role in determining the best life for the individual. In Aristotle, the best life is a life of reason, so practical reasoning has a straightforward and constitutive function, while even the best ways of living together involve more than reason. Political life requires persuasion and often compulsion. Practical reason in the *Politics* must be a more empirical and contingent business than it is in the *Ethics*. As we've seen hinted at in chapter 2, it is also more philosophical.

The priority of the right to the good, and so the attraction of politics as supplying a neutral framework in which ethical diversity can flourish, is a commonplace of modern ethics and politics that it is hard to understand the reversal that Aristotle constitutes.[3] The single best life of the *Ethics* is not a framework against which political diversity can be measured. Aristotle does not exhibit a variety of constitutions, all of which can equally be home to human flourishing. Instead, the *Politics* articulates a variety of possible ways of living together that have different connections to living well. Because of this flexibility and indeterminacy, Aristotle is not vulnerable to accusations of false neutrality that have plagued recent articulations of liberalism.

The argument of Book III puts into focus the relation between ethics and politics that has been a theme throughout this book. Rawls is the paradigm of modernity as he makes questions of justice as fairness prior to settling issues of the good life because a just society must admit plural and incompatible conceptions of good ways of living. Aristotle, good ancient that he is, does the opposite, and can be expected to show that we can't know what a good constitution is unless we first know the nature of the best life for individuals. *Politics* VII does just that.[4]

The trouble with this contrast is that *Politics* III doesn't fit. (In the next two chapters I will show that *Politics* IV–VI don't fit, either.) Book III defines the key terms of politics—*polis, citizen, constitution, sovereignty,* and even *justice* itself—with only the slightest attention to the purpose of politics and of the polis in individuals' living well. In contemporary terms, that means that this part of the *Politics* makes the right prior to the good. When he mentions the good life in *Politics* III, its use is merely formal: the theses that politics is about the good life and not just life itself and that good states work for the common interest while corrupt ones aim at the good of the rulers say nothing about the content of the good life. He instead seems to set his sights lower, declaring that the function of citizenship is preserving the state (III.4.1276b27; see *HA* I.1.488a9) instead of living well. Preserving the constitution as the function of citizenship does not look all that different from the modern project of securing a neutral framework of rights in which the good might flourish.

If the right is prior to the good in *Politics* III, the reason for that priority cannot be because true justice must leave room for the practice of plural and incompatible ways of living well, as moderns have it. Aristotelian justice has nothing to do with a neutral framework for distinct conceptions of the good life among which no rational resolution is possible. Rather, the right is prior to the good, justice to the good life, because man is a political animal, and so one cannot know the nature of the good life for the individual without first knowing what justice is. Justice and the right must then be prior to the good, not because justice is agnostic toward the good but because an understanding of justice will lead us to an understanding of the good. Man is a political animal before he is an ethical animal or a happiness-seeking animal. Human rationality is more intimately connected to man's political nature than to either virtue or happiness.

However, the account I just gave of the priority of justice to the good life creates new problems for making sense of Aristotle's thinking. We can't read the *Politics* as developing an idea of justice that will allow us to infer the nature of the good individual life. Although man is a political animal, the *Politics* relies on conclusions from the *Ethics* far more than the reverse, although still not very often. Ethics is prior to politics because the good life is led by individuals. Politics is prior to ethics because man is a political animal. Politics is a more noble and divine achievement than ethics (*kallion kai theioteron*) (*NE* I.2.1094b6–10, see too VIII.8.1159b7, IX.8.1169a33–34), but politics, unlike ethics, always aims at an end outside its own activity (X.7.1177b12). By looking at the complexities of the argument of Book III, we'll be able to spell out in more detail the Aristotelian relation between ethics and politics.[5]

The relations between ethics and politics are so complicated because of the gap, in practical science—both politics and ethics—between form and function. The formal and final causes of natural things are identical. The purpose of a pig is to live a porcine life. The form of a pig is its organization of flesh and bones that enables it to act like a pig. The purpose of politics and of the polis is the good life, but that end doesn't dictate how particular poleis should be structured. The formal cause of a polis is its constitution, the formula of justice by which a community determines who rules (e.g., III.3.1276b1–14, 4.1276b29). Man may be a political animal, but no one is a democratic or oligarchic animal.[6] (Analogously, people may be language-using animals, differing from other animals by having logos and not merely *phonē*, but no one speaks Language; we all speak English, or Xhosa, or Finnish.)

It is Aristotle's genius to convert this lack of smooth fit between form and function from a handicap into an advantage. The impossibility of any single normative political value makes politics into a practical science, not a technology. There is a broadening similar to what we saw in Book II, where Aristotle admits the opinions of philosophers and private citizens

about the ideal state in a way he would never listen to anyone but the virtuous and practically wise in the *Ethics*. Like modern political thinkers,
Aristotle in Book III takes disagreement seriously. He had no problem in
the *Ethics* saying that if people disagree, that is because most of them are
wrong. And yet the voices of democrats and oligarchs, those who argue that
people who are equal in one thing should be equal in all things, those who
contend that people who are unequal in one thing should be unequal in all
things—all these opinions enter into the arguments enacted in Book III.

Aristotle is no liberal or pluralist.[7] He doesn't put the right before the
good because of disagreement about the good, as moderns do. For us, the
priority of right to good is a stance we adopt because we cannot ground
things, as we would like, in the good. Instead, Aristotle sees plural constitutions resulting from the underdetermination of political structure by political goods, including the ultimate political good, living well; the final cause
does not determine the formal cause.[8] Only this underdetermination allows
the errors about justice that creates different constitutions to be more than
mistakes to be corrected. Therefore Isaiah Berlin is wrong when he answers
his question as he does:

> If we ask the Kantian question 'In what kind of world is political philoso-
> phy . . . in principle possible?' the answer must be 'Only in a world where
> ends collide.' In a society dominated by a single goal there could in prin-
> ciple [only] be arguments about the best means to attain this end. . . .
> It follows that the only society in which political philosophy . . . is possi-
> ble is a society in which there is no total acceptance of any single end.[9]

It is the burden of my argument that "political philosophy" can indeed exist
within a vision of the good life "dominated by a single goal." Contemporary
moral pluralism and the need for political neutrality come from disagreements about the good life. For Aristotle, plural constitutions and what he
calls political philosophy both result from the diversity of opinions about
justice, not about the good life. "All men hold that justice is some kind
of equality. . . . What we have to discover is equality and inequality for
what sort of persons. That is difficult, and calls for political philosophy"
(III.12.1282b18–23).

There is no need for such political philosophy in the household, and
therefore *Politics* III shows how political philosophy is generated not by the
collision of ends, but by the way political ends, unlike the economic ends of
the household, have an internal complexity that requires that deliberation
be more than the calculation of means. Political philosophy, deliberation

over the forms and functions of government, can go forward even where the nature of the good life is not in dispute, since we can still worry about the modalities of justice (oligarchic vs. democratic), the relations of citizenship to rule, and the relation between the good constitution and the good life. Book III shows how each of these relationships generates permanent political disputes and permanent places for deliberation.

The liberal idea that disagreement about the good is the reason to make the right prior to the good, assumes that if, on the contrary, one could affirm the nature of the good without dissent, then politics must be built on that foundation. The function of politics would therefore be to enforce and instantiate that good. There are then two kinds of politics, liberalism, and an alternative that could be called either perfectionism or totalitarianism. This seems to me a false and unhealthy opposition. Aristotle shows us how to do better.[10]

The *Ethics* recognizes that people disagree about the nature of the good life. That is because most people choose a vulgar life of pleasure; their opinions have no place in the philosophical inquiry into the best life. In the *Politics*, as we will see in more detail as we go, people disagree about the nature of justice; here too almost everyone is wrong. However, Aristotle doesn't dismiss those errors as he does in the *Ethics*. Those disagreements and errors generate the variety of constitutions, including good constitutions. No one can live well with a false idea of the good life, but constitutions can be good constitutions and promote the good life in spite of a partial conception of justice. There is no ambiguity for Aristotle in the question of how good the good life is, but from Book III on, the *Politics* exploits the ambiguity in how good a good constitution must be.[11]

The plurality that liberalism finds in good lives and ultimate values and the pluralism that Aristotle finds in good constitutions have one important similarity. Liberalism sometimes treats the fact of permanent disagreement, as a regrettable feature of human life, as in *Federalist* 10's definition of faction: "By a faction, I understand a number of citizens, whether amounting to a majority or a minority of the whole, who are united and actuated by some common impulse of passion, or of interest, adverse to the rights of other citizens, or to the permanent and aggregate interests of the community."[12] Aristotle too at times sees plural constitutions as coming from mistakes and so as a lamentable permanent feature of human life, but he also takes that plurality as a resource that the statesman can use to improve and reform a polis. That there are plural constitutions is in the first instance a matter of observation: "We see (*horōmen*) that constitutions differ in kind from one another" (III.1.1275a38). While there are only two kinds of justice, oligarchic and democratic, each is partial, partially correct, in the sense that they are to the advantage of their proponents. But he does not list a third kind, which captures proportion to merit or virtue, and would thus be doubly impartial. Under such a conception of justice, the relation between the good life and political organization would be smooth. We will encounter that smoothness in Book VII, and with it justice will disappear.

There are two kinds of proportion, arithmetic and geometric. Democrats assert one; oligarchs the other. Each of the two is imperfect. Each voices a partial truth, since political life always involves equality among citizens (VII.3.1325a28–30, VII.14.1332b12–27) and all communities require the inequality of rule (III.4.1276b29–31, I.5.1254a29–33). That is, even extreme and consistent oligarchs could not define political equality out of existence, nor could the most ardent democrat get rid of all political inequality. Each voices a partial truth, and therefore there can be good constitutions based on either arithmetic or geometric equality. There is no perfect formula for justice to place alongside these two forms of justice. Instead of settling these permanent contests about justice, he lays out the depth of that dispute as a resource for the statesman. There is no party of virtue, not in Book III or anywhere else in the *Politics*. "Those who are outstanding in virtue would engage in factional conflict most justifiably, yet they do it least of all" (V.1.1301a39–40; V.4.1304b1–5).[13] Virtue does not lead to a fighting faith. There will be a role for virtue and for the good man in politics, a role that, as we will see, varies as the argument of the *Politics* proceeds, but virtue is never an independent force.

Book III invokes a series of five distinct normative criteria for a good state, each of which is distinct from the good state's relation to the good life. Practical rationality becomes both possible and necessary because of these plural values and the problems Aristotle uncovers with each. Each of the five occupies a separate section of the text as it opens up space for deliberation:

1. The definition of *citizen*, the subject of chapters 1–3, applies most fully in a democracy. If a state that best exemplifies the definition of citizen were the best state, then democracy would arguably be the best state. Aristotle of course never draws this inference. From the first, then, we see normative criteria for the good state distinct from the good state's relation to the good life.
2. The best state is one in which all citizens are good *citizens*, not good men. "The virtue of the excellent citizen must exist in all, for it is necessarily in this way that the city is excellent" (III.4,1277a3). This criterion emerges out of the question of the relation between the

good man and the good citizen, and makes political standards even more distinct from political purposes, form from function. Chapters 4 and 5 define the best state by this relation between the good man and the good citizen. The common *function* of citizens in III.4 is preserving the constitution, not virtue, even though the *end* of the state is the good life rather than stability. But the most stable state of these chapters, like the most democratic state of 1–3, is not a state in which the best life would likely flourish. The relation between the value of stability and the value of promoting the best life is problematic, and will shift as Book III and the rest of the *Politics* develops.

3. Good *(orthoi)* constitutions are distinguished from deviant ones by working for the good of all rather than the good of the rulers, in apparent disregard of the content of that good, severing, again, the right from the good, form from substance. This is the criterion for a good constitution, as distinguished from the good citizen and the good state, and it forms the subject of chapters 6 and 7. The relation between a constitution aiming at the benefit of all and aiming at the good life is problematic, and it too shifts through the *Politics*.

4. Disputes arise between partisans of democracy and oligarchy about the nature of justice. These disputes are not silenced by the voice of virtue, either partisans of virtue within the state or Aristotle as the authoritative voice of reason outside it. Justice, therefore, seems doomed to characterizing imperfect regimes. But justice is proportional to merit, creating a different criterion for the goodness of a constitution from that in chapters 6–7, whether it is the rulers or the whole who benefits. Justice is the subject of chapters 8 through 13. There are six constitutions, and they arrange themselves in pairs. Aristocracy and oligarchy, polity and democracy, share a formula for justice, yet one of them aims at living well and one at life itself. (Monarchy and tyranny, the other two constitutions, have a more attenuated relation to justice.) Therefore, the difference between good and bad constitutions does not consist in different conceptions of justice.

5. Aristotle turns—without explanation—to a supposedly standing controversy over whether good laws or the exceptional ruler should rule. Whether the rule of law or the rule of the best man makes the best state, it will not be best because of an explicit connection to the end of the polis in living well. This section—chapters 14–18—tests Aristotle's procedure of deferring the question of what is best in favor of procedural questions of who rightly rules and decides.

Because of this project of understanding political structures without deriving conclusions from politics' purposes, the argument of Book III is very strange and difficult. Transitions seem abrupt, and what was established in one chapter seems ignored in the next. Aristotle proposes each item in my series of criteria independently of each other. Fundamental definitions and theses are asserted rather than argued for. The interrelations among citizen, constitution, and ruler seem to degenerate into circularities.

But once again, Aristotle converts these disadvantages into strengths. Political philosophy can occur in the rest of the *Politics* once Book III has freed space for deliberation by showing how constitutional form has no natural or inevitable ties to the other three causes. Where form follows function, there is no deliberation. "Art does not deliberate" (*Ph.* II.8.199b26). Where what is good determines what we should do, there is no deliberation necessary. Once form is sundered from purpose, right from good, then deliberation consists in finding practical causal ties between form and the other three kinds of causes. Aristotle's formula that we deliberate about means and not ends is more capacious than it might appear.[14]

II. THE MEANING OF "FORM" IN BOOK III

In nature, a thing's end and its form are identical. The constitution is the form of the state, the formal arrangement of sovereign (*kurios*) offices (e.g., III.6.1278b8–12, V.8.1308a6–7) based on particular conceptions of justice. But the fact that the number of rulers is the first criterion Aristotle uses to differentiate constitutions is a sign of trouble. Since how many people rule is accidental (*symbebēkos*, III.8.1279b36, *synbainei*, III.8.1280a3; see too *Republic* 4.445d4), it is hard to see how the number of rulers could constitute form.[15]

Politics I showed that to live well one must live in poleis, but that conclusion by itself says nothing about why poleis should be multiple discrete wholes. Biological life must be led by discrete self-organizing and self-sustaining organisms, but must political life? Why, for example, can someone be a member of only one such whole? I can be a member of a tragic and a comic chorus; I just can't perform in both simultaneously. I can own property in Thebes and in Athens, a situation far more critical today with global corporations who are, at least in the United States, legal "persons." Why can't I be a citizen in both poleis, as is becoming increasingly possible in today's nation-states? Each natural substance can have only one nature, and each nature can be realized in just one substance, but that one-one relation is just what it means to have a nature, an internal principle of motion. That one-one relation between form and substance does not apply to artifacts, where one form has multiple instantiations, and some instruments have multiple purposes.[16] Cannot there be overlapping organizations that aim at the highest good, the way people can have multiple loyalties to different communities of friends, or loyalties to gods and flags and to Mammon? Are the problems of dual loyalty that have so exercised people since the Reformation as inconceivable or uninteresting to Aristotle as the ethical questions about conflicts of virtues seemed to be? When democrats and oligarchs exist in a city, is there one city or two?[17] Why can't the whole of humanity be a community dedicated to the good life? All these questions arise from the lack of a natural or automatic connection between the forms of political life and the ends of politics in the good life.

The only explicit connection between constitutional form and the end of politics is that true (*orthos*) are distinguished from corrupt (*parekbasis*) constitutions by whether their end is the good life or life, which Aristotle makes equivalent to whether the rule is for the sake of the whole or only for the rulers. Aristocracy, for example, differs from oligarchy both because it aims at the good of the whole and because it selects its rulers on the basis of virtue rather than wealth. He doesn't try to prove that the two distinctions are equivalent. Aristotle provides no argument that there can be no constitution that aims at wealth but at the same time at the good of the whole—in fact there are such oligarchies in Book IV—or a constitution that selects its rulers on the basis of merit but aims at the good of the rulers, as slavery does. (He does raise the question of what to call a constitution in which the majority are wealthy, but that does not raise the issue of the connection between the two dichotomies, life versus the good life and ruling for the whole or for the rulers.) The three true constitutions, monarchy, aristocracy, and "polity," have the same end, the good life. Yet they are different constitutions. As I already mentioned, good and bad pairs of constitutions, aristocracies and oligarchies, polities and democracies, share the same constitutional form, the same conceptions of justice.

In addition, constitutions look like bad candidates for form because not only is there no connection between form and end, there is no connection between form and the generation of the polis. There is no reason at all to think that different constitutions come to be by different processes of generation. Aristotle rejects Plato's narrative in *Republic* VIII in which each constitution has its own characteristic genealogy. Man generates man, but poleis are not generated out of poleis. Aristotle never regards colonization as a paradigm for the genesis of states. Poleis are generated out of families and villages, as states come into existence for the sake of life but exist for the good life (I.2.1252b28–29). Once form is severed from both function and genesis, it is hard to see that anything is left of Aristotle's assertion of the naturalness of the polis.

Here is yet another place where Aristotle turns a difficulty into an advantage. The lack of connection between form and function isn't a weakness but a strength of politics. Thinking that form must be naturally connected to the other three causes is the practical mistake that defines degenerate states, analogous to pleonexia in injustice in the *Ethics*.[18] Pleonexia is a moral habit based on the idea that if something is good, then the more the better, and if something is good, it is good for me, and I therefore want it. Pleonexia comes from trying to solve practical problems by imitating nature and trying to create what nature has not given us, a smooth pathway from material to end. Unjust people think that because something is good, they should have it. Degenerate constitutions in *Politics* III try to take that same shortcut, making maximization a substitute for practical reason, and relying on the ambiguity in the idea of the desirable, from something worth desiring to something that I ought to desire. Deviant constitutions try to imitate nature by harmonizing efficient and final cause. By doing away with the need for political wisdom in adjusting these two criteria, they reduce praxis to making.

I can try to clarify how the distance between form and function affects Aristotle's argument by comparing it to his treatment of the family in Book I. In the family, function determines form, so that none of the questions that animate Book III through my five normative criteria can be raised about the family: (1) There is nothing parallel to the question of who is a citizen. Who is a member of a given family is not in dispute. (2) There is nothing parallel to the distinction between the good man and the good citizen within the family. There are no families, that is, in which there is a discrepancy between being a good father and head of household and being a good man. (3) The justice within the family does not have species, precisely because in that case function does determine form. There are no kinds of families. (There *is* something parallel to the distinction between states that aim at the advantage of the rulers and of the whole. That is the distinction between natural and conventional slaves. But that distinction does not generate a taxonomy of forms of the family.) (4) Because there are no kinds of families, there is nothing parallel in the family to the dispute between democratic and oligarchic justice. Justice may exist in the family, but the disputes about justice that call for political philosophy do not. (5) There is nothing parallel to the issue of whether the good man or good laws should rule, because the impersonality of good laws makes no sense within the family. The good is prior to the right in the family.[19]

States come into existence for life but are for the sake of the good life (I.2.1252b28). Degenerate states carry their efficient cause into their structure and being, and so continue to aim at life, and reduce the good life to life itself and aim at the advantage of the rulers. That would be fine if states were natural, like households, because then the natural end would also be life alone, not the good life. The household satisfies the ends it comes into existence to achieve.

The separation of form from function makes the right prior to the good. Each of the five sections of Book III is formal in a different way. Chapters 1–3 are formal because they abstract from the purpose of politics, and so the definitions of *polis, constitution*, and *citizen* revolve around nothing but the part/whole relation. These definitions and interrelations seem to have nothing specifically political about them, but apply to any community in which there is ruling and being ruled. Next, the relation of ruling and being ruled is a formal organizing principle. Chapters 4 and 5 introduce a formal end for the good citizen's participation—preserving the whole in which one participates—leaving unexplained the relation between this end and the end of politics itself, the good life. The relation between the state's two ends, self-preservation and the good life, is precisely as complicated as the relation of the good citizen to the good man. Chapters 6–8 offer formal criteria to distinguish different constitutions. Good constitutions are distinguished from bad ones by the formal criterion of who benefits from their rule, without saying what the benefits are, and good and bad constitutions admit of further differentiation by the formal and accidental criterion of how many rulers there are. Chapters 9–13 are formal because they approach justice by what partisans *say* about it, and then turn out to be formal in a more profound sense as Aristotle shows how incomplete and in need of further determination their formulas for justice are. The final section, 14–18, is formal, finally, in looking at a possibility of the man of incomparably great virtue without addressing how probable or realistic a possibility it is. The first thirteen chapters talk about forms independent of their end, while the last five chapters concern an end independent of its political form.

III. THE DEFINITION OF "CITIZEN": BOOK III.1–3

While people are political animals, it is not natural to live in any particular polis. No one is a natural democrat or a natural Corinthian, just as no one by nature speaks Xhosa or Finnish. Because of the gap between function and form, *Politics* III.1 begins concretely by asking how to distinguish the acts of a polis from the acts of its rulers (1274b34–35). There is no problem in ascribing acts to other agents, natural or ethical, including the household. Only for the polis is such an issue debatable. The definition of the polis in Book I as a community that aims at the best life cannot identify which acts are those of the polis.

A constitution is a certain arrangement (*taxis tis*) of those who inhabit the city (1274b39), a definition that not only employs none of his conclusions from Book I, but which also has no evident normative content at all, and nothing specifically political. He immediately recognizes that that definition is inadequate because the state is a composite and so its definition depends on that of citizen. Hence, he says, we have to define *citizen* before defining *constitution*. But in this case, the part seems defined wholly relative to the constitution, and so Aristotle's procedure looks circular, with *citizen* and *constitution* defining each other. If the constitution were a composite of men, or of households, it might make sense to say that a definition of the constitution depended on these prior terms. But the constitution is a composite of *citizens*, and *citizen* is defined relative to the constitution, so it seems odd to demand that *constitution* be defined in terms of *citizen*. One would not define a chorus by first defining a chorus member.[20]

Aristotle is not guilty of such circularity because the relation of part to whole is a practical one. The state is defined by what people do, not by why they do it, as an aristocratic politician might point to the good life, nor by what moves someone to become a citizen, as an oligarch might point to the desire for wealth or a democrat the desire for freedom. "The citizen in an unqualified sense is defined by no other thing so much as by sharing in decision and office (*krisis kai archē*)" (1275a22–23; see the slightly different formulation at 1275b18–19 where the citizen is "one for whom there is the freedom (*exousia*) to share in offices (*arches*), deliberation (*bouleutikēs*), and judging (*kritikés*)." Putting the citizen first places attention on the practical form, and not on motive or purpose, efficient or final cause.

Seeing the citizen/constitution relation as practical improves on a theoretical and static relation of parts and wholes. A state can change its constitution. (Again, think about how unintelligible all of this would be in a discussion of the family, where the part/whole relation is natural. Families might change or dissolve, but they couldn't change their form while still being a family.) While who is a citizen is relative to the constitution, and while constitutions are the forms of states (e.g., 1278b8–12, 1308a6–7), the

change from one constitution to another is not like a natural passing away
of one and the coming to be of a new substance. Citizens do not, during a
revolution, revert to a state of matter, parallel to a state of nature.[21] The
later idea of popular sovereignty might require a state of nature, but poleis
are made up of citizens, not individual men. In a revolutionary change, the
state changes from being, say, an oligarchy into being a tyranny, without an
interregnum in which citizens become matter without form.

Because of the nonnatural nature of the polis, it is unclear whether a
change in constitution is a change in substance or quality.[22] The ambiguity is there from the start of Book III. "For one investigating the constitution—what each sort is and what its quality (kai tis hekastē kai poia
tis)—virtually the first investigation concerns the city, to see what the city
is" (1274b32–34). A constitution in that respect resembles virtue in the Ethics: it is substantial enough that it is an energeia, but qualitative enough to
admit of degrees (Cat. 8.10b26–11a5).[23] Aristotle asks in III.3 about the continuing identity of a polis when it changes its constitution. He first decides
that an answer in terms of the material cause, the location and people, won't
do, calling it the "most superficial way" of investigating the problem.

> If a polis is a sort of community, a community of citizens sharing a consti-
> tution, then, when the constitution changes its form (eidos) and becomes
> different, it would seem that the polis too cannot remain the same. . . .
> We say that [any composite] is different if the form of the composite is
> different. . . . It is evident that we must look to the constitution above all
> when saying that the polis is the same. (III.3.1276b1–11)

This looks like a change in substance.[24] But in the Categories, "substance
does not admit of a more and a less," while qualities "admit of a more and
less" (5.3b33, 10b26–28). The kinds of democracy and oligarchy in Book IV
are differentiated by the more and the less, just like animal species. States
can be more or less democratic, oligarchic, et cetera, as one kind of bird
differs from another by the length of its wings or beak. But the differences
between correct and deviant constitutions cannot be a difference in pairs
of species as species are understood in the theoretical sciences. Monsters
and cripples don't form distinct species; they are simply failed members of
other species or genera, as we've seen for slaves. Animal species don't come
in pairs, one correct and one deviant. That the different constitutions are
not themselves species of a broader genus called constitutions makes their
transformation into one another more a change of quality rather than an
instance of generation and destruction.[25]

At III.3 Aristotle concludes: "It is looking to the constitution above all that the city must be said to be the same" (1276b12); the constitution is the form of which the state is the composite. That the constitution seems to be a form that fits somewhere between substance and quality comes from the complex relation between polis and citizen. Making the citizen basic shows that although the polis has an ethical end, which we knew from Book I, the ethical and intellectual qualities of its members, do not automatically contribute to the polis. A polis is not good because its members are good. We cannot simply add up the virtues of the members of a polis to get the virtue of the whole. As *Federalist* 55 put it, "had every Athenian citizen been a Socrates, every Athenian assembly would still have been a mob." In Book VII, but only there, will he say that "a polis is excellent by its citizens' being excellent" (VII.13.1332a32). In the rest of the *Politics*, that is false.

The goodness of a constitution is not a simple function of the goodness of its citizens. It is therefore natural for Aristotle to ask next about the relation between the good man or good person and the good citizen (III.4–5). But a problem remains. Not only does the definition of citizen best fit democracy, as Aristotle says (1.1275b6), only democrats would agree with it. Democrats, that is, define their principle of government as ruling and being ruled in turn, while others would define essential political activity and qualification for citizenship in terms other than participation, whether education in virtue or the protection of property, terms of prior claims or further purposes, efficient or final causes. According to the *Ethics*, justice and politics exist "among people naturally subject to law, . . . people who have an equal share in ruling and being ruled" (V.6.1134b15). The definition of citizen fits democracy best because democrats have this active definition of citizenship.

Democracy occupies a special place in Aristotle's analysis of politics, although this role carries no normative implications. The world had to wait for Spinoza to be the first to declare democracy the most natural form of government. Aristotle thinks that all constitutions from his time on must be democracies (III.15.1286b20–22), but gives no indication that this is either progress or decline. The status of democracy among the different constitutions will be a continuing problem in the *Politics*.[26]

IV. THE GOOD MAN AND THE GOOD CITIZEN: BOOK III.4–5

At the beginning of chapter 2, I pointed out that one reason the argument of the *Politics* is so complex is that the ergon argument Aristotle uses in the

Ethics fails here. In Book II we find that knowing what a polis is does not tell us what a good polis is. There is a similar gap here. If "the function of something is the same in kind as the function of a virtuous something . . . [so that] the function of a harpist is to play the harp, and the function of a good harpist to play it well" (*NE* I.7.1098a8–12), then what a good citizen is should follow simply from the definition of citizen. But Aristotle does not derive the good citizen from the definition of citizenship in 1–3 by asking what it takes to do a good job at the civic offices that had just defined citizenship. When good citizenship has its own normative criteria distinct from both citizenship and from ethical virtue, the gap between ethics and politics increases. What a good constitution is then becomes ambiguous in a way a good man in the *Ethics* is not.[27]

The purpose of citizenship surprisingly has nothing to do with the purpose of man and of the state, to live well. The function of citizens is to preserve the constitution. The argument is just as odd as that conclusion. Aristotle argues: in partnerships of dissimilar beings, each has a particular function and so a particular virtue. For that partnership to be a single community, though, there must be a common virtue, and that common virtue will be preservation of that community. Different sailors have different abilities but a common function (1276b21–28). If all "aim at" preservation, that aiming will not be conscious or intentional. Sailors do not know that they are aiming at a common goal, and citizens need not, either. But if aiming is not intentional, function seems reduced to result. At the extreme, we later learn that farmers make better citizens than mechanics and traders because they are busy with and enjoy farming and prefer it to politics (VI.4.1318b10–16). Do they preserve the state not through participation but through apathy? What is their civic excellence? All these difficulties arise because political form is distinct from function.[28]

The argument that makes security the common function applies to all communities, and not only the polis, so it is not citizen qua citizen whose good is preservation, but the far broader concept of the citizen qua part of a community made of dissimilars, including sailors. Ships and poleis have different purposes, but sailors and citizens both have the function of preserving their respective wholes.

Aristotle next does a little better by asking about the good man and the good citizen in a specifically political way, by asking if the good man is the good citizen in the best state (1276b36–37). He changes from the dissimilarity of sailors to the hierarchy of ruling and being ruled (1277a4).

There are really two questions here. First, Aristotle asks whether to *be* a good citizen you need to be a good man, and then whether *acting* as a good citizen is engaging in virtuous action. The first is about poleis in general, the second about the best polis. The first is about *dynamis*; the second about *energeia*. He rejects the first identity of the good man and good citizen by the argument from dissimilarity—there is one kind of good man but good citizens are relative to the constitution, and therefore good citizenship cannot require ethical goodness. The second identity of the good man and good citizen is rejected by the distinction of ruler and ruled.

Both of Aristotle's arguments against the identity of the good man and good citizen look very weak. The first simply asserts that there is one kind of good man but that good citizens are relative to the constitution, and therefore the two cannot be identical. But that doesn't follow. The virtuous person could be a good citizen, regardless of the constitution, the way a good sailor might be a good sailor on a variety of different ships. Second, just because ruler and ruled are different doesn't mean that the good person cannot be good at both. Being a good person doesn't *disqualify* anyone from being either a good ruler or a good ruled citizen. Aristotle's point is instead that being a virtuous person is not *necessary* for being a good citizen, while to be a good ruler you do have to be a good man.

Aristotle has good reason to deny that all good citizens will be good men, even in the best state. The state, made of dissimilar people, is a whole with structure and quality, not only quantity. In Book I he made this point by distinguishing political rule from rule over the family and in Book II by his arguments against Plato; in Book III the arguments against reducing the state to an alliance serve the same function (e.g., III.9.1280a31–b5). If good men were enough to make a good state, quantity would be enough, as it is with military strength. Therefore it cannot be qua containing good men that a state would be good. Even if all citizens were good men, the fact that they are all good men would not by itself make the state good. More pertinently and radically, being a good man will not make anyone a better citizen. Such additional virtue would be politically superfluous. Good men are neither necessary nor sufficient for a good state. Individual virtue of the citizens is a necessary condition for the ideal state of Books VII and VIII, but in one of the triumphs of the *Politics*, later in Book III and especially in Book IV, Aristotle will show how a constitution and a state can be *better* than its citizens, which would be impossible if the goodness of the constitution was derivative from the goodness of its citizens.

Aristotle has shown that the good man and the good citizen are distinct. It doesn't follow that the requirements of being a good man and being a good citizen can conflict. Aristotle never presents them as in conflict. There is no debate within the conscience of someone who is both a good man and good citizen.[29] Aristotle's man acts virtuously as a good man *by* acting politically as a good citizen. The good man contributes to the state by acting as a good citizen and so strengthening the constitution. The wealthy person with exquisite taste will not exhibit his virtue of magnificence (*megalopropria*) by equipping a chorus in a way that shows how lacking in good judgment his fellow wealthy citizens are since that could destabilize the constitution. The virtuous man displays his judgment by acting as a good citizen. Aristotle can therefore distinguish the good man and the good citizen—they have different functions—and yet not see their difference leading to conflict between the moral demands of conscience and the dictates of law. (For similar reasons, Aristotle never poses a conflict between natural and conventional justice.) As I will argue in detail when discussing Book V, the good man living in a democracy or an oligarchy will not seek to impose a rule of virtue, or withdraw from the state into his own realm of virtue, but will act as a good citizen in living well according to the constitution, and thereby, to the extent possible, transform being like-minded it into a correct constitution. Security is not law and order but *homonoia*, literally, of the same mind, and caring about each other's virtue (III.9.1280b6–8).

Caring for one another's virtue makes one's relation to fellow citizens a moral relation. While we today don't consider the distinction between one's fellow citizens and others a moral distinction, but only a political one, for Aristotle there is a moral difference between how we should treat other citizens and how we should treat everyone else. Justice, the primary ethical and political virtue, applies only between citizens.[30] Caring about each other's virtue is the mark of citizenship that enables Aristotle to avoid the dilemma that either sovereignty is distinct from citizenship, in which case citizenship seems to be reduced to being a beneficiary of the laws, a condition that could even apply to slaves, or all citizens should rule, collapsing the distinction between ruler and citizen. As I will argue soon, it makes sense for Aristotle to include within the constitution citizens who are not rulers, what can fairly be called second-class citizens.[31]

Therefore, while virtuous people aim at ethical excellence, good citizens aim at the security of the polis. All constitutions aim at stability. Good constitutions are distinguished from bad because they aim at the good life instead of mere life. Aristotle leaves unclear the critical relation between those two ends, security and the good life. Stephen Salkever puts the point exactly:

If those nomoi which were best suited to achieving the ultimate aim of politics (virtuous persons) were also those most appropriate for achieving its proximate goals (peace and integration), then social science could in principle provide precise answers to questions concerning the sorts of nomoi which could best serve the ends of the polis. Unfortunately, the antecedent of this hypothesis is usually not the case; at the heart of the problem of human affairs sits a tension which does not admit of precise theoretical resolution.[32]

The relation between stability and excellence sets a problem for politics that does not exist for ethics. The function of the good life in the *Ethics* is not to live as long as possible, but as well as possible. Aristotle would never assert that long life is a sign of the goodness of a person, but duration and stability are indeed signs of a successful constitution.[33] The *Ethics* says that a virtuous person "will choose . . . a year of living finely over many years of undistinguished life; and a single fine action over many small actions" (IX.8.1169a23–26); no statesman could make that choice, and they never follow principles they know to be self-destructive (*Politics* VI.10.1310a19–23). The three existing constitutions singled out for their reputation in Book II, those of Sparta, Crete, and Carthage, are known for their stability.

The original analogy to sailors on a ship is the start of the trouble. Sailors aboard ship will work to keep it afloat regardless of its cargo and destination. They don't have to endorse shipping heroin to Newark; they just don't want to drown. If stability is the common function of the citizen, then politics becomes truly amoral as the citizen's efforts to preserve the state have to bracket any opinions about the quality of that state.

V. THE KINDS OF CONSTITUTIONS: BOOK III.6–8

Book III began by establishing the autonomy of politics in a very weak sense. Polis, citizen (*politēs*), and constitution (*politeia*) define each other. That sort of autonomy is always in danger of becoming circularity. That danger is only slightly mitigated in chapters 4 and 5 with the relationship between the good man and the good citizen. It still looks like the constitutional act of defining a citizen is a performative in which saying makes it so; might makes right.

If the aim of the state is living well, and if only those communities can truly be called poleis that have the "power to make citizens good and just"

(III.9.1280b10), then why are corrupt constitutions forms of poleis at all and not business partnerships or mutual protection schemes? If a constitution aims at the benefit of the rulers, then "either we must not say that those who are part of the state are citizens, or those who are part of the state must share in the advantage of membership" (III.7.1279a31–32).[34]

> It is evident that a city that is correctly, not just verbally, so called must be concerned about virtue. For otherwise the community turns out to be an alliance and law turns out to be a contract, and, as Lycophron the sophist said, a mutual guarantor of what is just, but not such as to make the citizens good and just. (III.9 1280b8–12)

Earlier I noted that the different constitutional forms seemed to fall somewhere between substance and quality; here is a more concrete appearance of that same issue. As David Keyt puts it, "If the common advantage of a city were the advantage of its first-class citizens [i.e., the class from which rulers are drawn] only, a constitution that looks to the common advantage would look only to the rulers' own advantage, and the distinction between correct and deviant constitutions would collapse."[35] At stake is the status of citizens who are not rulers but who have to be distinct from all the other people protected by the state. At stake, too, is the status of corrupt constitutions, which, unlike true constitutions, don't aim at living well, but which still count as constitutions. Second-class citizens are still citizens, and corrupt constitutions are still constitutions. If the distinction between state and society was available, these problems would be simpler. But then they wouldn't be the same problems.[36]

   If Aristotle needs to show that nonruling citizens and corrupt constitutions are not contradictions in terms, III.6 starts off in what looks like an unpromising direction. It begins: "We come to the question whether to distinguish more than one constitution, and, if so, how many, what they are, and what the differences between them are" (1278b6–8). In the chapter before, Aristotle has just told us that "since there are several constitutions, there must also be several kinds of citizens, especially of the ruled kind" (III.5.1278a14–15). We already know, that is, *that* there are several constitutions, but we now need to know *what* they are. There is no obvious reason to expect that a taxonomy of constitutions will salvage the ideas of nonruling citizens or corrupt constitutions.

   The six constitutions Aristotle lists look innocent and uninteresting enough to invite comparisons to Polybius, *Republic* VIII, and the *Statesman*, and he admits that he takes them from exoteric discourses (III.6.1278b31). But there is something very powerful buried in the taxonomy. There are two independent variables, *who* rules and *for whom*, while in the *Republic* those two were tied together. Who is in authority and whether it is a good government are distinct, just because form and end are independent. Correct and corrupt constitutions can have the same principle of justice for selecting their rulers; the difference lies in who benefits. Aristocracy and oligarchy, on this account, share an account of who rules, and therefore a formula for justice, as do democracy and polity.

Aristotle has to be able to distinguish corrupt constitutions both from true constitutions and from partnerships that don't qualify as constitutions at all. Corrupt constitutions are still communities organized around justice, even if they fail to aim at the good life. There can be economic partnerships that aim at increasing the wealth of all participants, but which, no matter how economically self-sufficient, are not poleis. And distinct from those, there are poleis that aim at increasing the wealth of their rulers.

A community that considers wealth as its goal can organize itself around that goal without any pretensions that wealth is in its eyes the good life. That community is not a polis. There are no problems about justice; people are rewarded financially in proportion to their financial contributions. But another community organized around wealth can mistakenly conceive wealth as the good life, the ultimate good. Then it is a polis, a corrupt one. Its formula for justice will reward the rulers: the rich get richer through political activity.

This difference between misconceiving the accumulation of wealth as the good life, and aiming at wealth without any claims about the good life creates the difference between a corrupt constitution and an economic association that isn't a polis or a constitution at all. With that in mind, we are now in a position to understand the difference between corrupt and correct constitutions. Both the democratic principle of equality and justice according to numbers, and the oligarchic principle of inequality and justice according to wealth, can each be either an interpretation of justice as proportion to merit or a principle competing with it. In the first case, we have correct constitutions—in Book III called polity and aristocracy, in Book IV often called oligarchy and democracy—while the second case yields corrupt oligarchies and democracies.

Consider college admissions as an example. Parallel to Aristotle's analysis, merit is the principle of selection in good colleges. Wealth and numbers can be either forms of merit or alternatives to merit. A school might give

preferential treatment to children of alumni because their probable financial donations insure the continuing excellence of the school, benefiting all.
That's wealth as a form of merit. Another school could give the same preference, but in order to keep the school full of the right sort of people, keeping alumni happy. That's wealth as a principle distinct from desert. And
similarly on the democratic side. Diversity, the modern equivalent of the
ancient democratic principle of selection by lot, putatively improves the
educational experience for all students. Here diversity is an interpretation of
merit and desert. Alternatively, diversity challenges hierarchical assertions
of differentiations of worth in the name of democracy and makes a different constituency, not alumni but state governments and some foundations,
happy: here democratic equality opposes justice as proportion to merit.

Arithmetic equality makes freedom into the end of politics; geometric equality erects wealth into its end. "For one lot thinks that if they are
unequal in one respect (wealth, say), they are wholly unequal, whereas the
other lot thinks that if they are equal in one respect (freedom, say) they are
wholly equal" (III.9.1280a21–23). But where democracy makes freedom into
a principle of life, polity makes it into a principle of the good life. In democracy, freedom substitutes for merit, while in polity freedom is an index of
merit. The same holds for the difference between oligarchy and aristocracy.
Now we can see how Aristotle can argue that to act for the whole is to act
for the good life. Acting for the whole is our means of identifying aiming
at the good life. To act for the benefit of the rulers alone means that one is
acting for an end other than the good life. There can be no constitutions
whose rulers both aim at wealth and for the sake of the whole, and none
that select rulers by merit but rule for the sake of the rulers alone.

Now we can also see why correct constitutions are so rare, and why it is
so difficult to keep them from degenerating into corrupt constitutions. Degenerate constitutions collapse the distinction between the criterion for ruling and the purpose of ruling. Their rulers demand to rule because of wealth
or freedom, and they rule for the sake of wealth or freedom. In those states,
there is no distinction between sovereign and citizen because there is no
difference between generating principle and purpose. All who are not rulers
are not citizens, either. That is, only correct constitutions have second-class
citizens. In Book I, Aristotle said that barbarians collapse the distinctions
between women and slaves, and indeed between those people and domestic
animals (I.2.1252b4). So here, in degenerate constitutions those who aren't
rulers aren't part of the polis at all. It takes a good constitution to recognize
that those who are not rulers still participate in political and civic life.

In reading the *Ethics*, we have to understand why so few people fulfill their nature and live virtuously and happily. Similarly here. If people are political animals, why are most constitutions corrupt and so few correct? Starting in my first chapter, I've shown that despotism is a permanent temptation for individuals. These chapters of Book III show that despotism is also a permanent temptation for poleis and constitutions. More than a temptation, corrupt constitutions represent a fallback or default position. People who can, will live despotically, and constitutions that can get away with it will be despotic unless political intelligence intervenes.

VI. JUSTICE AS PROPORTIONAL TO MERIT: BOOK III.9–13

If a constitution can aim at living well if and only if it aims at the advantage of the whole, that identity places restrictions on the kind of whole the polis must be. Chapters 1–3 show the way in which the state as a whole is prior to its parts. On the other hand, these parts, unlike the parts of animals, have their own purposes, which cannot be ignored. Citizens not only have purposes, they have political opinions. They are political animals and have political logoi. People talk back. While who is a citizen might depend on the particular constitution, who is a political animal does not.

This section of Book III begins, as do the others, with no explanation for the change of subject: "The first thing to note is what marks (*horoi*) men give of oligarchy and democracy, and what are oligarchic and democratic justice" (1280a7–8). Justice comes into consideration because democrats and oligarchs define the principles of their constitutions by *speaking* about justice in certain ways (III.9.1280a7–12, anticipated in II.1273a21–b1; see too IV.8.1294a19–20, in which "there are three things *disputed* over equality in the constitution [*politeia*], freedom, wealth and virtue"). Their self-definitions are part of the problem of justice. The *politeia* or constitution is "the way of life" (*bios tis*) of the polis (IV.11.1295b1), and the disputes about justice are the connection between constitution as organization of offices and constitution as a way of life.[37] Unlike other ethical virtues and unlike other political goods, justice is intrinsically tied to talk about justice.[38] The gods have no justice, and they don't talk but only think. Like a liberal, Aristotle begins the treatment of justice from the fact of disagreement, but the implications he draws are very different.[39] Taking justice seriously does not mean preserving the phenomena or finding reflective equilibrium. It does mean that philosophy has a greater and different role to play in politics from what it does in ethics.

Justice, unlike the good life, is an intrinsically controversial idea. People always employ one form of justice as opposed to another. Therefore Aristotle immediately continues: "They all grasp justice of a sort, but they go only to a certain point and do not discuss the whole of what is just in the most authoritative sense" (1280a8–10). Because people are always partial when they talk about justice, Aristotle talks about principles of justice only for democracy and oligarchy. While democracy and oligarchy are distinguished from each other by their principles of justice, the three good constitutions are differentiated merely by numbers. Paradoxically, constitutional form seems more substantive for corrupt constitutions and more accidental for correct ones.[40] Justice is only a concern for the corrupt constitutions of democracy and oligarchy. Since justice in the *Ethics* is ethical virtue in general, toward someone else, justice plays a greater role in the best life for the individual than in the best state. Nothing could be further from the liberal justice expressed in Rawls.

Aristotle next says:

> Justice seems to be equality, and it is, but not for everyone, only for equals. Justice also seems to be inequality, and indeed it is, but not for everyone, only for unequals. They disregard the "for whom," however, and judge badly. The reason is that the judgment concerns themselves, and most people are pretty poor judges about what is their own. (1280a10–15)

On this account democracy and oligarchy are indeed the only constitutional forms possessing principles of justice. To have a principle of justice is necessarily to have a partial principle. Politically, justice according to merit is not another principle alongside arithmetic and geometric equality. Instead of correct constitutions having their own principles of justice distinct from democracy and oligarchy, they complete the respective partialities of arithmetic and geometric equality, as *energeiai* complete imperfect, instrumental activity in the *Ethics*. Aristocracy is the perfection of the oligarchic principle of justice, and polity the perfection of the democratic principle. Perfecting or completing the formulas for imperfect justice is what Aristotle does instead of saving the appearances or searching for reflective equilibrium.[41]

This relation between the correct and degenerate kinds of constitution justifies Aristotle's use of merely accidental distinctions of numbers to distinguish among the good forms of constitution (e.g., III.8.1279b34, III.15.1286b3–7, 18.1288a32–41, IV.2.1289a31–33). There are no essential differences among true constitutions. The perfections of democratic and oligarchic justice could be the same, so that polity and aristocracy are indistinguishable, as indeed they become in Book IV. Principles of individuation are principles of imperfection, of dominance by matter, not form, which makes corrupt constitutions rule for the sake of the rulers. The better the constitution, the less important what kind of constitution it is. At a maximum, this principle explains why Aristotle never refers to the ideal constitution of Books VII and VIII as an aristocracy; it isn't one kind of constitution as opposed to others. It has no principle of individuation, and no principle of justice, either. Virtue in this sense makes law superfluous.[42] Hence the difficulty I mentioned in placing constitutional forms squarely as substances or qualities. Dominance by matter is might making right, making a constitution corrupt. When form and function are distinct, as they are in praxis, then matter plays a more important and independent role than in natural objects. This accounts for the fact that, while monsters in nature are relatively rare, deviant constitutions are far more numerous than correct ones.

From chapter 9 on, Book III changes its argumentative method; it now presents a series of dialectical arguments for and against the rule of the many, of wealth, and of virtue, reaching its climax in chapter 13 when Aristotle says that the rich, the free, the well-born, the virtuous, and the many all have reasonable claims to rule, and then asks what happens "if all are present in a single polis" (1283b1). These disputes are followed by arguments, in chapters 14–18, for and against the rule of law versus the rule of the best man. The difference between correct and deviant constitutions is a settled principle, while the different constitutions and the difference between rule of law and rule of the best are topoi for continuing argument.

True justice is proportion to merit, but that fact carries no evident practical prescriptions. In the first eight chapters, we saw that knowing the content of the good life did not dictate the nature of the good constitution; here we discover that the nature of true justice doesn't tell us what the good constitution is either. The declaration of what full justice is concludes III.9.

> The purpose of the political community (tēn politiēn koinōnian) is not living together but good actions. Hence those who contribute most to such a society have a larger share in the city than those who are equal or

superior in freedom and birth but unequal in political goodness, or those
who are superior in wealth but inferior in goodness." (1281a2–7; see too
1280b10)

One might think that it follows that the virtuous should rule. But that declaration is immediately followed by chapter 10's opening: "There is a question as to what the authoritative element of the city should be, either the
multitude, the wealthy, the respectable, the one who is best of all, or the
tyrant; but all of these involve difficulties" (1281a12–15).

Whatever "having a larger share in the city" means, it does not determine the authoritative element. It isn't necessarily true that the best should
rule. Maybe the good person's scope for virtuous activity is greater when she
hands over the management of political affairs to people who are fulfilled
by that sort of thing, reserving for herself the opportunity to live nobly. The
virtuous person might prefer to see his friend ruling rather than rule himself
(NE IX.9.1169a29–30). (Tyranny emerges when the people think that the
best way to protect themselves against the rich is not by themselves ruling
but through a demagogue and tyrant [V.10.1310b12–14].) Justice as proportion to merit, however merit is conceived, has a connection to the right to
rule only if ruling is desirable for its own sake.[43]

There is a difference between desert, a backward-looking criterion that
justifies rule, and ability and contribution, forward-looking criteria that
make the demands of ruling prior to any pre-existent claims.[44] "Rule of . . .
a few is [called] 'aristocracy' either from the rulers' being the best men or
from its aiming at the best for the city and its participants" (III.7.1279a35–36).
Being the best and aiming at the best are distinct. Even if the best should
rule, ruling is not a reward for being good. Being good is not a status, like
being free or wealthy; it is the power to perform virtuous actions. If being
a ruler gives the virtuous person greater opportunity for virtuous action—
which is not self-evident—then having a larger share in the constitution
will mean ruling. Because virtue is not a status or a kind of property, like
freedom and wealth, but the potentiality for virtuous activity, having a
larger share in the constitution does not automatically mean ruling, as it
does in corrupt constitutions. Otherwise the good man would wish to rule
permanently. Sometimes my opportunity for virtuous action will increase
when I become a ruler and sometimes it will decrease. We don't necessarily honor the best teacher/scholar in a philosophy department by making
her the chairman. Ruling and being ruled in turn is the best solution for
the virtuous person, not having the largest possible share in ruling. Those
who want to rule permanently want to rule for their own advantage, that

is, want to rule under a corrupt constitution. No one, Aristotle thinks, wants to rule permanently for the good of other people. Hence the arguments on both sides of the issue between rule of law and rule of the best in chapters 14–18.[45]

Therefore, Aristotle faces the question of who should rule by pointing to a different kind of incompleteness, not the partiality that each formula is only one as opposed to another, but the indeterminacy within each formula itself. First, given a formula for justice, the things held proportional can be added together. The people have more of anything that offers a claim to rule, and so democracy can be the conclusion of an argument based on *any* form of justice. Equally, given a formula for justice, the things held proportional can be maximized, and so monarchy can be the conclusion of an argument based on any form of justice. See, thus, the following two passages, sometimes called the addition and maximization arguments:

> It is possible that the many, though not individually good men, yet when they come together may be better, not individually, but collectively, than those who are so, just as public dinners to which many contribute are better than those supplied at one man's cost; for where there are many, each individual, it may be argued, has some portion of virtue and wisdom, and when they have come together, just as the multitude becomes a single man with many feet and many hands and many senses, so also it becomes one personality as regards the moral and intellectual faculties. (III.11.1281b1–10; cf. 13.1283b27–34)[46]

> There is a certain difficulty (*aporia*) that confronts all claims for political honors. It would seem that wealth gives no right to rule, and birth gives none either. For if there is one man who is richer than all of them, then obviously by the same right he ought to rule alone. Similarly, he who excels in birth should be the sole ruler of those who claim on the ground of their freedom. And perhaps the same thing will occur even in aristocracies with regard to goodness; if there were one man who was better than the other good men in the government, he should rule by the same right. Similarly, if the masses should rule because they are stronger than the few, then, if there were one man, or a number of persons more than one but fewer than many, who were stronger than the rest, they ought to rule rather than the masses. (III.13.1283b13–26)[47]

From these additive and maximizing arguments, Aristotle concludes that no principle of justice—even proportion to merit—is determinative of a good constitution. These arguments take the principles of justice more seriously than its adherents do and thus exposes the partiality of these principles. While democratic and oligarchic justice are partial, there is no complete and impartial justice that should be the basis for the constitution instead. Partiality is not the problem. These arguments from addition and maximization show that any formula or proportion, not just defective ones, is incomplete. We can here see another difference between Aristotle's project and that of contemporary political theory. Theorists today start from something like the argument from addition and try to figure out the conditions—such as the Condorcet jury theorem—under which individual judgments will add up to a collective judgment that more confidently tracks the truth than the rationality possessed by any individual. Aristotle sees any such argument as part of a dialectical exchange that exposes the dilemmas of who should rule, and the limits of reason in supplying an answer to the question. Books IV–VI will illustrate ways in which the polis can be better, as well as wiser, than its citizens.[48]

Politics aims at the good life. What is unclear is how to embody the highest good in political life. Practical political philosophy consists in deliberating about how to connect that end to its appropriate matter, moving cause and form. Earlier I showed that the problems of politics were set by the fact that it had an end without natural connections to those three causes: people don't tend to achieve their end for the most part as do the subjects of natural science. The discussion of justice brings that predicament to a head. For that reason, he said that finding "what equality and inequality for what sort of persons . . . is difficult, and calls for political philosophy" (III.12.1282b18–23). We deliberate about how to connect the good man to the good citizen and to justice.[49]

Connecting form to function is the practical project for politics, signaled here by Aristotle's identification of aiming at the good life with aiming at the common advantage. The common advantage is identified with the political good (1282b14–18) and with absolute justice as well (III.7.1279a18–30, 12. 1282b16–18; cf. NE V.1.1129b14–19, VIII.9.1160a13–14). When Berlin upholds the cause of pluralism and liberalism in the lines I quoted earlier in this chapter, he does so against "single-minded monists, ruthless fanatics, men possessed by an all-embracing coherent vision." When Aristotle upholds the autonomy of politics, he does so against attempts to sidestep political philosophy through imitating nature by harmonizing efficient, formal, and final cause as corrupt constitutions do. Such ways of thinking, which I compared earlier to pleonexia as the vice associated with justice in the Ethics, therefore inevitably both reduce the good life to an external possession and makes rulers act for their own advantage. It is for this reason that Aristotle can uphold the thesis I noted before that when corrupt states aim only at the advantage of the rulers, it follows that they must aim at a degenerate and partial end. Aristotle's mode of argument stands as an example of deliberation and praxis coexisting with a single vision of the good life. Aristotle is no perfectionist; he shows us that liberalism and totalitarianism are not exclusive alternatives.

The addition and maximization arguments threaten the autonomy of politics as they would ultimately make the polis into an alliance, in which only quantity or the result counts. The danger exists because both arguments appeal to antecedent properties, and not, as with reciprocal equality and justice, to political activities themselves. If a polis had a limited purpose, as an alliance does and as partisans of partial constitutions suppose the polis has, there would be no problem in adjudicating between competing conceptions of justice and offering a correct one to replace them. Thus in chapter 9 after saying that both democratic and oligarchic justice are partly right and partly wrong, he first points to a resolution by supposing that "people constituted a community and came together for the sake of property. Then their participation in a polis would be proportional to their property" (1280a24–26), and the oligarchic idea of justice would be right. But if the purpose of the polis is living well (1280a31), then there is no such simple resolution. If we reduce the good life to life, then we no longer have to go through the trouble of deliberation and philosophy—there lies the purity characteristic of the factions that destroy the polis by failing to see the partiality of their conceptions of justice.

I have been characterizing the problem of praxis abstractly as the fact that in politics function and form are not naturally or automatically aligned. That problem reappears here in the fact that while true justice is proportional to virtue, true justice does not become a third formula for justice alongside democratic and oligarchic justice. The addition and maximization arguments show that democratic and oligarchic justice are both in principle incomplete. But they are all we have and what we need to deliberate with. Political philosophy does not settle things by adding the voice of an impartial umpire but instead shows the partiality of partially just claims so that they can contribute to true justice, either by leading, as in Book IV to a moderate constitution ruled by the middle class, or, as in Book V, to democracies and oligarchies whose rulers moderate their goals and stabilize the constitution.[50]

Aristotle does not reform politics by changing the attention of democratic and oligarchic advocates from life to the good life. Such a conversion, as I will argue in detail in chapter 5, would require further premises partisans of mere life should not accept. It would therefore make philosophy an authoritarian voice silencing the competition, as good a definition of utopian political philosophy as you can get. His procedure is more surreptitious, since he does not dispute with democratic or oligarchic opponents head on, and also more philosophical, as he recognizes that even these constitutions, although degenerate, are constitutions, and thus are capable of transformation, and self-transformation, into correct constitutions. He reforms politics by showing that if one changes the end of a constitution from benefiting the part to the whole, then the nature of the benefits will thereby be transformed. Correct constitutions are defined by aiming at the good of the whole, while still operating under the principles of democratic and oligarchic justice. This is Aristotle's priority of the right to the good.

In another apparent non sequitur, III.12 says that not all goods are commensurable. Height does not count as a political good.

> Someone might say, perhaps, that offices should be unequally distributed on the basis of superiority in any good whatsoever. . . . But if this is true, then those who are superior in complexion, or height, or any other good whatsoever will get more of the things with which political justice is concerned. And isn't that plainly false? . . . Besides, according to this argument every good would have to be commensurable with every other. For if being a certain height counted more, height in general would be in competition with both wealth and freedom. . . . Since this is impossible, it is clear that in political matters, too, it is reasonable not to dispute over political office on the basis of just any sort of inequality. (1282b22–1283a11)[51]

However, by denying that all goods are commensurable, he implies the more limited thesis that all *political* goods *are* commensurable. All goods, including freedom and wealth, that contribute to the state are commensurable in the sense that they create reasonable, although imperfect, claims to rule. They are political claims, while superior height is not. It is only thus that degenerate states still are states, not contracts or alliances or anything else.[52]

If all political goods are commensurable, then the statesman should not automatically choose virtue over wealth, but must somehow use all political goods in furthering the ultimate political purpose of the good life. Aristotle consequently expresses all these claims as *ethical* claims to show that they are indeed just, even though not absolutely. These are reasonable claims to honor (1283a17). The passage I quoted continues:

The rich are right in that they have a larger share in the land and the land is a public concern, also in that they are usually *more reliable* in business dealings. The free and the noble are right in the respect in which they are near together; the nobles are citizens to a greater degree than the ignoble, and nobility is always honoured in its own country. Also because the sons of better men are likely to be *better*, since nobility is goodness of stock. Similarly, we shall say that the claim of goodness is also just; for justice according to us is *social goodness (koinōnikēn aretēn)*, and on it all the other virtues must follow. The majority are right also in their claim against the minority, since when taken together they are stronger and richer and *better (beltious)* than the few. (1283a32–41; emphasis added)

Partial justice is just—it is reasonable to lay claims to political authority on the basis of things necessary for the state. But it is partial because its goods are necessary for the state's existence, not for its goodness. Therefore, deviant regimes are those that embody claims for existence that are not yet claims for goodness, which means that they aim at the advantage of the rulers, not the polis as a whole. Aristotle does not call these regimes deviant because they are based on claims of life, rather than the good life, but because they overgeneralize about equality: "Since equality in one point does not call for equality in all, and inequality in one point does not call for inequality in all, all such constitutions must be perversions" (III.13.1283a27–28). Yet, because these claims can become claims for contributing to the good life, their partial forms of justice can be the basis for good constitutions.

Aristotle presents us with a pair of partial forms of justice but no impartial or complete form. Democratic and oligarchic justice are the two formulas for justice, but democracy and oligarchy are only two among six constitutions. Therefore, we have to wonder whether democracy and oligarchy are forms of constitution in the sense that they are forms that any constitution has or can have, aspects of any constitution, or if they are forms that distinguish one constitution from another. Democracy and oligarchy could simply be ways of manifesting the essence of the political which any state can have. Any constitution is arguably democratic to the degree that it satisfies the definition of "citizen" that is true for constitutions in general but that some satisfy more than others (III.1.1275b3); in democracies above all ruling and ruled are shared (VI.2.1317b1–17), although that seems to mark all poleis at III.6.1279a7–10. Alternating ruling and being ruled is democratic, but it is also indicative of the rule of law in general

(III.16.1287a16–19). All states are, in addition, arguably oligarchic because political justice is distributive rather than corrective, and therefore geometric rather than arithmetic (III.1274b38, 6.1278b8–11, IV.1.1289a15–18). "All agree that the just in distribution must be according to worth of some sort, but all do not recognize the same sort of worth" (*NE* V.3.1131a25–28). All states are oligarchic, moreover, because in any state some are citizens and others are not. Since slaves are never citizens, even radical democracies have a tacit property qualification. In the same way, any constitution is monarchical to the degree that it maximizes whatever qualifications it depends on, and aristocratic to the extent that it aims, as all constitutions are supposed to do, at the good life. "Polity" is the name for one form of constitution and for constitution in general, and for the rule of law as opposed to the rule of men (cf. *NE* V.6.1134a35–b2).[53] Democracy and oligarchy embody partial conceptions of justice, and are two constitutions among others, because they take a feature common to all constitutions and erect it into an exclusive principle. The correct constitutions do not do that, and so are only individuated by the accident of the number of rulers.

Aristotle's discussion of justice in the *Politics* is surprisingly narrow, considering that justice holds cities together. This is justice as the way rulers are selected, and not how rulers or governments behave, and so justice distributes offices, not, as does distributive justice in the *Ethics*, "honors, wealth, or whatever can be divided among those who share in the political system" (V.2.1303b31–32).[54] Among those goods, though, honor is "the greatest of external goods" (IV.3.1123b22), the "prize of virtue, awarded to good people (b35–36), and almost the end (*telos*) of the political life" (I.5.1095b22–23; see too *Politics* VII.2.1324a29–31). "Just actions that aim at honors and prosperity are unqualifiedly the finest" (VII.13.1332a15–16).

If one is only distributing honors, distribution according to merit looks more appealing than it would for distributing wealth or security. One person might deserve an organ transplant more than another because she'll probably live longer, or because he didn't ruin his own liver through drinking. But no one *earns* the contested organ. Distribution according to merit is then more abstract when we're distributing something other than honor and rule.[55]

By the end of chapter 13, there are three distinct criteria for distinguishing good from bad constitutions: (1) in good constitutions rule is for the sake of the ruled, or the whole, while bad constitutions rule for the sake of the rulers; (2) in good constitutions justice is proportional to merit; and (3) good constitutions embody the rule of law, while corrupt ones are ruled by men.[56] The first is a difference in final causes, the second in form, and the third in moving causes. The first two, as I've argued, make the cut among constitutions in the same place, but the third has a more complex role. A constitution that doesn't aim at the true end of politics, living well, is still a constitution, but a constitution that doesn't embody rule of law is no longer a constitution. That is, constitutions can fail to aim at the end and still be constitutions, but constitutions that fail to maintain constitutional form through rule of law are not.

Good states recognize the need for political wisdom and praxis to connect the four different causes of political life just because the state is not natural. Only good states fully recognize that the causes are distinct, while corrupt states confuse form and end, making the state either into a means for enriching themselves or protecting their freedom. Only good states then are truly political, rather than an alliance or a contract to serve ulterior ends. In good states, consequently, citizens can be identified by a criterion other than ruling. Only in good states is there the political distinction between sovereign and citizen, a distinction among its citizens between rulers and ruled. Good states are then at a maximum distance from the condition of barbarians, whom, Aristotle says, collapse all distinctions, even between female and slave (I.2.1252b4, see *NE* VIII.10.1160b24-30). The more developed political life becomes, the more clear are distinctions between household and polis, master and ruler, ruler and citizen, citizen and the other inhabitants of the state. In good states, citizenship is a political activity, not a condition like being subject to or a beneficiary of the laws. It is caring about each other's virtue, a care manifested in participation in offices.[57]

VII. THE RULE OF THE BEST VERSUS THE RULE OF LAW: BOOK III.14–18

As I've been reading the argument of Book III, Aristotle shows the need for *phronēsis* because of the impossibility of directly enacting the good. However, there is a counterargument. The man of outstanding virtue is himself that counterargument, a reason to put the good prior to the right. Ruling and being ruled in turn constitute a sacrifice, and a greater sacrifice the more virtuous someone is. Already in Book II Aristotle made the central political phenomenon of ruling and being ruled in turn into an apparent second-best: "it is clearly better, where possible, for the same people always to rule. But among those where it is not possible, because all are naturally equal . . . it is at least possible to approximate to this if those who are equal take turns and are similar when out of office (II.2.1261a37–1261b2). That possibility recurs in Book VII: "When someone else has superior

virtue and his power to do the best things is also superior, it is noble to
follow and just to obey him. But he should possess not virtue alone, but
also the power he needs to do those things" (VII.3.1325b10–13). Therefore
it makes sense to end Book III by a consideration of monarchy and the conflicting claims of the rule of law and the rule of virtue, the right and the
good.

Moreover, even corrupt constitutions can exhibit ruling and being ruled
in turn. This remark from III.6 should make us hesitate before embracing
ruling and being ruled as an ultimate good.

> In the case of political office, where it has been established on the ba-
> sis of equality and similarity among the citizens, they think it right to
> take turns at ruling. In the past, as is natural, they thought it right to
> perform public service when their turn came, and then to have someone
> look to *their* good, just as they had earlier looked for his benefit when
> they were in office. Nowadays, however, because of the profits to be had
> from public funds and from office, people want to be in office continu-
> ously, as if they were sick and would be cured by being always in office.
> (III.6.1279a10–15)

In modern democracies, parties can take turns enriching themselves. That is
not what ruling and being ruled in turn means. Corrupt constitutions have
to be constitutions, and not a series of alternating temporary despotisms.

Heroic virtue appeared in *NE* VII.1 alongside virtue and self-control as
one of three desirable states of the soul, but once its existence is noted,
the *Ethics* makes nothing of it. *Politics* III ends with a discussion of the
strength of the claim to rule by such a man.[58] Aristotle uses the man of exceptional goodness to raise the question of whether the rule of law is only
of instrumental value, preventing rulers from ruling for their own benefit,
or whether the rule of law is a political value of its own in competition with
the rule of the best. This is the difference between moderation as a political
virtue and moderation as an unfortunate concession to necessity. This is
the necessity that John Stuart Mill says is the "necessary in both senses of
the term, being at once inevitable and indispensable."[59]

Rule of law is a value for a number of reasons: it is a sign of correct
rule; it embodies the security that is the common function of citizens; it
is, as this section maintains, reason without desire (III.16.1287a32). The
issue is whether those values are instrumental to the good life or should
be sought for their own sake, and if sought for their own sake, should they

be sought under all circumstances. The possibility of a ruler of outstanding virtue raises these questions. In the rest of the *Politics*, rule of law is a good because its alternative is the lawless versions of democracy, oligarchy, or tyranny. But here, as in Plato's *Statesman*, rule of law is opposed to rule by the best.[60] If rule of law can be valuable for its own sake even in contrast to rule by the best, then when it is, as is more usual, opposed to arbitrary rule, its goodness will be all the greater. Aristotle tells us that the laws should determine as much as possible; the image of the person of superlative virtue challenges that thesis. There need be no argument that rule of law is better than the real alternative of arbitrary rule, but whether it is better than the unlikely prospect of rule by the best person, while not an issue of direct practical urgency, will tell us about how good rule of law really is.

The topos of rule of law versus rule of men has a different meaning for true and for corrupt constitutions. The distinction is applied to the kinds of democracy and oligarchy in Book IV. Democracies and oligarchies without rule of law are the worst kinds of democracy and oligarchy. At that point the community stops being a polis, and government becomes an instrument by which the rulers rob and dominate the ruled. But when applied, as it is here, to true constitutions, rule of law is by no means obviously superior to rule by the good men who comprise those constitutions' rulers. Rule of law constrains the opinions and desires of the nonvirtuous. The function of law for the virtuous is not so clear. The complexity comes out in these lines from the *Ethics*: "Friendship seems to hold cities together, and legislators would seem to be more concerned about it than about justice. . . . If people are friends, they have no need of justice, but if they are just they need friendship in addition, and the justice that is most just seems to belong to friendship" (*NE* VIII.1.1155a24–29). If people are friends, they have no need of justice; if the rulers are virtuous, they have no need for law. After the inconclusive ending of Book III, the rest of the *Politics* in different ways shows itself "more concerned about friendship than justice," even though both justice and friendship come in for more extensive discussion in the *Ethics* than in the *Politics*. Book IV's emphasis on the middle class is a way of achieving concord and political friendship, Books V and VI are concerned with avoiding faction (the opposite of political friendship), and the final two books are circumstances in which citizens have no need of justice, but where friendship reigns without it.

Where the first thirteen chapters discussed forms independent of their end, the last five chapters concern an end independent of its political form. Therefore this section thematizes the issue of whether the right is prior to the good. The man of superlative virtue's claim to rule posits a good that is prior to the right, while those who uphold the rule of law counter by making the right prior to the good. While elsewhere in the *Politics* rule of law is superior to the rule of men, when the rule of men means rule by the man of superlative virtue, it isn't so clear which is superior.[61]

The section on justice, chapters 9–13, was inconclusive because of the addition and maximization arguments. The additive arguments show that different exemplars of a single good can be added together to produce a greater amount of any good, whether money, security, or even wisdom, but the maximization arguments show that using any good as a criterion for justice involves an arbitrary cutoff of a continuous quantity. If, thus, justice should be proportional to wealth, then there is no principled way of separating who should be a citizen, or ruler, on the basis of wealth.

At III.14–18 Aristotle deals with the consequences of such arguments with respect to a single good, the single good that is merit itself. The maximization argument is different when the value maximized is virtue. Aristotle does not raise the question about someone with excessive money, because rule based on excess of anything other than virtue would necessarily be despotic. Here is the unique case in which abandoning the rule of law would not be despotic:

> Those who are preeminent in the goods of fortune—strength, wealth, friends and the other things of this sort—neither wish to be ruled nor know how to be. . . . The ones do not know how to rule but only how to be ruled, and then only in the fashion of rule of a master, and the others do not know how to be ruled by any sort of rule, but only to rule in the fashion of rule of a master. What comes into being, then, is a city not of free persons but of slaves and masters, the ones consumed by envy, the others by contempt. Nothing is further removed from affection and from a political partnership, for partnership involves the element of affection. (IV.11.1295b13–24)

The question here is whether rule by heroic virtue is not similarly despotic, by being nonpolitical. Since for the man of superlative virtue, the good is prior to the right, his rule is a form of household management (III.14.1285b20–1286a1), where the ruler "acts in all things according to his own will" (III.16.1287a1–10, a30–40). When speaking about natural slaves and masters, Aristotle says: "Nor can the ruler and the ruled differ by the more and the less, for ruler and ruled differ in form (*eidos*), but the more and the less do not" (I.5. 1259b36, cf. VII.7.1325b3–5); and the question is whether such an argument can apply to the relation between the man of superior virtue in relation to the rest of us, who are not natural slaves. If his rule is not political, but still desirable, then politics and justice are a second-best solution to the problems of praxis, as in contemporary arguments that make the right prior because of a failure of the good to manifest itself. Monarchy establishes the simple proportion between ethical goodness and the excellence of a state that is so strikingly lacking in the rest of Book III: "It is in the same manner and through the same things that a man becomes good (*spoudaios*) and that a polis is established under an aristocracy or a kingship" (18.1288a32).

I think that Aristotle's answer to these problems runs this way: If I am ruled by a god or hero I am still ruled politically rather than despotically—on the condition that I have right opinion on matters about which the ruler has *phronēsis*, unlike the slavish ruled, who don't need right opinion but merely the ability to follow orders. "*Phronēsis* is the only virtue peculiar to the ruler. The other virtues, it would seem, must necessarily be common to both rulers and ruled, but prudence is not a virtue of one ruled, but rather true opinion (*doxa alēthēs*) [is]" (III.4.1277b25–29).[62] It is political rule, although permanent, because I live a virtuous and even happy life—missing only *phronēsis*. To act according to *phronēsis* without being a *phronimos* is to have right opinion, while to do virtuous deeds without being ethically virtuous is to be law-abiding.[63]

That only the rulers have, or exercise, *phronēsis* has a consequence for the practical purposes of the *Politics*. Aristotle has nothing to say to the nonruling citizens, no advice about why they should accept someone else as a ruler, nothing to say about the conditions, if any, under which they should try to change the constitution. This is not because there are no important practical issues about how nonruling citizens are to behave, but because political philosophy can only address those with *phronēsis*. Therefore, just as the *Ethics* speaks only to those who are already virtuous, the *Politics* speaks only to rulers.

While Aristotle does nothing with the possibility of heroic virtue in *NE* VII, the question about the rule of the best man as opposed to the rule of law is similar to the issue at the end of the *Ethics* about *theōria* as a practical life. The *Ethics* has to show how the acknowledgment of the superiority of *theōria* does not denigrate other praxeis. So here, being virtuous without ruling is both a perfectly good life and a second-best in which we forego when exercising certain central human capacities. Just as the exceptional man seems not to become a ruler through being ruled, we do not acquire *theōria* as we do practical virtues, by first performing the action for ulterior motives and then coming to do it for its own sake. Therefore, neither the rule of one man above the law nor *theōria* can be an object of deliberation; both are fortunate rather than deliberate. If *theōria* is better than practical virtue, it seems incomparably better; the heroic ruler seems similarly incomparably better than other citizens, and so justice, not to mention friendship, between ruler and ruled seems impossible.[64] And like *theōria*, the discussion of the heroic king has no further consequences for Aristotle's argument, which starts over again in Book IV as though these chapters did not exist. Where Book III began with democracy as the form of constitution that best fits the definition of "polis," it ends with the opposite extreme, the rule of the best man. The monarchy of superlative virtue is not a constitution in which the ruler is the only citizen. But to make that assertion takes away the distinction between citizen and sovereign that *Politics* III achieves. "Jason was hungry except when he was a tyrant, as one who did not know how to be a private individual" (III.4.1277a24–25). Monarchy, as distinct from despotism and tyranny, is possible only if there are citizens who are ruled and not rulers.

Because Aristotle is inconclusive about whether rule by the man of outstanding virtue can be political rule, and because I think he is right to be inconclusive, let me offer an example that illustrates the problem. Wilt Chamberlain stood to ordinary mortal basketball players much as the man of superlative virtue stood to other citizens. He was so much bigger, stronger, and more skilled than anyone else, that he could score and rebound at will, although in his case "at will" was a seriously complicating factor not relevant to the analogy. Such a basketball player created two distinct kinds of problems. First, there was the worry about whether to change the rules so that basketball would still remain competitive even with the presence of such a player. That problem looks at the man of superlative virtue not as a fellow citizen would regard him but as someone making judgments from the outside. The issue of fair and entertaining competition is not relevant to the analogy I want to draw. The more interesting problem is not how to protect the rest of us against the man of superlative virtue but what to do if he's on our side. And in fact that was a serious problem that teams had with Chamberlain. Until his skills diminished with age, no one could figure out how to use him as part of a winning basketball team. It was true that he was a basketball player of superlative ability. It was also true that his value, as measured by the players his teams could get in a trade—equivalent to ostracism in Aristotle's discussion—was quite limited. The distinction I noted earlier between forward- and backward-looking criteria for rule, between ruling as something that one deserves to do and something that one can do well, comes back here. The fable of Chamberlain is a paradigm for Aristotle's ambivalence about the man of superlative virtue and his place in a community.[65]

I want to note one more thing about this discussion of monarchy. It contains no discussion of any possible motivations someone might have for being a monarch, nor for consenting to the establishment of a monarchy. In particular, we find no connection between the treatment of monarchy and the desire for domination that might lead to tyranny. Instead, Aristotle's only question is whether monarchy can be best for some polis. It is hard to imagine someone having a choice of becoming Wilt Chamberlain or not, but teams did choose whether or not to trade for him. It is one thing to say that a team will win more games with him than without him, or with the players they would need to exchange for him. An absolute monarchy ruled by a virtuous man, by analogy, might be more secure and prosperous than any available alternative. But it is quite another thing to say that his presence makes the other players better. I will be healthier by listening to my doctor than by making my own decisions; the issue for politics is whether my community or I can become more virtuous by the presence of the supremely virtuous ruler, or whether instead his presence would diminish our opportunities for virtue. A closer analogy than basketball would be the great teacher: sometimes great teachers make their students into disciples, and sometimes into people who are capable thinkers in their own right. Both are possibilities. Both are possibilities for rule by the virtuous, which is why Aristotle is right to leave the question unsettled.[66]

VIII. CONCLUSION

Throughout I have been claiming that the incompleteness of the normative sets the problem for praxis that makes deliberation both possible and necessary. *Politics* III is political philosophy, carefully keeping to what political philosophy can achieve, and leaving to statesmen what is appropriate for statesmen. The second half of the book exhibits a series of dialectical arguments on both sides of several issues; the statesman converts them into rhetorical arguments designed to persuade citizens by giving weight, depending on the circumstances, to the different probable arguments Aristotle assembles. The weight given to different considerations is a matter of character, *ēthos*, that takes argument beyond logos and rationality into the ethical and the concrete.

This difference between dialectic and rhetoric, between political philosophy and political *phronēsis*, comes out in a curious paragraph in chapter 13.

> If they were (*ei eien*) all present in a single polis, therefore (I mean, for example, the good, the rich, the well-born, and a political multitude in addition), will there be a dispute as to who should rule or not? Within each of the constitutions we have mentioned, to be sure, the decision as to who should rule is indisputable, since these differ from one another because of what is in authority. . . . But . . . we are investigating how the matter is to be determined *when* (*hotan*) all these are present simultaneously . . ." (1283b1–9)

I find this paragraph odd because it seems that all these claimants to rule are always present in a single polis. The best translation of Aristotle's conditional, which varies between the subjunctive and the optative, is the English idiom "if and when." The question is how, if and when all these claims are simultaneously present, can there ever be "indisputable" rule. Actual statesmen face the issue in a more concrete form: "Suppose, for example (*ei eien*), that those who possess virtue are extremely few in number; how should the matter be settled? Should their fewness be considered in relation to the task . . . or to whether there are enough of them to constitute a polis by themselves?" (1283b10–13). The weight of the respective claims to rule can only be determined circumstantially. The *Politics* presents dialectical arguments; in particular circumstances they become rhetorical arguments that require political, not philosophical, judgment. "None of the definitions on the basis of which people claim that they themselves deserve to rule, whereas everyone else deserves to be ruled by them, is correct" (1283b23–27). I will point to further implications of the distinction between dialectic and rhetoric in my next two chapters.

What, finally, does this presentation of *Politics* III have to do with modern arguments about the right and the good? Once the right is prior to the good, there is a tendency for goodness to become subjective and optional, for the good to remain good at the price of becoming extramoral. This is the tendency to slide from toleration and pluralism to skepticism, indifferentism, and nihilism. The right is prior to the good because of what Rawls calls "the fact of pluralism." It seems to follow that were there no disagreements about the good, then the right would not have to be prior. The right is prior to the good if and only if there are permanent disputes about the good, which seems to have the further implication that these disputes are irrational, since taking part in them will never lead to resolution. *Politics* III stands as a refutation to these ideas.

In *Politics* III the right is prior to the good although there is a true good, a best life for man. The partisans of justice assert partial truths, a claim no modern advocate of the priority of the right to the good could make. There is a whole truth of which the partisans of democratic and oligarchic justice grasp a part, but that whole truth cannot be directly instantiated. The right is prior to the good without any fact of pluralism. Aristotle does not claim that there is a variety of constitutions all of which can equally be home to human flourishing. Instead the *Politics* articulates a variety of possible ways of living together that have different possible connections to living well. Because of this flexibility and indeterminacy, Aristotle is not subject to accusations of false neutrality that have plagued recent articulations of liberalisms.

Book III is primarily aporetic and formal. It clears space for deliberation and makes politics autonomous. Book I showed that the polis is natural; Book II explained the unity of the polis. Book III makes nature and unity into qualities that attach primarily to the polis itself, rather than to any antecedent conditions, ethical, psychological, or historical. After Book III we are ready for the scientific treatment of politics in Books IV–VIII. Book III shows that the statesman must enact practical connections between the constitutional form of the polis and the other three causes. In more substantive language, the statesman must, after Book III, develop connections between people's material interests in life itself and the formulations of justice they can accept and see as realizing both life and the good life. That is Book IV. The statesman must develop connections between the causes of security and faction and the stability of the state. Those connections form the subject of Books V and VI. Finally, the statesman must develop connections between the good life and the state's power of developing and rewarding virtue, which connections form the subject of Books VII and VIII. Relative to each of those purposes, the meaning of "form" changes, from justice through the parts of government and then stability and finally to the state's educational powers. Book III therefore leads to the ambiguity of the "best constitution" that Aristotle explicates in the opening paragraphs of Book IV. *Politics* III opens up the possibility of political philosophy that occupies the rest of the *Politics*.

Book III leaves the statesman with a problem. People "all grasp justice of a sort, but they go only to a certain point and do not discuss the whole of what is just in the most authoritative sense" (III.9.1280a8–10). How can we respond to this inevitable partiality? One could, first, recognize that democratic and oligarchic justice are partial and incomplete, and articulate the principles of true justice. At the opposite extreme, one could acknowledge that one's own conception of justice is partial, and defend it all the more militantly for that reason. Third, one could argue that there are poleis for which democratic justice is appropriate, and others that are better off with oligarchic justice. Finally, one could look for a constitution in which partisans of different conceptions of justice could live together. Those four possible responses become the four kinds of best that, from IV.1 on, organize the rest of the *Politics*.

CHAPTER FOUR

Practical Knowledge and
the Four Orientations to the Best

In the introduction I looked briefly at the first two chapters of Book IV and their presentation of four dimensions of politics, what I've called four kinds of best. I noted that the four inquiries he outlines correspond to the four causes. The first, "that which is best in the abstract" (*haplōs*) (1288b26), orients politics around the end of politics, the best life. The second, the best relative to circumstances, starts with the material cause and organizes political inquiry around the best that can be made out of given material. The third, the best on a hypothesis, starts not from the true end of politics, but any posited end, and so looks for means and devices that will preserve any given constitution. The final inquiry, the search for "the form of constitution which is best suited to states in general," articulates a formal cause that can organize almost any material, any kind of people.

It is easy to see how two of those orientations lead to practical knowledge. The best constitution in the abstract leads to what is often called utopian thinking. By knowing the best state, just like knowing the best life, we have a target to aim at, an ideal to aspire to, a standard by which other constitutions can be measured. The best on a hypothesis is practical in an even more obvious way, by identifying the resources that the statesman can use to maintain the existing constitution, whatever it is. The other two kinds of best are less obvious kinds of practical projects, and just how they are practical will be one of my main concerns in this chapter. They focus on material and formal causes, and it is harder to see how those orientations can be practical than making the final or efficient cause basic. These two are less obviously practical because they understand political life as neither natural nor artificial. The more natural a polis, the closer the four causes come to coinciding.[1] That is the ideal of Books VII and VIII. If the state is natural, then there is no process of making that can bring it about, and so we have to pray for its enabling conditions. The more the polis seems an artifact, the more distinct the causes have to be, as the argument of Books V and VI displays. When the polis is a work of art, the statesman is a maker, standing apart from other citizens and treating them as material to be organized, and sometimes manipulated. Book I showed how the state is natural, but also showed some of the limitations of understanding the state as natural. Book II looked at the state as an artifact, and showed the limitations of that mode of understanding. It is because the constitution is neither natural nor artificial that the four causes have the practical independence they do, which allows the articulation of the four distinct kinds of best.

Aristotle's third kind of best, the best relative to circumstances, is oriented to the material cause: given the material of a state, in particular the different classes that comprise the body of citizens, what is the best possible constitution for that state? That inquiry resembles the project of Book V in its emphasis on circumstances, but the crucial difference is that the practical project in Book V is subordinate to the *desires* (*epithumia*) of the rulers (1288b17) rather than what in fact harmonizes (*harmottousa*) with the people (1288b25).[2] For the circumstantial best of Book IV, the trainer might see that one person's absence of fast twitch muscles will make her into a good distance runner, not a good sprinter; the statesman here will similarly see in the material of a state's social and economic classes what the best constitution for that material would be.

The best in general, finally, looks for a formal cause, an organization of the constitution suitable for most conditions. I own a book that contains a daily program to prepare in twenty-four weeks to compete in an ironman triathlon. No variations are built in because of the athlete's age, body type, or skill level. No doubt, the book's advice would not be the best advice for world-class athletes who have personal trainers; on the other side, there are some people who, even if they wanted to, couldn't follow the regimen. The program is general enough to be useful to all between those extremes, although it might not be perfect for any.

It is my thesis that these last two inquiries, the formal and material, the best in general and the best in particular circumstances, are both accomplished in Book IV. As Aristotle announces the general program in IV.1–2, he suggests that there will be four distinct treatments of the best constitution, corresponding to the four kinds of best. But that is not what happens. Instead, by knowing about what constitution best suits a given people, we can draw as a corollary what is the best constitution in general, that is, the best constitution for poleis that are not unusually lucky, like the polis of

Books VII and VIII, or unusually constrained in their choices, as the constitutions of Books V and VI are.

Book IV presents a coherent argument by tying together those two orientations to the best. Aristotle ties them together through another aspect of the program he announces in the first chapter, the discovery of species of the different constitutions, and of democracy and oligarchy in particular. After enumerating the four kinds of best, he says:

> And therefore, in addition to the qualifications of the statesman already mentioned, he should be able to help existing constitutions, as has been said before. This he cannot do unless he knows how many forms of constitution there are. It is often supposed that there is only one kind of democracy and one of oligarchy. But this is a mistake; and, in order to avoid such mistakes, we must ascertain what differences there are in the constitutions of states, and in how many ways they are combined. (IV.1.1289a5–11)

Knowing the kinds of constitutions has a second practical purpose in addition to being able to improve existing constitutions:

> The same practical wisdom (phronēsis) will enable a man to know which laws are the best, and which are suited to different constitutions; for the laws are, and ought to be, relative to the constitution, and not the constitution to the laws. (1289a12–14)

Aristotle here seems to promise that once we know the kinds of constitutions, and especially the kinds of democracy and oligarchy, we will be able to "help existing constitutions." But the argument of Book IV is more complicated. One thread that connects its various stages of his argument is the subtle interrelation between the middle constitution, the mixed constitution, the middle class, and the moderate statesman. First, the differentiation of species of the different constitutions leads to Aristotle's discovery of which constitution is best in general, culminating in chapter 11. That discovery leads in turn to knowing what is best for different peoples, starting in chapter 12. The kinds of constitution give the legislator a manifold of possibilities, and they can be mixed according to their material cause (IV.12–13) or their formal cause (IV.14–16) to make them suit the population of a particular polis. While as kinds of best, the best in circumstances and the best in general are distinct, they really form a single kind of practical knowledge. This is signaled by the conclusion to IV.13:

We have said, then, why there are several constitutions—there are others besides those spoken of (for democracy is not one in number, and
similarly with the others), what their varieties are, and why they arise.
In addition, we have said which constitution is best, for the majority
of cases, and among the other constitutions which suits which sort of
people. (IV.13.1297b29–33)

My concern in this chapter is to understand Aristotle's use of the four senses
of the best in the *Politics* and in particular as *Politics* IV unfolds. But before
turning to that argument, I want to digress for a moment and ask an obvious
question. Why is there nothing parallel to this organization of four orientations to the best in Aristotle's *Ethics*? The *Ethics*—I see no difference here
between the *Eudemian* and the *Nicomachean Ethics*—seems limited to
what Aristotle here calls the best constitution *haplōs*, or according to one's
prayers, "[that] the best is necessarily fitting for the body that is naturally
the finest and is most finely equipped" (*Pol.* IV.1.1288b13–14). Only citizens, property-owning males in well-ordered cities, need apply. The *Ethics*
contains no considerations of the best in circumstances, the best in general,
or the best given certain undesirable conditions. There is no treatment of
the best in circumstances, as in the idea of virtue connected to "my station
and its duties."[3] Aristotelian virtues are not traits that are generally useful
in all sorts of situations, as in many contemporary conceptions of virtue
ethics. And Aristotle gives us nothing to help us understand how to do one's
best in tragic circumstances or how to act morally in an immoral world. By
the standards of *Politics* IV.1, Aristotelian ethics is not a complete art or
science.[4]

There is another possibility. It may be that there is some special reason,
a reason which does not apply to practical arts and sciences in general, that
applies to the individual good life and lets these four be satisfied together.
The virtuous life has its own kind of reliability attached to it, not, as in the
Politics, of lasting as long as possible, but in that someone who is courageous in the strict sense will also be able to be courageous in more extended
ways (III.6.1115a35–b2). Sincerely, "A lover of the truth who is truthful
even when nothing is at stake will be keener to tell the truth when something is at stake (*en hois diapherei*), since he will avoid falsehood as shameful (*aischron*) [when something is at stake] having already avoided it in
itself [when nothing was at stake]" (1127b3–7).[5] Happiness "will be widely
shared; for anyone who is not deformed [in his capacity] for virtue will be
able to achieve happiness" (I.9.1099b18–20). The fact that the virtuous life
is not always happy—recall the case of Priam in I.12—does not mean that

some other life in those circumstances would be happy, and therefore that fact does not count against the virtuous life being the best life regardless of circumstances. So it may be that the ambiguity that in politics generates the four orientations to the best becomes univocal in ethics.

I think that that's correct. It follows that there is a smaller role in ethics for philosophy, as distinct from *phronēsis*.[6] The good person must be able to think of all four orientations to the good, but practical philosophy has nothing distinctive to say about any of them except the best absolutely. In that sense, politics is more abstract, as well as more concrete in its attention to particular circumstances, than ethics. Its abstraction opens up the possibility that practical knowledge and practical experience may not be aligned as neatly as asserted in the *Ethics*. The *Ethics* is as complete as a science dealing with individual conduct can be, but is incomplete relative to the *Politics*.[7]

I. THE KINDS OF CONSTITUTIONS: BOOK IV.3–10

Helping existing constitutions is impossible without knowing how many kinds of constitutions there are. The list of six constitutions—in Book III monarchy, aristocracy, polity, democracy, oligarchy, and tyranny—while not conventional wisdom of the time, is not a fundamental innovation, either. The only novelty is making polity (*politeia*) into one constitution (*politeia*) among others. But that novelty was masked by the way it emerged for the sake of formal completeness. In Book IV, as I will show, *politeia* becomes something different altogether; here it will be a true Aristotelian innovation.[8] In Aristotle's eyes the discovery that these constitutions themselves have species is an important achievement. People see themselves as democrats and oligarchs; they don't see themselves as members or partisans of particular species of democracy or oligarchy. Aristotle rarely trumpets something he says as a discovery, and so we should pay attention to the few times when he does so.[9] According to 1289a5–11, making a constitution better requires knowing how many kinds of constitution there are. Figuring out the nature of the ideal state does not take knowledge of the kinds of constitutions, but knowing the other kinds of best does depend on knowing that democracy and oligarchy have species, and what those species are.[10] Knowing the best in circumstances, the best on a hypothesis, and the best in general requires knowledge of the kinds of constitutions. Therefore, Book IV must begin with an enumeration of the kinds of democracy and oligarchy, and of the other constitutions. In the case of democracy and oligarchy, this enumeration depends on a listing of the parts of the state, the different classes of people.

Chapter 3 of Book IV begins by saying that "the reason why there are several constitutions is that every polis has several parts" (1289b28). The ambiguity of the four kinds of best infects this statement. At different points in the *Politics* Aristotle will list different parts of the polis, and will give different answers to "why there are several constitutions." Only VI.3 shows the connection between the plural parts of the polis and the existence of plural constitutions.[11] Once we know that in different poleis, these different parts will have greater or lesser power—in some the farmers will be stronger, others contain more wealthy people—then we find that democracies and oligarchies, the most common constitutions, actually each have species. Chapters 4–10 then enumerate and rank the species of the different constitutions.

"That there are a number of constitutions and why this is so has been stated earlier. But we may now say that there are also several kinds of democracy and oligarchy" (IV.4.1291b13–15, see IV.11.1299b3–4, V.12.1316b25). Aristotle only rarely refers to monarchy, aristocracy, polity, democracy, oligarchy, and tyranny as *kinds* of constitution; he simply calls them different constitutions.[12] In the last chapter, when I noted that some of the complications of politics as a practical science come from the fact that while people are political animals, they don't live in poleis but in, for example, democratic or oligarchic poleis, I drew the analogy to language. While people might differ from other animals by possessing logos as opposed to mere *phonē*, no one speaks Language. We speak English, or Swahili, or some particular language. We don't refer to English and Swahili as kinds of languages, but as languages. Similarly here. Democracy and oligarchy are constitutions, not kinds of constitutions. In the introduction, I also suggested an analogy to the ethical virtues in the *Ethics*: they are never *kinds* of virtues, but are simply different virtues. Like the ethical virtues, the six different constitutions have different ends, but the species of democracy and oligarchy all share the same end—all democracies aim at freedom and all oligarchies at wealth. The ends of constitutions, therefore, do not differentiate species.[13]

At IV.3 Aristotle announces that democracy and oligarchy each has several species because every polis has several parts, and IV.4 elaborates on that point through an extended analogy to the kinds of animals (1290b25–38) that leads to a more detailed listing of the parts of the state than he gave in chapter 3.[14] But the analogy to biological kinds seems quite weak and inapt. First and most important, living things come in species because reproduction transmits form and end. Man comes from man, but democracies do not come from democracies. The plurality of constitutions comes from the different possible ways of "organizing offices on the basis of the superiority and varieties of the parts" (1290a11–12). Species are a given in natural science, but their existence has to be demonstrated in politics. Democracies and oligarchies come in different kinds because their material causes differ.[15]

> There must be several constitutions that differ in kind from one another (eidei diapherousias allēlōn), since these parts themselves also differ in kind (eidei diapherei ta merē). For a constitution is the organization of offices, and all constitutions distribute these either on the basis of the power of the participants or on the basis of some sort of equality common to them . . . Therefore there must be as many constitutions as there are ways of organizing offices on the basis of the superiority and varieties of the parts. (1290a5)[16]

Second, the enumeration of species of democracy and oligarchy differs in an obvious way from the species of animals after which it is supposedly modeled in IV.4. There is no implication that some animals will be better than others because they have better mouths, yet to list the kinds of democracy and oligarchy is to evaluate them. Third, different biological species have different ends as well as different forms, but the kinds of democracy and oligarchy share the ends of democracy and oligarchy. The analogy will have real value in the final three chapters of Book IV, and fortunately Aristotle does nothing with it until then.

A more helpful analogy than that to biological species is Aristotle's own procedure in the *Poetics*. Its first three chapters show that tragedy has a unique combination of means, object, and manner that sets it off from other imitations. The six constitutions of Book III are separated from each other in a similar manner. In chapter 4, tragedy becomes a species when, through a process of historical development, it attains its natural form (hautēs phusin). At that point tragedy has a form and an end. Imitation and the delight people take in imitation are natural, and so people make mimetic artifacts. But it doesn't follow that they make tragedies, and the form and end of tragedy do not unfold from the impulse and pleasure of imitation. Similarly in the *Politics*: natural impulses and natural need, plus the right circumstances, are enough to get to poleis, but not to democracy and oligarchy. The genealogy in Book I showed that it is natural for people to live in poleis, but there is no reason to expect from *Politics* I that there are either different constitutions or different kinds of constitutions. There is a difference, though. *Poetics* 4 traces a history that culminates in tragedy achieving that natural form. There are no such natural forms in the *Politics*; instead, Aristotle simply offers histories that show why monarchies used to be more common and why almost all poleis in his day were democratic.

I don't think it's all that important whether or not the six constitutions are *kinds* of constitution or not; it doesn't matter whether we call Finnish and Spanish *languages* or *kinds* of languages. But that democracy and oligarchy have kinds is practically very important. If the different democracies and oligarchies did not differ in kind, then one might think that legislators should try to make all democracies approximate the best democracy, all oligarchies the best oligarchy. Instead, the different constitutions have species because those species are the proper objects toward which the statesman should deliberate, and in that sense they are ends, even though all the kinds of democracy share a common end, freedom, and the same for oligarchy and wealth.

The broader the oligarchy, and the narrower the democracy, the better. But since there are species of democracy and oligarchy, then the best in circumstances must be the best way for a particular kind of democracy or oligarchy to be, not for democracy or oligarchy in general to be. In breeding sheep, we should aim at the best sheep possible, not at sheep that approximate some better species of mammal, such as us. The statesman is to make each kind of democracy and oligarchy the best it can be. Even the worst kind of democracy, the extreme democracy in which rule of law gives way to the rule of men, has a best condition: there "it is beneficial from the point of view of improving deliberation to do precisely the same thing as is done in oligarchies in regard to the courts" (IV.14.1298a13–17); oligarchies fine people who don't serve on juries to ensure that they do serve, and democracies should do the same to make people attend the assemblies.

He lists the kinds of democracy and oligarchy twice, democracy in chapter 4 and again, with some variations, in chapter 6, oligarchy in chapter 5 and then in chapter 6. In no case does he find one kind of democracy or oligarchy better than others because their citizens are more virtuous. The absolute best constitution of Books VII and VIII might be best because its citizens are virtuous—"the better character is always the cause of a better constitution" (VIII.1.1337a17–18)—but what makes a constitution best in particular circumstances or best in general is not the virtue of its citizens. With Rousseau, this part of the *Politics* takes people as they are and laws as they ought to be.

Instead of arguing that one democracy or oligarchy is better than another because its citizens are more virtuous, in an analysis that prefigures his conception of the rule by the middle class as best (IV.12), those democracies and oligarchies are best in which citizens do not have leisure and, in case of democracies, states do not have the revenue (1292b37), to involve many citizens in politics. The good citizen relative to these constitutions is someone who avoids participation in politics. If this doesn't refute the thesis that man is a political animal, it at least shows that being a political animal takes unexpected forms. While many critics of modern American politics criticize its citizens for "apathy," and government policies and the tactics of political parties for discouraging participation, Aristotle thinks that some constitutions are stable because their citizens do not participate much in politics. Note, though, that if it is lack of leisure that prevents political participation, it isn't because of lack of interest, as in contemporary accounts of apathy, and it isn't because these people find greater satisfaction and greater outlets for virtue in their private lives. Under these circumstances, instead, involvement leads to abandoning the rule of law for the rule of men and thus to despotism.

II. POLITY AND THE BEST IN GENERAL

Democracies and oligarchies come in species because different democracies and oligarchies include and exclude different numbers and classes of people. Aristotle continues by showing the species of aristocracy in chapter 7 and tyranny, only for the sake of completeness, he says, in chapter 10. In between comes his discussion of polity, which has no species, and which will be the subject of this section. The principle of speciation is different for these other constitutions. Unlike democracy and oligarchy, the kinds of other constitutions have no economic or social base that distinguishes the kinds, and no distinction of numbers of rulers. The kinds of aristocracy, thus, differ from each other in IV.7 on which other criteria are combined with merit in determining who should rule. The kinds of aristocracy, then, are not arranged in a series as those of democracy and oligarchy are. Of the three kinds of tyranny, only the last, and worst, the counterpart of absolute kingship, is found among the Greeks.

At IV.1.1289a5–11 we were told that we have to know about the kinds of constitution, especially the kinds of democracy and oligarchy, in order to help existing constitutions. Book IV accomplishes that task by circuitously moving from the kinds of constitutions to articulating the best constitution in general in chapter 11, and then using that understanding in the rest of Book IV to see what is the best constitution in particular circumstances. The best in general is practical, then, only via the best in circumstances.

The relation between (1) enumerating and ranking the kinds of constitutions and determining the best constitution, (2) best in general, and (3) best in particular circumstances, comes to a head, then, with the following natural question. The best constitution in general that Aristotle finds in IV.11, the middle constitution, seems to be the same as the polity of IV.8–9. He certainly finds the best constitution in general via a discussion of polity. But Aristotle never explicitly identifies them. What is the relation between them?

Polity is the only constitution he discusses without explicitly identified kinds. Instead, there are three principles (*horoi*) of mixture (9.1294a35) that allow polity to emerge from democracy and oligarchy. One can (1) "take legislation from both constitutions" (1294a36), finding what is common; one can (2) take "the mean between the organizations of each" (1294b1), or (3) "take elements from both organizations, some from oligarchic law and others from democratic law" (1294b5–6).

Therefore polity and the middle constitution are not identical. The best constitution in IV.11 cannot be identified with polity as polity was defined in Book III, the correct version of democracy, in the way aristocracy there was the correct counterpart of oligarchy. The polity of IV.9, a mixture of democracy and oligarchy, cannot correspond to the polity of Book III either. Only the second of those three principles creates a constitution that relies on the middle class, so the mixed and the middle constitution of IV.11 are not identical. There are mixed constitutions that are not the middle constitution. If the best in general will soon be the norm that allows us to determine what is the best constitution in particular circumstances, it is wise of Aristotle not to identify that middle constitution with any particular constitution. The two are not identical; instead, understanding the principles of the mixed constitution allows Aristotle to understand the middle constitution.[17]

Polity has a feature we should worry about. It is a mixture of democracy and oligarchy (IV.8.1293b33). But if polity is a good constitution and democracy and oligarchy corrupt, how can two corrupt things when mixed become good? More specifically, the principles of arithmetic and geometric justice that characterize democracy and oligarchy are incommensurable, and so cannot be combined.[18] A polity made by mixing democracy and oligarchy becomes good not because of the goodness of its materials, which are corrupt constitutions, but because of the practical wisdom of the legislator doing the mixing. "The more numerous the elements, the better the constitution" (II.6.1266a4–5). The goodness of polities and aristocracies is a practical good attributable to the goodness of the constitutional form, not the matter. We have, in polity, a correct constitution that neither depends on nor aims at virtue.

Once the mixed constitution can be a good combination of bad elements, and can be a good constitution without depending on virtue among its citizens, it looks as though Aristotle has made politics even more separate from ethics than he did when he distinguished the good citizen from the virtuous person in Book III. If democracy aims at benefiting the poor, and oligarchy at the advantage of the wealthy, then their proper mixture aims at the good of all. It still lacks justice as proportional to merit. The constitution achieves the common good without anyone aiming at it, almost as the modern economy supposedly serves the common good without anyone aiming at it. The state has ends that are not the ends of its citizens. The mixed constitution is better than the constitutions mixed into it (1294b17), better than democracy and oligarchy. It is also better than its citizens. They will still aim at wealth or freedom, but the constitution is organized to benefit the whole.[19] If "the better character is always the cause of a better constitution (aei to beltion ēthos beltionos aition politeais)" (VIII.1.1337a–18), Book IV discovers that there are other causes of a good constitution besides the good character of its citizens. Similarly, we might wish for people who act according to these lines from *Ethics* IX.8.1169a6–11, and might encounter them in Books VII and VIII, but Book IV discovers more indirect ways of achieving a good state without fully virtuous citizens:

> Those who are unusually eager to do noble actions are welcomed and praised by everyone: for when everyone contends for what is noble and strains to accomplish the very best, everything that is necessary will be done for the community, and each person individually receives the greatest of goods, since that is the character of virtue.

Democracy is rule by the poor, oligarchy by the wealthy. Democracies affirm an arithmetic conception of justice, oligarchies geometrical justice. Aristotle is in a sense optimistic here; he has no idea of false consciousness by which people have political opinions at odds with their interests; there are no poor people who advocate geometric justice or wealthy in favor of arithmetic justice.[20] The optimism might be justified in a political community small enough that people can judge each other's character and in an agonistic political culture in which people know where they stand. People see and want to act on their material interests. The alignment between material interests and ideas of justice makes polity more available than it

might be for us, given contemporary evidence of systematic divergence between people's interests and their political preferences.

The discussion of polity prepares the way for the discussion of the best
in general, the middle constitution, in another way. Aristotle lists species
of the other constitutions, because, he told us in IV.1, we need to know
about the kinds of constitution to figure out what is best in particular circumstances. Polity doesn't fit that account because it has no species. On
the other hand, the discussion of polity is uniquely and directly practical. It
begins: "Let us next discuss how, in addition to democracy and oligarchy,
so-called polity arises, *and how it should be established*" (IV.9.1294a29–
31). Democracies and oligarchies just are; they don't "arise" in Aristotle's
presentation. Polity exists only when it is intentionally established.[21]

Polity thus differs from democracy and oligarchy because one cannot account for it by identifying the powerful material interests behind it. Polities
owe their existence to wise activities of the statesman. However, those wise
activities need support. Aristotle finds this support in the middle class in
chapter 11. When he classified the kinds of democracies and oligarchies in
chapters 4–6, material circumstances determined the kind of constitution.
By the time he gets to the best in general and the best in circumstances in
11–13, the form of the constitution, and the intelligence needed to realize
the form, determine the appropriate material support.

Polity also differs from kingship and aristocracy, the other two correct
constitutions. At IV.2 Aristotle separates polity off from the other two:

> Since in our first inquiry concerning constitutions we distinguished
> three correct constitutions—kingship, aristocracy, and polity—and
> three deviations from these—tyranny from kingship, oligarchy from ar-
> istocracy, and democracy from polity; and since aristocracy and king-
> ship have been spoken of—for to study the best regime is the same as
> to speak about these, as each of them wishes to be established on the
> basis of virtue that is furnished with equipment . . . (1289a28–33; see too
> III.18.1288a41)

Polity, thus, is a correct constitution, but not, according to that quotation,
the best constitution.[22] Kingship and aristocracy depend on antecedent virtue, so they are the best constitutions *haplōs*, while polity is the best constitution that depends not on positing such qualities but on the constitution
itself. This constitution is generally available because any city can, by the
careful actions of the statesman, come to have a powerful middle class.
Therefore, there is a pathway from any state to this constitution, which is

why it can be called the best in general. It is a good constitution that can be reached from almost any starting point. There can, consequently, be a practical pathway to the polity, but not to monarchy or aristocracy.

Were Aristotle to identify the best constitution in general with any particular constitution, his analysis would be less practical because it would then be less suited to all circumstances. To identify the best constitution in general with any particular constitution, including polity, would make it harder to reach from some constitutions than from others, and then it wouldn't be the best in general. Some kinds of democracy and oligarchy are further removed from the best in general, but there is no ranking of democracy and oligarchy in terms of distance from the best in general.

Polity is rare (IV.7.1293a40). Its rarity has an easy explanation. "Rich and poor are held above all to be the parts of a polis. . . . Consequently, constitutions are established on the basis of the superiority of these, and there are held to be two constitutions, democracy and oligarchy" (IV.4.1291b7–12). In contrast to polity, though, he says that the middle constitution which is the best constitution in general is both rare (IV.11.1295b40, 1296a22, 14.1296a21–b1) and widely available. If it weren't widely available, it couldn't be the best constitution in general. Widely available, but not widely realized. How it can be both is our next question.

I think I can answer that question by recalling something similar in the *Ethics*. Happiness "will be widely shared; for anyone who is not unfit for virtue will be able to achieve happiness through some sort of learning and attention" (I.9.1099b18–20). In another sense virtue and happiness are evidently rare, and most men lead lives ruled by pleasure and not thought (I.5.1095b19–30). And the resolution is the same in the two cases. Happiness can be widely shared, because it does not require exceptional resources. You don't have to be extremely wealthy, well-born, or handsome to be happy. You just have to be virtuous. Similarly, the polity and the middle constitution do not take special equipment, as the constitution of our prayers does, but they do require *phronēsis*, political wisdom, on the part of the statesman and the rulers. Instituting a polity does not depend on special conditions; it depends on the knowledge and virtue of the legislator.

Polity possesses a level of virtue open to most people because it simply avoids the vices of poverty and wealth, and consequently listens to reason. Here Aristotle's argument comes dangerously close to the identification of the moderate and the middle with the mediocre, a rhetorical mean rather than one that belongs to a practical science. It is only for a low standard of virtue that avoiding the vices of poverty and wealth would be enough to guarantee virtue. But wealth and poverty are the two chief reasons people don't listen to reason. Because men in the middle class listen to reason, they are able to rule and be ruled (IV.11.1295b8–21). Consequently, poleis with a powerful middle class are both the best governed and the most stable:[23]

> A polis tends to consist as much as possible of people who are equal and similar, and this condition especially belongs to those in the middle. Consequently this polis . . . must of necessity be best governed. Moreover, of all citizens, those in the middle survive best in poleis. For they do not desire other people's property as the poor do, nor do other people desire theirs, as the poor desire that of the rich. And because they are neither plotted against nor engage in plotting, they live out of their lives free from danger. (1295b25–33)[24]

It says something about the nature of this practical project that while the polis with a powerful middle class is desirable, being a member of the middle class is never put forward as a claim to rule alongside freedom, wealth, virtue, and good birth. Men in the middle are virtuous, relative to this constitution, simply because they lack the two principal causes of vice, wealth and poverty. Such virtue doesn't fit the definition of virtue in the *Ethics*; the standard of virtue and political excellence is relatively low here. Such virtue is widely available because the conditions in which it can flourish are widely available; it is rare because those conditions are not by themselves enough. The actions required to bring a polity into existence are rare, but not inherently rare.

The middle class of the best constitution in general not only lacks the vices associated with economic poverty or plenty, but the associated political vices too, the faults that make oligarchies despotic and democracies soft (IV.3.1290a24–28): "The middle classes are least inclined either to avoid ruling or to pursue it, both of which are harmful to poleis" (1295b11–12). I said a little while ago that Aristotle skirts the danger of conflating moderation with mediocrity; here is the payoff of his playing with fire. In the absolutely best constitution in Books VII and VIII, all citizens must be virtuous. The three other kinds of best uncover constitutions that can be better than their citizens, can be good constitutions without their citizens being good. When the rich or the poor align themselves politically with the middle class, they also align themselves psychologically, and then they lack the vices associated with wealth or poverty. In that way, this constitution makes its citizens better. True, the middle class is not virtuous simply because it lacks the vices of wealth and poverty. But they don't need to be virtuous so long as, when they rule, the constitution aims at the good of the whole. Democracy and oligarchy can aspire to this constitution. If most constitutions are democratic or oligarchic, then this constitution, as the best that democracy and oligarchy can become, is the best in general.

The polity and the generally best constitution exemplify and explain a curious remark of Aristotle's in Book III. Several times in Book III, as I discussed in the last chapter, he says that a plurality of partial views and opinions can somehow add up to wisdom. He never justifies or explains these remarks, and they are not self-evidently true. Hobbes, for example, counters:

> It is easier to gull the multitude, than any one man amongst them. For what one man, that has not his natural judgment depraved by accident, could be so easily cozened in a matter that concerns his purse, had he not been passionately carried away by the rest to change of government, or rather to a liberty of everyone to govern himself.[25]

Therefore we should ask, although Aristotle himself does not, for the conditions under which it is plausible to assert that "the many, though not individually good men, yet when they come together may be better, not individually, but collectively, than those who are so, . . . for where there are many, each individual, it may be argued, has some portion of virtue and wisdom, and when they have come together" (III.11.1281b1–7, see too 1282a14, a34–41, 13.1283b27–34, 15.1286a27–31, IV.4.1292a10–14, as well as *Metaphysics* II.993b1–6). Immediately afterward, he says that "excellent men differ from each of the many, just as beautiful people are said to differ from those who are not beautiful, and as things painted by craft are superior to real things: they bring together what is scattered and separate into one" (1281b10–13). It is a work of art, that is, a constitution whose goodness derives from the efforts of statesman, superior to the works of nature—democracy and oligarchy—which come to be without anyone bringing them into existence. The constitution that is the best in general is a correct constitution that does not depend on antecedent virtue but instead "brings together what is scattered and separate into one." The best constitution in general is the one in which Aristotle's remarks about the summing of virtue and intelligence is plausible.

That the project in Books IV–VI is to find constitutions that are morally superior to their citizens shows how far Aristotle's orientation is from modern approaches to politics. We today typically ask about the plight of people—like us—who are better than their states or governments, who are intelligent or virtuous enough to question and criticize their governments and rise above the social pressures toward mediocrity. Should we rebel? Withdraw and cultivate our own gardens? Hold our noses and obey? We also worry about imposing our constitutional values and rule of law on nations that somehow "aren't ready for it." Aristotle's orientation in IV–VI is the opposite.

III. THE BEST IN PARTICULAR CIRCUMSTANCES: BOOK IV.12–13

Knowing the best constitution in general, we can now compare particular constitutions, and indeed confirm the rankings of democracy and oligarchy that Aristotle made earlier. So IV.11 begins its conclusion by saying:

> What the best constitution is, and why it is so is evident from these considerations. As for the other constitutions (for there are, as we say, several kinds of democracies and oligarchies), which of them is to be put first, which second, and so on in the same way, according to whether it is better or worse, is not hard to see now that the best has been determined. For the one nearest to this must of necessity always be better and one further from the middle worse. (1296b2–7)

But the section ends with a caveat:

> [P]rovided one is not judging on the basis of certain assumptions (*pros hypothesin*). I say "on the basis of certain assumptions" because it often happens that, while one constitution is more choiceworthy (*hairetoteras*), nothing prevents a different one from being more beneficial (*sympherein*) for some. (1296b10–12)

After that distinction between the choiceworthy and the beneficial, chapter 12 begins to consider "which constitution is beneficial (*sympherei*) for which people" (1296b13). Distinguishing the choiceworthy from the beneficial is part of Aristotle's project of making the *Politics* a practical work.[26] The distinction between the good man and the good citizen, and between virtue *haplōs* and virtue relative to a particular constitution, are variations on the same theme in which knowing what is best does not automatically tell us what to do. If there is a difference between the choiceworthy and the beneficial, then one cannot simply deduce what constitution will be best in particular circumstances from the best in general. It will take deliberation and practical wisdom. Each of the three kinds of best explored in Books IV–VI is increasingly closer to the deliberations of the statesman.[27]

Determining the best in particular circumstances is a practical inquiry. It begins in chapter 12 with two obvious points. First, "the part of the polis that wishes the constitution to continue must be stronger than any part that does not" (1296b14–15), advice that he had given earlier and which looks true and indeed obvious apart from the argument up to here. Second, "the legislator should always include the middle" (1296b34), whether establishing oligarchic or democratic laws (nomoi). But the chapter ends, and chapter 13 continues, with a much more interesting remark: "Those who wish to establish aristocratic constitutions" often make a mistake of giving more to the rich and deceiving the people (12.1297a7–12).

It is no surprise that democracies and oligarchies have their own characteristic vices; they are corrupt constitutions, founded on errors. But it is a surprise that aristocracies too possess an associated vice. Moreover, there are vices associated with being too wealthy and too poor, but none correlated with being in the middle, making the idea of aristocratic vices even more unlikely.[28]

There is an oddity here, and paying attention to it will let us see Aristotle at work in formulating a practical science of politics. First, he lists the sophisms that aristocracies—and other constitutions—use to deceive the people (IV.13.1297a6–9; see too V.8.1307b40). Since these sophisms are oligarchic (1297a36), he finds democracy using opposite devices (antisophizontai). Out of these competing sophisms—"clever devices" seems to me the best translation—come the principles for a just mixture: "If one wants to mix justly, it is evident that one must combine elements from either side" (1397a37–40). As sophisms, they are forms that can be applied cleverly without regard for appropriateness; as means of building a middle constitution, they require phronēsis to construct a just mixture. He even refers, at IV.13.1297a39, to a just (dikaiōs) mixture of sophisms. Just as two deviant constitutions, democracy and oligarchy, can combine to produce a well-formed one, balancing these sophisms results in stable and appropriate constitutional institutions. Justly mixing sophisms comes as close as Aristotle will come to the modern idea of a beneficial result coming from private vices. Here, though, it is not an invisible hand that coordinates the sophisms into a just mixture, but the wisdom of the statesman.[29]

The point of these devices is not for the other citizens to accept the rulers, but for people to be induced to rule. Such devices are not, as in modern

constitutions, things to constrain the rulers once they are rulers, in that way
substituting for knowledge and for virtue on the part of the rulers. Nonvirtuous people do not want to rule and be ruled in turn. They want to rule
or to avoid ruling for all kinds of reasons, but most of these are reasons the
statesman doesn't want to encourage. These devices are institutionalized
substitutes for the knowledge possessed by those who govern the best state.
In that way, the constitution can be better than the people who make it up.
The focus on ways of getting people to rule correctly, rather than accept
others as rulers, or to rule correctly once in office is a piece with the narrow
sense of justice at work in the *Politics*, where justice is concerned with how
rulers are selected, not what they do once they are ruling. (Aristotle does offer advice about what rulers should and shouldn't do to preserve the constitution, but these are not for him a matter of justice but political wisdom.)

IV. FORMAL POSSIBILITIES AND THE BEST IN PARTICULAR CIRCUMSTANCES: BOOK IV.14–16

I want to return for the last time to the programmatic remarks at the beginning of IV.1. After listing the four kinds of best, which he says apply to all
complete arts and sciences, he presents two projects that are uniquely political: defining the species of different constitutions, especially democracies
and oligarchies, and seeing which laws are appropriate for which constitutions. At least the first of these is uniquely philosophical: common opinion
asserts a difference between democracy and oligarchy, but in understanding
their differences the philosopher discovers that the different constitutions
have species. That discovery offers a framework for the *phronimos* and
statesman to see which laws are appropriate for which constitutions, the
second uniquely political enterprise. This last section of Book IV is specifically concerned with that latter project.[30] Instead of the parts of the state,
it looks at the parts of the constitution. This is the part of the *Politics* in
which Aristotle will do well at what the sophists do badly. They think it
is easy to legislate by collecting generally approved laws without worrying
about their suitability to particular constitutions or circumstances (*Ethics*
X.9.1181a12-b3).

Earlier I criticized the biological analogy of IV.4 as inappropriate. Here,
finally, it makes sense because of this shift from the parts of the state to the
parts of the constitution.

If we were going to speak of the different species of animals, we should
first of all determine the organs which are indispensable to every animal,

as for example some organs of sense and the instruments of receiving and digesting food, such as the mouth and the stomach, besides organs of locomotion. Assuming now that there are only so many kinds of organs, but that there may be differences in them—I mean different kinds of mouths, and stomachs, and perceptive and locomotive organs—the possible combinations of these differences will necessarily furnish many varieties of animals. (For animals cannot be the same which have different kinds of mouths or of ears.) And when all the combinations are exhausted, there will be as many sorts of animals as there are combinations of the necessary organs. The same, then, is true of the forms of government which have been described; states, as I have repeatedly said, are composed, not of one, but of many elements. (IV.4.1290b25–38)

As we saw earlier, he did not use this methodological remark to show how different kinds of democracy and oligarchy are generated out of different kinds of farmers, soldiers, et cetera. But the biological method of IV.4 is at work here in IV.14–16. While he never looked at how different kinds of craftsmen or farmers lead to different constitutions, he does show in these chapters how there are different kinds of deliberative organs, magistrates, and judicial powers, some more democratic and some more oligarchic. This makes sense, since IV.14–16, centering on the formal cause, would naturally present a series of possibilities. There are different mouths and ears. While the analogy to biological species seemed to break down because Aristotle ranked the kinds of democracy and oligarchy but wouldn't call one kind of fish a better fish than another species—there is no analogue in biology to the opposition of rule of law to rule of men!—the kinds of offices in 14–16 lends itself more closely to the biological kind of inquiry.

At the beginning of this chapter, I said that the programmatic statement of IV.1 suggested that the philosopher should treat the four kinds of best *seriatem*, but that in fact the best in general and the best in particular circumstances are treated together in Book IV. The first thirteen chapters of Book IV, which concern both the best in general (IV.11) and the best in particular circumstances (IV.12–13), use an analysis by material cause, the parts of the state, to tell us about both those kinds of best. The final three chapters, IV.14-16, look at formal rather than material parts and possibilities, parts of the constitution rather than parts of the state. They do so in order to show the best constitutional arrangements of offices for different particular circumstances. There is nothing in those three chapters about the best in general. There is no formal solution to the best constitution in general—unlike contemporary hopes for exporting written constitutions and bills of rights. There is only a solution that depends on the material of a powerful middle class.

In addition, the final chapters of Book IV, unlike the earlier chapters, tell the legislator what is best for democracy and what for oligarchy. We no longer have to think about the different species of democracy and oligarchy which seemed so important earlier in Book IV. Instead the statesman learns to mix democratic and oligarchic aspects of the different parts of government, much like the different ways of mixing democracy and oligarchy to generate polities in chapter 9, and mixing the sophisms in chapter 13.

Each chapter, 14–16, has three parts. First Aristotle enumerates the different parts of the constitution, and then describes the part which is characteristic of which constitution and of which kind of democracy and oligarchy, and finally what is most useful for each constitution. "All constitutions have three parts by reference to which an excellent legislator must study what is beneficial for each of them" (IV.14.1297b37). "One should be able to determine how many ways all these [offices] can be handled, and then fit the kinds of offices to the kinds of constitutions for which they are beneficial (IV.15.1299a12–14).

Reading these chapters feels like going through a mechanical exercise. Isn't it obvious when a constitutional arrangement is democratic, and when oligarchic? Here is a contemporary example that makes such answers less obvious. There is a current popular movement to curb the powers of juries in civil litigation cases, especially those involving product liability. Legislatures, it is argued, rather than juries should decide the sizes of damage awards. In thinking about this issue, how do we decide which is more democratic, a legislative rule or a jury verdict? At the same time, there is a popular movement to curb the discretion for judges in criminal sentencing, and have legislatures devise formulas for calculating sentences instead. Which would be more democratic? Neither question is ever raised; people argue over the imagined consequences for judicial decisions instead. It may not always be obvious whether a given institutional arrangement is democratic or not.

V. CONCLUSION

Book IV becomes increasingly practical as it moves from the declaration of its program through its determination of the kinds of constitution to the best constitution in general, and then the best in circumstances, and finally the best arrangements of ruling functions for different constitutions. Each stage in that argument is more practical than the last. Those three determinations—the best in general, the best in circumstances, and the best laws to suit different constitutions—were, recall, preceded by Aristotle enumerating and ranking the different species of the different constitutions in IV.4–10. That treatment of the species of constitutions ended with polity, because polities and aristocracies are made, while democracies and oligarchies are given. Therefore knowing the principles of polities and the species of aristocracies is more practical than knowing the species of democracies and oligarchies. After chapter 12 identifies the best constitution in general as the constitution with a powerful middle class, chapter 13 lists devices at the disposal of the legislator to ensure that the middle class is indeed dominant, making practical the treatment of the best in general. The treatments, then, of the material and formal causes both become more practical as they proceed. These final chapters look mechanical precisely because they enumerate possibilities from which the statesman can choose, unlike the different parts that constitute the different species of democracy and oligarchy.

Aristotle began Book IV by looking at material parts, and ends with formal parts. Chapters 14–16 shows how to put into good condition the parts of the constitution. You can't make material parts good—except through education, which is not a subject of Book IV but only of Books VII and VIII. The legislator can make a good democratic or oligarchic judiciary, but he cannot make a good farming class or a good wealthy class. As we saw in my second chapter, and as we see around us all the time, there is a temptation for people founding or reforming constitutions—whether in ancient colonies or in modern attempts to foster democracy after the overthrow of a tyranny—to manipulate these formal parts and ignore the material circumstances, which are much more difficult to treat practically. That temptation then gives way to disparaging formal arrangements as what Madison in *Federalist* 48 called parchment barriers: since they are formal, they must be impotent. Aristotle avoids these mistakes by treating matter and form together.

In IV.14–16, Aristotle can tell us which constitutional choices are beneficial for which constitution. There are no answers to questions of which choices are best in general. There may be a best constitution in general, but how to organize the deliberative part, the officers, and the judiciary depends on the particular constitution in question. The political wisdom exhibited in the *Politics* cannot be specific enough to deal with such an issue; that task must be left for the statesman. The description of the middle constitution in IV.12 and the devices listed in IV.13 are as far as the philosophical inquiry into the best in general can go. This is another good reason for Aristotle not to identify the middle constitution, the best in general, with any particular constitution, including the mixed polity. The best in general is a mixed and moderate regime. The best in particular circumstances will preserve a constitution as democratic or oligarchic and will moderate and stabilize it. Both call for moderation, but of different sorts.

Foregrounding the importance of moderation in the *Politics* might seem surprising. One reason for the prominence of moderation is the equally surprising limited meaning and function of justice in the *Politics*. If justice is limited to the principles of deciding who rules under a given constitution, Aristotle does not regard justice—as opposed to avoiding injustice—as one of the properties of the good ruler's actions and decisions. The vacuum left by the absence of justice is filled, at least in Book IV, by moderation.

Therefore, throughout the *Politics* and especially in Book IV, Aristotle has to be sure, as I mentioned before, that moderation does not mean mediocrity. The best way to fortify the middle class is by making moderation honorable. The complex relations between the mixed constitution and polity enact the difficulties with moderation. The statesman aims at a moderate democracy or oligarchy not because he isn't powerful enough to achieve an extreme democracy or oligarchy but because moderation is a sign of a good constitution, just as the virtuous person chooses to rule and be ruled in turn not because he is too weak to rule permanently, but because he recognizes that such mutuality and reciprocity makes friendship and further acts of virtue possible. The committed democrat or oligarch should prefer moderate democracy or oligarchy to their pure forms, and not out of respect for minority rights or fear of revolution by the disenfranchised, but because democracy and oligarchy best achieve their ends when they take a moderate, not a pure, form. Extreme democracy and oligarchy are self-destructive in ways similar to the way an object can destroy the sense faculty by being too bright to look at. Generally, the brighter the light, the better we can see, but taken to an extreme, the organ of sight is destroyed. When we look at the sun we don't see it, but instead the eye is in effect burned by it. Similarly, the more pure the oligarchy or democracy, the better, but at an extreme, pure oligarchy and democracy are no longer constitutions at all.[31]

Book III's taxonomy of constitutions placed democracy and oligarchy as corrupt constitutions, but Aristotle seems to ignore that teaching in Book IV. We can now square those two accounts. Because democracy and oligarchy are corrupt constitution, aiming at the good of rulers rather than the good of the whole polis, their moderate forms are better than their extreme versions. To say that moderate stinginess or cowardice is preferable to extreme stinginess or cowardice is not to say much. It could be that moderate overindulgence is the best one can get out of some individual, but to call that the best in circumstances would not point to a "best in circumstances" as a form of best that could be studied as part of the statesman's art and science. Aristotle goes much further here. Moderate democracy and oligarchy are good constitutions, the best possible in circumstances. They are good constitutions because they allow citizens to lead good lives.

Moderation must not be a political end distinct from living well. Book V will have to show that the more stable a constitution, the better. Book IV has to have shown that the more moderate a constitution, the better. Moderate democracy and oligarchy become legitimately good constitutions because they make it possible for their citizens to lead good lives. These are good lives, not just the best such creatures are capable of leading. The most inclusive oligarchy and the most exclusive democracy are the best oligarchies and democracies. Moderate democracy and oligarchy are not only moderate in their policies, but they are only moderately democratic and oligarchic.[32]

None of this applies to the aristocracies and polities of chapters 7–9. There is no argument in those chapters that the more moderate aristocracy or polity is best. Aristocracies and polities are already correct constitutions by the standards of Book III. There is no normative ranking at all of the two kinds of aristocracy or the three ways of establishing polities. Instead of moderation, the three kinds of polities are three ways of mixing the principles of democracy and oligarchy.

As Book IV becomes increasingly practical, Aristotle demonstrates a continuity between the practical knowledge of the philosopher presented here and the practical knowledge of the statesman. "It is with the same phronēsis that one should try to see both which laws are best and which are appropriate for each of the constitutions. For laws should be established, and all do establish them, to suit the constitution and not the constitution to suit the laws" (IV.1.1289a12; see NE VI.8.1141b25–29). The same phronēsis is involved in both the science of legislation and in deliberation. Book IV ends at the point where the philosopher can say no more and the practical knowledge of the statesman must take over, where practical knowledge must be embedded, particular knowledge. As I will show in the next chapter, this means that at this point practical knowledge must become ethical, involving the character as well as the knowledge of the agent.

In this chapter I've shown why there are different kinds of the various constitutions, and glanced at the different accounts Aristotle gives of why there are several constitutions in the first place. I want to end by asking why there are four kinds of best, or four orientations to the best. He says that any complete art or science studies these four, and I've traced them to

the four causes. But in a more substantive sense, they are four responses to
a predicament uncovered in Book III.[33] There we learn that one's conception
of justice is not the only one possible, and—a separate point—that it is imperfect. A politician could draw four possible practical conclusions from
that predicament, and these four generate the four kinds of best that organize *Politics* IV–VIII. Each of the four involves moderation in defense of
one's conception of justice, but moderation of different kinds. First, one can
modestly see that one's ideas of justice are partial, and aim to correct that
by reformulating justice until it is complete. I complete my idea of justice
by dissolving it into the final cause, the best life in ideal circumstances.
Once I know that my idea of justice is imperfect, I aim at the perfect idea
instead. I can have only modest expectations that that ideal will have much
embodiment in practical politics, expectations that I will clarify in my final
chapter. I exercise moderation by pursuing the ideal without becoming a
fanatic. Moderation appears in the relation between the political and philosophical lives. This is the project of Books VII and VIII.

At the other extreme, once I know that my idea of justice is not the only
one possible, I might think that I have to defend it all the more tenaciously
against others who think that their cause is just no less than I believe in
mine. That is the project of stability in Books V and VI, making justice and
assertions of justice into weapons aiming at staying in power, and wonder-
ing whether in such circumstances ideas about justice can be anything more
than weapons. Far from seeing one's idea of justice as one among others
leading to toleration, it can instead lead to militancy in its defense.[34] The
Aristotelian lesson is that while courageously defending my own, I moderate its claims in order to make the constitution more stable. My loyalty is
less to the particular constitution than to constitutional government and
the rule of law. In this way a life even under conditions of factions can be
a good life.

Third, I can engage in the moderating project of rule of law, and aiming
at the best kind of whatever constitution and idea of justice I am committed to, not the best constitution possible, but the best democracy, oligarchy,
or any of the others. The middle class and mixed constitution yield the
best constitutions. Thus the argument of IV.1–13, which ties various conceptions of justice to the social material that grounds those ideas. I don't
aim at being as democratic or oligarchic as possible but recognize that the
best democratic or oligarchic constitution is a moderate one of rule by the
middle class.

Finally, in IV.14–16, I can gain moderation through flexibility, seeing
the various democratic and oligarchic possibilities of different sorts of ar-

rangements of the parts of government, seeing justice as a formal property of constitutions and institutions, becoming a technician rather than an ideologue. Altogether, the practical wisdom of the statesman requires this complete unfolding of the four kinds of best as four ways of understanding the place of justice and inevitable partiality in the good life and the good community.

CHAPTER FIVE

Factions and the Paradox of Aristotelian Practical Science

Books V and VI continue the practical project of Book IV of showing how a constitution can be better than its citizens and its rulers. At the same time, these books seem to have much lower standards than the *Ethics* and the rest of the *Politics*. While someone who chooses life over the good life is vicious—the coward saving his skin, the self-indulgent gratifying appetites that prevent him from acting well, the miser, the boaster, etc.—Aristotle gives advice in the *Politics* and especially in Books V and VI about how to make the state stable and secure instead of how it can aim at a good life, and even in opposition to the good life. The democrat or oligarch who acts on Aristotle's counsels will forgo what he regards as the good life in favor of stability. Stability as the goal of politics seems to reject the identification of the end of the state with living well. Instead, the stable state is then only a necessary condition for human flourishing, much like the contemporary liberal state. There could be nothing noble about political activity under that understanding.[1]

In spite of that apparent similarity between modern liberalism and Aristotle's project in Books V and VI, there is a striking difference. The democracies and oligarchies that are the main subjects of this project are regimes that aim not only at life rather than the good life, but at the advantage of the rulers rather than a common good. Even if the modern state limits its horizons to aiming at life, modern political ideology condemns rulers who aim only at their own benefit. Giving up our civil liberties in the name of security is one thing; abandoning them for the profit of defense contractors, quite another.

The emphasis on stability and preservation points to another difference between the *Ethics* and the *Politics*. The *Ethics* is about virtue, not virtue and vice. The vices are explored only as consequences of what we learn about virtue or as ways of knowing about virtue. Vicious people fail to live up to the standards of virtue: there is no sense that anything other than vice itself could cause a person to prefer vice to virtue. But in the *Politics*, corrupt constitutions get at least equal time with correct constitutions. People want to live in bad states, especially bad forms of democracy and oligarchy, and especially to be rulers of such states.

Stability then becomes an end worth aiming at distinct from virtue and living well. In the *Ethics* Aristotle says that the good man, like Achilles in the *Iliad*, "will choose intense pleasure for a short time over slight pleasure for a long time; a year of living finely over many years of undistinguished life; and a single fine and great action over many small actions" (IX.8.1169a23–26). In the *Politics*, by contrast, stability is a measure of the excellence of a constitution. The constitution that chooses a brief but glorious existence over indefinite duration is not a good constitution (IV.1.1288b28–30, V.1.1302a2–4, V.7.1307a26–27, VI.5.1320a1–3).[2] The emergence of stability as a measure of excellence in politics but not in ethics would seem to make ethical and political thinking different, in spite of the fact that Aristotle maintains that they are the same (*NE* VI.8.1141b24).

I. ASYMMETRIES, EPISTEMOLOGICAL AND ETHICAL

Book V has a simple organization. "It is clear that if we know the causes by which constitutions are destroyed we also know the causes by which they are preserved; for opposites create opposites, and destruction is the opposite of security" (V.8.1307b26–29). Its first seven chapters present the causes by which constitutions are destroyed, and chapters 8 and 9 then show the causes by which they are preserved. Yet in important ways, the dictum is false: knowing the causes of constitutional change is not equivalent to knowing how constitutions are preserved. More radically, destruction and security are not the only alternatives facing someone in potentially revolutionary situations: constitutions could be reformed and improved as well as preserved and destroyed. The many ways in which knowledge of the causes of factions and knowledge of the methods of preservation are *not* equivalent supply the energy and interest that drives Book V's argument.[3]

Aristotle claims that knowing the causes of faction (*stasis*) will tell us how to resist them. His actual argument belies that assertion. But we don't have to look at the *Politics* to see that often knowing how something is caused does not tell us about what remedies there could be. Psychologists may discover that early childhood trauma has caused certain pathologies. Short of reversing time's arrow and stopping those traumas from happening in the first place, there is no direct path from such a discovery to having any idea of how to heal such a person. The demolitions expert is not necessarily an architect, and the heckler who effectively disrupts a speaker's performance is not necessarily a persuasive speaker himself.

I don't think this is a simple error on Aristotle's part. There is a difference between a causal analysis, such as we find in the first seven chapters, and a first-person deliberative understanding that the *Politics* overall aims at and which Book V finally arrives at in chapters 8 and 9. Knowing how people decide and choose does not tell me how to choose and decide. Knowing what causes people to form factions doesn't necessarily tell the statesman how to prevent them from arising. Historical knowledge is not necessarily practical knowledge. As we will see, Aristotle illustrates this difference between analysis and deliberation, for example, in the sequence of causes of faction in the pivotal V.3, which moves from avoidable mistakes to inevitable or unforeseeable events.

The lack of equivalence between knowing how constitutions are destroyed and knowing how to preserve them has ties to another, morally troubling, asymmetry. Regardless of how just or deviant a given constitution is, Aristotle writes as though preserving it is good and destroying it is bad. The programmatic statement at the beginning of Book V presents preservation and destructions as alternatives, with the former always to be pursued:

> What things bring about revolution (*metabolē*) in constitutions and how many and of what sort they are; what are the sources of destruction for each sort of constitution and into what sort of constitution a constitution is most particularly transformed; further, what are the sources of preservation both [for constitutions] in common and for each sort of constitution separately; and further, by what things each sort of constitution might most particularly be preserved—these matters must be investigated in conformity with what has been spoken of. (V.1.1301a20–25)[4]

The only practical task listed in that program is preservation. We are never invited to deliberate about whether to become a revolutionary. There is never an invitation that the people shall judge whether a government should be overthrown. How did stability become such an overriding value? Is this an intrusion of the author's own political conservatism rather than something that is integral to his method and thought?[5]

The first asymmetry was epistemological. Differences between knowing the causes of faction and knowing how to preserve constitutions drive the argument. The second asymmetry is ethical. Its effect on the argument is less obvious, but it is especially troubling ethically. Since the seventeenth century we are used to thinking of warring factions as being in a state of nature. Each argues in the name of justice, but there is no justice available to settle the dispute, except maybe an appeal to heaven. People still have the language of justice but can only use it strategically. No privileges go to those in power just because they got there first. It seems that we should value stability exactly in proportion to how worth saving the given constitution is. This asymmetry is troubling because obligation and legitimacy are central to modern political philosophy, which is written from the perspective of the good, or at least the rational, person in a questionable regime, not from that of the statesman. Book V seems to eschew such moral considerations, which for us are the only moral considerations. There is no right of revolution. Nor is there a duty of absolute obedience to the ruler. That is, knowing that factions are bad does not imply for Aristotle, as it does, say, for Hobbes, that we should therefore always support the government in power. The lesson Aristotle draws from the idea that statesmen should always aim at stability is, as we will see, quite different.[6]

Aristotle's project confronts the opposite moral difficulty from that faced in the *Rhetoric*. There we learn that the power to uphold and to refute a given proposition is a single power. There is no art of refutation distinct from an art of demonstration, and no art of advancing reasons for a given proposition that knows anything not equally available to someone seeking to overthrow that claim.[7] "The orator should have the power to convince about opposites, as in syllogisms . . . not that we should do both (for one ought not to convince people to do wrong), but that we will not miss the way things really are" (I.1.1355a29–32).

The trouble with the *Rhetoric* was that the moral injunction—one ought not to convince people to do wrong—seemed distinct from the art and power to convince about opposites, so distinct that it sounds like adventitious piety. In *Politics* V the moral difficulty comes from the fact that the science Aristotle teaches does *not* work equally both ways. While we have to know the causes of faction, we are never invited to join in one, while on the other side, stability becomes a value apart from all regard for the justice of the constitution to be defended. The *Rhetoric* claims that "true and better facts are by nature always more productive of good syllogisms and more persuasive" (I.1.1355a29). *Politics* V asserts an asymmetry on behalf of a much lower value—it's not easier to argue for the truth, but better to defend any constitution, regardless of how it measures up against absolute standards of justice. Defense is better than offense, regardless of the cause.

The relativism of stability seems ethically neutral, and so the project of preserving states ethically dubious, in a way that *justice* relative to a constitution is not. Justice may be a relative concept, but it isn't an arbitrary one. The goodness of the good citizen is not purely instrumental, like the goodness of a good slave. Stability seems to go beyond the relative to the arbitrary. Partial justice is still justice in a way that does not seem to have a parallel for stability. "All men grasp justice to some extent but they only go part of the way, and they do not state the whole of absolute justice" (III.9.1280a9–11). That idea seems repeated at the beginning of Book V: "We must first assume as a principle that many different constitutions have come into being because, though all agree about the just and the proportionately equal, they make a mistake (*hamartia*) about it" (V.1.1301a25–26). But there is a difference. Book V omits a normative consideration present in Book III. In III.9, democrats and oligarchs are doubly mistaken. They not only generalize about equality and inequality, thinking either that someone equal in some respect is simply equal, or that someone unequal in some respect is simply unequal, but in addition, "of the most authoritative consideration they say nothing" (1280a25). Like the democrats and oligarchs, Aristotle himself in Book V says nothing of justice according to merit and its connection to the end of the city, the good life.

Hence the conclusion of III.9 is absent from Book V: "Those who contribute most to a partnership [in living well] have a greater part in the city than those who are equal or greater in freedom and family but unequal in political virtue, or those who outdo them in wealth but are outdone in virtue" (1281a3–7). Book V is silent where Book III offered normative standards. We are left simply with errors causing factions which in turn cause revolutions. If particular constitutions and forms of justice are founded on error, modern remedies such as compromise and a modus vivendi make no sense: what would be the point of neutrality between a pair of errors? There are two kinds of justice, arithmetic and geometrical, democratic and oligarchic. Both kinds are partial, but there is no third kind of justice, true justice or justice according to merit, alongside those two, nor is there the indirect guidance we get from recognizing that neither form of justice is true justice. The solution to the problem of factions is not to abandon partial conceptions of justice in favor of complete justice. We need to understand why not.[8]

If we could tie stability to justice, that would help overcome the suspicion of relativism here. Unfortunately, while people's conceptions of justice may cause factions, justice itself plays little role in *Politics* V. Emphasizing stability makes us neglect justice.

II. FACTION AND CONSTITUTIONAL CHANGE

These asymmetries—that knowing how to preserve a constitution is not equivalent to knowing the causes of faction, and that preserving a constitution is always worthwhile—propel the argument of Book V. There are two differences between the programmatic plan of IV.1 and the first paragraph of V.1, which announces the subject for Book V. First, IV.1 does contemplate the possibility of reform: "To reform (*epanorthôsai*) a constitution is no less a task than to frame one from the beginning . . . The political expert should be able to assist existing regimes" (1289a3–7). Second, faction did not appear in IV.1. Stability is its subject instead. In one sense, the shift from preserving the constitution to focusing on factions seems innocent and obvious. Factions destroy constitutions, and so the statesman interested in stability must defeat factions. Aristotle makes the connection between factions and constitutional change more complex, and eventually discovers modes of constitutional change that have nothing to do with faction.

Once again: "We must first assume as a principle that many different constitutions have come into being because, though all agree about the just and the proportionately equal, they make a mistake about it" (V.1.1301a25–26). While plurality and particularity come from initial errors, these mistakes are not always fatal, and the causal analysis in V.1–4 shows that factions are caused as much by the emotions and actions of those outside the constitution as by errors internal to the constitution. Unlike Socrates, Aristotle never suggests that constitutions are unstable because they are imperfect. Instead, constitutions are unstable because of factions, while factions come into existence because constitutions are imperfect. Aristotle's argument is one step longer than Socrates's, with factions as an intermediate cause between imperfection and instability. That is how Aristotle makes his argument more ethical and practical. Preservation does not require perfection, only the suppression of faction.

Constitutional change is therefore a form of motion with an external cause, namely, faction. Aristotle differs from Plato on this count. But this external cause is not fully alien to the constitution. If it were, we would have to worry about the role of chance and ask, with Machiavelli in chapter 25 of *The Prince*, what the statesman can do to oppose fortune. Factions could come from outside agitators and foreign powers, or from unexpected changes in the proportions of rich and poor or other groups within the state, and not from any mistake in the constitution itself. Identifying constitutional change with faction avoids those Platonic and Machiavellian extremes, which agree that only internal causes of constitutional change can be understood, and that external causes are fortuitous and irrational. Aristotle shows how the statesman can understand external causes, since they are external to the constitution yet responses to a mistake about equality within the constitution. His analysis gives the statesman an intelligible yet external cause of constitutional change.

When factions become intelligible, as opposed to fortuitous or irrational, the outsiders become, if not citizens, part of the constitution. These outsiders, with the possibility of faction and revolt, and their claims about justice and injustice, have a political voice that makes them different from outsiders such as resident aliens or Spartan helots, who might threaten the stability of a polis but who have no political standing. Constitutions define who is a citizen, but it does not follow that such definitions are beyond practical criticism. The constitution's defining who is a citizen looks like a performative utterance, in which saying something makes it so, but this act appeals to normative standards of justice, and so the constitution cannot simply define who is a citizen (III.2.1275b26–30). Constitutions define citizens, and therefore all constitutions exclude some who might be citizens.[9] Citizens as defined by the constitution deny that they have relations of justice to the excluded and worry that the outsiders might return the favor. Aristotle's analytic framework accurately reflects the very unstable position of these outsiders. Making factions intelligible is a first step to controlling them.[10]

A brief analogy to the *Poetics* might help place Aristotle's analysis. Just as Socrates claimed that all constitutional change comes from an error within the ruling class, someone might think that all tragic downfalls were due to errors on the part of the person who will suffer the tragedy. One's errors become one's fate. Imperfection causes instability and loss. Tragedy is, then, the unfolding of the inevitable consequences of a tragic flaw. Such an understanding is parallel to my Platonic analysis of revolution. On the other hand, what I just called the Machiavellian analysis of factions resembles those who think that tragedy comes from moral luck, from the contingencies of clashes between people, projects, or values, from unforeseeable consequences, among other things. Aristotle's analysis of tragedy, like his analysis of factions, mediates between these possibilities. Tragedy results from an error, but the error is not blameworthy, nor is the plot a predictable outcome of the error. Similarly, constitutions are unstable because of factions, while factions come into existence because constitutions are imperfect.

Determinism and chance both defeat Aristotelian tragedy. There is noth-

ing noble, and nothing of the proper magnitude for tragedy, in an agent facing either a deterministic or a fortuitous universe. Similarly, there is drama
and even pathos in Aristotle's analysis of faction. In a situation where people
act in the name of justice without fully understanding its connection to true
merit, stability is a less likely outcome than continuous civil war. It is not
helpful simply to assert that the better the constitution, the more stable,
so that stability is acquired through making the constitution better. That
assertion doesn't take stability as a serious problem in its own right, and
doesn't take seriously the situation in which factions occur. That would be
something like Socrates's claims that the better the person, the less others
can harm him, which sounds too much like wishful thinking for Aristotle.

III. BOOK V.1–4: FACTION IN GENERAL

Chapters 1 through 4 of Book V concern the general causes of faction and
constitutional change, as opposed to those specific to a particular kind of
constitution. The argument within these chapters moves increasingly to
causes of faction that have no counterpart in methods of preservation, eventually separating constitutional change from factions altogether, although
those two were initially associated as effect and cause. Separating factions
from constitutional change opens up the difference between knowing the
causes of faction and knowing the causes of stability, between analysis and
deliberation.

The first three chapters look at the four Aristotelian causes of faction.
In chapter 1 we learn that factions have the same formal cause as the mul-
tiplicity and variety of constitutions themselves. He begins with lines I
quoted above: "We must first assume as a principle that many different constitutions have come into being because, though all agree about the just and
the proportionately equal, they make a mistake about it" (V.1.1301a25–26).
Given that mistakes as the formal cause of factions, we will understand factions practically by grasping the other three causes, the material, final, and
efficient causes:[11]

And since we are considering what circumstances give rise to party factions (*staseis*) and revolutions (*metabolai*) in constitutions, we must first
ascertain their origins and causes generally. They are, roughly speaking,
three in number, which we must mark out each by itself in outline first.
For we must understand (1) the disposition of those who form factions,
and (2) for the sake of what, and thirdly, (3) what are the origins of political tumults and of factions against one another. (V.2.1302a16–21)

This delicate status of factions as an external cause intimately related to the constitutions converts this taxonomy into an argument. The three successive causes move increasingly away from the formal cause of errors about justice and closer to things within the statesman's power. Aristotle is not wrong to assert that knowledge of destruction is knowledge of preservation. But as we come to understand the claim, we see that it points beyond itself to causes of destruction that have no counterpart in preservation—that's the bad news, since that means there are things we can't do anything about—and modes of preservation that are not simply contraries of causes of faction, which will turn out to be ways of preserving the state that at the same time make it better. Those modes will be ways of improving the constitution. The other three causes are increasingly distant from the formal cause, as they should be for a phenomenon that is an external cause related to the constitution itself.

Thus Aristotle says that the dispositions, the first cause on the list, follow from the general cause. That is, the material cause is almost identical to the formal cause of partial conceptions of equality: "We must lay it down that the general cause of men being themselves somehow disposed towards change is mainly the one we have in fact already spoken of" (1302a22). The ends of faction, the next cause considered, are also generated by the different interpretations of justice, but they are much less abstract and formal than the material causes. Partisans of inequality and equality aim at honor and profit (1302a31–33). Democrats and oligarchs assert two partial interpretations of equality; democrats typically aim at wealth, oligarchs at honor, and therefore the ends of factions are honor and profit. (See too III.15.1286b15: "Oligarchies made wealth a thing of honor.") Aristotle gives content to the purely mathematical description of the two formal possibilities by tying them to these ends. Notice that these two aims are different from other characterizations of the differences between democratic and oligarchic justice, which has democracy aiming at freedom and oligarchy at wealth. That is, democratic and oligarchic constitutions aim at freedom and wealth, respectively, while democratic and oligarchic *factions* aim at wealth and honor, respectively.[12]

At this point the discussion of factions in Book V directly teaches us something about the account in Book I of people as political animals. Recall that "speech is for making clear what is beneficial or harmful, and hence also what is just or unjust" (I.2.1253a8–18). There are no factions concerning what is beneficial or harmful, not because people don't make mistakes about what profits them but because they don't connect the useful with merit, while justice always relates to merit and desert. People can quarrel over anything, but citizens only form factions because of differences over justice.

The falsehood in the proof-text I quoted at the beginning—"It is clear that if we know the causes by which constitutions are destroyed we also know the causes by which they are preserved; for opposites create opposites, and destruction is the opposite of security" (V.8.1307b26–29)—starts to emerge with the efficient causes of faction. The variety of different efficient causes looks indefinite: the first few Aristotle mentions, we will see, follow from the analysis of the material and final cause, but as chapter 3 progresses, the causes he enumerates increasingly seem to emerge from historical examples, not Aristotle's own structure. As the kinds of cause become more historical, the connection between faction and constitutional change becomes more attenuated. These causes aren't tied to the particular constitution and its faults. He finally notes that there are kinds of constitutional change that don't come from faction at all, in spite of his earlier claiming that constitutional changes must occur through stasis (1301b6–7): "constitutions change even without faction" (3.1303a13, see too 6.1306b6ff, 8.1308a35ff).

A closer look at chapter 3 shows the dynamics of Aristotle's argument at work. Before going on to causes of constitutional change not related to faction, he first lists six efficient causes of constitutional change tied to faction, and the series exhibits a decreasing symmetry between cause and remedy. These causes of faction are less and less a response to a mistake by the rulers or the constitution.

1. "What sort of power insolence and profit have and how they are a cause is pretty clear" (1302b5–6). Good rulers can guard against insolence and profit, and so factions exist and succeed solely due to a culpable mistake by the ruler.

2. "It is also clear what honor is capable of and how it is a cause of faction. For both when men are themselves dishonored and when they see others honored, they form a faction" (1302b10–11). The simple connection present in the case of insolence and profit between cause and remedy disappears; even worse, by showing that the virtuous can be on either side of a revolt caused by honor, it invites questions about what *phronēsis* can do at all in these conditions. Factions "occur unjustly when certain men are either honored or dishonored contrary to their worth, but justly when according to their worth" (1302b12–14). The justice of a faction has no bearing on how the statesman should treat it.

3. "Men form a faction because of superiority when someone (either one person or more than one) is greater in power than accords with the city and the power of the governing class" (1302b15–17). This is a common enough cause of faction that it has generated its own characteristic remedy, ostracism, but Aristotle criticizes that countermeasure. "It is better to see to it from the beginning that no men become so pre-eminent than to supply a remedy later" (1302b19–20). It looks as though preeminence is an avoidable mistake, although Aristotle doesn't tell us how to insure that no one becomes pre-eminent.

4. "Men form a faction because of fear: both those who have committed an injustice, fearing that they will be punished, and those who are about to suffer an injustice, wishing to act first before they suffer it" (1302b21–23). Fear can be well motivated or not. Since justice is irrelevant to whether fear makes people want to overthrow a constitution, this cause begs for a treatment that relies purely on appearance, disregarding actual merit. What matters is whether people feel insulted. However, driving a wedge between appearance and merit separates the cause from the remedy as well. Not only, then, is there a difference between stability and excellence, but a difference between the arts of appearance that lead to stability, and the real virtues of the good constitution.

5. "Men also form a faction because of contempt" (1302b25). Contempt resembles the first cause, insolence and profit, in coming from a mistake made by the rulers. But contempt looks like an inevitable consequence of the mistake of forming a democracy or oligarchy in the first place and so an unavoidable feature of those forms of government. Aristotle's initial claim that the causes of instability were the causes of particularity (V.1.1301a25–26) looks vindicated: *all* constitutions have insiders and outsiders, and contempt seems a necessary by-product of having some people within the constitution and others outside. If there is a remedy, it won't have anything to do with the cause itself. Governments have to make the excluded feel nonexcluded, at least to the extent of not being objects of contempt. As with fear, appearance becomes important, making justice and virtue more irrelevant.

6. "Changes of constitution also arise because of disproportionate growth" (1302b33). "A city is composed of parts, the growth of one of which often escapes notice . . . and this often happens because of

chance" (1303a1–3). The statesman seems doomed because nothing could be more of a cause without a cure than this.

These causes cast into doubt the symmetry that knowing why men form factions will tell us what to do about them. It is increasingly unclear whether the mistakes that generate particular forms of constitution are avoidable or inevitable errors. The more irrelevant the justice of the insurgent's complaints, the less clear the connection between the constitution's mistake and its instability.

Things get even worse when Aristotle next turns to constitutional change without faction. Electioneering and belittlement, "small differences," and racial and territorial differences are sources of constitutional change that need not occur through factions at all, or in which factions arise without connection to any original error in the constitution or the rulers. These are clearly causes that are external to Aristotle's own treatment of constitutional change. Once there are sources of constitutional change outside of faction, the causes truly become indefinite. Whether or not they have anything to do with factions, they have nothing to do with the constitution revolted against. Aristotle's idea of factions as an external cause intimately related to the constitutions themselves has disappeared.

The partial and growing independence of the four causes in V.1–3 is significant. It is another consequence of the fact that poleis are neither natural nor artificial. Among natural things, formal, final, and moving causes are identical, and matter is correlative to form. In the arts, the four causes are fully independent of each other. The four causes of faction lie between those options, since faction is an external phenomenon tied to the internal nature of the constitution. We can deduce the material cause from the formal, as in nature, and can get at least partway toward understanding the final cause from those two, as honor and profit, the two final causes, have at least a correlation with the two forms of equality, arithmetic and geometrical. The moving cause is more independent, and the variety of possible moving causes that Aristotle presents cannot be read off from the formal cause that led to multiple constitutions in the first place. The moving cause must be more independent: since factions destroy states, the moving cause must be in some way extrinsic to the ruling principle of the constitution.

Faction is the practical subject for understanding constitutional change in almost the same way that virtue is the practical subject for understanding happiness in the *Ethics*. Virtue isn't all there is to happiness, but it is all that we can *practically* know about it. Happiness is virtuous activity in a complete life, but we can't do anything about the fortune that might interfere with leading a complete life. Similarly, factions aren't all there is to the destruction of regimes, but they are the substance of practical knowledge of preservation. In the two cases, virtue and factions not only are the only factors for happiness or preservation that can be an object of practical knowledge. In addition, knowing them must also be enough to act successfully. Should fortune dominate over virtue as the cause of happiness, we would leave Aristotle's world behind. We'd not only have a new kind of tragedy, but also a new kind of ethics in which the virtuous person confronts massive irrational or unjust forces, the ethics of the Stoics or of Machiavelli. Should these last causes of constitutional change apart from factions become dominant, we might have the consolations of history, but Aristotelian practical science would be impossible.

IV. BOOK V.4: A FIFTH CAUSE?

Chapter V.4 makes things even worse. Understanding why constitutions are overthrown becomes less and less useful for knowing how to preserve states the more we doubt that factions are the sole cause of constitutional change. The statesman in V.4 faces contingencies of history that lie beyond practical knowledge. Chapter 4 begins: "Factions arise, then, not concerning small things, but from small things; men form factions only concerning great things" (1303b17–18).[13] The causes of V.4 are occasions in which potential causes become actual causes. The disproportion between insignificant occasion and large effect, and the importance of causes that have nothing to do with faction and disputes about equality, grow out of the last few moving causes in V.3. None of the things that occasion revolution in V.4 relates to the first two causes, the material and final cause, outlined in V.2. The occasions listed in this chapter are ways in which potential *moving* causes become actual moving causes.[14]

If we only consider the potential moving causes of V.3, revolution looks inevitable, but turning to these occasions of constitutional change presented in this chapter makes it seem avoidable. His standard four causes are not sufficient for Aristotle's purposes here, even though the four causes are supposed to be exhaustive. We think we know when we know the cause (*Post. An.* II.11.94a20, *Ph.* II.3.194b18–20, *Met.* I.3.983a25–26); there are, therefore, limits to what we can *know* about factions. This chapter offers the possibility of action, not just understanding. As the relation between factions and constitutional change becomes attenuated, the declared symmetry between knowing the causes of factions and knowing how to keep constitutions stable disappears.

The asymmetry between knowing the causes of constitutional change and knowing how constitutions are preserved can be brought out by a comparison to the treatment of the passions in *Rhetoric* II.2–11. While each presents a trio of causes, there of emotion and here of faction, the *Rhetoric* contains nothing parallel to V.4. Once the orator knows the "state of mind" of someone with a certain emotion, "against whom" the emotion is usually felt, and "for what sort of reasons," he knows enough to cause the emotion in an audience. The definition of each emotion, plus these three causes, is enough to constitute practical knowledge of persuasion. But the statesman isn't trying to cause faction, as the orator causes emotion, but to prevent it. What is enough for the art of rhetoric is only the beginning for a science of politics.

In the *Rhetoric*, the three causes of emotion are all the rhetorician needs to know, and all there is to know. The end of the art of rhetoric is finding the available means of persuasion, doing all that is within the speaker's power to convince, and not persuasion itself. Having the three causes of a given emotion within one's power does not guarantee that one can cause the emotion. The statesman in V.4 learns something not knowable to the rhetorician—how the potential causes within the power of the rhetorician or the insurgent politician sometimes lead to the rhetorical victory or the constitutional overthrow they aim at, and sometimes do not. The rhetorician knows *that* his best efforts won't always succeed, but cannot know *why*; more precisely, he cannot do anything to cross the gap between exercising the power of finding the available means of persuasion and successfully persuading. *Politics* V is not interested in causing factions but in understanding how they occur and how to prevent them. The occasions listed in V.4 are not causes like the three causes already analyzed; they are explanations of why those causes sometimes cause factions and constitutional change and sometimes do not. This has no counterpart in the *Rhetoric*. *Politics* V.4 is both more and less practical than the *Rhetoric*, more in finding this additional, occasional, cause, and less in aiming at understanding factions, not creating them.

Before moving to look at what happens later in *Politics* V, another analogy to the *Rhetoric* will drive a further wedge between knowing how constitutions are changed and how to maintain them. Recall my proof-text: "It is clear that if we know the causes by which constitutions are destroyed we also know the causes by which they are preserved; for opposites create opposites, and destruction is the opposite of security" (1307b26–29). The practical meaning of "opposites create opposites" contains ambiguities that Aristotle's treatment of the emotions helps to uncover. Immediately after treating the first emotion, anger, Aristotle turns to a discussion of calm. The speaker needs to know how to provoke anger and how to remove it and counter the provocations of others. The orator who knows how to cause anger in others knows how to create calm, too. Anger and calm are opposites: calm is the privation of anger.

An audience might become angry because the clever speaker knows how to get them angry, or they might grow angry on their own account without anyone manipulating them. Even if anger is spontaneous, removing the anger can be a deliberate act by the rhetorician. Similarly, not all factions come from culpable or avoidable errors, since we saw that there are just factions. However, while the people engaged in faction can be seen as responding to situations without deliberation, removing those causes is a deliberative enterprise for the statesman.[15] The statesman's knowledge can extend to things people engaging in factions do without knowing. By knowing how anger comes about, the rhetorician knows how to create calm. If everything the politician could do to preserve the state stood to the causes of faction as anger stands to calm, there would be no difficulty in accepting the dictum of symmetry.

But neither the *Rhetoric* in its treatment of the emotions nor *Politics* V can stay with that simplicity for long. Aristotle turns from anger and calm to love and hate. Hate is not the absence of love, and we don't cause hatred by removing love, or cause love by removing hate. Knowing how to provoke hatred does not follow from knowing how to cause love, and knowing how to make others love me does not follow from knowing how to provoke hatred. We don't always know the methods of stability by knowing the causes of faction.

V. BOOK V.5–7: FACTION AND PARTICULAR CONSTITUTIONS

If the argument of chapters 1–4 shows that there are ways in which we can understand factions without any corresponding practical implications, the argument of chapters 8 and 9 present a different asymmetry that is grounds for optimism. They find methods of preservation that do more than remove the causes and effects of faction so these two chapters are the real climax of Book V. But before turning from the causes of faction in V.1–4 to the causes of stability in V.8–9, Aristotle in chapters 5–7 considers the causes of faction peculiar to particular constitutions. We learn in these chapters that the particular kind of constitution plays little role in causing factions. The only additional problem facing polities and aristocracies is that they are mixtures, polity of democracy and oligarchy, and aristocracy "of those two and virtue, but especially of the two" (V.7.1307a9), and therefore can be undone by being a bad mixture.

If the purpose of *Politics* V overall is to encourage statesmen to transform democracies and oligarchies into their correct counterparts, polity and aristocracy, then showing that for the purposes of confronting factions, polity and aristocracy aren't much different from democracy and oligarchy helps to smooth the way toward that transformation. Chapter 7 treats both aristocracies and polities as variants of oligarchy and democracy, with no special problems at all. Since aristocracies mix democracy, oligarchy, and virtue, "some are less and some are more enduring" (7.1304a16). Polities and aristocracies have no moral exemption from faction and the distinction between correct and corrupt constitutions is not in play here. When Aristotle talks about the measures statesmen can take to improve the constitution, it is unclear whether the reformed democracy or oligarchy becomes a polity or aristocracy or simply a better democracy or oligarchy, unclear because those distinctions do not exist for the statesman of Book V. In chapter 3 I noted the ambiguity in the relation of constitution to polis: was the constitution the substantial form of the polis or a quality of it? Here it looks like a revolution is a change in substance, while reform is a change of quality in a substance that stays the same. The statesman and other citizens will think that the improvement leads to a better democracy or oligarchy; only an outsider would make the distinction between these and polity and aristocracy.[16]

Aristotle takes that partial truth grasped by democrats and oligarchs and makes it into a complete truth, as methods of preservation become methods of converting corrupt into correct constitutions. Once again I see a parallel to the *Rhetoric*. Rhetoric is a faculty for arguing both sides of any question, but still is oriented to truth. The *Rhetoric* shows how finding arguments, even in aid of a bad or losing cause, can be a noble activity. Political wisdom encounters a situation in which both sides grasp partial truths about justice. It is the task of political wisdom to preserve existing constitutions. *Politics* V shows how preserving the constitution can be a noble activity.

If factions and constitutional change were caused by internal defects, each constitution would have its own way of passing away, and when a given constitution passed away, it would pass into a specifiable new constitutional form, which is just what happens in *Republic* VIII.[17] But, as I argued before, factions are an external cause of constitutional change derived from the constitution. Constitutions are unstable because of factions, while factions come into existence because constitutions are imperfect. Aristotle's argument, recall, was one step longer than Socrates's, with factions as an intermediate cause between imperfection and instability. Factions are outside the constitution, but the reasons for faction mostly come from the nature of the constitution and its characteristic mistakes. Therefore, it is an important discovery that the causes of faction do not vary with changes in the constitution. The methods of stability will mostly be methods that apply to all constitutions, both oligarchic and democratic. (Where the differences between aristocracy and oligarchy and between polity and democracy are mostly effaced, this is not so far monarchy and tyranny. They find stability through contrary means [V.10.1312b18–19; but see V.11.1314a32].)

VI. BOOK V.8–9: PRESERVATION (AND IMPROVEMENT?)

The argument of chapters 8 and 9 shows us that knowledge of preservation can outrun the causes of faction. While chapter 8 is mostly responsive to the causes of faction in the way predicted by my proof-text, the remedies of chapter 9 offer the statesman ways of making the constitution secure that are more than responses to or anticipations of factional threats. Then preservation can be more than fighting against faction. Both preservation and the knowledge of preservation can be things worth having in their own right, and not just necessities compelled by the need to fight against factions. Once preservation is more than preventing faction, Aristotle could have good reason to make preservation always preferable to constitutional change, regardless of the quality of the given constitution. Preservation will include reform, while revolution in his eyes cannot.

The trouble with that formulation is that it isn't easy to tell when a change is a reform, and when a revolution; we are brought back again to asking whether a constitutional change is a change in quality or in substance? The difference seems to be that reforms are carried out by the rulers, and revolutions by insurgents. Book III distinguished the virtues of the ruler and of other citizens as the difference between *phronēsis* and true opinion (III.4.1277b25–29). Only the ruler, operating with *phronēsis*, can improve a constitution without destroying it. It isn't the quality of the constitution that makes preserving it a good, but the quality of the activity of preservation that makes preserving the constitution a good. Preserving an imperfect constitution isn't good because that constitution is good but because preserving it is good. This might sound like throwing good money after bad, or acting courageously and heroically while engaged in an unjust war, so we will have to be careful and precise on this crucial point, as Aristotle himself is not, neither here nor in the *Ethics*, where he lists courage as a virtue without limiting it to a just war. The ethical virtue doesn't seem to look to the justice of its cause, and the statesman's duty to preserve the constitution similarly seems indifferent to the justice of the constitution he is given in the best on a hypothesis. If making it better means making it more stable, then it is only by accident that reforming a constitution would move it from a corrupt to a correct one, unless someone can show that a more stable constitution is always a better one.

As I said at the beginning, the power and direction of Aristotle's argument comes from the asymmetry between causes of destruction and of stability. One nice example of the asymmetry comes right after he tells the statesman to be on guard against minor violations of the law, the first way to preserve the constitution. "The next point is that we must not put faith in the sophisms strung together for the sake of tricking the multitude" (V.8.1307b40).[18] Factions succeed by deception as well as force (IV.4.1304b5–7), but deception will not work to counter factions. Destruction and preservation are not practical opposites, because some of the means that work for destruction are inappropriate for preservation. The statesman must master the arts of appearance—hubris and contempt are at least partly in the eye of the beholder—so that moderation and friendship must be seen as signs of strength, but those appearances must not be deceptive appearances. The statesman foregoes the use of sophisms in order to use true arts of appearance. Just as Aristotle's rhetorician will not do just anything to win, and discovers in the *Rhetoric* limitations to the kinds of means of persuasion he can artfully employ, so the statesman in Book V learns that only certain means will preserve the state. The statesman will then act moderately and with restraint, not out of exiguous moral considerations, but in order to preserve the state, avoiding means that might look useful but which in fact backfire. The statesman needs practical wisdom and not cleverness.[19]

Since those outside the constitution revolt if injustice is done to them, the obvious remedy is not to commit injustice. But Aristotle goes further, and the third means of preserving the constitution—after guarding against minor violations of the law and avoiding sophisms—recommends bringing outsiders into the constitution. The remedy goes deeper than the cause of faction. The statesman might not want to do so, but he learns that bringing outsiders into the constitution strengths it. In addition, people within the constitution should be treated democratically, whatever the constitution. "For what democracies seek to extend to the multitude, namely, equality, is not only just for those who are similar but also beneficial" (1308a10–12).

The democratic *ēthos* is essential to preserving *all* constitutions, since *philia*, friendship, and *homonoia*, consensus, come most naturally to a democracy. As usual, Aristotle fails to trumpet his important discoveries. The democratic *ēthos* is not unique to democracy, although of course many people, democrats and their opponents, wrongly think so.[20] That these remedies have no corresponding cause of factions should tell us that something important is going on.

The need for a democratic *ēthos* and for *philia* within all stable constitutions explains an odd feature of the definition of *polis, constitution,* and *citizen* in Book III. Aristotle defines *citizen* by saying that "the citizen proper (*haplōs*) is distinguished by having a share in giving judgment and exercising office. . . . We take a citizen to be one who shares in 'indefinite' offices" (III.1.1275a22–32). He then comments that this definition applies best in a democracy. He does not take a hint from that observation and go on to reason that democracy must therefore be the most natural form of constitution. But here in Book V a milder privileging of democracy does come. The route to stability is not for all constitutions to become more democratic, but for the *ēthos* of each constitution to include this democratic feature.

Finding means of preserving the constitution that are more than simply defeating the causes of instability makes all the difference. If the particular conception of justice in a given constitution causes faction, and faction in turn causes constitutional change, then stability would be reduced to preventing and fighting off factions. We would be in Machiavelli's world, in which stability is nothing but an episodic series of responses to crises. But in Aristotle's two-step analysis, constitutions are unstable because of factions, while factions come into existence because constitutions are imperfect. Just because each of those connections is not necessary and so can be severed—particular conceptions of justice need not lead to factions, and factions are neither a necessary nor a sufficient cause of constitutional change—stability can be more than the temporary duration of a constitution between revolutions. Therefore what the statesman does and knows can be more than the pragmatic knowledge of how to respond to factions.

Chapters 1–4 showed that some of our knowledge of how constitutions change has no counterpart in how they are preserved. Chapters 8 and 9 showed that we can know things about preservation without counterpart in destruction. It therefore makes sense that chapters 8 and 9 should be far more prescriptive than the rest of Book V. These chapters, unlike chapters 1–7, set up a pattern for deliberation. These asymmetries between knowledge of constitutional change and of constitutional preservation put us in a position to understand the normative asymmetry between destruction and preservation that makes stability such an overriding good.

VII. PRESERVING THE CONSTITUTION AND THE ARTS OF APPEARANCE

In my analysis of Book III, I characterized the difference between Aristotle's activity in the *Politics* and the activity of the statesman as a difference between dialectic and rhetoric. *Politics* III presents reasonable arguments for different conclusions regarding justice, but which conclusion would be the most appropriate in any particular circumstances requires weighing those probable arguments. Arguments carry different weight in different circumstances, and are more or less probable in different situations. Book V shows another way in which the statesman must act rhetorically, while the political philosopher presents either dialectical arguments, as in Book III, or political philosophy, in Book IV. The statesman must master the arts of appearance. He cannot appear to commit injustices. In particular, as I've already mentioned, the statesman must make it appear that the moderation he exercises in preserving the constitution is a sign of strength and wisdom rather than weakness. It is easy to interpret moderation as weakness, and the statesman must make the state secure by changing that interpretation. The ending of VI.3 can be taken as a theme for the entire argument, then:

> Concerning equality and justice, even though it is very difficult to find the truth about these matters, it is still easier to hit on it than it is to persuade those who are capable of aggrandizing themselves. The inferior always seek equality and justice; those who dominate them take no thought for it. (1318b2–5)

To persuade the powerful to act with equality and justice is to persuade them that moderation is a virtue. Moderation as a virtue pervades the *Politics*; in Book V it takes the form of choosing a stable and moderate democracy or oligarchy over a constitution that would be more purely democratic or oligarchic and therefore an extreme democracy or oligarchy. "Many of the things that are held to be democratic destroy democracies, and many that are held to be oligarchic destroy oligarchies. But those who think that this is the only kind of virtue push the constitution to extremes" (V.9.1309b19–24). Living democratically means doing as one likes; living oligarchically means organizing one's life around wealth and honor. But *ruling* democratically or oligarchically means aiming at the preservation of the democratic or oligarchic

constitution, and subordinating—not suppressing—one's other goals, of freedom, wealth, or honor. "Isn't democracy's insatiable desire for what it defines as the good also what destroys it?" (*Republic* VIII 562b).

"One should not think it slavery to live in harmony with the constitution, but safety" (V.9.1310a34–36, see *Met.* I.2.982b25–26, XII.10.1075a18–23).
Living in harmony with the constitution feels like a restraint to someone
who wants to do as he would like. Such a person experiences living in harmony with any constitution as slavery. But even democratic constitutions
demand doing something other than whatever one likes. "To be educated
relative to the constitution is not to do the things enjoyed by oligarchs
or proponents of democracy, but rather to do the things that will enable
the rulers, respectively, to govern in an oligarchic or democratic way"
(V.9.1310a19–22).[21] This is Book V's definition of the good life, the end of
politics and the state, and these definitions are appropriate when the aim
of the statesman is the stability of the state. Acting politically is a good life
of justice and friendship. The ruler who aims at life alone aims at domination or living as he likes, while the good life is a political life of mutuality
and reciprocity. In stable poleis, citizens act as political animals. Making
man's political nature dominate other aspects of human nature is the key to
stability and the reason preserving a constitution is a noble activity.

"The most important of all the things that have been mentioned for
the endurance of constitutions, which all men now make light of, is to be
educated in harmony with the constitution" (V.9.1310a12–14). Education
in harmony with a constitution is education in moderation, in becoming a
moderate democrat or oligarch. This education orients the citizen toward
ruling democratically or oligarchically, instead of living democratically or
oligarchically, and therefore education in harmony with the constitution
means becoming a fully politicized being. Stability and moderation are ways
in which people become political animals in difficult circumstances. "All
men now make light of" such education because they prefer living democratically or oligarchically to ruling democratically or oligarchically. Even
if man is by nature a political animal, living politically is demanding, and
people will resist fulfilling their nature. Constitutions become stable when
rulers fully realize their nature as political animals. In Book V at least, one
cannot often live politically except by living democratically or oligarchically. One can certainly never live politically except by living under some
particular constitution. If the *Ethics* is about how to be happy, the *Politics*
is about how to be a political animal. Being a political animal is as much a
full-time job as being virtuous is, and as difficult.

The distinctions Aristotle drew in Book III between correct and deviant constitutions become more determinate in the specific inquiry of Book V. Rule of law, as opposed to rule of men, is the domination of ruling according to the constitution over living according to the ends of the constitution. Ruling for the good of the whole, as opposed to ruling for the rulers' own benefit, becomes rule according to the constitutional *ēthos*. Even more radically, the distinction from Book III (and Book I) between living and living well is now made determinate as the distinction between living and ruling according to the constitution.

In the same way, the taxonomy of six constitutions functions differently in Book V. Book III presents a clear distinction between three correct constitutions—monarchy, aristocracy, and polity—and three corresponding deviant ones—tyranny, oligarchy, and democracy. I've already explored the complications of Book IV. All six constitutions appear again in Book V, but they play different roles in the argument. Aristotle does not say that his more stable democracies and oligarchies will really be polities and aristocracies without knowing it, as though the statesman hides his political wisdom and induces the masses to act for their own good. Instead, as the treatment of polities and aristocracies in V 7—and indeed the treatment of monarchy and tyranny in V 10–11—show, the correct/deviant distinction is not at work in the politics of *stasis* and stability of Book V. Constitutions become stable by becoming constitutions first of all, and democracies or oligarchies secondarily. People live in democracies and oligarchies, not under constitutions in general, but by ruling moderately and in accordance with the constitutional *ēthos*, they realize their nature as political animals, not democratic or oligarchic animals. When rulers and other citizens act by the constitutional *ēthos*, they will transform all constitutions into polities, the name Aristotle uses both for the general name for constitution in general and for the correct counterpart of democracy.

Others have drawn parallels between *Politics* V and Machiavelli, but I want to offer a different parallel between the two than the usual imputations of amorality. *The Prince* has to make vice attractive by showing how it takes skill and will, while virtue is easy and cheap. Machiavelli presumes, reasonably, that his audience thinks the opposite. Vice, they think, is backsliding to the default position; virtue takes constant attention and dedication. He shows instead that virtue consists in taking the easy way out, keeping one's hands and conscience clean, winning a victory in the narrow internal court of judgment instead of risking oneself in trying to win out in reality. Vice takes constant work, risking failure, risking one's soul. Therefore vice is admirable, while we should pity the virtuous. In a similar way, *Politics* V cannot make moderation and antidespotic action heroic, but Aristotle can make them prudent and desirable. Being a political animal will not be the second-best solution for those too weak to make it as tyrants, as Glaucon asserts in *Republic* II. Being a political animal, and therefore moderate in the appropriate sense, is a way of living well. Hence the difficult teaching of the lines: "Many of the things that are held to be democratic destroy democracies, and many that are held to be oligarchic destroy oligarchies. But those who think that this is the only kind of virtue push the constitution to extremes" (V.9.1309b19–24).

I nominate another analogy to Aristotle's project besides Machiavelli. Jackie Robinson, the first black athlete to play major league baseball, needed a heroic sort of courage to restrain himself from retaliating, to absorb insults and not respond to injustices. Besides courage, though, he needed to be able to make clear that his not retaliating was an act of courage and self-restraint, not of cowardice or weakness—here is the art of appearance in action. In order to be a successful baseball player, he had to convince people that it took more courage to refrain from responding to insults than to fight back.

Both ruler and ruled in *Politics* V have to master the arts of appearance. Thinking of moderation and stability as noble goals is the ethical solution to the problem of faction, the solution through character and *ēthos*. Rulers make the state stable through moderation, but that strategy will work only if the people see it as a sign of strength, not weakness, and so become moderate themselves. Nonrulers make the state stable through moderating their own demands and desires. Even though they are nonrulers, they will be citizens first, and aim at citizenship and not necessarily at rule. Nonrulers, like rulers, are understandably reluctant to moderate their demands, because any such restraint on their part looks similarly self-defeating—the squeaky wheel gets greased. Proof that the statesman has mastered the arts of appearance is that his moderation makes citizens moderate.

Philia and *homonoia* between ruler and ruled consist in being able to see moderation as virtue, not weakness. I suspect that Jackie Robinson was able to have his restraint seen as courage because of his evident great physical ability that made people think that fighting back would be easy, and therefore he must be choosing not to. The task for rulers and ruled in the *Politics* is even more daunting.

In the *Ethics*, Aristotle shows that *thumos*, the spirited and restless part of the soul, is satisfied not in *pleonexia*, never-ending acquisition, but in virtuous and even intellectual activity. In the *Politics*, in a similar way, he shows that the aspirations for equality and inequality are satisfied by justice according to merit, and not the more partial forms of justice that aim at equality or inequality while forgetting about merit. We learn that the freedom that democrats aim at can best be achieved through constitutional rule, and the democratic *ēthos* must be redefined so that alternating ruling and being ruled is not thought a compromise, but as something better. It permits better actions than either never ruling but being a free rider, or always ruling and in that way getting what one likes. (Aristotle thinks that the latter is the serious political problem, at least for his audience, while we have to take the former more seriously today.) The honor that oligarchs seek can be best achieved through constitutional rule too, so that the oligarchic *ēthos* must be redefined to desire meriting political honors and not just getting them. As democracy and oligarchy are transformed into forms of political activity worth doing for their own sake, they are at the same time transformed into more stable constitutions. They are stable precisely because they are constituted by activity worth doing for its own sake. Regarding political activity as instrumental towards some further goal, such as freedom or wealth, makes the constitution unstable. This is a fundamental and nontrivial conclusion on Aristotle's part.

Aristotle must show his audience the satisfactions of moderation and constitutionalism, but equally the convinced Aristotelian statesman then has to convince his fellow-citizens of the same. In Book IV the challenge was to see the appeal of the middle class: not simply that they avoid the characteristic vices of excess wealth and poverty but that they have political virtues that make for a good state. Similarly here, the attractions of moderation have to go beyond stability as the absence of stasis. Moderation and stability have to be worth pursuing for their own sake. They have to be noble. And, to make things harder, it's not enough that these new activities of moderation and stability be virtuous; they have to be seen as virtuous.

VIII. STOPPING FACTIONS VERSUS PRESERVING THE CONSTITUTION

Before discussing the rhetorical dimensions of the project of Book V as arts of appearance, I want to point to a serious philosophical problem. The asymmetries between knowing the causes of destruction and knowing how to preserve constitutions come from the fact that factions are unlimited in the means they choose to overthrow the constitution, and so amenable to a causal analysis, while, as we saw, the statesman is limited to means that improve the constitution through fortifying the constitutional *ēthos*, even sometimes at the expense of doing as one likes. The bar against deception is only the most obvious limitation. Insurgents and those who want to keep power have different ends. "The aim of the tyrant is the pleasant, that of a king, the noble" (V.10.1311a5), but "the ends [of the assailants] are also the same for tyrannies and kingships as for constitutions."

Since V.10 is at pains to insist that "the things that happen within kingships and tyrannies are much the same as those we have described as happening within constitutions" (1310a41), I assert the generalization on Aristotle's behalf: good constitutions aim at the noble, deviant constitutions aim at the advantage of the rulers, but *all* insurgents—even those who justly revolt because of dishonor—aim at honor or profit (V.2.1302a31–33). They might have high-minded motives, but in the narrow sense of a final cause, only honor and profit, not virtue, can be the ends of revolutionaries. Those who aim at overthrowing a constitution, no matter how good they are, and no matter how bad the constitution is, *must* aim at these lower ends, even if the whole point of overthrowing the constitution is to establish a better one. To succeed in overthrowing the constitution, they have to deliberate toward the ends of honor or profit. We therefore have a paradox that goes to the heart of Aristotle's thought. States can be good or bad. People can engage in faction justly or unjustly. And yet insurgents always have low motives, while defending the constitution can at least possibly be a noble activity. Its nobility does not depend on the quality of the constitution it defends, but the quality of actions it employs to defend whenever constitution it is given.

Making stability into a political end and a mark of a good constitution is still odd, though. Duration can measure motions, but not activities. One motion could be better than another if it lasts longer. Since activities are complete at every instant, how long they last is not part of their nature or value. And yet instability can be a sign that a regime is a bad one; the longer a constitution lasts, the better it must be. "For a constitution to be structured simply in all respects according to either sort of equality is bad. This is evident from what happens. For none of these sorts of constitutions is enduring" (V.1.1302a2–4; see too VI.5.1320a1–3). The statesman's job in Book V is defined in IV.1 as "considering both how some given constitution could be brought into existence originally and also in what way having been brought into existence it could be preserved for the longest time" (IV.1.1288b28–30). When the preservation or stability of the constitution is an activity, duration will be an excellence of this activity. "It is only equality according to worth that having one's own that is enduring" (V.7.1307a26–27).

As it aims at self-preservation, a state can call on individuals to risk their lives for the sake of the continuing existence of the state and constitution. The virtuous man prefers a short, glorious life (*NE* IX.8.1169b18–29), but the polis has no higher values in the face of which it could sacrifice its continuing existence. The state never risks its existence in order to let someone act virtuously, although the purpose of the state is that its citizens lead good lives. It never sacrifices its own life for the sake of this end.

IX. THE REVOLT OF THE JUST

The focus on stability raises two more questions, one of which I've already been talking about. First, this focus, as we've seen, makes it more difficult for virtue to play any role. "The greatest division perhaps is virtue and vice, then wealth and poverty, and so on, one being greater than another" (V.3.1303b15–17). Although virtue versus vice might be the greatest division, it's not one that characterizes faction or is a consideration for either ruler or ruled. Second, the same focus on moderation and stability seems to deny any role in politics for philosophy and the kind of arguments Aristotle supplies in the *Politics*. Philosophy either appears as an outside, imperial and neutral judge, in which case politics itself is no longer an activity, or the philosopher is an advocate no different from any other partisan, and philosophy becomes rhetoric.[22] In this section I will look more carefully at the role of virtue in politics, and then in the final section at the place of philosophy.

Book V's concerns with the politics of faction, then, are a particularly crucial place to see at work Aristotle's radical thesis that one can act virtuously only by acting as a citizen. More radically, trying to overthrow the constitution can never be the action of a citizen acting as a citizen. Those theses are especially hard to swallow—and have especially severe consequences—in situations of stasis and constitutional change. Aristotle's project in Books IV–VI is to show how an intelligent statesman can make the constitution better than the moral material he has to work with in the citizens. A role for citizens who are better than their constitution would interfere with this project.

Identifying a good man living in a bad state requires moral standards independent of the given constitution. Relying on such standards would prohibit the development of a fully political conception of the good life proper to Book V. Instead, the statesman should concentrate fully on stability and should not be distracted by his own conception of the good life, or anyone else's. Even if he has a better understanding of the good life than that embodied in the constitution, he is not better off acting on that conception. Deliberation must be concerned with what is best to do in a given situation, not what is best in abstraction. Compare these two remarks:

Those who excel in virtue would form a faction with the most justice of
anyone (though they do this least of all), for it is most reasonable to
regard as unequal without qualification these alone. (V.1.1301a40)
Those who excel in virtue do not cause faction, generally speaking; for
they are few against many. (V.4.1304b4–5)

The first gives no explanation for why there is no party of virtue. It only
says that the virtuous would be justified if they did form a faction. The second offers an explanation, but it has nothing to do with their being virtuous,
only being outnumbered. Aristotle gives no *principled* reason why there
should be no party of virtue.[23]

For Aristotle to succeed at demonstrating the unlikely truth that stability and progress come about through the development of the constitutional
ēthos of mutuality, he has to marginalize the very limited role that more
direct moral considerations play in destroying and preserving constitutions, even partially effacing the difference between monarchy and tyranny,
which otherwise are the constitutions at the greatest distance from each
other. Consider, for just one example, the parenthesis: "Men are stirred up
against one another by profit and by honor—not in order to acquire them
for themselves . . . but because they see others aggrandizing themselves
(whether justly or unjustly) with respect to these things" (V.2.1302a36–38).
The power of the politics of envy and righteous indignation is independent
of the validity of the accusations. It doesn't matter whether others are getting ahead justly. *Politics* V has its own moral purpose: to show how people's political nature can be fulfilled through an orientation to stability and
moderation. To explore how the moral qualities of particular actors within
political struggles affect their behavior would distract from his own moral
project. There is no room for philosopher-kings here. More importantly,
taking those moral qualities into account would distract from the moral
project of the statesman who aims at improving the state through stabiliz-
ing the constitution.

Constitutional stability and a constitution that aims at the good life
through aiming at stability is its own ethical project. Aristotle has removed
one relation between ethics and politics in order to establish another. The
world of faction is a world in which democrats and oligarchs struggle against
each other, and the virtuous must line up with one party or the other. There
isn't anywhere else to go in such a situation. Declarations that one is not a
democrat or an oligarch but acting for virtue alone would, probably rightly,
be regarded as deceptive partisanship. Disinterested virtue may have its
place in the more limited justice of the judge in the law courts, but the good

citizen and the good statesman are by definition partisans, and partisans who act in the name of impartial justice are no less partisans for that. The virtuous play no distinctive role in this sort of politics.

By refusing to recognize any special role for antecedent virtue or for justice as proportion to merit, Aristotle clears the way for his own kind of moral politics. In one sense, Aristotle lowers his ambitions to the best life one can have starting with the material the statesman is given: what counts here as living well might, by other standards and in other contexts, fall short of the best life. In another way, though, to show that a life of loyalty to a given constitution is a good life is a thoroughly ambitious project, one that makes moderation noble. This form of statesmanship persuades its followers and opponents that moderation is a political virtue and that the *ēthos* of acting politically should dominate the *ēthos* of any particular constitution.

Therefore the difference between the *Politics* and our own interests is more than simply perspectival. It isn't just that Aristotle is interested in the statesman's point of view while modern political theory, centering on obligation, takes the part of the citizen, the good or at least rational person compelled to do things he'd rather not do and even that he thinks are wrong or foolish. Aristotle's political philosophy has connections to the political wisdom of the statesman because the statesman's activities are intelligible, while those of the outsider, virtuous or not, are not knowable. The more knowable something is, the better it is. The causes of preservation are more knowable than the causes of destruction. Therefore preservation is a better activity than destruction. The activity of preserving a democracy or oligarchy—maybe even the monarchies and tyrannies discussed in the final chapters of Book V—can be a better activity than overthrowing these constitutions, regardless of how good the constitution itself is. The end product of destruction might be a better state than the result of preservation, but the activity is inferior. Book V is about that activity.

The rebel might, however, reply, so what? Isn't it simply moral fastidiousness always to do the best activity instead of aim at the best result? Aristotle must show that the difference in the quality of activity justifies the lack of a level playing field between insurgents and the defenders of the constitution. I don't think it is only readers coming to the *Politics* with our modern prejudices who should find this asymmetry, this categorical preference for virtuous action over good consequences, morally hard to swallow.

This predicament is familiar to readers of the *Rhetoric* and the *Ethics*. Aristotle's consistent lack of worry about the problem reveals an enormous gap between his thinking and ours. The *Rhetoric* argues for the superiority of persuasion through reasoning over other causes of persuasion. Rational persuasion is better than persuasion by any possible means because rational persuasion can aim at, and deliberate toward, a rational object, the internal end, finding the available means of persuasion. Aristotle doesn't assert that the rational rhetorician will necessarily or even probably win over his sophistic competitors, although he must believe that the rational rhetorician will win with sufficient regularity that its superiority isn't a matter of aristocratic disdain for consequences.

And similarly in the *Ethics*. Acting virtuously has good consequences, yet people who aim at making money will make more than the virtuous person, and professionals and people with nothing to lose sometimes make better soldiers (III.9.1117b17–20, see III.8.1116b13–15). He appeals to a sort of theodicy to maintain that happiness comes more from virtue than luck (e.g. I.9.1099b20–24; see *Top.* III.3.118b8–10, *Pol.* VII.13.1332a32, 1323b24–29, *EE* I.3.1215a13–19). In no case does Aristotle have anything to say about the person who faces an obvious dilemma. Given my opponent's sophistic tricks, if I stick to argument alone I will surely lose. How do I choose between the end of arguing as I should and the end of winning? If I act courageously against this superior force, my city will experience a glorious defeat. If I get up in the middle of the night and poison their food, I won't be courageous, but the city will be saved. Which good should I choose?

In the same way, *Politics* V has nothing to say about the virtuous person unjustly harmed by the rulers. This inquiry is about how to preserve constitutions, and if our sympathies today are sometimes with the righteous outsider, Aristotle has nothing to offer. He doesn't notice moral dilemmas because he's after bigger game. Looking to the larger project of constructing a political *science* makes Aristotle turn away from questions about deliberation in difficult circumstances. Aristotelian practical knowledge has a price.

The orator will uphold whatever position he is assigned. Such a person can't limit his trade to noble causes. However, in the process of defending the given cause, he will restrict himself to making arguments, not corrupting the audience through emotional appeals, bribes, or sophistical tricks. Rhetoric, then, develops its own ethics of argument, appreciating the value of rational argument over other means of victory. Such an ethical development is possible only if the speaker ignores antecedent morality, which would only be a distraction, both for himself, in making ethical choices, and for the audience, who must see external moral claims as irrational appeals to authority.[24]

Similarly, the statesman will defend the constitution he is given against faction. However, in the process of defending the given constitution, he will restrict himself to those means of stability that do more than counter the causes of faction. He will concentrate on those means that make the state stable by embodying the constitutional ēthos, ruling democratically or oligarchically rather than living democratically or oligarchically. The person of political wisdom chooses the right means for achieving stability. The right means are those that improve the state. There are no restrictions on the causes that may lead to the formation of factions or to their being successful—like the sophist, insurgents can do anything. But preserving the state requires more restricted means. They are limited to the constitutional ethos. While Aristotle does recommend some institutional devices that will achieve stability, the fundamental means of preserving constitutions is ethical, not institutional.

Should this satisfy my rebel who accused Aristotle of moral fastidiousness in promoting the best activity, even when opposed to a better result? Perhaps not. Aristotle's practical works are as little designed to overthrow that approach to practice as his theoretical works are meant to refute the skeptic. But at least we now can see that Aristotelian practical knowledge stands and falls with that correlation of goodness, knowability, and being. Since I can only know about being happy through acting virtuously, and not through being lucky, I should prefer to be happy through acting virtuously. This is a huge inference; if it is licit, it accounts for our paradox. I need to be ready to look a gift horse in the mouth. Since I can only know how to find the available means of persuasion, and not how to persuade, I should aim at finding the available means of persuasion. The more knowable something is, the more worth doing.

I think we can do a little better still in the political case than in either rhetoric or ethics. At V.7, Aristotle finds one difference between factions in aristocracies and polities and those already analyzed from democracy and oligarchy. Justice according to virtue can make these states more unstable than democracy and oligarchy, because it gives outsiders yet another reason to revolt. Aristotle lists three causes of faction unique to aristocracies. The first reason aristocracies fall is because "there are a number of men who are swollen with pride on the ground of being equal in virtue" (1306b27). Such men destabilize aristocracy more than democracy or oligarchy. The second is differences between rich and poor. All states contain such a difference, but in an aristocracy it is easier for the poor to make arguments from desert as well as need, since merit is supposed to be the principle of justice (1307a2). The poor man has nothing to complain about when told that justice is proportional to wealth, but anyone might feel injured by being excluded on the basis of virtue. Finally, "if someone is great and capable of being still greater, he may stir up faction in order to rule alone" (1307a3–4). Virtue can be a cause of instability, especially in constitutions that promise justice proportioned to virtue. In all these respects, aristocracy's commitment to justice as proportion to merit makes things worse.[25]

Earlier I mentioned the possibility that while the art of politics might be limited to preserving the state, the virtuous man might be able to judge that in a given case, he should overthrow the constitution. While the art of medicine is an art of healing, the physician can kill or cure; similarly, while the art of politics aims at preserving the constitution, any particular politician might choose to preserve or to overthrow one. Here, finally, we are in a position to see that that suggestion won't work. As the *Ethics* says: "In *technē* voluntary error (*ho hekōn hamartia*) is not so bad as involuntary, whereas in the sphere of *phronēsis* it is worse, as it is in the sphere of the virtues" (VI.5.1140b22–24; see *EE* VIII.1.1246a37–b8, *Met.* V.29.1025a6–13, *Poet.* 25.1461b9–12). To override stability, the end of politics, in the name of virtue is equivalent to a voluntary error, and a voluntary error in "the sphere of the virtues" is a self-destructive idea. If "it is with the same *phronēsis* that one should try to see both which laws are best and which are appropriate for each of the constitutions" (IV.1.1289a12), and if successful political life requires cooperation as well as a division of labor between the lawgiver and others acting with political wisdom, then the wise politician is not like the physician who might either kill or cure. There is never a conflict between the good man and the good citizen, and there is no higher law that tells an individual to reject the demands of his polis and its constitution. Aristotelian practical knowledge prevents us from doing some things that we would like to do, such as overthrow an imperfect constitution in the hopes of establishing a better one. By so doing, it also prevents the self-righteousness that often accompanies attempts to institute the rule of the just or the party of virtue. Finally, though, this orientation to practice allows us to do better things we couldn't do otherwise. Engaging in the moral project of *Politics* V is one of those better things.

My maxim that there is no party of virtue brings together a couple of the themes I see running throughout the *Politics*. The virtuous have no desire to rule over unwilling subjects, while ruling over unwilling subjects is the point of democratic and oligarchic factions. The virtuous have no desire to rule in such conditions because there's nothing in it for them. They will only rule when they can rule and be ruled in turn, exactly the opposite situation from stasis.

Therefore there is a gap, as I noted in chapter 3, between deserving the larger share in a constitution, because of merit, and deserving to rule. It isn't necessarily or always best, either for the virtuous or for the community, for the virtuous to rule. People involved in stasis see no gap, but that is because they want to rule in order to profit from it. Only someone with a desire to rule for its own sake could see the gap between being virtuous and deserving to rule and will attempt to supply a connection.

The question of why the virtuous should rule is the Aristotelian variation of Plato's philosopher reluctantly returning to the cave and not finding himself welcome. On analogy to the *Republic*, we need to ask why the virtuous should want to rule, or at least agree to do so, in any but the best of circumstances, and why they should be any good at it. The good man wants to rule in order to realize his nature as a political animal, who is someone who alternately rules and is ruled among equals. But then we have to ask to what extent being a political animal can be realized in the contentious and unstable world of factions, where ruling and being ruled in turn is the last thing on anyone's mind. Especially in the circumstances faced by the statesman in Book V, in addition to wanting to rule, why should either the virtuous person or the rest of the polis think that the virtuous person knows how to rule? The returning philosopher in the cave isn't very good at identifying shadows. Why should the virtuous person know what rulers should do under conditions of stasis? Machiavelli teaches that the successful ruler in such conditions—which he thinks is the human condition—must know how to be bad.

The asymmetry in *Politics* V, that statesmanship consists only in preserving, and never in changing, the constitution, has a counterpart in *Ethics* V's discussion of equity. Justice is itself asymmetrical: the just person will not always stand on her rights and take all she is entitled to; sometimes she will act justly by demanding less than she might (V.9.1136b20–21), while the unjust person seeks more than her share, never less (V.1.1129b1–5). This asymmetry lacks the morally problematic look of *Politics* V's prescriptions that we always act to preserve and strengthen the constitution, never to overthrow it, but the same one-sidedness is actually at work in both cases. And this asymmetry of justice carries over into the more specific actions of equity, in the following way.

The equitable person acts justly. He will correct the errors that come from the need for the law to state generalities. But those corrections only go in one direction. "The legislator falls short, and has made an error by making an unqualified rule (*hē paraleipei ho nomothetēs kai hamarten haplōs eipōn)*" (V.10.1137b21–22). An equitable decision only loosens the law, never tightens it. The equitable decision can say: the law dictates that this person should be found guilty, but had the lawmakers seen this particular case, they would have found him innocent. The equitable person acts justly and carries out the spirit of the laws. There is nothing equivalent on the other side. If the law dictates that this person should be found innocent, the equitable person can never override the law and find him guilty. That would not be acting lawfully or justly. It would be making a new law, not justly carrying out an existing one.[26] Later appeals to natural law might cut both ways, but equity does not.

There is a partnership, *homonoia*, between the lawmaker and the equitable judge, a partnership possible only if equity is one-sided. The statesman can institute good laws only by assuming that good men living under them will always try to uphold them and never overthrow them. The intelligent and virtuous lawmaker will recognize that his need to state the law in general terms will sometimes result in injustice in the particular. He will not object to the equitable judge acting in those cases. Knowing that in a good state the judges will be equitable, he can do his own job better, confident that they will do what he would have wanted to do. He can state the proper generalities of the law without worrying about having to specify every possibility because the law will be literally applied. In this way, the authors of the written U.S. Constitution could state some propositions in general form, using abstractions such as due process and equal protection, confident that judges and politicians will act equitably in obeying the Constitution. Someone writing a constitution who distrusted those who will execute the laws would have to write a different, and less just, document. Lawmakers who saw judges as competitors would be less successful as lawmakers.[27]

In the same way, the constitution and the person making it more stable are partners in a common activity. The statesman supporting the existing constitution is not a competitor to the constitution, while those engaged in faction, no matter how virtuous they suppose themselves to be, cannot be partners with the constitution. Such partnership is the friendship Aristotle mentions in V.9 when he lists the "three things that those who are to hold the supreme offices ought to have: first, *friendliness toward the established constitution (philian pros tēn kathestōsan politeian)*; next, great ability in the tasks of the office; and thirdly, virtue and justice—in each constitution the kind pertaining to that constitution" (V.9.1309a33–36). Trying to overthrow the constitution cannot be an act of friendship, and therefore cannot be an act of virtue. The good constitution will then leave room for the statesman, as the good lawmaker left room for the equitable judge.

X. POLITICAL PHILOSOPHY: INSIDE OR OUTSIDE THE POLIS?

In the last section I argued that virtue has no special role to play in the politics of factions. While true justice is proportion to merit, and the function of the state is to promote virtue, the statesman aims at stability, and the virtuous do not aim at remaking the state according to their own, better, understanding of politics. But it is worth asking the same questions about the authority of philosophy, whether philosophy knows something that the statesman needs to know.

The role of philosophy, like the role of virtue, faces the epistemological and ethical asymmetry I began with. Either the philosopher is a partisan, upholding one conception of justice as opposed to others, or a neutral judge, standing outside, and imposing his conception of justice on the others. Neither suits Aristotle's purposes.

Constitutions are unstable because the position of those excluded from the constitution is unstable; they are not citizens, since they do not participate in constitutional office, but they are citizens, as opposed to aliens, metics, slaves, and other noncitizen categories. While for purposes of governance someone excluded from citizenship is not a part of the state, for purposes of understanding factions, people who fail the test of a particular constitution but who could be citizens in other poleis still are citizens. There may be natural masters and slaves, but there are no natural citizens or noncitizens.[28] Those excluded from ruling still are citizens in the sense that they have to be persuaded, not commanded. Greeks show how civilized they are by distinguishing political from despotic rule, and consequently between political and despotic kinds of persuasion. While *Ethics* V.6.1134b10–17 says that we can only have full relations of justice and injustice among fellow citizens, *Politics* V.8 shows that we have to have relations of justice toward the free men who are not citizens under a particular constitution. This is not a shift from a more idealistic to a more realistic view, but a new challenge to political wisdom and to the uses of philosophy.

> One should see that not only some aristocracies but even some oligarchies last, not because the constitutions are stable, but because those occupying the offices treat well those outside the regime as well as those in the governing body—those who do not have a share, but not acting unjustly toward them and by bringing into the constitution those among them who have the mark of leaders, not acting unjustly toward the ambitious

by depriving them of prerogatives or toward the many with regard to profit. (*Pol.* V.8.1308a3–9)

The partial definitions of democracy and oligarchy put those whom they exclude into a practically unstable position, not quite out of the state and not quite in it, either, citizens by one standard and not by another. Faction is the rational response to such an ambiguous position.

Once the democrats and oligarchs in power realize the unstable status of the excluded, they have to rethink how to treat the opposition. While the distinction between correct and corrupt constitutions disappears from Book V, recognizing that one's constitution is one among many possibilities can make any constitution better. When I know that my democratic or oligarchic justice is only partial justice, I will extend relations of justice to noncitizens.

The great lesson philosophy has for political wisdom is that the statesman should not imitate the philosopher. The political science of Book III constructs the strongest scientific connections between terms: necessary connections. The strongest corresponding practical connection is a performative utterance. Science succeeds when its opposition is silenced. There are no counterarguments against necessary connections. Performative utterances, in which saying makes it so, similarly admit no rejoinders. But praxis fails when it tries to silence the opposition. Necessary connections become coercive. Tyranny, we learn at the end of Book V, is unstable. The statesman is better off with a logically weaker connection between constitution, city, and citizen, not a definition of constitution in which saying makes it so, but a persuasive and circumstantial definition of constitution that establishes probable, and desirable, connections between constitution, city, and citizen. Logically weaker connections can be ethically stronger. "Erotic necessities are probably better than geometrical necessities at persuading and compelling most people" (*Republic* V.458d). Aristotle repeats Plato's point, but as usual, toning down the passion.[29] The politician who tries to rely on philosophical authority or succeed by definitional fiat lives by logos alone. The statesman should instead make Aristotle's thesis, that constitutions define citizens, into an ethical proposition: constitutions define citizens not by fiat but by education which shapes the character.

It sounds odd to prefer a weaker argument, but there is an important sense in which we should. Politicians should not think that they can profit from the necessary connections of the philosopher because outsiders have to be persuaded that they will not be injured by being excluded, and that others should rule. "People governed in this way are necessarily governed well; the offices will always be in the hands of the best, while the people being willing and not envious of the respectable" (VI.4.1318b33–36).

Philosophical arguments become practical by becoming ethical. Aristotle contrasts Socratic dialogues with mathematical reasoning, the latter having no *ēthos* (*Rh.* III.15.1417a19–21). The *Politics* lays out arguments without *ēthos*, which the statesman then converts into ethical arguments. This, I suggest, is the way to understand Aristotle's claims that ethics and politics are practical sciences, ways of knowing that aim at action, without reducing practical discourse to rhetorical exhortation. That the *Politics* presents logoi to which the statesman's *ēthos* makes them into practical reasoning seems to me a more fruitful and accurate understanding of their relation than the idea that the statesman must "apply" the truths of the *Politics*.

In three respects, philosophy stands to the activity of the statesman as dialectical stands to rhetorical reasoning. First, the statesman has to weigh the probabilities of the likely arguments the philosopher presents. Thus we saw in Book III where Aristotle presented arguments for and against different constitutions, ranging from arguments for full democracy to those for an absolute king. All these arguments are plausible in the abstract, and the statesman has to decide their likelihood and probability in particular circumstances. Second, as we saw especially in this chapter, the philosopher only has to state the truth, while the statesman has to convince other citizens, and so has to not only be wise and good but appear to be wise and good. Finally, the statesman must convert the philosopher's logical arguments into ethical arguments, reasonings that require character as well as intelligence.

XI. PHILOSOPHY AND *PHRONĒSIS*: LOGOS AND *ĒTHOS*

Therefore I want to end this chapter by exploring this difference between ethical and logical argument, and so between what the philosopher knows and what the statesman knows. Thinking that some connection among ideas is necessary removes the need to create, develop, and fortify the relationship between people. Justice then makes friendship unnecessary. Philosophy makes bad rhetoric—certainty is unpersuasive—because it makes us think our job is done once we have made connections among ideas. When people refuse to accept putatively necessary relationships, the temptation is then to use compulsion, to force people to be free. Necessary connections remove the need for engaging the *ēthos* and passions of the parties being related. We should be glad that attempts to depopulate the moral world by replacing people with ideas fail.

In the face of constitutional change, the interdependence between constitution, city, and citizen that was a scientific virtue in Book III becomes a vicious circle. Noncitizens have no reason to accept the claims of the constitution, since those claims are partisan. *Anything* said in such a context is partisan, regardless of the truth or honesty, the virtue or the wisdom, of the speaker. In disputes between factions, both sides uphold competing conceptions of justice. In the context of factions, claims to justice as proportion to merit cannot exist as anything other than a partisan statement, which is why Aristotle does not promote a party of virtue. Using performative definitions to imitate Aristotle is an attempt to escape the world of partisanship into a pure realm of truth and justice. Demonstrative necessities become the pretext for silence and coercion. That is almost a definition of self-righteousness.

The crucial issue, then, is how the statesman can convert logical truths into ethical ones. Since practical argument will be more sensitive to circumstances, a single logical truth can be embodied in several different ethical arguments. How the necessary connections of Book III become practical truths depends on the *ēthos* of the particular constitution (IV.11.1295a40–b1, VII.8.1328a41–b2). *Ethos* gives meaning to abstract propositions; it determines which of the logically possible implications of a given proposition can be affirmed. In this case, an ethical argument must begin with the constitution that defines who is a citizen, and, via the democratic or oligarchic *ēthos*, leads to the conclusion that rulers must treat noncitizens well. That seems like a long distance to travel.

The philosopher offers two discoveries to statesmen about the relations between their respective activities. First, philosophy is incomplete. Except in rare circumstances—exemplified by the role of nature in *Politics* I and again in VII and VIII—philosophical truths cannot be directly instantiated; except in such circumstances it is an ethical and practical mistake to try. The incompleteness of philosophy creates an opportunity for autonomous decisions by the statesman. Deliberation concerns things that are up to us.

Second, the statesman has to learn the harder truth that the lack of constraint by philosophy or science does not mean the freedom to do as one likes, as democrats like to believe, or that might makes right, as oligarchs tend to think. The indeterminate nature of philosophical truth is an opportunity for practical deliberation about what is best in the circumstances. Philosophical truths are incomplete, but true nevertheless; they cannot be ignored but have to be incorporated into the statesman's character. "Man, as a principle of action, is a union of desire and intellect" (*NE* VI.2.1139b4–5). Practical philosophy is incomplete without *ēthos*.

The function of philosophy is to provide logoi that are made determinate through a particular *ēthos*. "Decision requires both understanding and thought and also a state of character; for acting well or badly requires both thought and character" (*NE* VI.2.1139a35). Practical wisdom acknowledges that the constitution defines who is a citizen, but it sees that thesis as raising the question of how citizenship *should* be defined. When we leave the realm of necessity we don't enter that of the arbitrary but the field of deliberation. This is the field of the probable, and it takes *ēthos* to judge probabilities. The constitution defines who is a citizen, and therefore the *ēthos* of the particular constitution will lead from the general principles of Book III to decisions about what to do. The particular *ēthos* of a particular constitution will lead from general principles to determinate decisions. It goes where philosophy cannot.

All deliberation is guided by a conception of what is best. The best, though, we learned at the beginning of IV.1, is ambiguous. The meaning of best appropriate for Book V is "best on a hypothesis" (IV.1.1288b17–33). The statesman who finds himself in a democracy or an oligarchy aims at the best by aiming at preserving the given constitution. Democratic and oligarchic constitutions are best maintained through an education in harmony with the constitution (V.9.1310a12–14). The ruler with a constitutional *ēthos* will treat outsiders well, not out of sympathy or interest, but because mutuality and friendship are part of his character, his *ēthos* as a ruler within this constitution.

The ethical and practical argument of Book V draws on another feature of the reasoning in Book III. The definition of citizen in Book III applies best in a democracy. There is no implication there, or elsewhere, that we should therefore prefer democracy. But we learn at V.8.1308a15 that *all* constitutions contain a *dēmos*, a people, within the rulers, who should treat each other equally and democratically. Even without the indefinite offices that Aristotle says define the constitution most properly in a democracy, there is an element of democratic *ēthos* in every constitution. Since factions arise not only from the people excluded from the constitution, but, especially in oligarchies, from within the ruling class (V.6.1305b11–37, 1306a13–20), preservation is as much a matter of how best to treat fellow citizens as how to treat the outsiders as equals.

Rulers treat fellow rulers democratically. Although they can't extend that courtesy to those excluded from the constitution, they still can treat these outsiders politically. While the strategy with regard to slavery is to maximize the distance between masters and slaves, the statesman aiming at security and trying to dampen the threat of factions should behave in the opposite way. Treating outsiders politically means, minimally, refraining from injustice. Injustice is only possible toward fellow members of a community. Therefore, however the constitution defines citizenship, and however justice is limited to fellow citizens, the constitution should never define our relations to noncitizens despotically. The statesman will maintain his constitution's distinction between citizens and noncitizens, but will not identify that distinction as a line between people one must treat justly and those outside the law whom one can treat despotically. Restricting justice in the full sense to the relations among fellow citizens does not preclude, but indeed implies, the application of justice in a looser sense to the other free people in the polis. The constitution may be restrictive, but the moderate *ēthos* of its rulers makes them extend friendship more widely.

Book V contains no answer to who should be a citizen apart from the partisan claims of democrats and oligarchs. The crux of the ethical argument comes in the discovery in V.9 that the best means of preserving states improve them. From the beginning of Book V we knew that the best means of preserving states makes them more stable and long-lasting. But I have only gradually argued for a connection between the stable constitution and the good constitution, because that connection is far from evident. In the *Rhetoric* Aristotle rejects the uses of *ēthos* defined outside the argument, one's reputation, or the trappings of character—for a modern example, the need of contemporary politicians to surround themselves with a multiracial backdrop—to make room for an *ēthos* developed by the argument itself (I.2.1356a8–13). An ethical argument is a better argument. Similarly, *Politics* V rejects antecedent distinctions of better and worse—some states are better than others, some revolts more justified—in order to develop the goodness of a constitution that comes from choosing the right methods of achieving stability. Insisting on the distinctions of Book III between correct and corrupt constitutions, between aiming at life and the good life, would only impede the ethical project of Book V.

This, then, is an ethical argument not only because the character of those making and receiving the argument is involved—the extreme democrats and oligarchs who see their position as the opportunity for despotism reveal their *ēthos* too—but in the more restricted and normative sense that such an argument engages *phronēsis*. The *phronimos* abandons what are here external standards of value in order to develop forms of political goodness within ethical activities of the statesman. He knows that the considerations of Book III are not by themselves a complete guide to action and that he must also rely on ethical considerations. Just as the statesman discovers democratic equality within any constitution, so he discovers justice as proportion to merit within the operations of stability.

Aristotle investigates the circumstances under which noncitizens will be satisfied with the rule of others, since that is how constitutions are preserved. For most people, he thinks, not being treated unjustly is good enough, and they are happy to avoid heavy burdens of active citizenship, especially if they can't make a profit from being in office (see too IV.13.1297b6–10). Instead of relying on definitional fiat, the statesman gets rid of faction by aiming at the good life, the good life under the flag of preservation.

Aristotle's own argument in *Politics* V embodies no *ēthos*. It has to be judged by scientific, not ethical, standards. The statesman using it takes those logoi and thinks through them ethically, deliberates about how they can lead to decisions and actions. He has to figure out what they mean in particular circumstances. The statesman will know how to mollify outsiders, making them less disposed to engage in faction, prevent the injustices against which factions react, and remove the occasions of faction that give them hope of success. That is the practical use of philosophy.

The *Politics* begins and ends with practical situations in which argument is unnecessary, the household of Book I and the ideal state of Books VII and VIII.[30] Slaves must be made to obey. If words work better than force, by all means the master should use words. But commands are not arguments, and there is no talking back. Wives, children and slaves who dispute the head of household's claim to rule should be punished and put in their place. At the other extreme, in the perfect state, since claims to rule based on freedom, wealth, and virtue coincide, there are no disputes about justice. Slaves may be necessary, as Book I argues, but can never be parts of the state. In the ideal state of Books VII and VIII, mechanics and laborers are similarly necessary conditions that are not parts of the state, while other states include such people as citizens. Under those constitutions, part of the virtue of political wisdom consists in the power of persuasion.

CHAPTER SIX

The Best Life and the Common Life

The last two books of the *Politics* explore the state and constitution that IV.1 calls "that which is best (for the best is necessarily fitting for the body that is naturally the finest and is most finely equipped)" (IV.1.1288a13–14), answering the questions of the "best regime, and what quality it should have to be what one would pray for above all, with external things providing no impediment" (a21). Here at the start of Book VII it is called the best constitution (VII.1.1323a14), and the city according to prayer (VII.1.1325b36). Describing such an ideal seems a pointless exercise in fantasy, so different from the down-to-earth character of the rest of the *Politics* that some commentators immediately infer that it must come from a more "Platonic" period in Aristotle's development. For me, instead it raises in its most acute form the question of how this inquiry into the ideal, and how political philosophy in general, could be practical. Politics almost by definition seems to be concerned with how to act in nonideal, constrained situations. Politics is the art of compromise and coercion and so is by definition circumstantial and contingent. There is a danger that when we abstract from those particular constraints, there will be nothing left for politics to think about—no disputes about justice threatening civil war, no scarcity or luxury to cause bad habits of arrogance or despair.[1] Spinoza is not alone in maintaining that if all people were rational, there would be no need for politics; in most formulations politics is necessary only because of human imperfections.

Aristotle opens Book VII saying that the statesman's judgments about the structure of the best state will be informed by knowledge of the best life. "Anyone who intends properly to investigate the best constitution must first determine which life is most choiceworthy" (VII.1.1323a14–16; see too VII.14.1333a14–16). Books III–VI studied good constitutions without first determining which life is most choiceworthy, and whatever he does here should not vitiate those other inquiries.[2] When he says that the best constitution requires knowledge of the best life, he must accept as a corollary that *only* an investigation of the best constitution requires that knowledge. The absence of undesirable and constraining conditions obliges the statesman to put the good life into clearer focus than needed, or possible, before. The natural question to ask about the beginning of Book VII is, why does understanding the best constitution, and only the best constitution, require knowledge of the nature of the best life? To answer that question is to understand the connection between the best constitution and the best life. I think the best way to move toward an answer is to follow Aristotle's argument in these Books, and in particular to notice precisely how Aristotle uses knowledge of the best life in discussing the best constitution.

For Aristotle, the focus of attention on the ideal constitution is that question of the relation between the best constitution and the best life. As we try to understand Aristotle, we must address a further, second-order question: how can considering the city of our prayers be practical? Unlike the proposed cities of Book II, this is not a model to be instantiated, nor an ideal to approximate: if the best state has very exclusive standards for citizenship, it does not follow that we can improve other states by tightening their requirements for citizenship. Aristotle recommends in the best state that all citizens own property both on the frontier and in the center, but there is no reason to think that approximating that condition would make other states better.[3]

Asking how this consideration of the best constitution can be practical recalls a puzzle I noted earlier. I mentioned in chapter 2 that while *Politics* II looks at the opinions of philosophers and private citizens (*hai men idiōtōnon hai de philosophōn* (II.7.1266a31–32), in the *Ethics* only people of practical wisdom and practical experience are worth listening to. What we know about the best life in the *Ethics* comes from generally acknowledged precepts and examples, nothing invented or discovered by the philosopher. The same holds for *Politics* III–VI; Aristotle's recommendations would be no surprise to a good statesman. The better the constitution, the greater the surplus of what the philosopher knows over what good statesmen know already. We come to know the ideal constitution in a different way, which allows more room for speculation not tied to practical experience; corresponding to the different access to the ideal constitution, our understanding the ideal constitution will lead to action in a different way as well.

This chapter's treatment of the city of prayer in Books VII and VIII turns on two textual questions, both concerning the relation between the best life and the best constitution, and both of which make the argument of Book VII much more complicated than apparently necessary. Here, as in the rest of my inquiry into the *Politics*, textual puzzles give us access to philosophical problems. I will first examine the first three chapters of Book VII, which Aristotle calls his preface, to show how their complex argument entitles him to talk about a constitution as happy and virtuous without falling into circularity and the fallacy of composition. The use of such predicates allows Aristotle to infer from the best life to the best constitution, and equally, from the best constitution to the best life.

However, those first three chapters are not Book VII's only discussion of the best life. Book VII in fact contains three separate examinations of the best life, not only in the first three chapters but again in chapters 8 and 13. I want to look in turn at each of the three discussions of happiness, to identify exactly what can be inferred from them in constructing the best state. Each of them is followed by a discussion of the kind of people who comprise the citizens of the best state, but those three discussions are quite different from each other. Chapters VII.1–3 poses the problem of how Aristotle moves to the nature of the best constitution from the nature of the best life. The rest of *Politics* VII and VIII raises the question of how he starts from both the best constitution and the best life and searches for their necessary conditions. Taken together, those two textual questions will illuminate the relation between the happy life and the best constitution, and so between ethics and politics. Then I will finally be in a position to show how the inquiry into the ideal can be practical.

I. BOOK VII.1

"Anyone who intends to investigate the best constitution in the proper way must first determine which life is most choiceworthy." Innocuous as the first sentence of Book VII might seem, in the context of the *Politics* it is surprising. Everything in the *Politics* until this point argued against making politics depend on an understanding of ethics.[4] Worse still, determining the best constitution by looking at the best life, as the beginning of VII.1 promises, suggests a fallacy of composition. Knowing who the best basketball player is, if there were such a thing, would not tell us what the best basketball team is—recall my example of Wilt Chamberlain in chapter 3. Knowing the best way for an individual to worship God does not dictate the structure of the best religious institutions. The *Iliad* shows that the best soldier does not dictate the best military organization.

That opening sentence seems to promise that Aristotle is about to derive the nature of the best constitution by presupposing his understanding of the best life. Nothing of the sort occurs. Aristotle never infers: Since the best life is a contemplative one, the state should be organized as follows: . . . Or, Since the best life is a political one, the constitution should contain the following features: . . . Instead, he examines the political life—and only the political life—to determine whether the same or a different way of life is choiceworthy in common and separately, and to sort through the ambiguities of that question. The question facing VII.1–3 is not, Which is the best life, but, Whether the best life is the same for an individual and "in common."

> Hence there should first be agreement on which is the most choice-worthy way of life for all, so to speak, and after this, whether the best kind of life common to all and to each citizen taken separately (*poteron koinēi kai chōris ho hautos hē heteros*) is the same or not the same. (1323a19–21)[5]

Aristotle's question looks pointless once we identify the best life. How could "agreement on the most choiceworthy way of life" not determine "whether the best kind of life common to all and to each citizen taken separately" are the same or not? Why do we need the intermediate step of agreeing on "whether the best kind of life common to all and to each citizen taken separately"? If the most choiceworthy life is a philosophical one, and if that is a life that is necessarily led separately—a supposition I will contest later—then the best life in common will be inferior to the best life. Conversely, if the best life is a political one, then a life lived separately would be second-best. If these two are the only plausible candidates for the most choiceworthy way of life for all, then the best life in common and separately will never be the same. Determining the best life will simply settle Aristotle's question about the individual and the common. That question, then, seems a distraction.

Here, in brief, is what I think is going on instead of the promised inference of the best constitution from the best life. The common life will show us the connection between the best life and the best constitution; it is the *relation* among those three—the best life, the common life, and the best constitution—that allows reasoning from one to another. He finds a best life that is the same for people living whether in common or separately. That life cannot be either the political or the philosophical life as commonly understood, since the political life is taken by definition to be common and the philosophical is taken to be necessarily separate.

The relation between the common life and either the best life or the best constitution is not straightforward, though, since "the common life" is ambiguous. Aristotle poses oppositions between the common and the separate seven times in the first three chapters. These oppositions contain two distinct issues between the common and the separate, but it takes until the end of chapter 3 before the two issues are clearly distinct.[6] The two issues are: First, is the best life for the individual the same whether it is the individual considered as living in common or as living apart? Second, is the best life of the individual the same as the best life for the polis? The best life for the *citizen*—the common life—is compared, alternately, to the best life for the individual and for the polis.

Here are the seven passages in VII.1–3 that oppose the individual to the common.

1. "Whether the same or a different way of life is choiceworthy [for men] in common and separately (*poteron koinēi kai chōris ho hautos hē heteros*)." (1323a19–21)

2. "Let us presuppose this much, that the best way of life both separately for each individual and in common for cities is that accompanied by virtue . . . (*kai chōris hekastōi kai koinēi tais polesin*)." (1323b40–1324a1)

3. "Whether happiness must be asserted to be the same both for a single individual human being and for a city (*hekastou tōn anthrōpon kai poleōs*) or not the same, however, remains to be spoken of." (VII.2.1324a5–6)

4. "A sensible person must necessarily organize matters with a view to the better aim both in the case of human beings individually and for the regime in common (*hekaston kai koinēi tēn politeian*)." (1324a35)

5. Those who advocate the political life as the best life argue "that in the case of each sort of virtue there is no more room for action on the part of private individuals than on the part of those who are active with respect to common matters and engage in politics (*eph' hekastēs aretēs ouk einai praxeis mallon tois idiōtais hē tois ta koina prattousi kai politeuomenois*)." (1324a40–1324b1)

6. "If these things are argued rightly and happiness is to be regarded as [the same as] acting well, the best way of life both in common for every city and for the individual would be the active one (*kai koinēi pasēs poleōs kai kath' hekaston*)." (VII.3.1325b15)

7. "It is evident, then, that the same life is necessarily best both for each human being and for poleis and human beings collectively (*ton auton bion anagkaion einai ton ariston hekastōi te tōn anthrōpōn kai koinēi tais polesi kai tois anthrōpois*)." (1325b30–32)[7]

I want to begin by concentrating on the first two passages, which begin and end chapter 1. The last two words of the chapter, *tais polesin*, have two possible meanings. To speak about life in common for cities could mean in common to men in cities, or it could be a common life led by the city itself, the "men in common." That latter reading is possible because from the beginning, Aristotle assumes without argument that poleis are the kind of thing one can talk about as virtuous and happy.

> It is impossible for those who do not do noble deeds (*ta kala prattousin*) to act nobly (*kalōs prattein*); and no action (*ergon*), whether a man's or a city's, is noble when separate from virtue and *phronēsis*. But the courage, justice, and *phronēsis* of a polis have the same capacity and are of the same kind (*dynamin kai morphēn*) as those possessed by each human being who is said to be just, practically wise, and temperate. (VII.1.1323b31–36)[8]

Aristotle takes it as obvious that poleis are the sort of thing to which the predicate "happy" applies, making the connection between the best life and the best polis seem more obvious than it really is. He should know better. He criticizes Plato for making happiness apply to the whole without necessarily applying to the parts, saying that happiness is not like "evenness" (II.5.1264b15–24), and criticizes the Spartan constitution for making the polis poor and private individuals into lovers of money (II.9.1271b15–16). We have to see whether Aristotle can plausibly talk about happy and virtuous poleis without committing the fallacy of composition. Unless virtue and happiness apply to states more than just metaphorically, there isn't any argument here.

Leaving that assumption aside for the moment, the next step in the argument is more interesting. The inference to the conclusion that cities and people must both be virtuous is licensed by the axiom that potentialities are proportional to activities, *dynameis* to *energeiai*. (Without that axiom, Aristotle could never infer from a potentiality to an actuality or the other way around.) If a state acts nobly, and if noble actions are the same for the polis and the individual, then the *dynamis* that makes noble actions possible for the state must mirror the *dynamis* for the virtues in an individual.

For this argument to work, however, Aristotle must ignore the fact that the ethical virtues are themselves *energeiai* of a prior *dynamis*, the powers inherent in the appetitive and persuadable part of the soul. The virtues of the state cannot be the *energeiai* of that part of its soul, because even happy states don't have souls.[9] That is, Aristotle's argument, which depends on the assumption that *energeiai* are proportional to *dynameis*, requires us paradoxically to *deny* that *energeiai* are proportional to *dynameis* when we look at the ethical virtues, which are, for individuals, the *energeiai* of a previous psychic *dynamis*, and which in states are not. The argument of the *Ethics* reveals the nature of happiness by exploring the virtues; it doesn't determine the nature of the virtues by looking at some independently understood happiness. Here Aristotle reverses that order of inference: for the state to be happy, it must have the ethical virtues.

The idea that states can be happy and virtuous depends, then, on both affirming and denying the idea that *dynameis* are proportional to *energeiai*. Aristotle can do both without contradiction only if the *Politics* has even less psychological depth than the *Ethics*, and the treatment of the absolutely best state even less than the rest of the *Politics*.[10] If polis and individual have the same virtues without having the same underlying *dynameis*, then the psychological aspects of the virtues central to the *Ethics* become politically irrelevant.

The first important consequence of this lack of psychological depth is that while through the rest of the *Politics* Aristotle distinguishes economic acquisition from despotism, in Book VII they are interconnected.[11] An individual might want an unlimited accumulation of external goods but have no interest in mastering other people, except as that furthers his material ambition. Another might desire to rule over others but not care about amassing possessions, except as instruments of rule over people. Sometimes they are even incompatible: "People resort to faction because of inequality not only of property but of honors, although in opposite ways in each case: the many do so because of inequality of property; cultivated people because of honors, if they happen to be equal. . . . No one becomes a tyrant to escape the cold" (II.7.1266b36–1267a14). When it comes to poleis, though, the ambitions to rule other men and own external goods coincide.

There is another difference between virtue as it appears in *Politics* VII and VIII and in the *Ethics*. In the *Ethics* we become virtuous by performing virtuous actions of the same kind. We become just by acting justly, witty by acting wittily, temperate by acting temperately, and so forth. There is no general education for virtue. But in *Politics* VII and VIII, music is precisely that general moral education. It develops character. Music does not develop capacities for action: we don't become able to act courageously by hearing music in the right modes or by watching Achilles. But music develops our capacities for responding with pleasure and pain to the appropriate objects, and in that way develops character. Music develops the love for the noble that the end of the *Ethics* tells us is necessary prior to the habituation that leads to the specific virtues. At the end of this chapter I will look more closely at music, which is not mentioned until Book VIII.

Aristotle can talk about states being virtuous and happy only because of this psychological superficiality. It is for that reason that Aristotle ends this argument by begging off talking about it further, in a passage that ends VII.1 with my second passage:

> So much, then, for the preface to our discussions. For we cannot avoid talking about these issues altogether, but neither can we go through all the arguments pertaining to them, since this is a task for another type of study. Let us presuppose this much, that the best way of life both separately for each individual and in common for cities (*kai chōris hekastōi kai koinēi tais polesin*) is that accompanied by virtue. (1323b37–1324a1)

II. NATURE VERSUS JUSTICE

Along with psychological depth, something else is absent from the treatment of the best state—justice. In Books VII and VIII, Aristotle uses the language of nature to talk about the best life, as he did in Book I, while in Books III–VI, the language of justice framed the good constitution. After the invention of individual rights, these two languages are connected, but in Aristotle's thought they are incompatible.[12] (That incompatibility prevents Books VII and VIII having as an unintended consequence a refutation of Books III–VI, since the languages of justice and nature do not meet.) The lack of attention to justice leads to problems: it seems to contradict his criticism of the *Republic* in Book II for forgetting that a polis is made up of people both equal and different in kind (II.2.1262a22–24, see too III.4.1276b20–1277a10,

IV.3.1290a2–7). Ignoring justice, that is, is a lack of attention to the nature of the specifically political community since justice *is* the political relation of part and whole. Aristotle's shift from the language of justice to the language of nature makes it easier to neglect issues of distribution that would question the part/whole analogy.[13]

For that reason, Aristotle's arguments for the identity of happy and virtuous communities and happy individuals work equally well for families, which are made up of people who are different but unequal, and for alliances and exchange relations, which are made up of people who are equal, equal enough to enter into voluntary contractual relations rather than relations of domination and despotism (II.2.1261a24–29). But there are no happy alliances and exchange relations because such things do not have enough unity to be happy or for other moral predicates to attach to them. None of these is self-sufficient, and only self-sufficient communities and individuals can be happy. None of them has something common in the right way. Aristotle seems guilty of the same fallacy he accuses Plato of committing.[14]

Whether poleis are literally happy and virtuous points to the philosophical problem that animates *Politics* VII. In contrast to other kinds of association, for the polis and only for the polis, self-sufficiency for the individual and the community are not at odds, and yet neither is simply derivative from the other. The more self-sufficient and virtuous the citizens, the better and more self-sufficient the polis.[15] "What is more self-sufficient is more choiceworthy, what is less a unity is more choiceworthy than what is more so" (II.2.1261b14–15). People need to join communities, including the polis, because they are *not* self-sufficient but need each other: the polis "comes to be for the sake of living, but it remains in existence for the sake of living well" (I.2.1252b28). People enter exchange relations because they are not self-sufficient, but they don't become self-sufficient as a result of their commerce.[16]

The fundamental problem of the entire *Politics* is to work out the difficult dimensions of the apparently innocuous claim that humans are political animals. People lead complete, self-sufficient, and happy lives by being part of a complete and self-sufficient community (*NE* I.7.1097a8–11, IX.8.1169b16–19). Every stage in Aristotle's argument has to avoid the dangers of one side of self-sufficiency obliterating the other, either the state providing the background conditions in which individuals can lead autonomous lives or individuals sacrificing themselves for the good of the whole, what could be called the liberal and totalitarian (or republican) options. If the virtue of the part is simply derivative from the virtue of the whole, then the individual won't be truly virtuous or self-sufficient. Private vices could be public benefits. If the virtue of the polis is a collective idea, as the wealth of nations derives from the aggregate wealth of citizens, then the polis won't have enough unity to be self-sufficient. In neither of these cases will the fact that the polis is made up of people different in kind be relevant. In those cases, inference from the best life to the best constitution is easy, and there are no dangers of the fallacy of composition. According to philosophers such as Rawls, it is to prevent such inferences that liberalism was invented. If so, Aristotle is not open to the liberal criticism.[17]

If poleis and individuals are both kinds of things to which happiness applies, it seems we have a substance made of substances, which the *Metaphysics* declared impossible (VII.13.1039a3–6; see VII.11.1036b30–32, 10.1035b23–25, VII.16.1041a3–5, 1040b14).[18] This is an abstract way of putting the problem of self-sufficient people coming together in a self-sufficient whole. The argument of Books VII and VIII must come to terms with the connection between the self-sufficiency of the individual and of the polis, so that a happy and complete polis can be made up of happy and complete human beings, without reducing the one self-sufficiency to the other, as occurs in forms of association other than the polis. The *economic* self-sufficiency of the polis can be defined apart from any economic self-sufficiency on the part of citizens or families, since these parts are never economically self-sufficient. But the political self-sufficiency of the polis is simply a structure in which people can lead happy lives.

The contrasts between the separate and the common allow Aristotle to explore those connections between the self-sufficiency of the polis and the individual without circularity, but only when discussing the ideal constitution. For the rest of the *Politics*, what makes something a state and what makes it a particular state are distinct, and that divergence drives individual and communal self-sufficiency apart. While reciprocal equality is called the preservative of cities (II.2.1261a29–31, *NE* V.8.1132b31–34, 1133a1–2, 11, 24–28, 1133b5–8, 15–16; see *Laws* 757b–d), *distributive* justice gives each constitution its specific identity. Only for the ideal constitution is Aristotle entitled to ignore questions of distributive justice. The constitution of Books VII and VIII has no specific identity.

Justice leaves the discussion as happiness and the good life enter. Books III–VI approach questions of the good constitution by looking at constitutional *forms*, which is where we find justice. Books VII and VIII articulate the best constitution instead by looking at its *ends*, the best life. *Politics* III–VI defines the best life, the end, as an expression, an *energeia*, of a good form. Therefore, all we know about the good life in those books is through the contrast between living and living well, which was allied at different points with the contrasts between constitutions that aim at the good of the whole versus the good of the rulers, proper versus degenerate constitutions, and rule of law versus the rule of men. In *Politics* VII–VIII, when the end is discussed explicitly, formal structure becomes secondary, and Aristotle has to flesh out what it is to live well.

A sign of the shift from a focus on the forms of political life to direct attention to the end of political life is that where Book III claims that the specifically "political good" is justice, which is equivalent to the common advantage (III.12.1282b16), VII.8 argues instead that citizens of the best state share in happiness (1328a27–37). Books III–VI almost never mention happiness, while VII and VIII are silent about justice. We have come a long way from concerns about shared property in Book II.

So far, then, I see two important differences between the treatment of the ideal state and the rest of the *Politics*: Books VII and VIII claim that you have to know about the best life in detail to identify the best constitution, and they shift attention from the form of the good constitution, and therefore justice, to the end of the good constitution, and therefore nature. Before we're done with the "preface," we will see a third.

III. BOOK VII.2

Aristotle continues to dismiss these questions of distribution and causation even when he distinguishes ethical and political issues. It is evident, VII.2 begins, that "the happiness of each individual is the same as that of a polis" (1324a5). He continues:

> Two questions need to be investigated, however. First, which life is more choiceworthy, the one that involves taking part in politics with other people and participating in a polis, or the life of an alien cut off from the political community? Second, and regardless of whether participating in a polis is more choiceworthy for everyone or for most but not for all, which constitution, which conditions of the polis, is best? This second question, and not the one about what is choiceworthy for the individual, is a task for *political* thought (*tēs politikēs dianoias kai theōrias*). (1324a14–20)

At VII.1 Aristotle seemed to deny the separation of ethical and political questions asserted here. Separating them, as he just did, rejects the immediate inference from best life to best constitution. But how can he ask the political question, which constitution is best, "regardless of whether participating in a polis is" the best life? Isn't that decision fundamental to the choice of the best constitution? We can't directly derive the best constitution from the best life, but can't think of the best constitution as neutral among competing conceptions of happiness, either. Finding a third alternative besides those two, which could be called Platonist and liberal, is Aristotle's contribution to practical political science.

Aristotle seems to be trying to have it both ways, making politics fundamental to ethics and ethics basic to politics, which is why, after answering a question in chapter 1, he raises it again at the start of chapter 2—"which life is more choiceworthy"—and then says the answer is obvious.

> Whether happiness must be asserted to be the same both for a single individual human being and for a city (*hekastou tō anthrōpon kai poleōs*) or not the same, however, remains to be spoken of. But this too is evident: all would agree that it is the same" (1324a5–6).[19]

After saying that it is obvious that happiness is the same for the individual and for the polis, chapter 2 immediately goes on to argue for that identity anyway, but the argument here differs from that in chapter 1. There the definition of happiness as virtuous activity applied to both state and individual. The beginning of chapter 2 argues more broadly that, whatever end people pick—wealth, despotism, or virtue—they will still see the same end for city and individual. Chapter 1, thus, argues: since the best life is one of virtuous activity, it must be the same for the individual and the polis. Chapter 2 argues: since the best life is to be the same for the individual and the polis, it must be a life of virtuous activity.[20] Combining the two creates a biconditional that allows not only for the inferences Aristotle claims to make from the best life to the best polis, but also inferences from the best polis to the best life.

Aristotle really does get to have it both ways. The treatment of the best city and the common life makes clear how ethics and politics require each other, an idea that has more teeth now than ever. The interrelations Aristotle develops between ethics and politics uncovers the inadequacy of the usual staged debate between the political and the philosophical lives. Advocates of both lives deny the connection between ethics and politics. Partisans of philosophy assume the philosophical life is not informed by its political context, and devotees of the political life deny an ethical dimension to politics, since the only existing states that organize themselves toward a coherent aim identify the active life with the life of domination and hegemony (1324b5–22). If the definitions of the best life for the individual and for the city implicate each other, then both groups of partisans will need to be corrected; the payoff will be a new understanding of both the political and the philosophical lives.[21]

We have to figure out what the best life is, he says, because that will guide us in making the best constitution: "a sensible person must necessarily organize matters with a view to the better both in the case of human beings individually and for the regime in common" (*hekaston kai koinēi tēn politeian*) (1324a35). But a few lines later the opposition is slightly different. Advocates of the political life as the best life argue "that in the case of each sort of virtue there is no more room for action on the part of private individuals than on the part of those who are active with respect to common matters and engage in politics" (*eph' hekastēs aretēs ouk einai praxeis mallon tois idiōtais hē tois ta koina prattousi kai politeuomenois*) (1324a40–1324b1; see *NE* X.8.1179a3–6). These were my fourth and fifth citations. This fifth contrast is stated only for those who think that the political life is the best life. One must wonder whether it would be equally true, or even make sense, for those who think the philosophical life the best. Is there a difference, that is, between contemplation engaged in by a private individual and by political men? At the end of this chapter, I will argue that the treatment of music in Book VIII shows what the contemplation conducted by citizens looks like.

IV. BOOK VII.3

Which is more choiceworthy, Aristotle asks, "the life of politics and action (*ho politicos kai praktikos bios*) or a life detached from all external affairs, for example, a theoretical life (*theōrētikos*), which some say is the only life for the philosopher" (1324a25–29)?[22] By the terms of the debate that Aristotle inherits, the practical life *is* the political life, while the theoretical life is not a common life or a civic life at all; it is the life of an alien removed from political community (*ho xenikos kai tēs politikēs koinōnias apolelumenos*) (1324a17). Neither side of the debate thinks the other is truly active: those who favor the philosophical life think all political activity is despotic and constrained, and those on the side of politics think it the only way of being active. These partisans are more extreme than Aristotle in the *Ethics*, who, after settling on *theōria* as the best life, calls the political life happy "in a secondary way" (X.8.1178a9).[23]

Chapter 3 discards those partisan identities: "Some reject the idea of holding political offices in the city, believing that the life of the free man differs from that of the political man" (*tou eleutherou bion heteron tina einai tou politikou*) (1325a18). Some people, at least, think there can be a good private, nonpolitical, but practical life, a good life that is neither political nor philosophical. If that is possible, what about the final option, a life that is both political and theoretical? Book VIII, the life of leisure (*scholē*) centering on music is not the life of a stranger but of a citizen, and this life presents exactly this possibility: life that is neither recognizably political nor philosophical, but which satisfies the criteria he offers here for both those lives. The life of leisure is the political life, stripped of its commonly misunderstood tendency to despotism, and it is the philosophical life, stripped of its connotation of isolation. Properly understood, we now see the two competing lives, or at least what is best about them, are the same. The life of leisure is a perfectly active life. Aristotle the political philosopher puts both the political and the philosophical lives in their proper places.

In this way Aristotle does in Books VII and VIII something he never does in Books III–VI. The philosopher stands above a dispute and then offers his own mediation. In Book III he said that all poleis, or at least all democracies and oligarchies, are based on partial ideas of justice, but he refused to see the possibility of embodying a nonpartial idea, and in Book V he said that factions and instability come from partiality, but he did not there offer completeness as a remedy. Political philosophy cannot overcome disputes about justice; the philosopher will not be on the side of democratic or oligarchic justice, arithmetic or geometric equality. In chapter 5 I looked at the political function of philosophy in the situations of factions that Books V and VI explore, and remarked how the philosopher could be neither a partisan nor a neutral judge. Here, in contrast to disputes about justice, philosophy does settle questions about the best life. Philosophy, then, has more to say when attention turns from the best constitutional form to the best end. Not only does the best constitution have room for philosophical activity within the state, the statesman thinks about philosophical problems in establishing the constitution.

As the standing of the political philosopher changes, so too does the way in which political philosophy can be practical. Philosophy has a more independent role in thinking about the ideal state. Paradoxically, it has no independent role in the state itself. The contemplative life in the ideal state is a common life of enjoying music instead of contemplating unmoved movers or other worthy objects by oneself. At the beginning of the chapter, I noted the psychological thinness of the *Politics*. Not only does it not look very deep, it doesn't look very high, either. That is, while ethical activity eventually points beyond itself to the contemplative life at the end of the *Ethics*, political life is more strongly self-contained. There is nothing in the *Politics* parallel to the remark in the *Ethics* that "man is not the best thing in the universe" (VI.7.1141a20–21).

Aristotle answers the specifically political question about the best individual life, not by comparing the political and philosophical lives, as he does in the *Ethics*, but by focusing on the political life alone, asking how it can be a happy life, active and noble, worth choosing for its own sake. Only the political life comes in for scrutiny here because, as he shows later, the philosophical life makes no claims with political consequences. At VII.14.1333a28, he will tell us that exercising theoretical reason "must be more choiceworthy to anyone who can carry [it] out." All citizens in the best state can engage in choiceworthy acts of practical reason. Some of them, though, aren't up to philosophy. Such inequality however, is practically irrelevant. Those capable of *theōria* have no special political privileges or prerogatives.[24] Once we understand the true nature of the best practical life, we know all we need to know, for planning the best constitution, about philosophy. In the *Ethics* we learn about the nature of the philosophical life from a comparison to the gods, but in the *Politics* we learn about the political life from a comparison of individuals to *poleis*.[25]

Chapter 3 of Book VII ends with an inference from the best state to the best individual: because cities can be active by themselves (*kath hautas*), so can individuals. Activity "can come about on the basis of [a city's] parts: there are many sorts of community that belong to the parts of a city in relation to one another. This is available in a similar way to any individual human being as well." He therefore concludes that "it is evident that the same life is necessarily best both for each human being and for *poleis* and human beings collectively" (1325b30–32), my seventh and final quotation. Aristotle now sees himself in a position to proceed from his "preface" about the best life to considering the best constitution, and the conditions necessary for the best state.

By the end of chapter 3, my seven passages comparing the individual and the common have led to formulating two distinct issues: (a) whether the best life for the individual is the same as the best life for the polis, and (b) whether the best life for the individual considered in isolation is the same as the best life for the person who lives with others. Confusing the two issues creates the standard clash between partisans of the political and the contemplative lives.[26] Gradually separating the two issues, Aristotle develops his argument about a best life that must be active but not necessarily political. We can now think about happy, *common* lives, not political as opposed to philosophical or philosophical as opposed to political lives.

Book VII began with the announcement that it was going to reason from part to whole, from the best individual life to the best constitution. In fact, the crux of the argument goes in the other direction. Thinking about the polis as happy and virtuous helps us to see how a political life can be happy because Aristotle's argument clarifies the relation between activity and virtue. VII.1 says that "the virtues are not acquired and preserved by means of external goods, but the other way around, and that a happy life for human beings . . . is possessed more often by those who have cultivated their characters and minds to an excessive degree, but have been moderate in their acquisition of external goods" (1323a38–1323b4).[27] Chapters 2 and 3 argue at length for the same point, but for the polis rather than the individual. The happy life is the most active life. But most active, we learn by looking at the happy polis, does not mean most dominating. The attention of the happy polis will be on the internal political activities of peace, especially education, not the foreign relations of war and commerce. Seeing happiness writ large in the polis helps us to understand happiness in individuals. The polis shows that activity need not be toward another, a truth easier to grasp and accept for poleis than for individuals. If "a single polis can be happy all by itself, provided it is well-governed" (1325a1), then so can an individual.

The individual zealous for virtuous activity might wonder why he should be restrained by the demands of mutuality involved in ruling and being ruled. But the polis will not conquer other poleis whenever it has the opportunity, despite the fact that the restraint on poleis seems even less than on individuals: poleis do not have relations of justice toward each other and owe each other nothing. If states shouldn't aim at domination, then neither should individuals. There is equality among states, even though it is not equality under law. Rather, it is equality in neither ruling nor being ruled. Aristotle supplies an argument against domination that does not depend on universal human rights, national sovereignty and self-determination, or any other modern idea. Similarly, then, so long as there is an equality among people, it will be unjust to rule permanently, even if ruling is the fullest exercise of one's own virtue.

In the best state, the good man will be happy through ruling. He will not infer, though, that to rule more—ruling permanently or ruling over more people—will make him happier. He can be "excessively cultivated," in the words I just quoted from VII.1, without that leading to domination. In my first chapter I said that in Aristotle's mind, slavishness could not be an attractive option, while despotism was a permanently appealing possibility. Despotism may be wrong, and it is a wrong interpretation of self-sufficiency, but people, especially the young, ambitious men who are Aristotle's audience, don't see it as disgraceful. In chapter 1, I examined the passage in VII.7 in which Aristotle states that the same combination of thought and *thumos* allows for both friendship and domination. Therefore, ruling and being ruled in turn has throughout the *Politics* appeared on the verge of becoming a compromise between the ideal of always ruling and the greatest evil, always being ruled by another. Domination must be a temptation even for the virtuous, as it appears to afford more opportunity for virtuous activity.

At this point Aristotle can offer a response to that temptation that doesn't rely on the analogy to poleis. Ruling more would mean forfeiting the relations of equality necessary for friendship and happiness. If ruling over equals is the best activity, one has to insure that that rule will not make the others unequal. One lives a complete and self-sufficient life by being part of a complete and self-sufficient community, and permanent rule prevents such a community.

> Perhaps one might come to believe that authority is the best of all, for it is in such a way [i.e. with authority] that one could perform the greatest number of the most noble actions. So a man who is able to rule should not give it up to a neighbor but rather take it away from him . . .
>
> Now perhaps it is true for them to say this, if indeed the most choiceworthy things can be attained by plunderers and men who use violence. But certainly this cannot be the case and is falsely assumed; for if the ruler is not as much superior to the one ruled as a man is to his wife or a father is to his children or a master is to his slaves, his actions may no longer be noble. So a transgressor might not succeed later in recouping as much as he has already lost by deviating from virtue; for, among peers, the noble and the just should be shared by turns, as this is fair and alike to all. (VII.3.1325a34–b8; see *NE* 1122a3–7)[28]

Good citizens place the right value on political activity, and so neither desire to rule permanently nor to avoid rule. They have learned the hard lesson that just because an activity is intrinsically good doesn't mean that one should engage in it as much as possible, regardless of circumstances.[29] Good people don't so much desire to rule as desire to participate in a community of alternating ruling and being ruled. The rulers in such a polis are then simply people of the right age. The organization of the best polis is so minimal that a natural distinction between young and old is enough to distinguish ruler and ruled. Constitutional form is unnecessary, and Books VII and VIII contain none of the detailed descriptions of different offices we find in IV–VI.[30]

People with political wisdom understand why they should resist the temptations of permanent rule and despotism. The virtues must create and preserve their own enabling conditions, the conditions under which they can be successful.[31] If the function of virtue were not to foster its own enabling conditions, then having to engage in politics would constrain my best life, or I would forfeit opportunities to engage in the best activity, politics, by letting others have their turn at ruling. True, at any moment, I give up something by ruling and being ruled in turn. I forfeit opportunities not only for profit and honor, but for exercising virtue, by letting others rule instead of doing as much as I can myself. But if virtue sustains the conditions for its development and success, I give nothing up in alternating ruling and being ruled. Ruling over equals is a better, a more fulfilling, activity than ruling over unequals. Since one shouldn't desire to rule over unequals, one shouldn't desire to be unequal. The price one pays for ruling over equals is not to rule permanently but to rule and be ruled in turn.[32] Therefore, finally, chapters 1–3 show us that the best human life is a common life, and therefore a political life, but not a political life as usually conceived. The common life is a practical life that is its own end.

V. BOOK VII.4–7

After establishing what happiness and the best life is, Aristotle appears to be in a position to explore its political consequences and figure out what the ideal constitution and state look like. But chapters 1–3 must somehow be inadequate because Book VII contains two further discussions of happiness, in chapters 8 and 13, and he gives no reason for this movement back and forth between considerations of happiness and of the best state.[33] To make things worse, the connection between the discussions of happiness and the discussions that follow concerning the material relative to that end is not obvious. Aristotle never argues along the lines of hypothetical necessity outlined in *Physics* II.9.200a11–15: Since the end of the state is happiness, these consequences follow for the nature of citizens, laws, territory, education, or anything else. When we looked at chapters 1–3, I asked how Aristotle explores the nature of the best constitution by starting from the nature of the best life. Here I wonder how he starts from both the best constitution and the best life and figures out their necessary conditions. We will find that there must be a difference between reasoning about means toward ends in general and reasoning about means toward ends that are activities chosen for their own sakes. Looking at how Aristotle reasons will help us understand the relation between political philosophy and the knowledge and activities of the statesman. That, finally, will put us in a position to understand how political activity can be chosen for its own sake, and how music can provide the education to produce virtuous citizens and at the same time the highest activity for citizens, both political and philosophical.

The first three chapters contain the *Politics*'s most extended discussion of the best life. Once that discussion is over, Aristotle seems to begin again without drawing on what he has just argued. Chapter 4 begins: "Since what has just been said was by way of a preface, . . . the starting point for the remainder of our investigation is first to discuss the conditions that should be presupposed to exist in the ideal polis we are about to construct" (1325b33–36). It is hard to see any connection between the preface and this inquiry into the presupposed conditions. First among such conditions is the population. Aristotle rejects the idea that the more, the better. A bigger state is not a better one: chapter 4 begins by refuting the idea that "a happy polis must be a great one. . . . They judge a polis to be great if the number of its inhabitants is large, whereas they ought to look not to number but to ability (*dynamis*)" (1326a8–13). When looking at Book V, I noted that the longer-lasting a polis, the better, while that criterion did not apply to good individuals. What is true for time is not true for space: the more long-lasting the constitution the better, but it is not true that the bigger the state, the better. "A city made up of too many persons with respect to the necessary things may be self-sufficient (*en tois men anagkaiois autarkēs*) like a nation, but it is not a polis, for it is not easy for a constitution to be present" (VII.4.1326b3–5).

Looking at VII.1–3, we saw that just because ruling was an activity worth doing for its own sake, it did not follow that the more one ruled, the better one's life. Similarly here. The argument of 1–3, and in a different way the argument of chapter 4, make happiness, virtue, and self-sufficiency into threshold conditions: once one is free rather than a slave, it doesn't make

sense to talk about further degrees of freedom. Self-sufficiency has one contrary: conditions that fall short of self-sufficiency. Self-sufficiency is not a
mean between extremes.[34] Otherwise freedom would be relative: the free
man would become, in the presence of the individual of outstanding virtue,
a natural slave. "It cannot be that the difference [between master and slave]
is one of degree. Ruling and being ruled differ in kind" (I.13.1259b36–37).[35]
A bigger state will not necessarily be a happier state.

This conclusion doesn't seem profound. But it is a clear example of the
mode of practical reasoning Aristotle has been practicing less obviously in
the first three chapters, and in the rest of VII and VIII, and the distinction
between the economic autarchy of a nation and the ethical and political
self-sufficiency of a polis helps explain the odd form of argument Aristotle undertakes. Maximization has an entirely different meaning from what
it would be if the chief good were something that could be bought, con-
quered, seduced, or otherwise acquired. An end which can be acquired and
possessed is different from an end which is an activity chosen for its own
sake. The deliberation about what to do for the first kind of end has to be
different from the thinking about the second. Therefore, chapters 4–7 and
the remainder of Book VII do not have the appearance of reasoning from
hypothetical necessity or practical deliberation, but in fact reason in a way
appropriate to an active highest good.

The ideal state shouldn't be too small or too large. But there is an asymmetry here. Once a polis is self-sufficient, it is not obvious that making it
bigger does any harm, just as the individual striving for more opportunities to exercise virtue is not obviously wrong. The issue is whether self-
sufficiency is a threshold concept, whether an organized whole can lose its
self-sufficiency by being too large. Aristotle's reasons for claiming that a
polis cannot be too large look quite weak.

> A polis that consists of too few people is not self-sufficient (whereas a
> polis is self-sufficient), but one that consists of too many, while it is self-
> sufficient in the necessities, the way a nation is, is still no polis, since it
> is not easy for it to have a constitution. For who will be the general of its
> excessively large multitude, and who, unless he has the voice of Stentor,
> will serve as its herald? (VII.4.1326b1–5)

If "an excessively large number of things cannot share in organization"
(1326a30), it seems that this is a barrier that could be overcome by technological progress, giving heralds amplified voices and generals better means

of oversight. Aristotle therefore moves to a better argument, that people have to know each other in order to make the moral judgments essential to his polis (VII.4.1326b14–18)—as opposed to the modern state.[36] This latter argument is specific to the polis, not to all organized wholes.

Technology and other factors could expand the upper, but not the lower, bound of self-sufficiency. But the more important asymmetry here is that the deficiency is obvious, connected as it is with the lack of economic self-sufficiency, while making the polis better by making it bigger must be a permanent temptation, precisely the permanent temptation of pleonexia, having more goods and dominating others. Pleonexia is not obviously irrational, and doesn't need refutation so much as the presentation of a world in which there are greater satisfactions. It is not obvious that an "excessive" amount of goods, if that expression makes sense, is harmful in the way that deficient amounts obviously are. It is hard to see how a polis could have too many resources to be economically self-sufficient. A polis might have so much wealth that it becomes a tempting target for other poleis, or a standard of living that required for its maintenance a distortion of other policies, but it wouldn't cease being self-sufficient because of an excess of resources. There might be disadvantages to having too large a polis, but these drawbacks would not stop the state from being self-sufficient. Yet Aristotle claims that they would. The theme of moderation, which we saw at work in the last chapter, appears to reenter here without justification.[37]

The difference between states being too small and too large recalls the pair of virtues concerned with one's property in Book II, liberality and temperance. While the self-sufficient man needs temperance to hold on to his property and remain self-sufficient, it is liberality that allows self-sufficient people to enter into a self-sufficient community. In one sense, the temperate person is the person with moderate desires, but in a more radical way, both temperance and liberality are needed for moderate desires. People who "have been adequately educated by the laws" have moderate and equal desires, while "it is the special business (ergon idion) of the legislator to create in men the disposition to use private property in common" (II.5.1263a39–40). One could be temperate without caring about other people, but liberality requires a concern for others. Temperance, therefore, would not by itself unify a state; for that one needs liberality as well. One needs a minimum of property to be temperate and have enough property to hold on to, but it is much harder to specify an amount of property one needs in order to be liberal.

Taken together, VII.4–5 lets us make a first cut on the question of how a discussion of the ideal state can be practical. Statesmen rarely have a choice about how large a polis can be or where to locate it, but any statesman can see how Aristotle reasons about these issues and make it a model for practical reasoning. How to find an upper limit for self-sufficient activity and how to distinguish self-sufficiency from isolation—these are issues the statesman must confront all the time. We learn here something about how to think through such issues.

Chapter 6 seems to discuss things farther removed from happiness and the ideal constitution. "There is much dispute about whether access to the sea is beneficial or harmful to well-governed poleis" (1327a10). Maybe so, but that by itself doesn't justify discussing the issue in the *Politics*. Just as economic self-sufficiency does not mean isolation, neither does moral and political self-sufficiency. One theme of Books VII and VIII is how the philosophical life can be a common life and not an isolated one. Aristotle makes a similar determination about the polis here. Economic self-sufficiency is not isolation, but it has to avoid the danger of commerce leading not to self-sufficiency but to interdependence and a loss of self-sufficiency, as happens when trade becomes dominant. Such an outcome models the difficulty the politically and ethically self-sufficient polis faces—and the ethically self-sufficient person as well—avoiding the interpretation of self-sufficiency as the isolation of the philosopher.

After saying all that he thinks needs to be said about "territory, harbors, poleis, the sea, and naval force" (6.1327b16), Aristotle returns in chapter 7 to talking about population and citizens, as he did in chapter 4. Here, though, he does not ask about numbers but about nature. "We spoke earlier about what limit there should be on the number of citizens. Let us now discuss what sort of nature they should have" (7.1327b18), and there follows the notorious geography that puts the Greeks at the moral center of the world that I discussed in my first chapter. To say that citizens should have intelligence and *thumos* does not depend on substantive conclusions about the nature of happiness, from either VII.1–3 or from the *Ethics*. Even worse, the psychological nature that distinguishes Greeks from barbarians is flexible enough to allow for all sorts of lives besides that of virtuous activity. In particular, the same combination of thought and *thumos* allows for both friendship and domination, citizenship and despotism. "*Thumos* is the capacity of the soul by which we feel friendship" (VII.7.1327b40). If one thought that the chief good consisted in possessing the most possible external goods, it would still be the case that a combination of intelligence and *thumos* would be necessary to achieve happiness under that description. This moral psychology may identify the nature of citizens in the best state, but that nature is not a *dynamis* that leads smoothly and unequivocally to good citizens.

VI. BOOK VII.8

Chapter 8 returns, therefore, to fundamentals to look again at the best life and its implications for the material of the best state. Chapters 8–12 represent a halfway point in the progression from matter as something presupposed to matter as subject to the deliberations of constitutional design.

For that reason chapters 8–12 are the most recognizably political and constitutional chapters of Books VII and VIII. Chapters 1–7 were relatively prepolitical, outlining the material preconditions for the ideal state, and so nothing yet differentiated the people of the ideal state from Greeks as a people rather than a political organization. The combination of thought and *thumos*, Aristotle says, lets Greeks govern themselves, but we still need an argument to connect that to political self-rule.[38] Once we finish these intermediate chapters, chapters 13 will in turn simply presuppose all issues of constitutional design to focus on the development of the best citizens through education, the discussion that continues through Book VIII. It is only these middle chapters, and especially 8–10, that discuss anything that resembles constitutions as institutions.

Chapters 1–3 were organized around the question of whether the best life is a common life. Chapter 8 also organizes its discussion of happiness around questions of the common life, but in a different way. "Communities should have one thing that is common and the same for all their members (*kai koinon kai tauto tois koinōnois*), whether they share in it equally or unequally" (1328a27–29). The chapter begins by separating necessary conditions from parts, a distinction that, he says, applies to all "naturally constituted wholes" (*kata physin synestōtōn*). If that is the case, then other human associations such as alliances and nations are not naturally constituted wholes. (While slaves are part of the household in Book I, they are not parts of the polis.) Citizens have something in common, while the other people in the city, and people who are members of other wholes, do not. "Happiness is the best thing" (1328a37), and happiness is therefore what is shared by citizens, and only by citizens, even if unequally. We have come a long way from the similar-sounding question of Book II, in which what citizens had in common was the common use of private property. Here citizens, unlike noncitizens, all share in happiness.

In the ideal state, people seek happiness in the best way, and so have the best way of life and constitution. In that ideal state, people will share in happiness and in political rule to different degrees. The surprising point is that this inequality is without political significance. In the *Republic*, people of different classes share in happiness to different degrees, and those differences structure the state. Nothing like that occurs here. Citizens being happy to different degrees does not cause factions, since each is as happy as he can be and would gain nothing by trying to make others more or less happy, and those differences do not structure the state, either. Equality, and therefore justice, are in these circumstances beside the point.

Chapters 8 and 9, after saying that all citizens share in happiness, turn to a new question of the common, "investigating how many of these things there are that a polis cannot exist without" (8.1328b2–3). Once we know, by the end of chapter 8, which are the necessary tasks within a self-sufficient community, chapter 9 asks which of those are performed in common by all the citizens. Chapter 8 concluded by listing the necessary tasks: "there should be farmers, craftsmen, soldiers, rich people (*to euporon*), priests, and people to decide matters of necessity and benefit" (1328b20–21). Chapter 9 starts with a shorter list: "It remains to investigate whether everyone should share in all the tasks we mentioned (for it is possible for all the same people to be farmers, craftsmen, deliberators and judges)" (1328b24–25; see too VI.8.1322a29–34). Soldiers, rich people, and priests are not in this new list. Soldiers return immediately in chapter 9, and priests later in the chapter. Farmers and craftsmen are eliminated from citizenship, for different reasons: farmers because they cannot have the necessary leisure and craftsmen because their lives are "ignoble and inimical to virtue." Rich people are not mentioned again.

The question for chapter 9 is which of these occupations—farmers, craftsmen, deliberators and judges—should be performed by all citizens in common. Here too, he says, there is variation from constitution to constitution: "in democracies everyone shares in everything, whereas in oligarchies it is the opposite" (1328b31–32). Applied to economics, his remark is false. Neither in democracies nor anywhere else does everyone share in all economic activities. However, in democracy everyone does share in political activities. Oligarchies, organized around wealth, treat political offices like they treat economic roles, as subject to specialization; politics again reduces to economics.[39]

The contrast between democracy and oligarchy seems out of place here, where we're supposed to be learning about the ideal state, not about democracy and oligarchy. Chapter 8 also had something that looks irrelevant. At the beginning of the chapter, he said: "It is by seeking happiness in different ways and by different means that individual groups of people create different ways of life and different constitutions," which seems to have nothing to do with the ideal state, either. Those different conceptions of happiness appear in differences between democracy and oligarchy concerning which necessary activities are compatible with happiness and therefore with citizenship.

He then seems to recognize that these more general remarks look tangential: "Since we are investigating the best constitution . . ." (1328b34). For the first time in Book VII, Aristotle makes use of a specific Aristotelian teaching about happiness. (VII.1 relied on the "exoteric discourses."[40]) Since happiness is virtuous activity, tasks that are incompatible with virtue should not be done by citizens. Aristotle implicitly sides with the oligarchs here.[41] It seems that being virtuous or acting virtuously is a full-time job, leaving no room for activities that aim at lower ends, while leaving time, as we will see, for leisure.[42] But that's not Aristotle's point.

> Since we are investigating the best constitution, however, the one that would make a polis most happy . . . it evidently follows that . . . the citizens should not live the life of a vulgar craftsman or tradesman. For lives of these sorts are ignoble and inimical to virtue. Nor should those who are going to be citizens engage in farming, since leisure is needed both to develop virtue and to engage in political actions. (1328b34–1329a2)

Aristotle seems to be arguing that since such economic actions don't require virtue, they instead require a state of character incompatible with virtue. For such an argument to be right, most people's lives—the lives of all but the best—have to be defined by their economic life. Only then can Aristotle say that a given economic activity is incompatible with citizenship. Being a farmer or a craftsman, then, isn't something one does; it is something that one *is*.

But Aristotle claims that his argument holds only in the best state. Other states have lower standards for virtue, and those standards can be met by working people. Farmers and craftsmen can be courageous and liberal, but their lives, according to Aristotle, require states of character incompatible with the exercise of virtue in leisure.[43]

In chapter 4 I noted that the constitution Aristotle calls the best in general can be reached starting from almost any existing constitution—that is what makes it the best in general. The contrast to the best *haplōs* couldn't be greater. There is no pathway from any other constitution to the ideal constitution articulated in Books VII and VIII. Correspondingly, there is no pathway from the ethical virtues as they are normally exercised to those appropriate for the ideal state. This is the reason people whose virtues would be good enough for citizenship under other constitutions are excluded here. Under all other circumstances, the ethical challenge for the virtues is to do something for its own sake despite the fact that it is necessary. I have no choice about whether to defend my city, but I still have a choice about acting courageously for its own sake. Virtue is difficult because the necessity of an action can easily make it impossible to take pleasure in it and choose it for the sake of the noble.

Plato describes the situation beautifully in the *Laws*:

> Notwithstanding that human affairs are unworthy of earnest effort, necessity counsels us to be in earnest; and that is our misfortune. (803b)

The ethical challenge for the virtues of leisure is the opposite—to do something for its own sake even though it is not necessary, instead of thinking that the only alternative to the realm of necessity is rest and recreation. I said at the beginning of the chapter that the challenge in imagining the ideal constitution was to find anything left for politics to do once all the usual problems of compromise, scarcity, competition, and conflict had been left behind. Aristotle finally reaches the point in his argument for addressing that challenge. In *Ethics* X.7 he rates the political life inferior to the contemplative life because politics is always constrained political action always has an end outside itself (1177b5–27). Here in *Politics* VII–VIII he searches for a kind of political life that is not constrained.

Once economic activities are excluded, there is nothing left of the question of whether political activities should be common except for the relation between the military and the more narrowly political offices. "Since the best polis contains both a military part and one that deliberates about what is beneficial and makes judgments about what is just, and since it is evident that these, more than anything else, are parts of the polis, should these tasks be assigned to different people or are both to be assigned to the same people?" (1329a3–6; see IV.4.1291a24–28). The young engage in military activities. Being a soldier is not the best activity, nor is it necessary in the same way that economic activities are. Military activity is necessary the way some virtuous activities are: courage is worth displaying for its own sake, but only if circumstances, themselves undesirable, make it necessary. The same holds for corrective justice. Military activities do not disqualify people for citizenship the way moneymaking does because military activities require ethical virtues. On the other hand, engaging in those virtuous but necessary activities do not seem to equip people for acting virtuously in leisure: here, then, is a case in which we do not become rulers by being ruled.

Chapters 10–12 turn from citizens sharing happiness to a series of different means for unifying the polis, common messes, distribution of the ownership of land, and location and fortification of the city. Chapter 10 ends by saying that "farmers, ideally speaking, should be racially heterogeneous and spiritless slaves. . . . As a second best, they should be non-Greek subject peoples, similar in nature to the slaves just mentioned" (1330a25–29). In Books IV–VI Aristotle had recommended farmers as citizens on the ground that they will not have the leisure to participate in government, but would still support the constitution (e.g., IV.6.1292b25–29, VI.4.1318b11–16); there the project was to find people who could do good *for* the constitution without being good themselves, and farmer-citizens fit the bill perfectly. What made farmers good citizens was not virtue but preoccupation. Books IV–VI studied forms of best constitution where stability was the mark of a good constitution. Book VII shows what happens when stability as a distinct consideration no longer comes into play. Farmers are no longer citizens, since quiescence is no longer a political value.

VII. BOOK VII.13

Chapter 13 is Book VII's final consideration of happiness, and it makes considerable progress over the earlier ones. The first discussion in chapters 1–3 related self-sufficiency with regard to life to the self-sufficiency of living well, and so determined what sort of people could be citizens, culminating in the moral geography of chapter 7. The second, in chapter 8, related different necessary activities to the noble activities of military activity, deliberation, and judgment to decide which activities fit some for citizenship and disqualified others. The distinction was then not between economic and political self-sufficiency of the polis, but between economically and politically necessary *activities*. But in chapter 13 Aristotle goes further and raises the stakes of virtue. Happiness is not only *energeia kat'aretēn*, but an unqualified (*haplōs*) *energeia* and use (*krēsis*) of virtue. As Book VII progresses, its discussions of happiness become more Aristotelian.

The division among the uses of virtue between those that are noble and those that are not makes a cut within the area regarded as noble that chapter 8 used to exclude some people from citizenship. We saw in the first chapter how Aristotle's polis differentiated among things conflated in lesser forms of organization; the best polis makes distinctions that are irrelevant in lesser constitutions. Barbarians, he tells us, conflate women and slaves (I.2.1252b4), and corrupt poleis divide the population into rulers and noncitizens, leaving no room for citizens who aren't rulers. Similarly, the partisans of philosophy in VII.1–3 think that virtuous actions must be worth doing regardless of circumstances and so see politics as constrained, and devotees of the political life think that because it is the highest good, nothing else is worth doing. By searching here for the absolutely virtuous, while recognizing that there are lesser forms of virtue, chapter 13 further develops the dialectical arguments in 1–3 against identifying political activity with acquisition and conquest. The best citizens live virtuous lives. Not all virtuous lives are equal. The best citizens live the *best* virtuous lives. These center around worth doing in the best of circumstances. Other people can be fully virtuous, but not lead the most virtuous life, because their activity is praiseworthy and worth choosing in circumstances that are themselves undesirable, such as the justice which corrects injustices, but worth doing in the best of circumstances.[44] At the beginning of this chapter I wondered whether ideal politics wasn't an oxymoron because the politics most of us experience most of the time is directed toward conditions that are unjust, threatening, or otherwise undesirable. While in chapters 8–12 Aristotle asked whether different economic activities had consequences that made people unfit for virtue and so for happiness, from this point on he asks which activities are themselves the activities of virtuous and happy people.

Thus the first treatment of happiness in 1–3 relies on a distinction of internal and external goods, the second, in chapter 8, distinguishes the necessary conditions of living well from the parts of the constitution, and the final one, in chapter 13, distinguishes unqualified from merely relative uses of virtue. A sign of the progress among these three treatments of the best life is the final resolution of the question of resources in chapter 13. "We need resources in order to live a good life, although we need fewer of them if we are in a better condition, more if we are in a worse one" (VII.13.1332a1–2). In the earlier treatments of resources, Aristotle looked at territory and other materials as conditions of virtue and happiness. Here the resources are no longer a prior independent variable. They vary with virtue. Now Aristotle will try to formulate a system of education that will allow people to be happy with fewer resources. The *state* might require considerable resources to bring it about that individuals do not need many resources. Paradoxically, the fewer resources the virtuous man needs to be happy, the more noncitizens he needs to support him. Sparta impoverished its citizens so that the state could be wealthy; Aristotle makes the state rich so that its citizens don't have to be. The apparently facile part/whole analogies at the beginning of Book VII have led to something much more subtle.

Why are there exactly three considerations of happiness in Book VII? In what sense does the third consideration, in VII.13, make Aristotle's inquiry complete? Starting with the most abstract, everything that is, is either a *dynamis* or an *energeia*. For living things, there is a third possibility, something that can be both potency and act, what the *de Anima* calls a first actuality. These three possibilities are three ways of treating human nature developed in response to three discussions of the best life. They are three different analyses of the means and material for the end, human happiness. Since happiness is not only an end but an *energeia*, we need this complex deliberation on the practical relation of means and material to the end. First, material is a question of prayer. Then it becomes a subject of choice, of selecting which kinds of work are compatible with virtue. Finally, matter becomes a subject of deliberation in the fullest sense, where the citizens themselves are the product of the constitution's educational system. The third consideration of happiness presents us with a last matter that can be the object of planning, and so shifts the subject from constitutions to education. In the third part of Book VII and in its continuation in Book VIII, Aristotle looks at this last matter by seeing how the statesman and the constitution can create virtue in citizens.

The first time people and territory are, relative to political action, matter beyond which one cannot practically look. People have psychic capacities that either suit them for or disqualify them from political life. The first treatment of happiness precedes a discussion of the people in terms of the ideal quantity, making self-sufficiency a matter of numbers, discussing people in terms of natural practical powers. In the next stage of inquiry, people are more than a bundle of psychic capacities. Here Aristotle examines men at work, in terms of economic self-sufficiency. The issue is which economic and nonpolitical *activities* make possible or impossible the further activities that comprise living well. Finally, the last investigation of happiness introduces the rest of Books VII and VIII and their investigation of education, as we look at people in terms of ethical self-sufficiency, where the legislator creates the matter by education for virtue. Here the issue is the relation between education, and music in particular, and *scholē*, leisure, absolutely noble activity. Once Aristotle has finally determined the *nature* of the citizens of the best state, he can turn to the two other factors for virtue, habit and reason (VII.15.1334b6–8, see too VII.13.1332a38–b11), which occupy the rest of the *Politics*. Thus at VIII.3.1338a9–12 he says that "we should learn and be taught certain things that promote leisured activity.

And these subjects and studies are undertaken for their own sake, whereas those relating to work are necessary and for the sake of things other than themselves." Music both promotes leisure and is undertaken for its own sake. Music has two distinct roles: it constitutes the education that leads to civic virtue, and it is also the activity appropriate to virtuous people in their leisure. The relation of ruler and ruled makes it final appearance in the *Politics* as the relation between performing music and listening to it. It is easier to be virtuous in war than in peace; most people need a constitution with a lower standard of virtue because they can't handle leisure.

Finally, then, the third discussion of the best life in chapter 13 allows Aristotle to draw the explicit connection between the best life and the best state that he has been promising all along. The inference goes exactly in the opposite direction from what he has promised. The soul has parts, and those parts are themselves arranged in means/ends fashion. The body exists for the sake of the soul; appetite and emotion for the sake of reason, and *phronēsis* for the sake of *nous* and *sophia*. Similarly, "war is for the sake of peace, occupation for the sake of leisure, and necessary and useful things for the sake of noble things" (VII.14.1333a33–36). Here, but not earlier in Book VII, the structure of the ideal state mirrors the structure of the happy soul and the good life. Paradoxically, though, Aristotle does not derive these political hierarchies from psychic hierarchies. Instead, at this point Aristotle has finally secured these political hierarchies, arguing directly and without recourse to the psychic analogy. He can then turn to their psychic instantiation by discussing the educational policies by which the ideal will reproduce its political hierarchies within the souls of its citizens.

The three treatments of happiness are all ways of talking about matter relative to an end. They are all about people as the material realized in the best state. But the relation of matter to end is different, and it develops as Aristotle moves along. The argument of these books deepens our understanding of happiness as an activity, and how to reason about the matter and means needed when the end is an activity.

VIII. BOOK VIII: VIRTUE AND MUSIC

The *Politics* does not end with a grand conclusion as the *Ethics* does with its transcendence of the political life by the philosophical, or the *Physics* with its ascent from the world of motion to the unmoved mover. Whether Book VIII is complete, or whether Aristotle went on to fill in more details about music and *scholē*, his readers have a right to feel unsatisfied.[45] By the time we are finished, we know much less about what the best life in the best circumstances looks like than we do about a life of the ethical virtues described in the *Ethics* or political life under the other constitutions outlined in the *Politics*, and so naturally we would like to know more.

There is good reason Aristotle cannot fill in the picture of what the life of leisure looks like. Even the noncourageous person can understand a philosophical discussion of courage. I don't have to be courageous to understand Aristotle's placing courage as a habit of choosing between the vicious habits of cowardice and recklessness, his exposition of courage as a habit of choosing the mean amount of fear and confidence, or his narrowing of courage to the greatest of evils, risking one's death in battle for one's state. The nonjust and even the unjust person can recognize examples of justice and understand why justice is a virtue. People who don't act virtuously can still understand what virtue is, because the virtues require doing for its own sake something that is valuable first of all regardless of whether it's done for its own sake or not: it is good to stand and fight in defense of one's polis even if out of shame, fear, experience, or ignorance, and it is good not to take other people's property, however attractive and useful it might be, whether out of fear of punishment, respect for the law, or ambition to have an upstanding reputation. The nonvirtuous can understand that the virtues are good without understanding the point of doing something for its own sake.

The virtuous life of *scholē* is not as easy to understand by the nonvirtuous, and the accounts of music in Book VIII do not help that much, either. As Aristotle repeatedly notes, states organized around virtue have been organized around courage, and generally neither states nor people know what to do with leisure. They interpret *scholē* as amusement or relaxation from the real business of life. Moreover, much of the understanding of music is not philosophical but technical, so Aristotle defers to expertise in associating different modes with different states of character. In particular, we learn nothing about the curriculum that parallels so much of the discussion in the *Republic*. We are told which musical modes imitate and lead to which sorts of character, but nothing about which stories of men, heroes, and gods should be imitated. This is a common curriculum without a list of books, not even a discussion of the place of Homer in the ideal education. I could understand an argument that the virtuous will watch *La Bohème* instead of *Rent*, but find no such argument in the *Politics*.

If we think about the *Poetics*, the direction of Aristotle's treatment is stranger still. The ethical and educational value of music for politics lies in its matter, the melodies and rhythms, rather than its form, the objects imitated. The *Poetics* lists the six parts of tragedy in descending order of importance: plot, character, thought, diction, melody, and spectacle. *Politics* VIII confines its attention to melody. What is accidental in the *Poetics* becomes primary in the *Politics*.[46]

> Since then music is a pleasure, and virtue consists in rejoicing and loving and hating aright, there is clearly nothing which we are so much concerned to acquire and to cultivate as the power of forming right judgments, and of taking delight in good dispositions and noble actions. Rhythm and melody supply imitations of anger and gentleness, and also of courage and temperance, and of all the qualities contrary to these, and of the other qualities of character, which hardly fall short of the actual affections, as we know from our own experience, for in listening to such strains our souls undergo a change. The habit of feeling pleasure or pain at mere representations is not far removed from the same feeling about realities . . . (VIII.5.1340a16–24)

In *Poetics* 4 Aristotle tells us that "poetry [making] in general comes from two causes in human nature, the pleasures of imitation and the instinct for harmony and rhythm" (1448b5–19). People are the most imitative of all animals. While earlier in *Politics* VIII he described learning, like any *kinēsis*, as arduous, here learning is pleasant because of the connection to imitation: "To learn gives the liveliest pleasure, not only to philosophers but to people in general. . . . In contemplating they find themselves learning or inferring (*theōrountas manthanein kai syllogizesthai*)." That last phrase hints at how music, and imitation in general, can function both in learning and in the activity of leisure, contemplation. Moreover, while it is in the *Poetics* that Aristotle tells us that imitation is associated with learning, he notoriously never claims that tragedy either teaches people or has ethical effects. It is in the *Politics* that he tells us that music, melody and rhythm, provides an ethical education.

Those few lines from the *Poetics* offer two more suggestions about the educational value of music. First "we enjoy looking at accurate likenesses even of things which are themselves painful to see." Courage is the virtue that involves pains, but many of the virtues are painful to the nonvirtuous. If our musical experience makes us more capable of becoming courageous, more ready to give our money to friends, and more likely to moderate our anger, then musical education can develop the love for the noble that makes possible the development of the particular virtues.

Second, "the reason why we enjoy seeing likenesses is that, as we look we learn and infer what each is. . . . If we have never happened to see the original, our pleasure is not due to the imitation as such but to the technique or the color or some other such cause." If this account of imitation fits *Politics* VIII, then we enjoy the musical imitation of character because we recognize the music as an imitation, and this means that we already have some knowledge of its models in human character. The movements of music imitate the emotional movements of the soul, and to experience music as an imitation depends on and develops our understanding of those psychic movements. Excessive technical proficiency corrupts both the performer and the audience because it diverts attention from this mimetic relation to other aspects of the performance.

In commenting on the beginning of Book VII, I noted that while Aristotle says that to identify the best constitution, one must start from our knowledge of the best life, it is *only* the best constitution that requires knowledge of the best life. Book VIII starts in a similar way. "Legislators should be particularly concerned with the education of the young," that "education should suit the particular constitution, and since the polis has a single end, education too should be one . . . and its supervision should be communal." It is only here that he recommends the revolutionary abandoning of the usual practice of education being under the authority of the parents. Only in the ideal state does the account I just gave of musical education make sense; in more corrupt states there is no reason for confidence that the young will be able to recognize the similarity between musical and emotional movements. Only in the ideal state will the best leisure activities be public rather than private.[47]

According to the distinction in the *Metaphysics* between *kinēsis* and *energeia*, education is a *kinēsis*. We learn for the sake of knowing, and therefore learning is not its own end. No one would learn Norwegian except in order to know Norwegian. Learning is arduous; knowing is pleasant. But while in that broad sense all education is instrumental and leads to a goal outside itself, the differences among goals make some sorts of education more instrumental than others, just as some virtuous activities are chosen for their own sake more than others.

And so Aristotle shifts in VIII.3 from education to leisured activity (*diagogē*) as his subject: "Nowadays, most people take part in music for the sake of pleasure. But those who originally included it as part of education did so, as has often been said, because nature itself aims not only at the correct use of work, but also at the capacity for noble leisured activity" (1337b28–32). Then the two, education and leisure activity, are combined:

"We should learn and be taught certain things that promote leisured activity. And these subjects and studies are undertaken for their own sake, whereas those relating to work are necessary and for the sake of things other than themselves. It is for this reason that our predecessors assigned music a place in education" (1338a9–14).

It would be a wonderful consummation of the *Politics* if Aristotle could show, as those last lines implied, that there was a side of education that was undertaken for its own sake. If that were so, that side of education need not be confined to the young, but could be a common kind of leisured activity. But Aristotle backs off from that affirmation in chapter 5. "It is not appropriate to give children leisured pursuits, since the end (something complete) is not appropriate for someone who is incomplete" (1339a29–30). (On the other hand, later in the chapter, "education in music is appropriate to their youthful nature. For on account of their age, the young are unwilling to put up with anything that is unsweetened with pleasure, and music is something naturally sweet" [1340b14–17].)

The rest of Book VIII as we have it focuses on music as a part of education, not music as what virtuous people practice as constituting their leisure. In Book VII, young men practiced the virtues of war, older men the virtues of deliberation. Here, young men perform music while older men enjoy and judge it. This is the final form of ruling and being ruled. If the young were to perform music for the sake of the enjoyment and judgment of the older, they would be corrupted through the effort to please and impress the audience. Instead, they perform music in order later to be able to judge it well, developing right opinion that can eventually become *phronēsis*. In that way, musical education becomes in a certain sense its own end: its purpose is to develop the very ethical character that is at work in the judgment of musical performances. Both musical performance and musical judgment are not what moderns would call aesthetic; the criteria for both are ethical. Citizens in the ideal state may not need to practice all the ethical virtues, but they have an ethical appreciation for them impossible for people outside the musical practices of the best constitution.

The issue for leisure is how an activity that doesn't produce any external good can still be serious and noble, not frivolous. The issue for education is how an activity of something imperfect and not yet fully formed can be worth choosing for its own sake. Music is supposed to solve both these problems.[48]

I want to try to clarify things a little by returning for the last time to Plato's *Republic*. The *Republic* has two discussions of poetry or music— music as opposed to gymnastic covers all intellectual as opposed to physical cultivation, and the discussion of poetry includes discussions of the musical modes. The first, in Book II, looks at poetry or music as part of the education of potential guardians. The second, in Book X, looks at poetry again, but this time without restriction to its preparatory role. And the *Politics* contains a single examination of music, the one in Book VIII. It therefore in a way does double duty, thinking about music both in education and in the leisurely activity of the virtuous. Our access to the best leisurely activities is through the education that gives people the capacities to practice those activities.

Neither education as preparation for citizenship nor music as the consummation of the best political life have anything at all to do with either preparation for philosophy or the practice of philosophy. This education is not dialectical; there are no debates and no testing of scientific principles. There is no indication that it prepares people for dialectic or for science. It has nothing in common with the education of the guardians in *Republic* VII. It doesn't lead to specialized professional musicians, nor to specialized scientists and philosophers.[49]

There isn't, then, much the philosopher can say about the best life. Instead, Aristotle has gradually built a case, first through the three discussions of happiness and the best life in Book VII, and then through the discussion of education in Book VIII, that opens up the life of leisure to those of us not living the best life in the best state. He cannot start with a fixed understanding of the best life as a principle from which to derive the best constitution, as he promises at the start of Book VII, he finds instead an aspect of the best life invisible except under the best constitution and that therefore couldn't be known first. That is the side of virtue and happiness connected with leisure rather than constraint.

It is canny of Aristotle to approach the discussion of music, as the activity pursued by the best people in the best circumstances, through a discussion of education. I've shown the way Book VII contains a series of variations on the idea of the common, ranging from happiness—the end—as what all citizens in the best state must have in common to the various materials—the right sort of ethnic stock—through common military political occupations. Book VIII talks about a final aspect of the common, a common education and culture shared by all citizens, and hence a common ethical formation conducted by the polis. In yet another instance where the *Politics* is more revisionary than the *Ethics*, Aristotle recommends that education be common.

Book VIII.1 begins by contending that "no one would dispute" that "the legislator should be concerned above all with the education of the young"

(1337a11). But the chapter quickly moves to more and more tendentious conclusions: "Since there is one end for the whole city, clearly it is necessary that education too be one and the same for all, and care for this education must be a common project and not a private matter, which is the present way of going about it" (1337a22–25). Why the arguments Aristotle himself makes in Book II against holding property in common do not apply to common education is not clear, since Aristotle moves so quickly here.[50] But the proposal to make education common not only contradicts the usual practice of education being the responsibility of parents, as Aristotle notes, but also the sort of individualized education exemplified by Socrates in Plato's dialogues.

The discussion of education in Book VIII is the closest Aristotle can come to his procedure in the *Ethics* of starting from goods desired for all kinds of reasons and discovering ways of choosing them for their own sakes. Education of the young develops the ethical responsiveness necessary for the more specific habituation in the ethical virtues and political capacities.[51] Since the end of education is the development of the ethical qualities of citizens, education cannot be its own end. However, Aristotle will discover aspects of education that are valuable for their own sakes. Those aspects are precisely the participation in music with which the *Politics* ends. While Book VII begins by promising to derive the nature of the best constitution from the nature of the best life, I have shown how the movement of thought for the most part goes the other way. It is only through understanding the best constitution that this side of the best life becomes visible to those of us who live outside such a polis.

The focus on education and leisure in Book VIII brings to attention questions of cultural reproduction that mirror the issues of political reproduction that make Aristotle concentrate so much on the stability of the constitution. In *Confronting Aristotle's Ethics* I argued that one of the functions of the virtues was to insure the continuation of their own enabling conditions, the conditions under which they can be successful. That didn't mean that the virtuous person must try to keep some people in poverty so that he can help them through exercising the virtue of liberality. It means insuring that the community understand liberality as a noble activity rather than sentimental weakness, and that the community see helping others financially as the proper use of money rather than a loss relative to the opportunities for indefinite accumulation. Education is the means by which a community reproduces itself. The best constitution reproduces its way of life through a system of unified, public education, in which the young participate through learning and the mature through leisurely enjoyment.

The surprising overall picture we get from Books VII and VIII is that we don't need to know much in detail about happiness for practical knowledge of the best state. Book VII requires us to think about two aspects of happiness, that it is active and common. It isn't interested in the particular ethical virtues that take so much of Aristotle's attention in the *Ethics*. Music is preparation for *virtue*, while we acquire the particular *virtues* through habituation in those specific virtues. Music is preparation for virtue, while we acquire the particular virtues through habituation in those specific virtues. Happiness is virtuous activity, and the virtuous life is a common life. If happiness had a different definition, it could function more as a premise from which to derive the best constitution, and then we would need a more detailed understanding of its nature to ground those deductions. If the best life, for example, was a life of conquest and unlimited acquisition, for example, there would be a more direct and obvious connection between the good life and the good constitution. We could reason instrumentally from such an end to the means necessary to accomplish it. Hence the qualified praise of Sparta. Since it has a definite end of conquest, unlike most states, which don't have a single end at all, they can at least plan the organization of the constitution and the education of citizens around that end.

The praise and criticism of Sparta is a leitmotif that recurs throughout the *Politics*, but comes to the fore especially when Aristotle is talking about the ideal constitution. Only the Spartans organized their constitution toward their conception of the good life, but that conception was limited to war and conquest and so "they did not know how to be at leisure" (II.9.1271b4). Spartan citizens did not know how to be at leisure and so had to make war their end. Given that limited end, their conception of practical reason was truncated, too: "although they think (rightly) that the good things that people compete for are won by virtue rather than by vice they also suppose (not rightly) that these goods are better than virtue itself" (1271b6–9; see too VII.2.1324b5–11, VII.13.1333b5–11, 1334a2–b5). Without Aristotle's philosophical understanding, people can at best organize their common lives around the virtues of war, since those virtues are commonly understood, while the virtues of leisure are not.

Political philosophy, exemplified by the *Politics*, has a practical role, then, that has no parallel in the *Ethics*. Without political philosophy, the statesman could only aim at the incomplete good life manifested in the Spartan constitution. Leisure turns into play. The Spartan women show what happens further: freedom from necessity degenerates into licentiousness and a love of luxury (II.9.1269b22–23, 1270a1–9).

At the beginning of this chapter I asked whether there is anything left of politics and political wisdom once all the normal constraints, which seem to define the circumstances of politics, were removed. Aristotle finally addresses this problem by showing what leisurely civic activity amounts to. Music certainly does not look like political action as it was conceived at the beginning of Book VII, nor does it resemble the life of the philosopher.[52] Not only are most people bad at handling leisure; they don't even understand what it is. Music is an activity that is civic and communal and at the same time is its own end. The rest of the *Politics* will elaborate on this picture, excluding the utilitarian parts of education until Aristotle finds kinds of learning worth undertaking for their own sake. "It is completely inappropriate for great-souled and free people to be always asking what use something is" (VIII.3.1338b2–3). Music is both a form of education for the young and a form of leisured activity for all. Just as he transformed the meaning of the political life from one of conquest into a self-sufficient and virtuous life, so he transforms the meaning of the philosophical life into the activities of common culture. The partisans of philosophy might see such activity as inferior to "real philosophy," just as devotees of the political life could see leisure as anything but the culmination of the political life, but Aristotle has radically redefined politics and philosophy so that musical activity is the highest political good.

At this point we can reframe Aristotle's problem of the ideal state this way. The only poleis that have truly unified laws, all organized around the state's purpose, are those states, like Sparta, which are organized for war. One has to wonder whether that sort of political unity, the full subordination of laws to the constitution, is only possible when the state aims as courage and military domination. Just as most people don't know what to do with leisure, no state has been able to be organized without that organization being forced on it by the exigencies of war. The noble, *to kalon*, will have to be redefined in order to see leisurely activities as worth choosing for their own sake.

The *Politics*, then ends not with the triumphant and dramatic endings of the *Republic* and even the *Ethics* but with a pair of banal-looking but profound questions that focus on two dimensions of the nature of unqualified activities. First, do citizens have to play musical instruments as well as observe and judge the performances of others?

Perhaps it might be held that what children seriously attend to is for the sake of their play once they have become men and complete. But if something of this sort is the case, for the sake of what would they have to learn it themselves, and not partake of the learning and the pleasure through others performing it, like the kings of the Persians and the Medes? For necessarily those who have made this their task and their craft produce something better than those who devote only as much time to music as is needed for learning it. But if they should exert themselves in such matters, they would themselves have to take up the activity of cooking; but this would be odd. (VIII.5.1339a31–b3)

The Oriental despot treats leisure as relaxation, paying others to act so that he can have pleasure. Second, is it possible to be too proficient, once again reducing an *energeia* to a *technē*?

It is evident that the learning [of music] should neither be an impediment with a view to later activities, nor make the body vulgar and useless with a view to military and political training—with a view on the one hand to the uses now, and on the other to the sorts of learning [to be undertaken] later. This would result in connection with the learning [of music] if they did not exert themselves to learn either what contributes to contests involving expertise in the art or those works that are difficult and extraordinary (which have now come into the contests, and from the contests into education), but learn such things . . . up to the point where they are capable of enjoying noble tunes and rhythms . . ." (VIII.6.1341a6–17)

(Aristotle asks this only for performers, seeing their activity degenerate as it aims at pleasing the audience, but one could also worry about judges becoming aesthetes and connoisseurs.) Both performing and observing music can degenerate. Both are hard to understand as activities rather than as labor and passive enjoyment. Book III ended with balanced arguments between the claims of the rule of law and rule of the person of heroic and superlative virtue. There is no such balance here. There is no place for professional expertise and superlative musicianship in the best constitution.

All the citizens of the best state, and only of the best state, delight in music and *scholē*, and in that sense all are wise. Only of the best state, because most people don't know what to do with leisure: we learn that it is easier to be virtuous in constrained circumstances than in the best situation, another reason to see the ideal constitution as only suitable for the best people. The virtues of war are more widely distributed than the virtues of peace. But in the best state, everyone sees *scholē* not as play or rest but as the highest activity. Not everyone in the best state is a philosopher, but all participate in the common form of wisdom appropriate to citizens. While there is an age for courage and for *phronēsis*, there is no age for philosophy, music, or leisure, another reason to think that philosophy is not a discrete activity, as its partisans maintain. Books VII and VIII understand the activity of living well through repeated contrasts to instrumental actions. That distinction finally dissolves in the discussion of music, since music both constitutes the ethical development of citizens—and as such has a goal outside itself—and is the use of leisure toward which all other political activities are directed.

What is *the* political problem in the ideal state? In all other poleis, the central political problem is justice. In the ideal state, the fundamental political activity is education, self-maintenance, and reproduction. Where all men make mistakes about justice, the best people are still prone to make mistakes about the best life, mistaking *kinēseis* for *energeiai*, through domination, or, more rarely, through withdrawal into philosophy. The difficulty of leading an active life culminates in the fact that most people cannot participate in leisure as an activity. Hence the possibilities of degeneracy canvassed at the end, expertise, connoisseurship, and relaxation.

IX. THE IDEAL AND THE PRACTICAL

At the beginning of this chapter, I rejected interpretations of Aristotle's city of prayer as an ideal to be approximated, let alone instantiated. Nor is it a standard against which to measure other constitutions. Our final challenge in understanding the *Politics* is seeing in just what way knowledge of such an absolutely best state can be practical. According to the ordering of the books of the *Politics* I have followed, we study the absolutely best state only after knowing how to develop the other dimensions of practical knowledge, the other three kinds of best. Only then are we able not to mistake the absolute best for the other kinds of best, and the practicality properly associated with the absolute best with the other kinds of practicality. The discussion of the best state seems constantly deferred in the *Politics*, and now we are finally ready for it.

The chief practical benefit is in following Aristotle's *argument* rather than taking his *conclusions* as precepts or recipes. The argument of VII and VIII lays bare the structure of political wisdom as it deliberates about the peculiar problems brought to light through thinking about the absolute best. As I put it in chapter 5, the *Politics* lays out arguments without *ēthos* which the statesman then converts into ethical arguments. Through making arguments ethical, the statesman will be able to take circumstances into account, weigh probabilities, and turn the philosopher's reasoning into deliberation. If the end of the state is wealth or something similar, then the statesman would not need *phronēsis; technē* would suffice. Praxis is always in danger of reduction to *technē*, and the *Politics* shows how precarious the idea of politics as an activity is. Book V started with stability as the absence of factions but moved to stability as a political activity and an excellence of the constitution. The particular virtues had technological counterparts: military skill might work better than courage, a science of distribution better than justice. The remedy against reducing politics to a science is the ability to follow Aristotle's argument so that we can read the *Politics* as an exercise in practical reason.

More specifically, though, what about the particular problems of making the treatment of the *ideal* constitution into practical knowledge? I mentioned the oddity that the political philosopher has a greater and more independent role in the ideal constitution than in less ambitious inquiries, so that Aristotle can decide what is the best life in a way that he never arbitrates decisions about justice. As the standards for virtue are higher in the ideal constitution than in others, so the *ēthos* necessary to embody Aristotle's argument here must meet a tougher standard.

There are two possible responses to a presentation of the ideal constitution by those of us not likely to live there. The first is to see the distance between the ideal and reality and either withdraw from politics or withdraw politics from having anything to do with the good life, what could be called the stoic and Machiavellian options, respectively. The second is to use the ideal to find the truly political in what is otherwise disappointing, and to see ways in which a common life is a noble one and reciprocity worth choosing for its own sake. Understanding the ideal state lets us see other good constitutions as good, not simply as compromises or products of error and partiality. Seeing the ideal, we then won't see political activity, wherever we find ourselves, as such a dirty business, or engage in it as such. We can instead see the connection between ordinary politics and the absolute best. We can now better understand what is truly political about our ordinary political activity.

Aristotle shows how to reason about the means and conditions for an end that is an activity. I've stressed the way the odd nature of Aristotle's argument comes from the way one cannot reason from end to means for happiness as *energeia kat'aretēn* as one could if happiness were identified with wealth, honor, or even security or stability. Hence the complex argument of chapters 1–3 and their significance for what follows. In addition, the three distinct treatments of happiness, in chapters 1–3, then 8, and finally 13, show a further, more refined feature of the same problem, as Aristotle shows the statesman three different relations between the end of happiness and its means and conditions, finishing finally with musical activity, which is both education for virtue and the consummation of virtue. When discussing the ideal state, the philosopher displays practical reason in action.

People as Political Animals

This book has looked at the problems of Aristotle's *Politics* a book or two at a time. I want to end by pointing to five themes that run through the *Politics* as ever-deepening ways of understanding how people are political animals. Each theme is a different way of exploring the complex interrelations between ethics and politics, between living well and living together. I call them themes because each is sometimes in the foreground, sometimes in the back, sometimes works as the beginning of an argument and sometimes as its goal. None can be captured by a single stable proposition. Their fluidity is not a sign of confusion but of their shifting roles within Aristotle's own overall argument. Ruling and being ruled in turn, for example, is sometimes presupposed, sometimes argued for, sometimes a criterion for judging suggested constitutional arrangements, sometimes a minimal requirement for politics, and sometimes a maximum, the fulfillment of political life, and sometimes something that we unfortunately have to settle for. One could even think of a lawless democracy as ruling and being ruled in turn, in which groups take turns getting rich from their turn in charge, and then it would be something to avoid.

My five themes are also ways of connecting Aristotle's political problems to our own. There is, for example, no single definitive answer to my first question, political animals as opposed to what? Slavish animals, despotic animals, philosophers, acquisitive animals are only a few of the candidates. Themes such as this one motivate and animate Aristotle's argument, and eventually allow us to construct our own variations on these themes, continuing Aristotle's project without trying to "apply" his conclusions, if we can find them, to our circumstances. One important alternative for Aristotle is despotic animals. Many people have argued that there is a crucial shift in modernity from war to commerce, and a contemporary alternative to political animals could be citizens as holders of rights protected by the state so that they can live private lives.[1]

If people are political animals, then Aristotelian politics is more comprehensive than modern politics. Otherwise political activity wouldn't satisfy the virtuous person as an activity that can constitute the good life. There is no realm of the private in principle outside the reach of politics. Mill's remark that "citizenship fills only a small place in modern life, and does not come near the daily habits or inmost sentiments" illustrates the divide.[2] Aristotle's dictum in the *Ethics* that achieving the good for the state is "a nobler and more divine" achievement than achieving the good for the individual (I.2.1094b7–10) is about as far from Mill's as possible. The thesis that people are political animals, elaborated in the *Politics*, stands as a challenge to contemporary ways of thinking and living.

1. People Are Political Animals. Political Animals as Opposed to What?

My first chapter began with Aristotle's ideas of slavery and mastery. We had to see why, although humans are political animals, only some people live in poleis, and of those, only some are fit to be citizens. If people are political animals, and if most people aren't citizens, it follows that most people do not fulfill their human nature. When people don't fulfill their nature, they don't become some other kind of animal. They are incomplete human beings. While that passage from *Politics* I.2 separates humans from other animals by the presence of logos, speech or thought, Aristotle's natural slaves don't lack logos. They have it, have the intelligence to engage in the crafts and to follow their masters' orders through listening to reason and being persuaded. They instead lack *thumos*, the spirited self-assertion that makes for citizenship, friendship, and tyranny.

Greeks are "both spirited and endowed with thought, and hence both remain free and govern themselves in the best manner and at the same time are capable of ruling all" (VII.7.1327b24–33). To be a citizen, then, requires this unique combination of logos and *thumos.* That civic nature lets us ask more productively than usual whether what Aristotle means by a political community must be restricted to the Greek poleis he is familiar with, with their slaves, primitive economies and bureaucracies, and frequent wars and civil wars. Can, instead, "political" be broader, including, for example, any social organization that allows for ruling and being ruled in turn, or broader still to include modern states, even liberal states that do not aim at the highest human good, or more narrowly, including only communities that aim at the good life, even if they don't possess the other properties of state-hood, such as a monopoly on legitimate violence and control of territory? In an Aristotelian spirit, we have to face this more morally challenging issue: can someone be a citizen without being at the same time the master of do-mestic slaves? Aristotle sees the same psychic capacities making possible both civic life and domination. In deciding whether the *Politics* has any rele-vance to contemporary problems, we have to think through the relation be-tween these capacities for thought and for spirited self-assertion. Since the seventeenth century we have made progress in living together by dampen-ing the operations of the *thumos* that Aristotle thought constitutive of be-ing a political animal. To take Aristotle seriously today we would have to examine the consequences of this transformation.

My second chapter followed Book II's discussion about what citizens in a state must have in common to raise a second question about political animals and their alternatives. At stake there was the uniqueness of the political community, especially as opposed to the family, but also to other kinds of organization, such as a military alliance or a trading agreement. To be a political animal is to form a community with others who are different in kind (II.2.1261a24). Man is a political animal means, among other things, that people are not family or economic animals. So-called communitarian followers of Aristotle have to confront the challenges of finding the locus of living well in a community that isn't at its heart an association with others different in kind.

Chapter 3 shows that, while it might be natural for people to live in poleis, there is a variety of ways of organizing the rulers and ruled of a polis, a variety not dictated by nature. The purpose of the polis, living well, does not determine the form the polis takes. In natural objects, end and form are identical; in ethics and politics they are not. Knowing that the polis is natu-ral and that man is by nature a political animal does not yet put us in a posi-tion to understand the forms political life takes, the different constitutions. That man is a political animal means, among other things, that people are not by nature democratic or oligarchic animals. On the other hand, people don't live in poleis, they live in democratic or oligarchic poleis. My chap-ters 4 and 5 look at the more empirical books of the *Politics*, Books IV V, and VI, and show that stability and a good constitution depend on people acting like political animals rather than democratic or oligarchic animals, placing loyalty to constitutional government, rule of law, and ruling and being ruled in turn above loyalty to the specific constitution.

Finally, chapter 6 looks at Aristotle's ideal state, and asks whether there is anything recognizably political about the life within such a state. If humans are political animals, it still might not follow that the best life is a political life. As he does at the end of the *Ethics*, Aristotle opens up the possibility that the best life for political animals is a life that in a certain way transcends politics. How this best life can be a common life without being political is another question that sets challenges for us today.

2. Do People Lead the Best and Most Satisfying Lives When They Are Acting as Political Animals? What Is Intrinsically Valuable about Ruling and Being Ruled in Turn?

"Humans are political animals" is limited not only because most people don't seem to fulfill their nature by living as citizens in a polis—my first theme—but because most people don't think they are most fully human when participating as citizens in political activity. Most people, even most citizens, do not think that their participation in politics defines who they are. While Aristotle insists that despotically ruling over others cannot be a good life, there is strong reason, already articulated in the *Republic*, to think that people would act despotically if they could get away with it. Accumulating great wealth through craft or trade, he argues, cannot be a good life, although some people then and maybe most people today think that it is. The family cannot be the site of living well, a refuge from the dirty hands and compromises of politics. Not only will only a minority of people be fully political animals but only a minority would choose to live politically. Most people would rather not be political animals.

The political life consists in ruling and being ruled in turn. That is both what makes it so fulfilling and so unusual and precarious. In chapter 1, I used Aristotle's accounts of masters and slaves to see how "mastery," "despotism," and "domination"—three translations of the Greek *despotēs*—have the same psychological root as friendship and the capacity for the mutuality of ruling and being ruled. Despotism remains a permanent threat to politics in a way that slavery and slavishness, in Aristotle's opinion, do not. He thought that slavishness held no attractions for his audience, while the same powers that made for political activity, friendship, and equality also could lead to the despotic life. Modern politics seems to have reversed this emphasis: we have anger management for potential tyrannical souls, but encourage what Aristotle would see as slavishness through treating life as the satisfaction of desires. The development of commercial society has refuted Aristotle's expectations that one doesn't have to worry about slavishness but only about despotism. Families have a permanent ruler instead of taking turns ruling and being ruled; most friendships have no rulers at all.

In Book II he says that "it is clearly better, where possible, for the same people always to rule. But among those where it is not possible, because all are naturally equal . . . it is at least possible to approximate to this if those who are equal take turns and are similar when out of office" (II.2.1261a37–1261b2). This passage makes it sound like the unfortunate fact of equality makes the ideal of permanent rule impractical. Yet both equality and ruling and being ruled in turn are the essence of political life. The aspiring despot would regard ruling and being ruled in turn as a second-best. The benefits of alternating ruling and being ruled are not obvious and have to be developed as Aristotle's argument progresses.

Book III shows that what separates correct from corrupt constitutions is not how many rule but the relation between rulers and the ruled. We begin to see how ruling and being ruled in turn can be desirable in its own right, while in corrupt constitutions authorities rule for their own sake, not for the sake of the whole. But Book III ends with the possibility of permanent rule by a supremely virtuous person or group of people. While in Book I there was a natural difference between people capable of ruling themselves and the slaves who need masters, here the difference between rulers and ruled is a matter of degree. That is, whether one can be a ruler or not depends on nothing intrinsic to the individual but whether the polis also contains someone supremely virtuous. Whether I will be permanently ruled depends not on my qualities but on whether there is a supremely virtuous person in the neighborhood. Ruling and being ruled in turn, equivalent here to the rule of law, is attractive because of the realistic improbability of finding supremely virtuous leaders.

Books IV–VI showed how to make constitutions correct without relying on their citizens either being or becoming virtuous. Here alternating between ruling and being ruled, and being "similar when out of office" was the effect of the right institutional arrangements instead of relying on citizens being good enough to want to rule and be ruled in turn. In Book IV he discovers in the middle class a group of people who are willing to rule without wanting to rule permanently. Without the vices of poverty and wealth, they are virtuous enough to be ideal citizens in these less than ideal constitutions. In Book V he advises democratic rulers to treat the wealthy well enough to make them loyal to the constitution, and oligarchic rulers to act the same way toward the people. Here a stable constitution seems to be a framework in which people can lead virtuous lives rather than political participation being the most fulfilling of lives. These stable constitutions then provide a full separation of ethics and politics, anticipating modern politics. Ruling and being ruled in turn means sharing an honorable burden, and most of all it means treating fellow citizens as partners in constituting a stable, continuing enterprise. Books VII and VIII provide a new interpretation of the idea of citizens both ruling and being ruled in turn—rulers and the ruled are distinguished only by age. The young men in the military eventually become old enough to rule, which is very different from alternating ruling and being ruled. None of these seem to embrace the idea of ruling and being ruled in turn as something worth doing in itself, the essence of political life.

3. While People Might Be Political Animals, They Don't Live in Poleis; They Live in Democracies, Oligarchies, Et Cetera. Why Are People Political Animals rather than Democratic or Oligarchic Animals?

Nothing in the nature of the best life as described either in the *Ethics* or in the *Politics*, nothing in the dictum that humans are political animals, and nothing in the genealogy of the polis in *Politics* I, gives any reason to expect a variety of legitimate constitutions. There is no such variety, for example, among families. Living democratically or oligarchically doesn't seem to be an accidental qualification of living politically, like having blue or brown eyes is an accidental property of beings with vision. The color of our eyes has nothing to do with how we see, but the kind of constitution we live under has a lot to do with how we live together. Aristotle needs a stronger explanation for the variety of constitutions. As we've seen, he provides several different accounts at different points in the *Politics*.

As I trace this third theme, we see a variety of connections and differences between ethics and politics. The *Ethics* displays a unique best life while the *Politics* is open to an array of good constitutions. In each of Aristotle's different explanations for why there is a plurality of constitutions, the reason is because people make mistakes about justice. It seems to follow that if people didn't make errors about justice, there would only be one best state. Just as it looked like ruling and being ruled in turn was necessary only because people, or Greeks, won't stand for being permanently ruled, so here it looks like the plurality of constitutional forms is a reflection of the way politics is as much a matter of opinion, force, and convention as it is of true justice. There are many constitutions because everyone has a partial conception of justice, either erasing differences in the name of equality or ignoring equality in order to do justice to differences.

But that argument from imperfection won't work. There are not only plural constitutions, but plural correct constitutions. The plurality of correct constitutions is of special interest because Aristotle reverses the relation of ethics and politics posited by modern liberalism. Today, we think that there are a variety of ways of living well, and that the individual is the best authority for judging how he or she should live. The task of liberal politics is then to construct neutral ways of coordinating such free individuals. Therefore politics is one, while there are many moralities. The *Ethics* presents a single good practical life, the life of active citizenship, while the *Politics* offers a diversity of possible ways communities can organize themselves to live well. We today have many ethical visions and a single politics, whereas Aristotle has a single ethical vision and many good constitutions.

While Aristotle says that plural constitutions come from errors about justice, we today assume that there are plural good lives because of the legitimate diversity of ultimate goods. For us, only the absence of such an evident single best life, according to this way of thinking, saves us from totalitarianism. Aristotle offers an alternative to this line of thought, which might help us in finding nontotalitarian ways of thinking about a single politics with room for plural ways of living well.

Books VII and VIII fit the commonplace contrast between ancients and moderns that claims that for the ancients ethics is prior to politics: it is only by knowing what the best human life is that we can figure out what the best state and the best constitution is. The rest of the *Politics* doesn't fit that picture at all. Book III overturns the commonplace that ancient politics is directed toward the good while modern politics aims at the right, since it explores justice and the variety of constitutions without referring to any details of the good life. It thereby sets the tone for Books IV–VI, which discuss a variety of good constitutions without attention to the nature of the good life. As these books discover constitutions that are better than the citizens who comprise them, they show that not only does *knowledge* of the best life not precede knowledge of the best constitution, but that virtuous people do not precede good constitutions.

Book III distinguishes correct from bad constitutions by four different criteria: good constitutions (1) rule for the sake of the whole, not just the ruling part, (2) they aim at the good life and not merely at life for their citizens, (3) justice in correct constitutions is proportion to merit, and (4) good constitutions appeal to the rule of law. Book III stands out from the rest of the *Politics* because only here does rule of law have two opponents, the rule of men ignoring law to do as they like, the antithesis of constitutional rule—this is the contrast that continues through the rest of the *Politics*—and also the rule of the best person, a rule by wisdom rather than the generalities of law. These two alternatives make ruling and being ruled both desirable in itself and a second-best.

In the rest of the *Politics* Aristotle relates those four criteria for correct constitutions to each other in different ways. Sometimes they are equivalent, and sometimes he uses them to separate constitutions along lines other than the correct/corrupt demarcation. Book III calls democracies and oligarchies corrupt constitutions, but as we move through Books IV–VI we encounter lawful and lawless democracies and oligarchies, so rule of law doesn't separate correct from deviant constitutions. The mixed constitution and the constitution dominated by the middle class in Book IV aim at the good of the whole, but not at the good life, and these constitutions do not embody justice as proportion to merit. Political philosophy doesn't purge democracy and oligarchy of their partial conceptions of justice; it shows how to orient those constitutions toward the common advantage.

The partial and imperfect nature of any particular conception of justice and the emphasis on stability in Books III–VI makes Aristotle uninterested in distinguishing between moral and conventional aspects of politics. There is no distinction between *mala in se* and *mala prohibita*, between natural and conventional aspects of justice. There is no effort to find a moral core to political life, with the rest having to do with coordination. There is no distinction between living together and living well.

4. If People Are Political Animals, What Is the Relation between Citizen and Polis? In Particular, What Is the Relation between the Moral Virtues of the Individual and the Virtues of the Good Citizen and the Good State?

Because people are political animals, they lead complete, self-sufficient, and happy lives by being part of a complete and self-sufficient community, the polis. "The complete good seems to be self-sufficient. What we count as self-sufficient is not what suffices for a solitary person by himself, living an isolated life, but what suffices also for parents, children, wife, and, in general, for friends and fellow citizens, since a human being is a naturally political animal" (*NE* I.7.1097b9–12). At every stage in Aristotle's inquiry, he shows us how to avoid the twin dangers of one side of self-sufficiency obliterating the other, of the state providing the background conditions in which individuals can lead free lives or of individuals sacrificing themselves for the good of the whole.

The polis is self-sufficient because individuals are, by themselves, not self-sufficient. If individuals were self-sufficient, the state would be the background condition for good lives and not a value in itself. In Books I and II, this theme takes the form of distinguishing economic from political self-sufficiency, the polis from the family. Individual citizens, unlike households, become ethically self-sufficient without being economically self-sufficient. Self-sufficient people living in a self-sufficient community means that in Book III "citizen" and "constitution" are defined in terms of each other. For either term to have an independent ground would destroy the self-sufficiency of the other. Books IV–VI show that the good constitution should not, and cannot, depend on the antecedent virtue of its citizens, but instead can be a better constitution than the citizens who make it up. If the goodness of a constitution doesn't derive from the goodness of its citizens, the self-sufficiency of the polis doesn't derive from that of its citizens either. Finally, in Books VII and VIII, the interrelations between self-sufficient citizens and the self-sufficient community takes the form of talking about the state itself as happy and virtuous. A city is virtuous (*spoudaios*) when its citizens are virtuous (*spoudaios*) (VII.13.1332a33–35). The individual can be self-sufficient and autonomous if and only if the community is.

The talk about a happy and virtuous polis raises questions about the relations between part and whole familiar to Aristotle and his listeners. In Book IV of the *Republic* we learn that states are just and moderate only if all their citizens have those virtues, but are courageous and wise because of the presence of courage and wisdom in only small classes of citizens. While there is nothing canonical about the four cardinal virtues for Aristotle, we can understand a lot of what is most challenging in the *Politics* by tracing what happens to the four virtues as they function in Aristotle's argument.[3] Already in Book II we see that it is relatively easy to organize states around the goal of courage; the reasons that make courage an attractive and attainable goal for states are exactly the reasons it is so difficult for states to achieve the others.

Justice is the obvious political problem. Negotiating through disputes about justice requires political philosophy. Particular constitutions emerge because of disputes and errors about justice. But I was constantly surprised to see how small a role justice plays in the *Politics*. Justice comes into consideration because democrats and oligarchs define the principles of their constitutions by *speaking* about justice in certain ways (III.9.1280a7–12). "Man is more of a political animal than a bee or any other gregarious animal . . . No animal has speech except a human being" (I.2.1253a8–10). Justice and arguments about justice are inextricably tied together. Justice disappears from view when, as in Books VII and VIII, it isn't something we argue about.[4]

More surprising still is how narrow Aristotle's conception of justice is. The justice Aristotle discusses has to do with the principle by which rulers are selected, not what rulers do once in office. Distributive justice distributes offices; it does not refer to the rulers distributing other goods, such as wealth, honor, or security. Bernard Williams says that "modern liberalism . . . has given itself the task of constructing a framework of social justice to control necessity and chance, in the sense both of mitigating their effects on the individual and of showing that what cannot be mitigated is not unjust. It is a distinctively modern achievement to have set the problem."[5] Modern justice is concerned with the distribution and redistribution of resources as well as offices. As we saw in the treatment of property in Book II, Aristotle does not regard the unequal distribution of wealth as unjust. It is simply given that some people are wealthy and others poor. Inequality can produce instability, and for that reason should be countered, and measures taken to try to prevent people from being too rich or poor, but not in the name of justice. In this respect, the political activity described in the *Politics* is less ambitious than contemporary politics.

Justice in the *Politics* is not only narrower than newer conceptions, it is also narrower than the justice Aristotle himself discusses in the *Ethics*, which distributes honors, wealth, and security (V.2.1030b31–32). Justice in the *Politics* is a one-way operation in which citizens select rulers. Rulers can act unjustly toward citizens by confiscating their property or humiliating them, but Aristotle doesn't talk much about this face of justice. That's not what democrats and oligarchs argue about.

While justice plays a smaller role in the *Politics* than one might expect, temperance or moderation (*sophrosynē*) does much more work. While there are obvious and explicit overlaps between the treatments of justice in the *Politics* and in the *Ethics*, the virtue of temperance in the *Politics* is not concerned with the pleasures of food, drink, and sex, as in the *Ethics*. In *Politics* II it is the virtue concerned with holding on to one's property. Beyond that, there is a specifically political virtue of maintaining political and potentially friendly relations with other citizens, especially between the rulers and the ruled and between members of different factions. If this isn't a cowardly and unprincipled retreat to the mediocre as a way of avoiding offense, or commitment, then a peculiarly Aristotelian form of political wisdom emerges as he displays the political virtue of moderation. Democracies and oligarchies naturally tend to become extreme species of those constitutions, and the virtue of political moderation counters that natural tendency. Political moderation consists in seeing alternating ruling and being ruled as worth doing for its own sake, and not as a second best. Williams talks about "the heroic Aristotelian capacity for compromise," and we need to see moderation, both on Aristotle's part and on the statesman's, as noble rather than weak.[6]

Much of the interest in the *Politics*, especially in Books IV–VI, comes in seeing Aristotle develop political forms of moderation that insure stability and at the same time move the constitution as close as possible to promoting the good life, so that aiming at stability does not become an amoral variant on *raison d'état*. Choosing to alternate ruling with being ruled, instead of trying to rule all the time—or to be a free rider and be ruled permanently, the modern worry that replaces the threat of despotism—exhibits a moderation that Aristotle must show isn't simply a second-best. Similarly for his dictum that "to be educated relative to the constitution is not to do the things enjoyed by oligarchs or proponents of democracy, but rather to do the things that will enable the rulers, respectively, to govern in an oligarchic or democratic way" (V.9.1310a19–22). Democrats and oligarchs should not try to act as democratically or oligarchically as possible, but act politically, constitutionally, and therefore moderately. It is always easy to see moderation understood as self-control as a necessary condition for good action. The challenge is to see moderation instead as a virtue, not just a necessary condition but something worth choosing for its own sake. This is the same issue as trying to see ruling and being ruled in turn as desirable in its own right and not as something forced on us by necessity.

In the *Politics* the alternative to moderation is a drive toward political extremes. Just as the capacity for political friendship and for domination have the same source in the combination of intelligence and *thumos* noted in VII.7 and which I discussed in my first chapter, the virtue of moderation and the vice of extremism are both rooted in the desire for justice and a community where people can live well. Moderate democracies and oligarchies will be seen as settling for a second best, or for mediocrity, by democratic and oligarchic purists. Democrats will insist on absolute equality or regard any deviations from it as unfortunate and temporary compromises necessary until their party is strong enough to discard them, and the same for oligarchs. In actual circumstances, the desire for the ideal constitution creates factions and revolution. The challenge is to see stable and moderate democracies and oligarchies as forms of the best constitution, under the appropriate sense of best.

Moderation, especially in Books IV–VI, presents another variation on the relation between individual ethical virtue and the virtues of the state.

In Book IV, Aristotle shows how there can be good states whose goodness doesn't come from the virtue of their citizens. States and constitutions can be better than the citizens who make them up. The ambitions of the statesman are moderated here; they don't include remaking the citizens into virtuous people. In Books V and VI, Aristotle gives advice on how to preserve any constitution, no matter how corrupt. Of special interest is the way that the virtuous have no special role in this vision of politics; as I like to put it, there is no party of virtue among the factions to which the statesman must attend.

Wisdom, finally, presents a different kind of problem. *Phronēsis*—practical and political wisdom—is said in Book III to be the virtue exclusively of rulers, and that *phronēsis* is exhibited for the statesman in Aristotle's own arguments. But there is another kind of wisdom, associated with the life of philosophy. There is no political community of philosophers, but the later parts of Book VII and all of Book VIII that we have are devoted to the political counterpart of philosophy, the development of music as both a form of ethical education and the way citizens spend their leisure together. Just as the virtuous have no special role in the *Politics*, philosophers have no special place in Aristotle's ideal state. The *Politics* ends by discovering the virtue of leisure suitable for citizens of the ideal state, a form of wisdom quite unlike the contemplation of the *Ethics* or of the *Metaphysics*.

5. What Is the Role of Philosophy in Politics, Including How Aristotle's *Politics* Can Be Practical?

One of the surprising conclusions of my study is that the best constitution is Aristotle's own discovery. No one prior to Aristotle had identified polity as a form of constitution, and no one would recognize the best state of Books VII and VIII the way they would acknowledge the life of virtuous activity in the *Ethics*. The best life of the *Ethics* is certainly not Aristotle's discovery: he would never say that up until he wrote the *Ethics* no one had yet lived the best life, but until Aristotle writes the *Politics*, no one had yet conceived his best constitution, let alone lived under it. This difference produces another of the great differences between the *Ethics* and the *Politics*: in the *Ethics* we are told to pay attention to the unarticulated sayings of the wise, and we see that practical wisdom rests on practical experience. One cannot become virtuous by attending lectures on virtue but by doing virtuous actions until they become second nature. The *Politics* is more willing than the *Ethics* to dictate to people; it contains many more explicit recommendations and precepts than the *Ethics*. It is more open to the possibility that someone can have political wisdom without direct political experience, and that one person's practical wisdom can be transmitted to another. One state can adopt useful laws from another polis; there is no equivalent for individuals. Therefore, Aristotle is willing to listen to the proposals of Plato, Phaleas, and Hippodamus in Book II and to rely on the 158 histories of constitutions he and his students collected as depositories of practical experience without ethical counterpart.

The *Politics* presents a form of practical knowledge that is more circumstantial than the *Ethics*, more interested in the practical problems of non-ideal situations, and more open to taking seriously a diversity of opinion. While most opinions about justice are wrong, they, unlike the wrong opinions in ethics, are part of the data of politics because the statesman, unlike the good person, needs to make them a part of his deliberations. If the *Ethics* is willing to dismiss divergent opinion as simply wrong, the way Aristotle handles different opinions in the *Politics* may make that book more useful to us than the *Ethics*.

Philosophy, then, has a greater role in politics than in ethics. In the *Ethics* the need for philosophy, and so the authority of the philosopher, comes from the need to infer from the "what" to the "why," the *hoti* to the *dioti*. "The political man should also not regard as irrelevant the inquiry that makes clear not only the *that*, but also the *why*. For that way of proceeding is the philosopher's way in every discipline" (*EE* I.6.1216b35–37). Aristotle's audience already knows what good action is and what is the good condition of the soul. Taking them as settled, the philosophical project of the *Ethics* is to show why the life with the soul in the best condition is the life of virtuous action in the political community. The philosopher can help people who are already leading good lives to see just where the goodness of their lives lies.

The data of politics are more unsettled, and so the function and authority of the political philosopher is greater. Thus in Book II, he justifies the examination of proposed constitutions, "any others described by another that are held to be good" on the grounds that "the currently available constitutions are not in good condition" (II.1.1260b30–35). In the *Ethics* Aristotle offers an array of the ethical virtues, which only slightly departs from a list most Greeks would agree to, but in the *Politics* he says: "Concerning the things relative to virtue, nothing is agreed. Indeed, to start with, not everyone honors the same virtue, so it is reasonable to expect them to differ as well in regard to the training of it" (VIII.2.1337b2).[7] Aristotle claims that observing that the different constitutions have species is his own discovery. Earlier I quoted these lines: "All men hold that justice is some kind of equality. . . . What we have to discover is equality and inequality for what sort of persons. That is difficult, and calls for *political philosophy*" (*EE* III.12.1282b18–23). There is nothing corresponding to this in the *Ethics*.

Just as Aristotle will take seriously the opinions of people who are not statesman, so the audience for the *Politics* will be correspondingly broader than that for the *Ethics*, where only people who are already good can profit from philosophical reflection. We can learn more from others' experience in politics than in ethics. Most people think that ruling and being ruled in turn is not desirable in its own right, and would, they think, rather rule all the time if they could get away with it. Most think that their idea of justice is the right one, and no one thinks with Aristotle that all conceptions of justice fall short of true justice.

The passage from *Politics* I that declared man a political animal continues: "Speech [logos as opposed to *phonē*] is for making clear what is beneficial or harmful, and hence also what is just or unjust. For it is peculiar to human beings, in comparison to the other animals, that they alone have perception of what is good or bad, just or unjust, and the rest. And it is community in these that makes a household and a polis" (I.2.1253a13–18). Here is another complication shared by ethics and politics, the complex interrelations between what is useful and what is just. In neither ethics nor politics is there the opposition between the useful and the just that leads some modern readers, especially those influenced by Arendt, to see the realm of the political as rising above necessity and the social.[8] In the *Ethics*, virtue consists in choosing for its own sake things that are in the first instance worth doing for other reasons: courage is worth choosing for its own sake because withstanding one's fears in battle and aiming at military victory is already something worth doing, for whatever reason. In the *Politics*, the relation between advantage and justice becomes the relation between stability and the good life as goals of the polis.

The purpose of the polis is for its citizens to lead virtuous and happy lives, but the common function of citizens aims at the security of the state, and political friendship is advantage friendship, not virtue friendship (VIII.9.1160a11, *EE* VII.10.1242a6).[9] In the *Politics*, democratic justice posits everyone as equal and oligarchic justice claims that offices should be distributed in proportion to wealth. Correct constitutions distribute offices in proportion to merit, but merit is not a third standard of justice in addition to numbers and wealth. Merit functions politically by taking those formulations for justice and reorienting them toward rule for the sake of the whole polis and not the rulers alone, toward the good life instead of life.

In the introduction I looked at the first two chapters of Book IV to outline the variety of ways in which philosophy can be practical. Aristotle delineated four different kinds of political inquiry based on four meanings of the term "best" in the "best constitution," and four distinct ways in which the *Politics* and political philosophy can be practical. Aristotle supplies the statesman with a flexible understanding of the best constitution and so of the relationship between ethics and politics. The *Politics* presents, then, a challenging example of how philosophy can be practical without being partisan or usurping the role of the statesman. The political philosopher presents arguments that must be completed by the statesman. The arguments of the philosopher are purely rational and lack ethical substance. Specifically, they don't have the weighted probabilities that circumstances allow the statesman to place on competing arguments. The statesman's arguments, unlike the philosopher's, must not only be cogent but must appear attractive to fellow citizens, making the statesman into a rhetorician as the philosopher is not. By this alliance with political wisdom, philosophy has something to contribute to practice.

> Concerning equality and justice, even though it is very difficult to find the truth about these matters, it is still easier to hit on it than it is to persuade those who are capable of aggrandizing themselves. The inferior always seek equality and justice; those who dominate them take no thought for it. (VI.3.1318b2–5)

Therefore philosophy has a huge range in the *Politics*. At one extreme, the philosopher stands outside the polis as an architect designing the best polis to conform to his philosophical vision. At the other extreme, in Books VII and VIII, the statesman has to wonder what to do with the philosophers in his midst, how to incorporate philosophical activity into the framework of the best state. In between lie the practical philosophical problems that make the statesman need to exercise *phronēsis*, practical wisdom. Philosophy makes statesmanship into a very demanding job.

The idea of practical philosophy faces obstacles on all fronts. First, praxis looks too variable and circumstantial, too dependent on force and opinion, to be knowable. Justice varies so much both with circumstances and with people's opinions that a philosophical understanding of justice seems impossible. On the other side, there seems to be nothing to know that the successful ethical agent or politician doesn't already know. The higher the value we place on political life, the less likely it is that we find a science knowable by the philosopher. If politics is about winning, or about coordination, maybe things will be predictable enough for there to be a science. But if politics has something to do with living a good life, political philosophy making a practical contribution to our lives will be far more difficult. Only at a few critical places does Aristotle promise that political philosophy will tell the statesman something he doesn't already know. Most of the time, philosophical knowledge of praxis seems either impossible or unnecessary. Whatever progress we've made politically since Aristotle's time, the difficulty of philosophy being practical remains with us.

NOTES

INTRODUCTION

1. I try, probably unsuccessfully, to use gendered language when talking about Aristotle's own statements in the *Politics*, and gender-neutral language when speaking in my own voice. That leaves open the question of whether by "men" Aristotle means "men" or "people." I think that he must almost always mean "men." Another brief matter I should clarify at the start: unless I explicitly state otherwise, when I refer to "the *Ethics*" I mean the *Nicomachean Ethics*. I do not think there are significant differences for my purposes between the *Nicomachean* and the *Eudemian Ethics*.

2. The treatment of the ideal state finds a kind of political activity that does not depend on correcting wrongs. Parallel to that conception of politics will be a conception of philosophy as an activity that is more than therapeutic and does more than solve problems left to it by the partial ideas of other disciplines and activities, what Dewey called "the problems of men."

3. That the best *haplōs* does not appear in this final enumeration is evidence, far from conclusive, that Book IV is meant to come after Books VII and VIII. For the purposes of my argument, the order of the books does not matter. I will assume, for the sake of clarity, the traditional ordering of the books in which the *Politics* ends with the treatment of the ideal state. Both the disputed orderings are consistent with my argument. Over the years, I have persuaded myself for and against both orderings. I will return to this textual question periodically in the rest of the book.

4. The four causes are enumerated at *Posterior Analytics* II.11.94a21–23, *Ph.* II.3.194b16–195a26, and *Met.* I.3.983a24–26.

5. Others do not see these four as consistently correlated as I do. Nor do they see the opening chapters of Book IV setting out a program for the rest of the *Politics*. One exception is Stephen G. Salkever, "Aristotle's Social Science," *Political Theory* 9 (1981): 479–508. For a different analysis, with references to other considerations of these passages, see Peter Simpson, *A Philosophical Commentary on the Politics of Aristotle* (Chapel Hill: University of North Carolina Press, 1998). For an understanding compatible with mine, and derived from the same ultimate source, see Anfinn Stigen, *The Structure of*

Aristotle's Thought (Oslo: Universitetsforlaget, 1966), 354–55: "In the first approach the problem concerns the best state absolutely, the discussion is carried out in terms of 'excellence' and the solutions proposed claim to be simply best. In the second approach the problem concerns what state is best in certain circumstances, the discussion is carried out in terms of 'appropriateness' rather than excellence, and the solutions proposed claim to be 'best' in the sense of most preferable, appropriate, fitting or suitable. In the third approach the problem concerns the best state in general, the discussion is carried out in terms of 'expediency' rather than excellence or appropriateness, and the solutions proposed claim to be best in the sense of most expedient, useful, advantageous or politic. In the fourth approach the problem concerns the best means to bring about, change or maintain a state; the discussion is carried out in terms of 'effectiveness,' and the advice given claims to be best in the sense of most efficient." For the source of Stigen's analysis, see Richard McKeon, "Aristotle's Conception of Moral and Political Philosophy," *Ethics* 51 (1941): 253–90.

6. Bernard Yack, "A Reinterpretation of Aristotle's Political Teleology," *History of Political Thought* 12 (1991): 15–33, at 6–7: "Nature seems to have chosen a most imperfect and inconvenient way for human beings to develop and perfect their characteristic capacities. For *no* actual political community is well-ordered according to Aristotle; consequently '"human affairs' [*pragmatōon*] most often work out badly" (*Pol.* 1260b35; *Rhetoric* 1389b16)." All actual political regimes fall short of unqualified justice, and Aristotle's recommendations for improvement would still leave them short of the mark."

7. W. L. Newman, *The Politics of Aristotle*, 4 vols. (Oxford, 1887–1902; reprint, New York: Arno Press, 1973), 2: 400: "There is no sign that Aristotle deduced from the *Politics* the lesson which it would seem clearly to imply, as to man's chance of attaining full virtue and happiness" except in the ideal state. Bernard Yack, "A Reinterpretation of Aristotle's Political Teleology," *History of Political Thought* 12 (1991): 15–33, stresses that the purpose of the polis is to make the good life possible. That relation of "possibility" contains ambiguities that I think need display.

8. Chapter 3 of *Confronting Aristotle's Ethics: Ancient and Modern Morality* (Chicago: University of Chicago Press, 2006), is an extended attempt to tease out these background conditions.

9. "In the case of human beings what seems to count as living together is this sharing of conversation and thought (*logon kai dianoias*)" (*NE* IX.9.1170b12).

10. The relation between the Greek polis and the modern state is the subject of a huge literature. See, among many others, M. I. Finley, *Politics and the Ancient World* (Cambridge: Cambridge University Press, 1983); and Mogens Herman Hansen, *The Tradition of Ancient Greek Democracy and Its Importance for Modern Democracy* (Copenhagen: Royal Danish Academy of Sciences and Letters, 2005).

11. It is easy to be polemical about this, arguing either that progress in knowledge makes Aristotle's accounts obsolete, or that his works offer perennial teachings unaffected by changes in the details of knowledge. For the former, see, e.g., M. F. Burnyeat, "Is an Aristotelian Philosophy of Mind Still Credible? A Draft," *Essays on Aristotle's de Anima*, ed. Martha C. Nussbaum and Amélie Oksenberg Rorty (Oxford: Clarendon Press, 1992), 15–26; Stephen Holmes, "Aristippus in and out of Athens," *American Political*

Science Review 73 (1979): 113–28; and Jeremy Waldron, "What Plato Would Allow," in *Theory and Practice: Nomos 37*, ed. Judith Wagner Decew and Ian Shapiro (New York: New York University Press, 1995), 138–79. For the latter, see Nussbaum and Putnam, "Changing Aristotle's Mind," 27–56. In *Confronting Aristotle's Ethics* I argued for a position much like Burnyeat's. I now think that the contrast between the *Ethics* and *Politics* allows the articulation of a more sophisticated position on this issue.

CHAPTER ONE

1. Schofield's comment sums up the consensus. "[It] is a common complaint among scholars that Aristotle's idea of natural slavery is an anomaly within his philosophical system. . . . [Although] it might be granted *argumenti causa* that there are persons who satisfy Aristotle's description of natural slaves . . . it is a massive error or pretence to assume that in the actual world (for Aristotle, the contemporary Greek world) slaves *are* what he calls natural slaves." Malcolm Schofield, "Ideology and Philosophy in Aristotle's Theory of Slavery," *Aristoteles' "Politike": Akten des XI. Symposium Aristotelicum* (Gottingen: Vandenhoeck & Ruprecht, 1990), 4.

2. In addition, Aristotle has no interest in discussing the legitimacy or justification for different kinds of constitution. As Finley put it, "the great theorists of antiquity felt no need to grapple with the problem of legitimacy, which today figures at the very heart of our concern with the nature and value of modern society as a main dimension of political culture." M. I. Finley, *Authority and Legitimacy in the Classical City-State* (Copenhagen: Munksgaard, 1982), 12–13.

3. *Politics* 1278a10–12: "The necessary people are either slaves who minister to the wants of individuals or mechanics and laborers who are the servants of the community."

4. Stephen Salkever, "Reading Aristotle's *Nicomachean Ethics* and *Politics* as a Single Course of Lectures: Rhetoric, Politics, Philosophy," in Stephen Salkever, ed., *The Cambridge Companion to Ancient Greek Political Thought* (Cambridge: Cambridge University Press, 2009), 209–42, at 225: "He makes the central claim in chapter 2 [of *Politics* I] that human beings are by nature political. But his assertion of our political nature is not based on a belief that political is an intrinsic good or that the political life is a natural ideal. The argument developed here (1253a) is that political activity, a uniquely human activity that is essentially connected to acquired respect for nomoi, for humanly made laws and customs, can, if properly organized, channel our inherited potentiality for living according to logoi in the direction of justice and practical reason rather than injustice and despotism." Jonathan Lear, *Aristotle: The Desire to Understand* (Cambridge: Cambridge University Press, 1988), 203, says that there "seems to be a pronounced tension between Aristotle's role as descriptive biologist and his role as teleological biologist." Yack, "A Reinterpretation of Aristotle's Political Teleology," at 15: "In all other natural species that Aristotle examines the individual members that fail to realize their complete natural form are the exceptions. If the polis almost always fails to complete its development, it seems impossible to justify Aristotle's description of it as natural. Aristotle makes nature responsible for the polis; but our actual political life seems to indicate that nature, as Aristotle understands it, cannot be responsible for the form of our political communities."

5. Aristotle, of course, never draws this explicit connection between the incompleteness of motion, as he explains it in the *Physics*, and the incompleteness of slaves, much less the connection of such incompleteness to slaves as instruments of praxis. He does notes the connection I am asserting between the completeness, and hence freedom and independence, of a person and of an activity, e.g., in *Met.* I.2.982b25: "As the man is free, we say, who exists for his own sake and not for another's, so we pursue [wisdom] as the only free science, for it alone exists for its own sake." And, even closer to my connection between completeness of person and of activity: "Even in the case of external actions we speak of those who by means of their thoughts are master craftsmen as acting in the authoritative (*kurios*) sense" (*Pol.* VII.3.1325b21–23).

6. See also *Pol.* III.1.1275a14–19, III.3.1278a4–6, VIII.4.1339a32: "It is not suitable to assign intellectual entertainment (*diagogē*) to boys and to the young; for a thing that is an end does not belong to anything that is imperfect (*outheni gar atelei prosekei telos*)." The "'incompleteness'" of women is obviously a subject in itself; Aristotle says that women have *phronēsis* but that it is not *kurios*; I would understand that by connecting it to the fact that women, not being full citizens, do not participate in the polis, which is the *kuriotatē* of all communities (I.1.1252a1–7). Barker denies these differences and so is committed to denying the existence of natural slaves. Ernest Barker, *The Political Thought of Plato and Aristotle* (New York: Dover, 1959), 365: "That reason should be present even in an imperfect form means a potentiality of reason in its fulness." Robert Schlaifer, "Greek Theories of Slavery from Homer to Aristotle," *Harvard Studies in Classical Philology*, supp. vol. (1941): 451–70, reprinted in M. I. Finley, ed., *Slavery in Classical Antiquity* (Cambridge: Heffer, 1960), 93–132, at 196–97: "For such a creature to be enslaved is of benefit to him as well as his master, for everything is benefited only by fulfilling its function, by reached the *energeia* in accordance with its own *aretē*. No attention, therefore, is paid consciously to the good of the slave; the master looks out for himself alone, but the relation is so intimate that a harm to one must be a harm to the other and the good of one likewise a good for the other."

7. For people as political animals, see R. G. Mulgan, "Aristotle's Doctrine that Man is a Political Animal," *Hermes* 104 (1974): 438–45; Wolfgang Kullmann, "Man as a Political Animal in Aristotle," in *A Companion to Aristotle's Politics*, ed. David Keyt and Fred D. Miller, Jr. (Oxford: Blackwell, 1991), 94–117; John M. Cooper, "Political Animals and Civic Friendship," in *Aristoteles' "Politik": Akten des XI. Symposium Aristotelicum*, ed. Gunter Patzig (Gottingen: Vandenhoeck & Ruprecht, 1990), 221–42, reprinted with modifications as John M. Cooper, "Political Animals and Civic Friendship," revised version, in *Aristotle's Politics: Critical Essays*, ed. Richard Kraut and Steven Skultety (Lanham, MD: Rowman & Littlefield, 2005), 65–90. I have found most helpful David Depew, "Humans and Other Political Animals in Aristotle's *History of Animals*," *Phronesis* 40 (1995): 156–81.

8. "We reject the education involving expertise in the art [of music] both in instruments and performance—we regard as involving expertise in the art that with a view to contests, for one who is active in this does not undertake it for the sake of his own virtue but for the sake of pleasure; hence we judge the performance as not belonging to free persons but being more characteristic of the laborer; and indeed the result is that they become vulgar, for the aim with a view to which they create the end for themselves is

a base one; the spectator, being crude himself, customarily alters the music, so that he makes the artisans engaging in it with a view to him of a certain quality themselves and with respect to their bodies" (VIII.6.1341b8–18, see III.4.1277b3–7, VII.16.1335b5–11). Note that while Aristotle finds slavish character in people who are not literally slaves, he rarely extends the term metaphorically as broadly as Plato does.

Josiah Ober, *Political Dissent in Democratic Athens* (Princeton: Princeton University Press, 1998), 308: "In the last chapter of book 1 (1.13.1259b18ff), in the midst of a consideration of the moral virtue of members of the household, Aristotle suddenly turns to the issue of the virtues of the craftsman (*technitēs*)/mechanic (*banausos*) and makes the radical suggestion that this category of individual 'has a kind of delimited slavery' (*aphōrismenēn tina echei douleian*, 1260b1) because 'virtue pertains him to the precise extent that slavery does.' Aristotle explains that the master/employer is the 'cause' of virtue in both the (actual) slave and the (nominally free) craftsman. Here Aristotle seemingly suggests that working men were not in fact free in an unqualified sense. Yet nor were working men enslaved in the simple sense of being natural slaves. They offered a troubling middle ground between the simply free and potentially virtuous leisured elite and the natural slave. They were psychologically complete humans and thus likely to act as free men in seeking a political role, yet they did not possess political virtue. What, then, was their proper place in the politeia?"

9. The restriction to praxis makes his argument more plausible than a more general claim would be, but it creates difficulties of its own, which I cannot explore here. Helpers in the realm of *poiēsis* can in theory be replaced by machines as technology progresses: Aristotle's example is shuttles that move themselves. Practical helpers seem, by contrast, in Aristotle's eyes a permanent part of praxis. If anything, though, it would seem to be the other way around. A hundred years ago, a gentleman could not properly devote himself to virtuous activity without having someone else to drive him around, because taking care of a carriage and horses took a fair amount of time and attention. Today, he can drive himself. But the workers who used to make carriages are still needed to make cars today. So it looks as though Aristotle has it backwards: progress has made human instruments of praxis unnecessary without displacing poetic instruments.

10. Simpson concludes that such craftsmen are "worse and lower than slaves, and only rise to the level of slavish virtue, when actually employed by someone," but I cannot see evidence for this conclusion. Simpson, *A Philosophical Commentary on the Politics of Aristotle*, 69.

11. Compare the pandering Aristotle finds in professional musicians with his comment at the beginning of the *Rhetoric*: "It is wrong to warp the jury by leading them into anger or envy or pity; that is the same as if someone made a straightedge rule crooked before using it" (I.1.1354a24–25).

12. Adam Smith, *An Inquiry into the Nature and Causes of the Wealth of Nations*, vol. 1 ed. R. H. Campbell and A. S. Skinner, vol. 2 of the Glasgow Edition of the Works and Correspondence of Adam Smith (Indianapolis: Liberty Fund, 1981), "CHAPTER II: Of the Principle which gives occasion to the Division of Labour." Accessed from http://oll .libertyfund.org/title/220/217387.

13. I discuss how the fulfillment of human nature can be rare in chapter 6 of *Confronting Aristotle's Ethics*. See also Salkever, "Aristotle's Social Science," 486–47: "In

general, an animal's pleasures are determined by its ergon (*Ethics*, 1176a5); most dogs, spiders, and mules take pleasure in the sorts of things that all members of their species desire. Human beings, however, are different: 'But among humans there is no small difference in pleasures. For the same things give enjoyment to some and pain to others, are painful and hateful to some and sweet and dear to others' (*Ethics*, 1176a10–12). With other animals, pleasures and apparent goods, the starting points of desire, vary mostly by species; with humans, they vary from individual to individual, and are the major source of human inequality." David Keyt, "Distributive Justice in Aristotle's *Ethics* and *Politics*," *Topoi* 4 (1985): 33: "A polis with a deviant constitution differs from a freak of nature in the animal kingdom in one important respect. A freak of nature in the animal kingdom is an anomaly, a deviation from what happens for the most part (*epi to polu*) (*GA* IV.4.770b9–13). That which is contrary to nature is the complement of that which is according to nature; and that which is according to nature, Aristotle holds, is that which happens always or for the most part (*Ph.* II.8.198b35–36; *Gen. Corr.* II.6.333b4–7 passim). Hence that which is contrary to nature is that which happens on those rare occasions when what happens for the most part does not happen (*Ph.* II.6.197b34–35, 8.198b36; and see *Met.* E.2.1026b27–1027a17). In Aristotle's political philosophy this situation is reversed. The best polis, the only one that strictly speaking is according to nature, occurs rarely, if ever, whereas polises that deviate from this norm and are contrary to nature are the rule." And Lear, *Aristotle: The Desire to Understand*, 207–8: "Humans tend to live in flawed societies. . . . Why are there not more good states? This ought to have been an urgent and troubling question for Aristotle."

14. "A household is more self-sufficient than one person, and a city than a household" (II.2.1261b11). See Elizabeth Belfiore, "Family Friendship in Aristotle's *Ethics*," *Ancient Philosophy* 21 (2001): 113–32.

15. The village as intermediate between the family and the polis should make us wary of assuming that the bonds of family become the bonds of the polis. That becomes the issue in Book II.

16. Similarly, should he find that slavery is conventional, that would not by itself be a reason for abandoning it. At I.9.1257b10 he notes that, as with slavery, there is a debate about whether money is natural or conventional. Should money turn out to be conventional, this would never be a reason to abolish it. Similarly, merely establishing that slavery is conventional is not by itself an argument against slavery.

17. See, e.g., I.1.1252b2 and *PA* 683a20–25. But see IV.15.1299b9 and *de Anima* II.8.420b20–23 for exceptions. Depew, "Humans and Other Political Animals in Aristotle's *History of Animals*," at 163, n.16: "Humans can appear in public as cooperative citizens only if they are able to preside over cooperative households in which different functions and roles are assigned to different persons: masters, free women, children, and slaves. Human rationality is, in several senses, the difference-maker."

18. Edmund Burke uses language very much like that of *Politics* VII.7 in criticizing Southern slave owners: "In such a people, the haughtiness of domination combines with the spirit of freedom, fortifies it, and renders it invincible." Edmund Burke, "On Conciliation with America," *The Works of Edmund Burke* (Boston: Little, Brown, 1880), 2: 124.

19. And yet owning slaves is desirable; people should do it whenever possible. "An ox is a poor man's servant" (I.2.1252b11).

20. VII.2.1324b29–36: "It is not the task of the doctor or the pilot to either persuade or [failing that] compel persons [to submit to their rule]—patients in the case of the one, voyagers in the case of the other. But the many seem to suppose that expertise in mastery [i.e., ruling over slaves] is [the same as] political expertise, and they are not ashamed to train [to do] in relation to others what they deny is just or advantageous for themselves. For among themselves they seek just rule, but they care nothing about justice toward others."

21. Salkever, "Reading Aristotle's *Nicomachean Ethics* and *Politics* as a Single Course of Lectures," 226: "The chances for genuinely human political life seem . . . to depend on our capacity for distinguish politics from various forms of mastery that resemble political life but threaten to distort and corrupt it."

22. I leave *thumos* untranslated. Aristotle himself doesn't define it; the closest I think he comes to a definition occurs when he says that *thumos* is the natural capacity that makes possible the "power to command and the love of freedom." "Spirit" is the English that comes closest; "will," while more controversial, is sometimes appealing. Some of the difficulties with the meaning of *thumos* are indicated in Angela Hobbs, *Plato and the Hero: Courage, Manliness and the Impersonal Good* (Cambridge: Cambridge University Press, 2000), 3: "At first sight the *thumos* of the *Republic* seems one of the more bizarre creations of an already bizarrely creative period in Plato's life. At different points it is connected with a very wide range of characteristics, not all of which obviously cohere: anger, aggression and courage; self-disgust and shame; a sense of justice, indignation and the desire for revenge; obedience to the political authorities though not necessarily to one's father; a longing for honor, glory and worldly success; some interest in the arts but a fear of intellectualism; a preference for war over peace and increasing meanness over money." See also P. A. Vander Waerdt, "The Political Intention of Aristotle's Moral Philosophy," *Ancient Philosophy* 5 (1985): 83, which says that Aristotle's "account of moral education in the *NE* abstracts from the forms of regime and from the natural role of thumos in education—from the political face of virtue, as it were." In Christian moral psychology, to oversimplify, *thumos* is replaced by the will as the supplement to reason and passion. In modern moral psychology, *thumos* is replaced as the supplement to reason and passion by interest. The virtues, especially temperance, are radically transformed under these newer psychologies.

Important reflections on the meaning and nature of *thumos* can be found in Jonathan Shay, *Odysseus in America: Combat Trauma and the Trials of Homecoming* (New York: Scribner, 2002). Discussions with Shay, as well as with Betty Belfiore and David O'Connor, have helped me formulate the argument in this section.

23. The earliest such modern thought-experiment occurs in Book II of Herodotus, where an infant is isolated with a wet nurse who has had her tongue cut out to see what language the child will "naturally" speak by itself. That the sense of nature involved in natural slaves is thin does not by itself decide whether the same is true for women, that is, whether the sexual differences noted in the biological works translate into political or ethical differences. Just as in the question of natural slaves, I see no evidence that Aristotle is interested in nature or human nature in a sense that would permit these modern questions to be raised. Nevertheless, the idea of counterfactuals comes into existence much later than Aristotle. I find most helpful on this important question of philosophical

method Amos Funkenstein, *Theology and the Scientific Imagination from the Middle Ages to the Seventeenth Century* (Princeton: Princeton University Press, 1986).

24. Thus the ancient topos of *physis* versus *nomos* is quite different from the modern distinction of nature versus nurture. As David Depew points out, we moderns need an "exceedingly thin notion of cultural transmission" to support democratic and individualist ideology, while "the entire issue is foreign for Aristotle, who . . . [has] an implicit notion of deep cultural transmission that betrays no dividing line from biological heritability" ("Barbarians, Natural Rulers and Natural Slaves," unpublished manuscript, p. 15). For this reason, I accept Bodéüs's claim that Aristotle's theses about barbarians, reason and *thumos* need not be a description of nature as opposed to the way barbarians are educated. Richard Bodéüs, "The Natural Foundations of Right and Aristotelian Philosophy," in *Action and Contemplation: Studies in the Moral and Political Thought of Aristotle*, ed. Robert C. Bartlett and Susan D. Collins (Albany: SUNY Press, 2000), 69–105.

Dewey, *Freedom and Culture* (New York: Capricorn Books, 1939), 103: "It is not accidental that the rise of interest in human nature coincided in time with the assertion in political matters of the rights of the people as a whole, over against the rights of a class supposedly ordained by God or Nature to exercise rule. The full scope and depth of the connection between assertion of democracy in government and new consciousness of human nature cannot be present without going into an opposite historical background, in which social arrangements and political forms were taken to be an expression of Nature— but most decidedly not of *human* nature.

"Regard for *human* nature as the source of legitimate political arrangements is comparatively late in European history; that when it arose it marked an almost revolutionary departure from previous theories about the basis of political rule and citizenship and subjection—so much so that the fundamental difference between even ancient republican and modern democratic governments has its source in the substitution of human nature for cosmic nature as the foundation of politics."

Ibid., 124: "Because of lack of an adequate theory of human nature in its relations to democracy, attachment to democratic ends and methods has tended to become a matter of tradition and habit—an excellent thing as far as it goes, but when it becomes routine is easily undermined when change of conditions changes other habits."

25. Newman, *The Politics of Aristotle*, 1: 286–87: "If Aristotle had said that the State exists not only for the realization of the highest quality of life, but also for the development in all within it of the best type of life of which they are capable, he would have made the elevation of the mass of men one of its ends. But this he hardly seems to do." See too Oswyn Murray, "*Polis* and *Politeia* in Aristotle," in *The Ancient Greek City-State*, ed. Mogens Herman Hansen (Copenhagen: Royal Danish Academy of Sciences and Letters, 1993), 201: "It is characteristic of Aristotle's theoretical focus that he does not stop to consider the interesting historical question, how other breeds of lesser humanity might reach their appropriate political forms."

26. In early modern thought, geographical differences among peoples were supplemented by temporal differences between the temporal and the civilized. This is an advance over Aristotle because one can think of the primitive as the not-yet-civilized, while there is no such progression in Aristotle's geography.

If Aristotle were more interested in the non-Greek world, he would run into trouble here. He can say that barbarian masters are not true masters; they are only masters in their barbarous situation. But he cannot get away with the same for slaves. In Persia, the despots might not have been real masters, but the slaves were surely still slaves. Moreover, he looks at, and even praises, the constitution of Carthage, a polis made up of non-Greek citizens (1272b24), and talks about the happiness of King Priam, another non-Greek, in the *Ethics*.

27. A parallel question arises in the *Metaphysics*. If, as its first line says, "man by nature desires to know," why do so few people choose to engage in philosophy? The difference is that the *Metaphysics* does not claim that that desire is constitutive of human beings, while the *Politics* does.

28. Newman notes that when Aristotle says that the Europeans are "freer," this means "free in comparison with Asiatics" (*The Politics of Aristotle*, 3: 364). See too III.14.1285a21. Carnes Lord, *Education and Culture in the Political Thought of Aristotle* (Ithaca: Cornell University Press, 1982), 164: "For Aristotle as for Plato . . . the phenomenon of spiritedness [*thumos*] appears to be of fundamental importance for understanding of nature of human sociality, and thereby the limits or the nature of political life in particular; and for both the phenomenon of spiritedness is profoundly problematic. Spiritedness is indispensable for the best city just as it is an inescapable fact of political life as such; but it represents at the same time a grave danger, as it constantly threatens the predominance in politics of prudence or reason." See too *Republic* 4.435e–436a: "It would be ridiculous if anyone imagined the spirited character didn't come to be in the cities from particular people who also have this attribute, like those in Thrace and Scythia, and pretty generally in the northern region, or similarly with the love of learning, which one might attribute especially to the region round about us, or the love of money that one might claim to be not least round about the Phoenicians and those in Egypt."

29. If slaves didn't have some rational capacity, including the capacity to be persuaded, they couldn't be tortured to tell the truth. There's no point in torturing animals to extract confessions. The modern conception of torture as not only violating the rule of law but violating the humane treatment of people reflects a change in our understanding of psychology. See, among many others, Paul W. Kahn, *Sacred Violence: Torture, Terror, and Sovereignty* (Ann Arbor: University of Michigan Press, 2008), and "Torture and Democratic Violence," *Ratio Juris* 22 (2009): 244–59, as well as John H. Langbein, "The Legal History of Torture," in *Torture*, ed. Sanford Levinson (Oxford: Oxford University Press, 2004), 93–104.

30. Modern bureaucracy exemplifies the ability to reason without *thumos* or having one's own ends. When Arendt says that Eichmann acted without thinking, her account is designed to explain how one can act rationally enough to administer the complexities of the Final Solution while in another sense lack the commitments that one attributes to the thoughtful person. Hannah Arendt, *Eichmann in Jerusalem* (New York: Viking, 1963).

31. In the *Ethics* too, slavishness is more shameful than action motivated by the *thumos* that is at the root of despotism. See VII.3.1149a30–b35.

32. An explanation for Aristotle's silence on natural masters occurs in Paul W. Kahn, *Out of Eden: Adam and Eve and the Problem of Evil* (Princeton: Princeton University

Press, 2007), 148. "The paradigm of slavery is at stake whenever the merely natural element of man's character is projected onto an other. The slave is what we are not: nature without culture. If the slave is pure nature, the master is not a product of nature at all. He creates himself by embodying an idea. To embody an idea in politics is to express a willingness to sacrifice for it. Not accidentally, the same American culture that practiced slavery was also one which thought of itself as particularly committed to the military virtues of honor and sacrifice."

33. The specifics of Aristotle's moral geography has the odd implication that the rest of the world contains lots of natural slaves running around without anyone naturally equipped to master them, setting a big job for the Greeks to master them all. Odd as this consequence is, it is consistent with his argument in Book I, which first demonstrates the necessity of the master/slave relation and only then asks whether there are any people who naturally till the waiting niche.

34. The relation of master to slave is the relation of form to matter. To be is to be something. Matter needs a form. Form is realized in matter, but is not deficient, qua form, without such realization. Matter is always potentially something, but an unrealized form is not a potential form. Thus a master would suffer no psychic loss if he lost his slaves, while the slave would suffer a large psychic loss if severed from his master. To pursue that analogy, one master can have many slaves but a slave can only serve one master, just as a single plan can be embodied in many buildings, but one heap of bricks can only take on a single form. The need of masters for slaves is dictated by necessity, while the need of slaves for masters is central to the purpose of the slave, since the slave can have no purposes of his own.

35. The connection between these two is developed in Bernard Williams, "Justice as a Virtue," in Williams, *The Sense of the Past: Essays in the History of Philosophy*, ed. and with an intro. by Myles Burnyeat (Princeton: Princeton University Press, 2006), reprinted from Amélie Rorty, *Essays on Aristotle's Ethics* (Berkeley: University of California Press, 1981), 189–99.

36. Newman also notes that "the mildness of the dog to those whom he knows is due to the philosophic element in his nature . . . ; Aristotle claims, on the contrary, that what Plato ascribes to the philosophic element is really due to *thumos*." Newman, *The Politics of Aristotle*, 3: 366–67.

37. If friendship is coextensive with *thumos*, this would account for the impossibility of masters and slaves being friends. If friendship is restricted to be coextensive with virtue and *prohairesis*, this would account for its moral significance. Masters and slaves are disqualified from friendship at IV.11.1295b14–24: "Those who are superior in the goods of luck (strength, wealth, friends, and other such things) neither wish to be ruled nor know how to be ruled. . . . Those, on the other hand, who are exceedingly deprived of such goods are too humble. Hence the latter do not know how to rule, but only how to be ruled in the way slaves are ruled, whereas the former do not know how to be ruled in any way, but only how to rule as maters rule. The result is a polis consisting not of free people but of slaves and masters, the one group full of envy and the other full of arrogance. Nothing is further removed from a friendship and a community that is political. For community involves friendship." Extreme democrats and oligarchs, then, are slavish and despotic, showing that slavishness is not confined to Asians, and therefore that the

psychological differences Aristotle traces here are not natural in the contemporary sense. In *Ethics* VIII Aristotle says that a master can be friends with a slave, not qua slave but qua man. But it is hard to see how a slave could reciprocate. "Insofar as he is a slave there is no friendship with him. But there is friendship with him insofar as he is a human being" (VIII.12.1161b7). A master could wish the slave good, for his own sake. But could a slave formulate such a wish? He cannot even wish himself good for his own sake, so the concept of something being good for its own sake must be incoherent to the slave.

38. In *Republic* IX *thumos* appears as a lion and a snake (588d, 590b). As Burnyeat points out, the lion's roar and the snake's hiss are both expressive and communicative, a feature of *thumos* as opposed to appetite (*epithumia*). Myles Burnyeat, "The Truth of Tripartition," *Proceedings of the Aristotelian Society* 106 (2006): 1–23, at 9.

39. Kraut's note is helpful. "One may wonder whether Plato's problem—how to combine those two opposed qualities—is a genuine difficulty. Why shouldn't it be possible to be both harsh (towards *A*) and gentle (towards *B*)? The problem becomes more interesting if one asks whether one can be gentle and harsh, friendly and angry, towards one and the same person: this is the phenomenon that Aristotle is discussing here." Richard Kraut, trans., *Aristotle: Politics, Books VII and VIII* (Oxford: Clarendon Press, 1997), 95.

40. *NE* VIII.1.1155a22–29: "Friendship would seem to hold cities together, and legislators would seem to be more concerned about it than about justice. For concord would seem to be similar to friendship and they aim at concord above all, while they try above all to expel civil conflict, which is enmity. Further, if people are friends, they have no need of justice, but if they are just they need friendship in addition; and the justice that is most just seems to belong to friendship." See also *Politics* IV.11.1295b20–25: In a state composed of excessively rich and excessively poor people, "the ones do not know how to rule but only how to be ruled, and then only in the fashion of rule of a master. What comes into being, then, is a city not of free persons but of slaves and masters, the ones consumed by envy, the others by contempt." Nothing is further removed from affection and from a political partnership; for a partnership involves the element of affection.

41. Something similar is at work at the end of *Ethics* VI. Ethical virtue and *phronēsis* are not the combination of natural virtue plus cleverness. The intelligence manifested in cleverness is not the intelligence of *phronēsis*, nor is the desire for good ends present in natural virtue the same desire as the desire for the noble at work in ethical virtue. These natural bases are transformed when they are part of the greater, and in that sense natural, whole. See too *Pol.* VIII.3.1338b24–32: The Spartans, so long as they persevered in their love of exertion, had preeminence over others, while at present they fall short of others in both gymnastic and military contests. For it was not be exercising the young in this manner that they stood out, but merely by the fact of their training against others who did not train. The element of nobility, not what is beastlike (*to kalon all' ou to thēriōdes*), should play the leading role. For it is not the wolf or any of the other beasts that would join the contest in any noble danger, but rather a good man.

42. Compare *Politics* VII with Thucydides, Pericles's funeral oration (2.40.2–3): "We do not consider words (*logoi*) to be an impediment to actions (*erga*), but rather [regard it] essential to be previously instructed by speech before embarking on necessary actions. We are peculiar also in that we hold that we are simultaneously persons who are daring and who vigorously debate what they will put their hands to. Among other men, ignorance

(*amathia*) leads to rashness, while reasoned debate (*logismos*) just bogs them down." See too Herodotus (7.50.1–2), where Xerxes says that we should act without thinking too much in order to accomplish anything.

That both logos and *thumos* are specifically human appears in *NE* III.1. "How are errors that express emotion (*thumos*) any less voluntary than those that express rational calculation (*logismos*)? For both sorts of errors are to be avoided; and since nonrational feelings seem to be no less human [than rational calculation], actions resulting from emotion or appetite (*thumos kai epithumia*) are also proper to a human being; it is absurd, then, to regard them as involuntary" (*NE* III.1.1111a35–b3). "Passion and will (*thumos kai boulesis*), and also appetite (*epithymia*), exist in children as soon as they are born, but it is the nature of reasoning and intelligence to arise in them as they grow older" (*Pol.* VII.13.1334b20–24).

43. Jean-Jacques Rousseau, "Discourse of the Origins of Inequality," *Basic Political Writings*, trans. Donald A. Cress (Indianapolis: Hackett, 1988), 64: "As soon as men had begun mutually to value one another, and the idea of esteem was formed in their minds, each one claimed to have a right to it. . . . From this every voluntary wrong became an outrage, because along with the harm that resulted from the injury, the offended party saw in it contempt for his person, which often was more insufferable than the harm itself."

44. A good example of the shift from ancient polis to modern state is found in Michael Walzer, "Drawing the Line: Religion and Politics," *Utah Law Review* 1999 (1999): 619–38, at 629: "This first critique of separation [of religion and politics] stresses the capacity of religion and its secular surrogates, such as Marxism and national, to engage people in a politics of large causes. This is contrasted with the merely technical or bureaucratic universality of the neutral state, which indeed serves all of its citizens but gives them no reason to serve themselves, to participate in the political process. Only religious or near-religious conviction can provide effective reasons." What Walzer says seems to me true for the modern state. The question for the *Politics* is under what conditions political participation can be a positive good, indeed an intrinsic good. To rule permanently is to destroy the very conditions under which political participation is its own end. This would be similar to the possibility raised in the *Ethics* of wishing goods to one's friends, so that they would become gods and so no longer friends.

45. "Men are not born to be free. . . . Liberty is a need felt by a small class of people whom nature has endowed with nobler minds than the mass of men. Consequently, it may be repressed with impunity. Equality, on the other hand, pleases the masses." Napoleon, quoted in J. Christopher Herold, ed., *The Mind of Napoleon* (New York: Columbia University Press, 1955), 73, and then quoted again by Lynn Hunt, *Inventing Human Rights* (New York and London: Norton, 2007), 180.

46. Put another way, the arguments concerning natural slavery have no implications for any positive institution of slavery or slavishness. For an articulation of that formulation, see Bodéüs, "The Natural Foundations of Right and Aristotelian Philosophy," 69–105. To say that capitalism and freedom can be at odds is not, of course, to deny that alternatives to capitalism can be even more inimical to freedom. Aristotle lists five economic ways of life in I.8.1256b1–2: nomadic, raiding, fishing, hunting, and farming. Only farming plays a role in the rest of the *Politics*, so I infer that he thinks, although without giving an explicit argument, that it is the only form of economic self-sufficiency that can lead to political self-sufficiency.

47. This is the difference, in Hegel's terms, between the bad and the good infinite.

48. One of the oddities of Book VII, which I will discuss in its proper place, is that there, when talking about the ideal state, Aristotle yokes together unlimited accumulation and domination over other people, while he distinguishes them in Book I.

49. *Aristotle's Rhetoric: An Art of Character* and *For the Sake of Argument* (Chicago: University of Chicago Press, 1994).

50. The seminal discussion is Benjamin Constant, "The Liberty of the Ancients Compared with That of the Moderns," in *Political Writings*, ed. and trans. by Biancamaria Fontana (Cambridge: Cambridge University Press, 1988), 308–28.

CHAPTER TWO

1. See chapter 6 of *Confronting Aristotle's Ethics*.

2. Barker's claim that "the State has its own life, and it has grown" misses, I think, this crucial point about both the organization of the *Politics* and its argument. Barker, *The Political Thought of Plato and Aristotle*, 281, n.1.

3. The one thing that most people seem to take away from the *Republic* is the idea of philosopher-kings. Barker claims that the guardians "were an attempt at once to differentiate 'State' from 'society,' and to discover an organ for the realization of the common good." Ernest Barker, *Greek Political Theory: Plato and His Predecessors* (London: Methuen, 1960), 14. If Barker is close to right, it would be very important to consider philosopher-kings. Without them, there is no "organ for the realization of the common good" in the *Politics*.

4. The lack of focus leads Stalley and others to construct hypotheses about the composition of Book II. For example, Stalley notes, in connection with II.5, that "most of the points made in this discussion have no direct bearing on the *Republic*" (194). "From 5.1264a1 or thereabouts the focus of Aristotle's argument becomes less clear" (196). R. F. Stalley, "Aristotle's Criticism of Plato's *Republic*," in *A Companion to Aristotle's Politics*, ed. David Keyt and Fred D. Miller (Oxford and Cambridge: Blackwell, 1991), 182–99. Salkever, "Reading Aristotle's *Nicomachean Ethics* and *Politics* as a Single Course of Lectures," 228–29, finds unity and focus. The constitutional proposals examined each exaggerate "the importance of one element of good politics. Plato exaggerates the importance of unity among citizens. Phaleas exaggerates the value of equality; Hippodamus exaggerates the value of abstract rationality as a guide to political action. Unity, equality, and theoretical rationality are all important aspects of a justifiable polis, goods that aim at enabling good human lives. Any praiseworthy political actor must attempt to incorporate them as much as possible into the life of the polis. But if we treat each of these desiderata in isolation from the others and from the acquisition of sufficient instrumental goods, we are on the road to failure. Plato's obsession with unity obscures the conditions necessary for good human development; Phaleas's focus on equality obscures the variety of, and some possible cures for, human vices; Hippodamus's devotion to the cause of rationality obscures the extent to which a degree of stable custom and habit are needed to hold citizen bodies together."

5. Book II is not Aristotle's last word on what citizens have in common. In Book III he says that the security and stability of the constitution is the common work (*ergon*) of

citizens (III.4.1276b28–30). Citizens, we also learn in Book III, have to care about each other's virtue, which places upward limits on the size of the state. Constitutions differ from each other by different conceptions of justice, and so different constitutions have different purposes or ends, and to be a citizen is to share in the ends of the state. And in Books VII and VIII, when discussing—again?—the ideal state and constitution, he discusses common education.

6. Lloyd Gerson, "Aristotle's Polis: A Community of the Virtuous," in *Proceedings of the Boston Area Colloquium in Ancient Philosophy*, ed. John Cleary, vol. 3 (Lanham, MD: University Press of America, 1988), 205–6: "In ethics Aristotle treats of means and ends ideally, since it is irrelevant to inquiry into the particular beliefs and desires of people except in a very general way. Politics treats of action concretely, by counting as scientifically relevant to action the conditions of people's lives. Theoretically, it is possible to conclude that men desire happiness, which is in fact the virtuous activity of the soul. Practically, it is important to know that some men, say, farmers, are conscious of desiring above all a successful harvest."

7. Recall Machiavelli's defense of his own right to be listened to. Machiavelli, *Discourses on Livy*, preface to Book II: "For it is the office of a good man to show others that good which because of the malignity of the times and of fortune, he has not been able to accomplish, so that (many being capable)) some of those more loved by Heaven can accomplish them." For discrepancies between the program of X.9 and the *Politics* as we have it, see especially Richard Bodéüs, "Le recherche poliqitue d'après le 'programme' de l'*Éthique à Nicomaque* d'Aristote," *Études classiques* 51 (1983): 23–33; and P. A. Vander Waert, "The Plan and Intention of Aristotle's Ethical and Political Writings," *Illinois Classical Studies* 16 (1991): 231–51.

This contrast between the *Politics* and the *Ethics* about whose opinions are worth attending to cannot be put aside by references to Aristotle's general procedure of examining *endoxa*, the opinions generally held or maintained by philosophers or other experts. I am therefore attempting something more fine-grained than the line of discussion initiated by G. E. L. Owen, "*Tithenai ta Phainomena*," in *Aristote et les Problemes de Methode*, ed. S. Mansion (Louvain: Publications universitaires, 1960), 83–103. There is a difference between theoretical and practical science. In the former, no special qualifications are needed for the experiences that form of the subject of the sciences. In the latter, though, practical knowledge is about phenomena not available to all. For some reason we have to determine, political knowledge does not require appropriate ethical habits, while ethical knowledge does. That the state is more like an artifact than the individual life does not itself imply that political science should be not more open than ethics. The *Poetics* contains no discussion of endoxa, even though it is about artifacts.

8. Barker, *The Political Thought of Plato and Aristotle*, 223: "That there should be . . . room for human co-operation obviously implies that there may be a certain defect in Nature. And Aristotle admits that this is the case (*PA* i.683a22; 683a22). . . . And the reason is that matter . . . is not always congruous with form; and Nature, as the force impelling matter to form, may therefore, and indeed must therefore, sometimes fall short of its aim. But Nature's defects are man's opportunities: it is through them that art gets a new sphere of operation." John Stuart Mill, *The Subjection of Women*, in *Essays on Politics and Society*, ed. J. M. Robson (Toronto: University of Toronto Press, 1977), 293–94:

"In the less advanced states of society, people hardly recognize any relation with their equals. To be an equal is to be an enemy. . . . Wherever he does not command he must obey. Existing moralities, accordingly, are mainly fitted to a relation of command and obedience. Yet command and obedience are but unfortunate necessities of human life: society in equality is its normal state."

9. In distributive and corrective justice, each gets what is his own. In fair exchange, each gets someone else's. See Scott Meikle, *Aristotle's Economic Thought* (Oxford: Clarendon Press, 1995), 131. Fred D. Miller, Jr., *Nature, Justice, and Rights in Aristotle's Politics* (Oxford: Clarendon Press, 1995), argues that the *Politics* does contain a theory of rights. However, I see no justification for private property here in terms of rights, but only in terms of its value in creating the right kind of political association.

10. Thomas J. Lewis, "Acquisition and Anxiety: Aristotle's Case against the Market," *Canadian Journal of Economics* 11 (1978): 69–90, at 71: "For Aristotle the justification of the right to property is grounded on the ability to use what is directed in a proper way. This has two different aspects: first the property must be used in a manner compatible with its nature, and thus to its own benefit; second, the use of property in this way must also benefit the owner of the property, in the sense of being a necessary means of his acting in accordance with his own nature. The property relationship exists only between those beings capable of directing themselves in accordance with their natures, and those beings incapable of such self-direction. The latter is the property of the former." See the contrasts drawn between English and Roman law in Alan Ryan, *Property and Political Theory* (Oxford: Blackwell, 1984), 7: "The English legal system discouraged a question which Roman law encouraged, namely, 'What is it to be the *owner* of something?' or 'How does a thing become Mine?' The English legal inclination to enquire what gave a man good title to possession and no more than that, seems to have diverted a certain psychological or metaphysical interest into other channels. It was left to a different philosophical tradition to enquire into the relationship of owner and owned," 11. "The British mainstream was not infected by the need to produce a theodicy. . . . Social institutions were neither justified as part of the redemptive process envisaged by Hegel and Marx, nor were they condemned for failing to be. The *matter-of-factness* about what *property* was, is, in this view, matched by an unwillingness to see in work much more than what the labourer saw in it. There is, in the European tradition, a concern for how work and ownerships unilaterally create a world more thoroughly human and therefore a world more permeated with (or better able to do without) the divine plan that is hardly visible in British thinking."

11. Miller, *Nature, Justice, and Rights in Aristotle's Politics*, 315–17, argues that property in the *Politics* means "rightful ownership." I maintain that property exists in a realm outside the world in which rights apply. While today we value earned over unearned wealth, a contemporary analogy to Aristotle's point could be found in beauty. No one deserves to be beautiful. If someone tries, and makes beauty into an achievement, it is by that fact less attractive. Part of the appeal of beauty is precisely that it is spontaneous and involuntary. Wealth does not have the charm that beauty has—beauty is pleasure objectified while wealth is frozen use—but when we dismiss certain political competitions as beauty contests, we are protesting against an exchange of beauty for political power, just as Aristotle would have protested against buying citizenship or political office.

12. Williams, "Justice as a Virtue," 189–99, at 212, notes this difference between Aristotelian and modern justice. "In discussing distributive justice, I will not always assume, as Aristotle does, that we are concerned with some unallocated good that is, so to speak, 'up for grabs,' and waiting to be distributed by some method or other to some class of recipients. We can, besides that, recognize also the case in which the good is already in somebody's hands, and the question is rather whether he justly holds it."

13. Stalley, "Aristotle's Criticism of Plato's *Republic*," 183, notes that while Aristotle says he is going to find both what is good and what is not helpful in earlier accounts, he in fact almost entirely concentrates on what is wrong with these earlier proposals. Part of the oddness of Book II comes from the fact that Aristotle does not contrast his predecessors' solutions with his own.

14. On redistribution, see III.10.1281a14–19, II.1.1318a11–26.

15. The argument in *Republic* IV that proves the existence of justice in the ideal state shows not only that the ideal state possesses the four virtues of wisdom, courage, temperance, and justice, but *also* that it possesses *only* those virtues. (Recall that Socrates claims that if they find courage, wisdom, and temperance, justice will be the one remaining [428a].) It is hard to imagine any of the other virtues Aristotle lists in the *Ethics* in Socrates's city.

16. See too the goods of fortune in *Politics* IV.11.1295b6–7, which include beauty, strength, good birth, and wealth. These are not goods that can be shared, the subject of Book II, or distributed, the subject of justice in the *Ethics*.

17. A contemporary account of what is unique about farming is found in Nicholas Wade, *Before the Dawn: Recovering the Lost History of Our Ancestors* (New York: Penguin, 2006), 130: "One advantage enjoyed by settled societies, and denied to foragers, is the ability to generate and store surpluses. Surpluses form the basis for trade. They can be exchanged for things considerably more vital than extra food, like weapons, or alliances, or prestige." Glaucon's desire for sauces and furniture in *Republic* II leads to a new kind of self-sufficiency possible only with an agricultural base.

18. Richard Bodéüs, "Law and the Regime in Aristotle," in *Essays on the Foundations of Aristotle's Political Science*, ed. Carnes Lord and David K. O'Connor (Berkeley: University of California Press, 1991), 234–48, at 242: "It is not the impossibility of actually establishing such a regime that motivates his basic criticism, but the irrationality of the means that are mobilized to serve a certain end. As he puts it, 'even if one were able to do this, one ought not do it, as it would destroy the city'" (1261a21).

19. "Actions that spring from virtue in general are in the main identical with actions that are according to law, since the law enjoins conduct displaying the various particular virtues and forbids conduct displaying the various particular vices. Also the regulations laid down for the education that fits a man for civic life (*pros to koinon*) are the rules productive of virtue in general" (*NE* V.2.1130b22–26; see too V.7.1138a4–7). Bodéüs, "Law and the Regime in Aristotle," 243: "The guarantee of the law, Aristotle believes, remains preferable to that which can be supplied by the (good) will of men. It is preferable above all to the situation that leaves to chance circumstances the responsibility of ensuring the survival of the political regime."

20. Similarly in Book III Aristotle will show that rule of law, unlike rule by another person, does not prevent citizens from ruling. Aristotle couldn't imagine that rule of law means rule by impersonal bureaucrats who prevent citizens from themselves ruling.

21. See Samuel Fleischacker, *A Short History of Distributive Justice* (Cambridge: Harvard University Press, 2004), for an account of how distributive justice came, relatively recently, to be concerned with distributing property as well as offices. The revenues of the polis were mostly derived not from taxes but from liturgies, voluntary contributions from wealthy citizens.

22. In chapter 4, I will consider ways in which, relative to the *Politics*, the *Ethics* is not "a complete art or science."

23. Lear, *Aristotle: The Desire to Understand*, 193: "It is tempting to think that in critical reflection one must somehow *step outside* one's beliefs and subject them to critical survey. Yet Aristotle self-consciously refuses to take any such step. His ethical and political arguments are directed toward people who are already virtuous, and are designed to show them that (from their own perspective) the virtuous life makes sense. This makes a radical departure from Plato. Plato thought that one had not fully secured the ethical life unless one could formulate an argument for it which would be compelling even to a person who stood outside it. . . ."

24. This was James Russell Lowell's description of the American Constitution. The phrase has become more widely known through Michael G. Kammen, *A Machine That Would Go of Itself: The Constitution in American Culture* (New York: Knopf, 1986).

25. A more extended account of this general education occurs in *Parts of Animals* I.1.639a1–8: "Every systematic science, the humblest and the noblest alike, seems to admit of two distinct kinds of proficiency; one of which may be properly called scientific knowledge of the subject, while the other is a kind of educational acquaintance with it. For an educated man should be able to form a fair off-hand judgment as to the goodness or badness of the method used by a professor in his exposition. . . . It is plain then that, as in other sciences, so in that which inquires into nature, there must be certain canons, by reference to which a hearer shall be able to criticize the method of a professed exposition, quite independently of the question whether the statements made be true or false." The good judge must be able to understand when to judge a given political action by standards of the best and when to judge by the criterion of necessity.

26. If the analogy helps, consider the Ten Commandments, which begins with the declaration that "I am the Lord your God," and ends with the injunction against coveting your neighbor's donkey.

27. If one thinks that Books VII and VIII should come before Book IV, then there will be four books that precede the elaboration of the four inquiries into the best constitution in IV.1. Book I takes the material cause, the natural genealogy of the polis. Book II deals with the efficient cause, the activity of the statesman. Book III looks to the formal cause, the conceptions of justice embodied in each particular constitution. Books VII and VIII examine the final cause, the best life and its implications for the political life.

CHAPTER THREE

1. John Rawls, *A Theory of Justice* (Cambridge, MA: Belknap Press, 1971), 211–16.

2. Bernard Yack, *Problems of a Political Animal: Community, Justice, and Conflict in Aristotelian Political Thought* (Berkeley and Los Angeles: University of California

Press, 1993), 168: "Although Aristotle seeks determinate and certain knowledge of the human good, he denies the existence of comparable standards of justice. As a result, he rejects a perfectionist understanding of human justice, even while advocating a perfectionist understanding of the human good . . . [Aristotle] differs from modern defenders of liberal distinctions between the right and the good in thinking that it is standards of justice, rather than standards of goodness, that must be left indeterminate and open to a variety of interpretations."

Richard Boyd, *Uncivil Society: The Perils of Pluralism and the Making of Modern Liberalism* (Lanham, MD: Lexington Books, 2004), 128–29: "In contrast to Aristotelian political thought, which relegated matters of accumulation to the *oikos*, which presumed some shared understanding of justice to be the defining characteristic of a political regime, and which denied any clear distinction between private religiosity and the religion of the city, eighteenth-century thought reverses this emphasis. Instead, the task of political life is restricted to the aggregation and compromising of private distributional conflicts, while the locus of morality shifts to the private sphere. In effect, any public disagreement that might conceivably invoke partisan passions is to be relegated to civil society or the realm of private opinion." I should note at the outset that the comparison I use to organize this chapter is an asymmetrical one. I am comparing Aristotle's *Politics* not to a modern work but to an abstraction called modernity or liberalism. My purpose is to understand the *Politics* and to use the *Politics* to help us understand our current political problems, and for this purpose the generalized contrast to Aristotle is useful and licit. Nothing here should minimize the differences among different modern or liberal thinkers.

3. The opposition of the right and the good received its canonical formulation in William David Ross, *The Right and the Good* (Oxford: Clarendon Press, 1930). See too Judith Jarvis Thomson, "The Right and the Good," *Journal of Philosophy* 94, no. 6 (June 1997): 273–98. The good consists in those things that it is most desirable to bring about. The right comprises the actions which one is free to do, given the constraints on action by obligations, duties, and the recognition of other people's rights.

4. 1.1323a14–16; see also 2.1324a13–23. Martha Nussbaum, "Nature, Function, and Capability: Aristotle on Political Deliberation," supplement, *Oxford Studies in Ancient Philosophy* (1988): 145–84, makes the contrast between Aristotle and Rawls on just this basis. Aristotle, she says judging from *Politics* VII, has the "idea that a rather full account of the human good and human functioning must precede and ground an account of political distribution, is alien to much recent work in political theory" (150), and she immediately draws the contrast with Rawls. Rawls himself draws the lines between himself and Aristotle in these terms as well. John Rawls, *Political Liberalism*, expanded edition (New York: Columbia University Press, 2005), 134: "One of the deepest distinctions between conceptions of justice is between those that allow for a plurality of reasonable though opposing comprehensive doctrines each with its own conception of the good, and those that hold that there is but one such conception to be recognized by all citizens who are fully reasonable and rational. Conceptions of justice that fall on opposite sides of this divide are distinct in many fundamental ways. Plato and Aristotle, and the Christian tradition as represented by Augustine and Aquinas, fall on the side of the one reasonable and rational good. Such views hold that institutions are justifiable to the extent that they effectively

promote that good. Indeed, beginning with Greek thought the dominant tradition seems to have been that there is but one reasonable and rational conception of the good."

Charles Larmore, *The Morals of Modernity* (Cambridge: Cambridge University Press, 1996), 19, suggests that the clearest exposition of the difference, which has set the subsequent terms of debate, is in Henry Sidgwick, *The Methods of Ethics* (1907; Indianapolis: Hackett, 2007), 105–15.

5. For a sustained argument about the relations between the *Ethics* and the *Politics* compatible with my analysis, see Larmore, *Morals of Modernity*.

6. There is a partial analogy to the *Poetics*. There may be a natural delight in imitation and in imitating, so that poetry is natural. But tragedy and the other *forms* of poetry cannot be derived from those natural bases. There is no natural impulse to make or to enjoy tragedies. By arguing that no one is democratic or oligarchic by nature, Aristotle departs from Plato's account of the different constitutions in *Republic* VIII, in which there is a homology between the constitution, its goals and its determination of who rules, and the nature of its citizens.

7. Charles Larmore, *The Autonomy of Morality* (Cambridge: Cambridge University Press, 2008), 142: "No longer are interest and passion alone the chief objects of concern, for the proliferation of reasonable views of the good life constitutes a political problem in its own right." We will see in this chapter just how novel this political problem is. Book VII differs from the rest of the *Politics* precisely because it is there that he says that different poleis emerge from different conceptions of happiness.

8. Josiah Ober, "Aristotle's Natural Democracy," in *Aristotle's Politics*, ed. Richard Kraut and Steven Skultety (Lanham, MD: Rowman & Littlefield, 2008), 228, claims that the plurality of constitutions must be either due to nature or history. I maintain that it is the demands of practical deliberation and practical science that creates the plurality: "The natural polis having achieved its *telos* in respect to social form [in Book I], it is ready to take on a political form, a *politeia*. Two possibilities present themselves: First is that the political *telos* is inherently a part of the social *telos* and thus that the 'natural *politeia*' of the natural polis will be manifest immediately upon the realization of the polis. In this case all subsequent regimes changes are devolutionary, corruptions of the pristine original form. This sort of story is familiar form Books VIII and IX of Plato's *Republic*, where Kallipolis is the original and ideal form, and all other regime-types (timocracy, oligarchy, democracy, tyranny) are devolutions. The other possibility is that, like the polis itself, the emergence of the political *telos* is historical and sequential, requiring a development from one natural stage to the next, until the *telos* is achieved. This second, sequential, story seems to be what Aristotle has in mind in the *Politics*."

9. Isaiah Berlin, *Against the Current: Essays in the History of Ideas* (New York: Penguin, 1980), 149–50.

10. Along similar lines, it is clear that the *Ethics* is not perfectionist, either, since Aristotle never derives the properties of virtue from the properties of happiness. Despite the fact that happiness is *energeia kat'aretēn*, it is virtue that tells us what happiness is, not the other way around. Peter Simpson, "Contemporary Virtue Ethics and Aristotle," *Review of Metaphysics* 45 (1992): 503–24, at 507: "According to [contemporary] virtue theorists, one is supposed to use the concept of flourishing to develop an account and justification of the virtues. Flourishing is the prior notion and the virtues are to be understood

in terms of it. But Aristotle's understanding of the relation between flourishing and the virtues is the opposite of this. Aristotle does not argue to the virtues from some prior notion of flourishing, nor does he even attempt to do this. The virtues fall into the definition of *eudaimonia*, but *eudaimonia* does not fall into the definition of the virtues." And see part of his footnote on that passage: "There is no justification given by Aristotle for the move from the definition of *eudaimonia* to the particular virtues. This is indeed true, for the movement of thought is the other way round: the virtues are the way to understand *eudaimonia*; *eudaimonia* is not the way to understand the virtues."

11. Salkever, "Reading Aristotle's *Nicomachean Ethics* and *Politics* as a Single Course of Lectures," at 226: the constitution, "the particular aspirations and institutions that defined the actuality of any polis, as Aristotle understands it, embodies an answer to the question apparently inseparable from human life, What is the best life for a human being? Thus Aristotle's claim about the priority of politics to individual life is not an assertion of the superiority of the collective to the individual interest, and it certainly does not mean that we should take our identity from our role as citizen of a particular regime. Instead, it is an assertion of the priority of living well to living, of the form of a human life to its matter, and of the centrality of the question of the best life."

12. Alexander, Hamilton, James Madison, John Jay, and Ian Shapiro, *The Federalist Papers: Alexander Hamilton, James Madison, John Jay* (New Haven: Yale University Press, 2009). Also available at http://www.constitution.org/fed/federa10.htm.

13. But see V.3.1303b15–17: "The greatest factional split is between virtue and depravity; then there is that between wealth and poverty, and so on with others in varying degree."

14. There is one more difference between Aristotle's *Politics* and modern political theory worth mentioning. It is the end, the good life, that distinguishes the polis from other communities, while today we think it is the means, the legitimate use of coercion, that differentiates the state from other associations. When Aristotle asks about means that are specially suited for the peculiarly political end, these are means not to secure obedience but to unify the political community. The locus classicus for the modern formulation is Max Weber, "Politics as a Vocation," in *From Max Weber*, ed. H. H. Gerth and C. Wright Mills (New York and Oxford: Oxford University Press, 1946), 77–78.

15. Harvey Mansfield, in his commentary on Gerson, "Aristotle's Polis: A Community of the Virtuous," sees Book I showing that the city is by nature, while Book III "sets forth the artificial character of the city." While I have argued that Book I goes as far as it can with the idea of the city as natural—as I think Mansfield agrees—I think that Book II shows the powers and limitations of thinking of the city as artificial, and Book III begins again with the city as a practical activity. That aside, Mansfield's remark is just right: In Book III, by contrast to Book I, Aristotle does not attempt at first to define the city (*polis*) by its end; rather he says that the city is chiefly its regime [*politeia*] (226). "The discussion in Book III takes account of human choice and of ruling in accordance with choice in the regime, matters that had merely been alluded to earlier" (227).

16. After naming the plot the soul of a tragedy, the last chapters of the *Poetics* show that tragedy and epic have the same end or purpose.

17. *Republic* 4.422e–423a: "Each of them is a whole bunch of cities. . . . Each of them is two things at war with each other, one made up of the poor, the other of the rich, and

in each of these there are a great many parts." See too *Republic* 4.415d; *Politics*
II.5.1264a25.

18. This point is central to the *Ethics*. See, for example, *NE* V.1.1129b1–6; see also
V.9.1137a26–30, VII.13.1153b7–25, VIII.2.1155b21–27, VIII.13.1162b35–37, *de Anima*
431b10–13, *Met.* VII.3.1029b6–7, *EE* I.1.1214a30–b5, I.4.1215b1–5, I.5.1216a10–37,
I.5.1216b18–25, VII.1.1234b23, VII.2.1236b38–1237a3, VII.1.1237b37–1238a8, VIII.3.1249a4–
7. I argue for the centrality of this thesis for the *Ethics* in *Confronting Aristotle's Ethics*.

19. "Aristotle's claims that the polis exists by nature implies a belief that it also
comes to be by nature." David Keyt, "Three Fundamental Theorems in Aristotle's Politics," *Phronesis* 32, no. 1 (1987): 54–79, at 58. Barker, *The Political Thought of Plato and
Aristotle*, 281, n.1: "Natural things develop from within, as the result of an immanent
force. As such a natural thing, the State has its own life, and has grown." R. G. Mulgan,
Aristotle's Political Theory: An Introduction for Students of Political Theory (Oxford:
Clarendon Press, 1977), 11, argues that Aristotle does try to discover the nature of the
polis "by examining the pattern of its growth and development." The trouble is that this
has nothing to do with the growth and development of any particular polis, and Book I
does not issue in a definition of the polis.

20. The connection among key terms is more obvious in Greek. The state is a *polis*;
the constitution is a *politeia*; a citizen is a *politēs*; a statesman is a *politikos*.

21. *Met.* H.5.1045a3–5: "All the things which change thus into one another must go
back to their matter; e.g., if from a corpse is produced an animal, the corpse must first
go back to its matter, and only then becomes an animal; and vinegar first goes back to
water, and only then becomes wine." Democracy and oligarchy are contraries, but not
related as positive to privative, so it is not clear whether that line from the *Metaphysics*
applies. It is not the case that before a democratic polis can become an oligarchic one, it
must revert to a state of nature by being stripped down to its matter, nothing but citizens,
or households, or people, and then reconstitutes itself as a new constitution and a new
polis.

22. Aristotle frequently uses artifacts as examples in the *Metaphysics* to explicate the
idea of substance, as he uses artifacts in explaining the definition of nature in *Physics* II,
but strictly speaking artifacts are not themselves substances. It is because form and
function are distinct that Aristotle has trouble in *Politics* III.1–3 saying whether there is
a single, continuing polis that changes its constitutional form, or whether each change
in constitution creates a different polis. For more on this question, see Murray, "*Polis*
and *Politeia* in Aristotle," 197–210. In the *Poetics*, tragedy and comedy are *eidē* (forms),
so when Aristotle uses the analogy of the chorus in Book III, the issue becomes whether
there is a single thing called a chorus that is first tragic and then comedic, or whether
there is only a set of people who form themselves first into the one and then into the
other. On the latter reading, in a revolution, people revert to the state of nature. In chapter 5, I will argue that is not the case. To follow out the analogy of constitutions further,
if tragic and comic choruses had different numbers of members, would the ones who sit
out while the smaller chorus performs still be members of the chorus?

23. See Edward Halper, "The Substance of Aristotle's Ethics," in *The Crossroads of
Norm and Nature: Essays on Aristotle's Ethics and Metaphysics*, ed. May Sim (Lanham,
MD: Rowman & Littlefield, 1995), 3–28, at 4: "Aristotle speaks of the state and happiness

as actualities because he regards them as quasi-substantial beings." See too p. 28, n.24: "Aristotle regularly treats nonsubstances as if they were substances. The paradigmatic example is mathematical entities, which he claims mathematicians treat as separate though they are not (*Met.* M.3.1078a17–31)."

24. Meikle, *Aristotle's Economic Thought*, 62: "The polis has some of the important characteristics of a substance; it is a subject of predications, it has form and matter, it has a process of coming-to-be, and so forth. Aristotle considers the polis to be a *suntheton* or substance for that reason, and not because of an analogy with some other kind of substance."

25. Aristotle almost never refers to the six constitutions as *kinds* of constitution, but just as constitutions. I will offer an explanation in chapter 4.

26. *NE* VIII.11.1161b8–10: "There are friendships and justice to only a slight degree in tyrannies, but to a much larger degree in democracies; for there people are equal, and so have much in common."

27. *NE* V.2.1130b26–29: "We must wait till later to determine whether the education that makes an individual an unqualifiedly good man is a task for political science or for another science; for, presumably, being a good man is not the same as being every sort of good citizen."

28. Similarly, the *Politics* begins by saying that the state, as the supreme partnership, "aims at" the highest good (I.1.1252a1–7). Such aiming cannot always be intentional, and the same goes for citizens aiming at security: "The polis wishes to be [made] 'out of' equal and similar people to the greatest extent possible" (IV.11.1295b25–26). Miller, *Nature, Justice, and Rights in Aristotle's Politics*, 54: "There are important differences between organisms and communities. In the former, the part typically has a function or end which is distinct from and subordinate to the end of the whole. . . . But in the community the end of the whole is a common good in which the parts must directly share in order to qualify as parts . . . Hence, the realization of the end of the whole must *include*, rather than transcend or supersede, the fulfillment of the ends of the parts." Rawls, *Political Liberalism*, 137, notes that "associations" are voluntary in ways that the political community is not. If the polis has an unlimited purpose, then citizens don't aim at that end in the same way they aim at, e.g., economic ends. Therefore the highest form of teleology is not intentional or voluntary. Gerson, "Aristotle's Polis: A Community of the Virtuous," 205–6: "The good in politics is not different from the good in ethics in the way the good for a species of animals is different from the good of an individual animal. For those may actually be opposed, as for example, when individuals are culled from a population to protect the herd."

29. Larmore, *The Morals of Modernity*, 32: "Recall Hegel's famous observation that conscience has had an importance in modern thought it never enjoyed in ancient ethics. Sidgwick himself agreed with this observation. Once the right is made prior to the good, a person can expect to find himself in situations where what he ought to do conflicts with what he wants to do, and where this conflict will not disappear (as it must on the ancient view) in the light of a deeper understanding of what he wants. From the moral point of view, his self-fulfillment must then give way before the claims of morality. And to have internalized the superiority of these claims is what it is to live under the authority of conscience." Yack, *Problems of a Political Animal*, 262: "One might think of the good

individual-good citizen dichotomy as Aristotle's way of representing the conflict between political and moral duties, but Aristotle never makes this distinction. General justice, the love of the common good of one's community and the primary virtue of a good citizen, is also a disposition that Aristotle expects from a good individual. A good individual should be *disposed* to promote the common good of the regime in which he participates as well as to obey its laws." Terence C. Irwin, *Aristotle's First Principles* (Oxford: Oxford University Press, 1988), 410: "These claims about the good man and the good citizen do not imply that the non-ideal states include good men who do not fit into that system as good citizens. Someone cannot be a good man without being a good citizen and without having the relations to others that make the full range of virtuous actions possible and reasonable." But see at 458: "Aristotle implies . . . that if the virtue of a citizen conflicts with the virtue of a man, we should give up the virtue of a citizen. He believes, however, that this is only a logical, not a practical, possibility. He is right to believe this if the best way to cultivate the virtue of a man, as far as we can, is to cultivate the virtue of a citizen in the political system we live in."

30. Paul W. Kahn, *Putting Liberalism in Its Place* (Princeton: Princeton University Press, 2005). *NE* VIII.11.1161b7–11: "Insofar as someone is a slave, there is no friendship between him [and a master]. But there is friendship with him insofar as he is a 'human being. For every human being seems to have some relation of justice with everyone who is capable of community in law and agreement; hence [every human being seems] also [to have] friendship [with every human being], to the extent that [every human being] is a human being." The bracketed additions, as well as the translation, are from Terence C. Irwin, trans., *Aristotle: Nicomachean Ethics* (Indianapolis: Hackett, 1985), 132.

31. The term *second-class* citizen is applied to Aristotle by David Keyt, "Supplementary Essay," in David Keyt, ed., *Aristotle: Politics, Books III and IV*, trans. by Richard Robinson (Oxford: Clarendon Press, 1995), 125–48. *NE* VIII.1.1155a22–29: "Friendship would seem to hold cities together, and legislators would seem to be more concerned about it than about justice. For concord would seem to be similar to friendship and they aim at concord above all, while they try above all to expel civil conflict, which is enmity. Further, if people are friends, they have no need of justice, but if they are just they need friendship in addition; and the justice that is most just seems to belong to friendship." That the good man will act as a good citizen and not directly try to impose the rule of virtue is yet another manifestation of the general Aristotelian phenomenon that what is best does not determine what to do.

32. Salkever, "Aristotle's Social Science," 492. My difference with Salkever is that I don't think that "not admitting of theoretical resolution" means that Aristotle either throws up his hands or passes the buck to the statesman. I think it still leaves work to be done by the practical philosophy of science of politics.

33. Machiavelli's *Discourses on Livy* is organized around the distinction between stability and glory as the ends of different republics. A republic that wants to last as long as possible should imitate Venice, while one that wants to expand and so achieve greatness should imitate Rome.

34. Irwin, *Aristotle's First Principles*, 627n15: "Every political system, Aristotle assumes, will claim to some degree that it is concerned with the common interest of its

citizens; this is part of the status of a citizen as opposed to a slave, 1279a30–32. However, not all systems are in fact designed to do what they say they are doing."

35. Keyt, "Supplementary Essay," 134. And at 131: "In at least two places Aristotle tacitly recognizes such a concept. In discussing kingship Aristotle, following normal Greek practice, twice refers to some of the king's subjects as citizens (III.14.1285 25–29, V.10.131 1a7–8). . . . But no subject of a king holds any deliberative or judicial office unless he is appointed by the king. So by Aristotle's definition of a full citizen there can be only one full citizen in a kingship, the king himself. Anyone else who is a citizen must be a second-class citizen." See also Miller, *Nature, Justice, and Rights in Aristotle's Politics*, 212; Mary P. Nichols, *Citizens and Statesmen: A Study of Aristotle's Politics* (Savage, MD: Rowman & Littlefield, 1992), 69. Cynthia Farrar, *The Origins of Democratic Thinking: The Invention of Politics in Classical Athens* (Cambridge: Cambridge University Press, 1988), 22: Athenians "came to regard . . . citizenship as an opportunity for more than acquiescence: for real participation. The significant political distinction no longer corresponded to the social divide between noble and commoner, nor even between free man and slave, but was defined in purely political terms: citizen versus non-citizen." Susan D. Collins, *Aristotle and the Rediscovery of Citizenship* (Cambridge: Cambridge University Press, 2006), 134: "As commentators have noted, Aristotle's schema is puzzling not least for the fact that, with regard to the fundamental criterion—the common advantage—the distinction between deviant and correct regimes would seem to collapse: If a citizen is one who shares in rule, and the city a multitude of citizens, then by definition the common advantage is the advantage of the rulers." For the commentators who have gone before, Collins refers to Newman, *The Politics of Aristotle*, 1: 216n2; Simpson, *A Philosophical Commentary on the Politics of Aristotle*, 151; and Donald Morrison, "Aristotle's Definition of Citizenship: A Problem and Some Solutions," *History of Philosophy Quarterly* 16, no. 22 (1999): 144–46.

36. The ambiguous status of second-class citizens is also signaled at III.5.1278a34–38: "There are several kinds of citizens, and that the one who participates in the offices is particularly said to be a citizen. . . . For people who do not participate in the offices *are* like resident aliens. When this is concealed, it is for the sake of deceiving coinhabitants." For a corrupt constitution that is so degenerate that it ceases being a constitution at all, see IV.4.1292a30–37: "The *Polis* was the state of the *politai*, the citizens. . . . *Andres gar polis* . . . it is the men who are the *Polis*. There were no subjects." Victor Ehrenberg, *The Greek State* (London: Methuen, 1974), 88–89.

37. See *EE* VII.9.1241b13–15: "All constitutions are a kind of justice; for [a constitution] is a community and every community is held together by what is just." Josiah Ober, *The Athenian Revolution: Essays on Ancient Greek Democracy and Political Theory* (Princeton: Princeton University Press, 1996), 165: "The term *politeia* embraces not only the constitution (legal arrangement of governmental institutions), but the ideology (the system of beliefs by which actions are organized), and the social practices promoted by the dominant subsociety within the *politeia*." Barker, *Greek Political Theory: Plato and His Predecessors*, 44: "The Greeks believed in the need of education to tune and harmonize social opinion to the spirit and the tone of a fixed and fundamental and sovereign law. The modern belief is in the need of representation to adjust and harmonize a fluid

and changing and subordinate law to the movement of a sovereign public opinion or 'general will.'"

38. There is an interesting antecedent in the views imputed to Protagoras in the *Theaetetus*. Protagoras argues that justice is a matter of persuasion: whatever we think is just is just. There are real answers, in contrast, to questions of advantage, and so the useful is not simply a matter of decision and persuasion. Aristotle sees a necessary connection between justice and talk about justice, a connection not found in the other ethical virtues. For a third party to see an act as, for example, courageous or witty, she must possess the concepts of these virtues, but the agent need not, and generally will not, use these ideas in deciding to act virtuously. But justice must be consciously present both for the judge and the agent. See Bernard Williams, "Acting as the Virtuous Person Acts," in Williams, *The Sense of the Past: Essays in the History of Philosophy*, ed. and with an intro. by Myles Burnyeat (Princeton: Princeton University Press, 2006), 189–97; reprinted from Robert Heinaman, ed., *Aristotle and Moral Realism* (London: UCL, 1995), 13–23.

39. See Joseph Raz, "Disagreement in Politics," *American Journal of Jurisprudence* 43 (1998): 25–52.

40. Ober, "Aristotle's Natural Democracy," 223–44, at 229: "Aristotle's long and sometimes torturous discussion of 'which regime is best' in Book III shows that the ranking remains disputed in respect to the uncorrupted regimes. There is a sense in which kingship is best, another sense in which aristocracy is best, and perhaps also a sense in which 'politeia' is best. But the rank ordering is clear in respect to the corrupted regimes: democracy is better than oligarchy, which is in turn better than tyranny."

41. That is not the case with tyranny and monarchy, which is why monarchy needs separate consideration at the end of Book III. What Ellen Meiksins Wood and Neal Wood, *Class Ideology and Ancient Political Theory: Socrates, Plato, and Aristotle in Social Context* (Oxford: Blackwell, 1978), 120, assert for Plato, I claim, in a very different sense, for Aristotle: "The revolutionary nature of Plato's political thought lies in his attempt to 'aristocratize' the polis, or 'politicize' aristocracy—that is, to synthesize what were in their very essence antithetical forces in the history of Athens, the *aristocratic* principle and the *political principle*." That good constitutions are completions of the bad and partial interpretations accounts for Keyt's claim that "Aristotle uses the expression [*kat'axian*] . . . sometimes contrasted with *kat'arithmon* and [then it] distinguishes *virtue and wealth* from freedom (*Pol.* V.1.1301b30–1302a8, VI.2.1317b3–4). Other times *kat'axian* is associated with *kat'aretēn* and marks *virtue* off from wealth and freedom (*Pol.* III.5.1278a19–20, V.1013 10b33)." David Keyt, "Aristotle's Theory of Distributive Justice," in *A Companion to Aristotle's Politics*, ed. David Keyt and Fred D. Miller, Jr. (Oxford: Blackwell, 1991), 238–78, at 242, n.15.

42. *NE* VIII.13.1162b5–10: "Complaints and recriminations occur solely or chiefly in friendships of utility. . . . In a friendship based on virtue each party is eager to benefit the other, for this is characteristic of virtue and friendship; and as they vie with each other in giving and not in getting benefit, no complaints nor quarrels can arise, since nobody is angry with one who loves him and benefits him."

43. See *Republic* 1.347b–c. Irwin, *Aristotle's First Principles*, 434–35: "It is . . . doubtful that Aristotle's favored distributive criterion actually follows from the moral

and political principles used to attack other criteria. In so far as he seems to believe, for instance, that superior virtue and service to the community justly claims greater goods as its reward (1281a4–7, 1282b30–1283a3), he argues too quickly. This principle that virtuous political activity is the goal of the state does not imply that past achievement in this activity should be the standard for distribution of goods. More needs to be said to show that such a criterion of distribution will best promote the goal of the state, and Aristotle does not say all that is needed." See P. A. Vander Waerdt, "Kingship and Philosophy in Aristotle's Best Regime," *Phronesis* 30 (1985): 249–73.

44. For the difference between forward- and backward-looking conceptions of merit, see Waldron, "What Plato Would Allow," 563–84, esp. 572; and Wolff, "L'unité structurelle du livre III," 279 and especially 292. One can see the difference between these two criteria in current affirmative action debates. Some opponents of affirmative action see it as wrong because it is unjust not to give some benefit, such as college admissions, to the most deserving. Supporters retort that the presence of members of minority groups improves the performance of the whole. See, for example, Waldron, "Redressing Historic Injustice," *University of Toronto Law Journal* 52 (2002): 135–60.

45. For more elaborations on the topos of the rule of law versus rule of the best, see the *Statesman*, esp. 293a. For an argument that the *Politics* does lead to the conclusion that a single best man should rule permanently, see Vander Waerdt, "Kingship and Philosophy in Aristotle's Best Regime." There are really two distinct issues, whether the single best man should rule permanently and whether he should *want* to rule permanently. In general, the better something is, the less is it possible to possess it to excess. Yet the *Politics* confronts this possibility not only in making alternating ruling and being ruled in turn a mark of the political, but earlier, in Book II, by arguing against too much unity.

46. For similar claims, see *Pol.* III.11.1282a14, a34–41, IV.4.1292a10–14. See also *Met.* II.993b1–6: "No one is able to attain the truth adequately, while, on the other hand, we do not collectively fail, but everyone says something true about the nature of things, and while individually we contribute little or nothing to the truth, by the union of all a considerable amount is amassed. Therefore, since the truth seems to be like the proverbial door, which no one can fail to hit, in this respect it must be easy, but the fact that we can have a whole truth and not a particular part we aim at shows the difficulty of it." III.15.1286a27–31: "When the law cannot determine a point at all, or not well, should the one best man or should all decide? According to our present practice assemblies meet, sit in judgment, deliberate, and decide, and their judgments all relate to individual cases. Now any member of the assembly, taken separately, is certainly inferior to the wise man. But the state is made up of many individuals. And as a feast to which all the guests contribute is better than a banquet furnished by a single man, so a multitude is a better judge of many things than any individual."

47. For the maximization argument, see Abraham Lincoln:

If A. can prove, however conclusively, that he may, of right, enslave B.—why may not B. snatch the same argument, and prove equally, that he may enslave A.?

You say A. is white, and B. is black. It is *color*, then; the lighter having the right to enslave the darker? Take care. By this rule, you are to be slave to the first man you meet, with a fairer skin than your own.

You do not mean color exactly?—You mean the whites are *intellectually* the superior of blacks, and, therefore, have the right to enslave them? Take care again. By this rule, you are to be slave to the first man you meet, with an intellect superior to your own.

Abraham Lincoln, "Fragment on Slavery," in Roy P. Basler, ed., *Collected Works of Abraham Lincoln*, vol. 2 (New Brunswick, NJ: Rutgers University Press, 1953), 222–23. See too Arnold Isenberg, "Natural Pride and Natural Shame," in *Explaining Emotions*, ed. Amelie Oksenberg Rorty (Berkeley: University of California Press, 1980), 382, n.5, who quotes Jefferson "on the Negroes: 'But whatever be their degree of talent it is no measure of their rights. Because Sir Isaac Newton was superior to others in understanding he was not therefore lord of the person or property of others.'"

48. See Jeremy Waldron, "The Wisdom of the Multitude: Some Reflections on Book 3, Chapter 11 of Aristotle's *Politics*," *Political Theory* 23 (1995): 563–84.

49. Yack, *Problems of a Political Animal*, 166: "Aristotle insists that we 'need political philosophy' to deal with competing claims to political power because we need to go beyond considerations of merit to draw any conclusions about them. Fairness and its fidelity to determinate standards of merit cannot be our guide in choosing standards of distributive justice. We must be guided, instead, by our much more indeterminate judgments about how an actively just individual would promote the common advantage of the community."

50. Yack, *Problems of a Political Animal*, 168: "Although Aristotle seeks determinate and certain knowledge of the human good, he denies the existence of comparable standards of justice. As a result, he rejects a perfectionist understanding of human justice, even while advocating a perfectionist understanding of the human good . . . [Aristotle] differs from modern defenders of liberal distinctions between the right and the good in thinking that it is standards of justice, rather than standards of goodness, that must be left indeterminate and open to a variety of interpretations." William Mathie, "Political and Distributive Justice in the Political Science of Aristotle," *Review of Politics* 49 (1987): 59–84: 76: "The intended effect of the teaching on political justice is to convert exclusive claims to rule into partial claims. As understood on the basis of the Aristotelian revision, the claims to rule become reasons why the claimants can and should recognize other claims as well. As the claims of the many becomes [sic] a claim based upon collective wealth and virtue, it can no longer justify the expropriation of the wealth of the few; as distributive justice looks to the just distribution of what is common rather than a redistribution of the possessions of citizens, one may even say the Aristotelian revision furnishes a foundation for distributive justice within the regime. . . . Similarly, the claim of the wealthy is now made on the basis of the contribution to the common good their property comprises (1283a33) and on the basis of their virtue as men generally honest in money matters (1283a34)."

51. Recall the argument Socrates makes in the *Gorgias* when he asks whether the doctor, the most knowledgeable about healthy food, should get the bigger share of such food (490b–c).

52. Bernard Yack, "Community and Conflict in Aristotle's Political Philosophy," in *Action and Contemplation: Studies in the Moral and Political Thought of Aristotle*, ed.

Robert C. Bartlett and Susan D. Collins (Albany: SUNY Press, 2000), 280–81: "In his classification of regimes, Aristotle distinguishes between two sets of three regimes, the right (orthos) and the divergent or erring regimes. This distinction between two sets of regimes does not represent a distinction between just and unjust regimes, let alone the distinction between legitimate and illegitimate regimes the modern reader is tempted to see in it. Each regime, with the exception of tyranny, is partly just, for a regime is a decision about the standards of political justice. As long as it establishes *some* proportion among claims to rule, a regime is lawful and just, no matter how much that proportion usually exaggerates the worth of equally or unequally held qualities."

53. When Bruni translated the *Politics* into Latin, he used *respublica* to translate *politeia* in both senses. While "polity" in English can also do such double duty, it is almost a calque. Those who prefer to translate *politeia* in the sense of constitution as "regime" convey more meaning, but then cannot use the same term for both senses.

54. See Fleischacker, *A Short History of Distributive Justice*, for an account of how distributive justice came, relatively recently, to be concerned with distributing property as well as offices. The revenues of the polis were mostly derived not from taxes but from liturgies, voluntary contributions from wealthy citizens. Gerson, "Aristotle's Polis: A Community of the Virtuous," 221n50: "Aristotle views distributive justice as a matter primarily of qualifications for offices and as instrumental to the final good of the state. Its range is much narrower than would perhaps be allowed today and certainly does not include the *redistribution* of goods." As he notes on pages 218–19, this narrowing is not due to the lack of many examples of redistribution in Athens and elsewhere. See too Zhu Rui, "Equality in Worth as a Pre-Condition for Justice in Greek Thought," *History of Political Thought* 24 (2003): 1–15, who nicely contrasts the postulation of equality of all people in modern political thought with the ancients' more "empirical" approach to equality.

55. David Charles notes that "in large parts of the *Politics*, Aristotle's positive proposals are concerned exclusively with the narrower issues of *who should rule?, who should be a citizen?*, or more generally with the question of who should be engaged in military affairs or matters of policy and justice (1291a36–b2, 1329a3–5). Indeed, this seems to him the major *political* question." His footnote goes on to recognize that this is the central question throughout Book III. "Thus, in Book III chs. 1–5 are concerned with the issue of the definition of citizenship, III.6 with political offices, III.7–13 with who should hold office, and III.14–17 with royalty...." David Charles, "Perfectionism in Aristotle's Political Theory: Reply to Martha Nussbaum," supplement, *Oxford Studies in Ancient Philosophy* VI (1988): 185–206, at 187. But Charles offers no explanation for this emphasis on Aristotle's part. It is the purpose of the present chapter to do so.

56. Just what Aristotle means by rule of law is not self-evident. It certainly does not mean balance of powers and other institutional structures that people point to today, such as judicial review. For some of the history of the idea of rule of law, see Brian Z. Tamanaha, *On the Rule of Law: History, Politics, Theory* (Cambridge: Cambridge University Press, 2005). "According to Aristotle a polis in which *hoi kyrioi* are above the laws ... is a perversion, and this view applies to all three types of constitution.... Aristotle equates being above the laws with disregarding the law in order to rule for one's own interest, just as he

equates ruling in accordance with the law with ruling in everybody's interest." Mogens Herman Hansen, *Polis and City-State: An Ancient Concept and Its Modern Equivalent* (Copenhagen: Munksgaard, 1998), 75.

57. Contrast this idea of justice, limited to the selection of rulers, to the modern idea of justice based on respect for property. Justice has become "a negative virtue, and only hinders us from injuring our neighbor. The man, who barely abstains from violating either the person, or the estate, or the reputation of his neighbors, has surely very little positive merit. He fulfills, however, all the rules of what is peculiarly called justice." Adam Smith, *Theory of Moral Sentiments*, part 2, section 2, chapter 1 (p. 82).

58. The identity between the person of heroic virtue in *NE* VII and the supremely able and virtuous person here in *Politics* III depends on the idea that the former would engage in political activity. That is doubtful, and its ambiguity points to the ambiguities of rule by such a person here.

59. John Stuart Mill, *On Liberty* (Indianapolis: Hackett, 1978), 42.

60. See especially *Statesman* 294a–b.

61. Harvey Mansfield, "Commentary on [Lloyd] Gerson," *Proceedings of the Boston Area Colloquium in Ancient Philosophy*, vol. 3 (University Press of America, 1988), 227: "Every actual regime implies the superiority of the absolute monarchy of the best man to itself."

62. The auxiliaries in *Republic* IV have true opinion, while the rulers have wisdom. Aristotle elevates all citizens into the position occupied only by the auxiliaries in the *Republic*. *Politics* I offers another example of rule which is permanent yet political rather than despotic. That is the rule of men over women in the household (1259a41). Permanent political rule by the person of outstanding virtue would be like a permanent rule of men over women in the household in which the women permanently ruled could still lead complete and happy lives. That is not a possibility Aristotle ever considers, and is exactly as plausible or implausible as permanent political rule by the person of outstanding virtue.

63. Vander Waerdt, "Kingship and Philosophy in Aristotle's Best Regime," 255: "To ostracize a man for his incomparable virtue therefore is incompatible with the best regime's end, the education of its citizens in accordance with the natural hierarchy of human goods." See too W. R. Newell, "Superlative Virtue: The Problem of Monarchy in Aristotle's Politics," in *Essays on the Foundations of Aristotelian Political Science*, ed. Carnes Lord and David K. O'Connor (Berkeley: University of California Press, 1991); and Newman, *The Politics of Aristotle*, 1: 268–83.

64. *NE* VIII.11.1161a34–b3: "Where ruler and ruled have nothing in common, they have no friendship, since they have no justice either." But see VIII.14.1163b13: "This is how we should treat unequals. If we are benefited in virtue or in money, we should return honor, and thereby make what return we can. *For friendship seeks what is possible, not what corresponds to worth*, since that is impossible in some cases, e.g., with honor to gods and parents. For no one could ever make a return corresponding to their worth, but someone who attends to them as far as he is able seems to be a decent person" (emphasis added).

65. For a similar analysis, see David K. O'Connor, "Wilt versus Russell: Excellence

on the Hardwood," in *Basketball and Philosophy: Thinking Outside the Paint*, ed. Jerry L. Walls and Gregory Bassham (Lexington: University Press of Kentucky, 2007), 116–28. Zhu Rui, "Equality in Worth as a Pre-Condition for Justice in Greek Thought," *History of Political Thought* 24 (2003): 10, notes that ostracism is "an ancient version of the Rawlsian 'veil of ignorance,' under which we choose to pretend ignorance of our own particular excellence."

66. Arlene Saxonhouse, *Fear of Diversity: The Birth of Political Science in Ancient Greek Thought* (Chicago: University of Chicago Press, 1992), 129: "It is best to be ruled by the one best suited to rule over others as a god but given the definition of the human being and of the citizen as one who shares in ruling and being ruled, the rule of the best does not allow for the political arena where we as humans can fulfill our natural human potential, attain our *telos*. There now appears a contradiction between what is best for the whole and what allows for the fulfillment of the nature of the many. Nature gives mixed signals: there is the natural hierarchy of the superior over the inferior (as in a city without citizens, namely a monarchy of the godlike man) and then there is the human being achieving his or her *telos* as the political animal exercising *logos* by making choices in the political realm."

CHAPTER FOUR

1. *Ph.* II.7.198a25–17, *PA* I.1.641a25–28, *GA* I.1.715a4, *Met.* XII.10.1075b8–10, *de Anima* II.4.415b12–21.

2. The difference might be clearer in a contrast between two kinds of rhetoric. In the first, corresponding to *Politics* IV, the speaker accommodates her arguments for what she thinks ought to be done to the opinions and values of the audience. I might need the biologist explaining evolution to me to take into account my ignorance of modern genetics. In the second, corresponding to *Politics* V, the speaker accepts the opinions and values of the audience as a starting point, and convinces them by telling them what they want to hear, showing how he's on their side. The lawyer trying to stop intelligent design from joining the biology curriculum might construct a narrative of progress that she thinks jurors might want to hear.

3. F. H. Bradley, *Ethical Studies* (Oxford: Oxford University Press, 1927). The treatment of akrasia in *Ethics* VII could correspond to the best on a hypothesis, both of them focusing on the efficient cause. Aristotle may well organize all his sciences—and all his arts, if we include the *Rhetoric*—according to the four causes, but only in the *Politics* do the four causes generate different kinds of best and separate inquiries.

4. On the other hand, there is an important affinity between the *Ethics* and *Pol.* IV–VI as opposed to VII and VIII. In those last two books, as in the contemplative life discussed at the end of the *Ethics*, actions that are their own end have no further ends. In the ethical virtues studied in the rest of the *Ethics*, things are done for their own sake and also done for the sake of some external goal, defending the city, helping friends, and so forth. In *Politics* IV–VI those who are citizens and live well also engage in occupations

that exclude them from citizenship in the last two books. To follow out this analogy, the life of contemplation with which the *Ethics* ends consists in activity which is done for its own sake and not in addition for some further end. Similarly, the citizens of the ideal state of Books VII and VIII do not engage in any instrumental activity. They leave farming and moneymaking to others.

5. Compare *Rh.* I.9.1367b5–6: "For if a person meets danger unnecessarily, he would be much more likely to do so where the danger is honorable." See Edward Halper, "The Unity of the Virtues in Aristotle," *Oxford Studies in Ancient Philosophy* 17 (1999): 115–43.

6. The place of philosophy in politics and ethics is obviously a larger subject than I can treat here without losing the thread of the argument, and I will look at it in more detail in the next two chapters. But we saw it already in Book II where Aristotle admitted the views of philosophers and private people about the best constitution in a way that has no parallel in the *Ethics*. We saw it again in Book III when he said: "Justice is a quality of a thing in relation to persons, and everyone holds that for persons that are equal the thing must be equal. But equality in what characteristics does this mean, and inequality in what? This must be made clear, since this too raises a difficulty, and calls for political philosophy" (III.12.1282b18–23). See too *EE* I.9.1216b35–37: "The political man should also not regard as irrelevant the inquiry that makes clear not only the "that," but also the "why." For that way of proceeding is the philosopher's way in every discipline." The relation between the "that" and the "why" is different in ethics and in politics, and so the function of philosophy is accordingly different.

7. The situation for the *Rhetoric* is more complicated than that for the *Ethics*. The *Rhetoric* might appear at first glance to limit itself, like *Politics* V–VI, to how best to advance any cause with which the speaker is presented, the hired gun theory of rhetoric. And indeed I will draw analogies between the *Rhetoric* and *Politics* V in my next chapter. But Aristotle limits the art of rhetoric to argument and thereby promises to consider more than persuasive success. He recognizes the existence of audiences so corrupt—often corrupted by orators—that they can't listen to reason. These would seem to be analogous to the best on a hypothesis here. There are modes of discourse and even of persuasion that are not governed by rhetoric, those in which one reasons from principles rather than from common opinion. Analysis of such reasoning is found in the *Analytics* and not in the *Rhetoric* at all, but that kind of reasoning most resembles the ideal of the absolutely best state of Books VII and VIII. II.12–17 shows how to modify one's appeals based on different kinds of audiences, analogous to the best in particular circumstances. The rest of the *Rhetoric*, I think, concerns the best in general.

8. See IV.7.1293a40–41, IV.11.1296a36–38.

9. He says that he invents logic, and is the first to see that reasoning is the heart of rhetorical persuasion. His rare claim of originality here should be compared to his reservations about political innovation at II.1.1260b27–38 and II.8.1269a14–27.

10. This gives another reason why it is difficult to determine the order of the books of the *Politics*. The treatment of the ideal state in Books VII and VIII is to this extent independent of the analysis in Book IV, and so could precede it as well as follow after that project is completed.

11. Books III, V, and VII contain different explanations for why there are several constitutions, since those books are parts of different inquiries. The purpose of Book III is to construct proper interrelations between citizen, polis, and constitution; there are several constitutions because one, few, or many can rule, and because different constitutions have different ends, freedom, wealth, or virtue. In Book V plurality comes from imperfection and error. "We must first assume as a principle that many different constitutions have come into being because, though all agree about the just and the proportionately equal, they make a mistake (*hamartia*) about it" (V.1.1301a25–26). Book V's account of why there are several constitutions is appropriate for an inquiry into the best on a hypothesis, using the efficient cause to engineer stability even in a context of imperfection and error. In Book VII, there are different constitutions because different people can participate in happiness in different degrees (VII.8.1328a38–41).

Chapter 3 of Book IV lists the necessary parts of a state (1289b28–1290a4; see VI.8.1321b6–7), and then IV.4 contains a more refined list (1290b38–1291b1). Different functions can be filled by the same people, except that no one can be rich and poor. Therefore, rich and poor are "especially held to be the parts of a state" (IV.4.1291b8), and there are two constitutions, democracy and oligarchy. In IV.3 he corrected this common opinion by saying that actually democracy and oligarchy exist alongside aristocracy and polity, which are distinct constitutions. In IV.4 he again corrects common opinion by saying that democracy and oligarchy themselves have species. The different sorts of rich and poor must themselves differ in kind, so that the fact that "there are several kinds (*eidē*) both of the people and of the so-called notables" implies "several kinds of democracy and oligarchy" (IV.4.1291b14–17).

12. Exceptions are IV.7.1293a37, 42, V.5.1304b18, and *NE* VIII.10.1160a31; III.3.1276b2 is ambiguous. He says that he bases the sixfold classification on *exoterikoi logoi* (non-esoteric discourses) (III.6.1278b31).

13. By contrast, in the *Poetics*, the different kinds of imitation have different ends, like the species of animals. The complication in the *Poetics* is that we learn in the final chapter that tragedy and epic have the same end. Here that complication becomes pervasive.

14. Contrast the quite different analogy between poleis and animals at *de Motu* 703a28–703b2.

15. Simpson, *A Philosophical Commentary on the Politics of Aristotle*, 294: "Aristotle has here traced the differences in regimes to differences, as it were, in material parts. But earlier he traced these differences to differences in the end the regime proposed to itself, wealth, freedom, virtue, or the like, or in what it supposed happiness to be (3.7, 4[7].8.1328a37–b2, 6[4].1.1289a15–18)."

16. Halper, "The Substance of Aristotle's Ethics," 17: "Aristotle's task through a good bit of the *Politics* is to determine how an activity that is in principle common can be divided and distributed among various people in ways that will allow each to exercise his ability to the greatest degree."

17. Curtis Johnson also argues against identifying them (*Aristotle's Theory of the State*, [New York: St. Martin's Press, 1990], 143–52), with counterargument by Miller, *Nature, Justice, and Rights in Aristotle's Politics*, 262–63, n.27. These arguments, though, turn on the relation between rule by the middle and rule by a combination of rich

and poor, while I am interested in the place of both constitutions in Aristotle's argument here for identifying the different kinds of best. Robinson looks at the arguments on both sides in detail (100–101).

18. Many commentators think that the mixed constitution must retain the principles of justice of the democracy and oligarchy out of which it is composed, rather than having its own principle of justice. At issue is the relation between the materials and the form of the mixed constitution. For such claims, see Barker, *The Political Thought of Plato and Aristotle*, 477; Miller, *Nature, Justice and Rights in Aristotle's Politics*, 256; and Simpson, *Philosophical Commentary on the Politics of Aristotle*, 316. Lockwood, I think, gets it right when he says that "political justice, at least to Aristotle's predecessors, appears so unusual because it combines things thought to be antithetical, namely the notion of rule (*archē*), which was thought to require excellence and expertise, and the notion of random rotation of office, which was thought to require democratic notions of equality. The novelty of political justice consists in seeing how excellence and equality can be combined. At the same time, Aristotle's regime of polity mixes elements of oligarchic and democratic regimes, and its novelty consists in the fact that those two regimes were also thought to be antithetical." T. C. Lockwood, "Polity, Political Justice and Political Mixing," *History of Political Thought* 27 (2006): 207–22, at 208.

19. Yack, *Problems of a Political Animal*, 104: "How can Aristotle insist that the polis naturally, which means 'for the most part,' aims at producing the conditions that promote the possibility of the good life, when actual political communities almost never consciously do so? If the polis naturally promotes the good life, than nature must display some cunning in its organization of political life. If ordinary, imperfect regimes make the good life possible, they must do so indirectly and unintentionally."

20. This is not to deny that demagogues were elite leaders of the people. It is the rich and poor as classes who at least try to advance the interests of their classes.

21. Simpson, *A Philosophical Commentary on the Politics of Aristotle*, 322: "Mixed regimes seem to be especially dependent, as oligarchies and democracies are not, on legislative action for their existence. For they require a mixing of very different parts (poverty and wealth and virtue), which mixing could hardly happen spontaneously but must be a deliberate and conscious act."

22. Recall, too, that in III.13 Aristotle distinguishes not between the best and merely correct constitutions, but between correct and the best claims to rule: "As regards the polis, all, or at any rate some, of these would seem to have a correct (*orthōs*) claim in the dispute. But as regards the good life, education and virtue would seem to have the most just claims (*malista dikaiōs*) of all in the dispute" (1283a24–25). In Book II's criticism of Plato's *Laws*, Aristotle notes that the constitution most generally acceptable is not necessarily the best constitution after the ideal one (II.6.1265b28–30).

23. Those two are connected by *kai de*, showing that they are distinct. See Pellegrin's comment on the passage: "Il y a peut-être une sort de jeu de mots sur le terme *sōzontai* (1295b28): ces gens a la fois sont la sauvegarde de la cité et en tirent leur propre sauvegarde." For more on the relations between the mean, the middle, and the mixed, see I. Evrigenis, "The Doctrine of the Mean in Aristotle's Ethical and Political Thought," *History of Political Thought* 20 (1999): 410–14. See Adam Smith, *The Theory of Moral*

Sentiments, ed. D. D. Raphael and A. L. Macfie (Oxford: Clarendon Press, 1976), 63: "In the middling and inferior stations of life, the road to virtue and that to fortune, to such fortune, at least, as men in such stations can reasonably expect to acquire, are, happily in most cases, very nearly the same. In all the middling and inferior professions, real and solid professional abilities, joined to prudent, just, firm, and temperate conduct, can very seldom fail of success. . . . Men in the inferior and middling stations of life, besides, can never be great enough to be above the law, which must generally overawe them into some sort of respect for, at least, the more important rules of justice."

24. Simpson, *A Philosophical Commentary on the Politics of Aristotle*, 331: "It is worth nothing, however, that these arguments about the superiority of the middle to the extremes are all about how the social position of those in the middle makes them behave in a moderate way. Those in the middle are not shown to be in the mean because they have been educated in virtue and possess the inner habit of virtue (such education only exists properly in the simply best regime). Someone taken from the middle and suddenly thrust among the poor or the wealthy is likely to behave as badly as the poor and the wealthy. But the socially conditioned virtue of the middle is precisely what Aristotle is now in search of, for it is something both good and within the reach of every city."

25. Thomas Hobbes, *Behemoth*, in *English Works of Thomas Hobbes*, VI: 211–12. See too Cass R. Sunstein, *Republic.com* (Princeton: Princeton University Press, 2001), and "The Law of Group Polarization," in *Debating Deliberative Democracy*, ed. James Fishkin and Peter Laslett (London: Blackwell, 2003).

26. See *NE* V.1.1129b1–6, V.9.1137a26–30, *EE* VII.2.1236b38–1237a3. I explore the ethical significance of the distinction between what is good *haplōs* and what is good for us in the first chapter of *Confronting Aristotle's Ethics*.

27. I take this as a reason to end the *Politics* with Book VI, and to place Books VII and VIII earlier. As I note elsewhere, there are arguments on the other side, too, which indicate that we should stay with the traditional ordering. There is a continuing dispute because there really are good reasons on both sides of the controversy.

28. The aristocratic vice here resembles some of the traits of the virtuous man of *NE* IV, who speaks ironically to his inferiors, holds them in contempt, sure that they can't understand him.

29. As Aristotle proceeds to generate principles of good mixtures out of the sophisms, we could also recall the difference between rhetoric and sophistic in the *Rhetoric*. The sophist has no argumentative principles of his own; he simply uses rational principles, but uses them as tactics rather than as principles. For details, see the second chapter of *Aristotle's Rhetoric: An Art of Character*.

30. Richard Robinson, ed., *Aristotle: Politics, Books III and IV* (Oxford: Clarendon Press, [1962] 1995), 17, while stating the point tentatively, seems to me to get it just right: "It is just possible that Aristotle intended IV 14–16 as an answer to the sixth question of IV 1, which was which laws are the best and which laws fit each of the constitutions. There is no other question listed in IV 1 or IV 2 to which IV 14–16 is a conceivable answer."

31. Avishai Margalit, *On Compromise and Rotten Compromise* (Princeton: Princeton University Press, 2010), 5: "Ideals may tell us something important about what we would like to be. But compromises tell us who we are."

32. These two sorts of moderation correspond to the two senses of the mean in the *Ethics*, virtue as a mean between extreme vices and virtue as *about* the mean amount of actions and passions, the difference between *meson* and *mesotēs*. Generally, *mesotēs* refers to the mean state of character and *to meson* to actions that lie between extremes. Over many years of conversation, Charles Young has taught me the value of this distinction.

33. McKeon, "Aristotle's Conception of Moral and Political Philosophy," at 282: "It would be a mistake . . . to think of Aristotle's massive classification of states simply as function and mathematical determinations of conceivable political combinations, institutions, and ends. They are, rather, the multiple development, by means of the four causes, of answers to the problem, basic to politics as Aristotle conceived it, of how institutions and constitutions depend on and influence citizens associated in communities."

34. It has become common over the years to recognize the similarities between Book V and Machiavelli, but not this particular affinity. Isaiah Berlin, "The Originality of Machiavelli," first published *Studies on Machiavelli*, ed. Myron P. Gilmore (Florence: Sansoni, 1972), and reprinted in Berlin, *Against the Current: Essays in the History of Ideas* (New York: Penguin, 1980), 25–79, at 79: "If not all values are compatible with one another . . . then a picture emerges different from that constructed round the ancient principle that there is only one good for men. . . . If there is only one solution to the puzzle, then the only problems are firstly how to find it, then how to realize it, and finally how to convert others to the solution by persuasion or by force. But if this is not so . . . then, the path is open to empiricism, pluralism, toleration, compromise. Toleration is historically the product of the realisation of the irreconcilability of equally dogmatic faiths, and the practical impossibility of complete victory of one over the other. Those who wished to survive realised that they had to tolerate error. They gradually came to see merits in diversity, and so became skeptical about definitive solutions in human affairs. . . . [Machiavelli's] intellectual consequences, wholly unintended by its originator, were, by a fortunate irony of history (which some call its dialectic), the bases of the very liberalism that Machiavelli would surely have condemned." I have criticized Berlin's reading of Machiavelli on just this point in "After *Virtù*: Rhetoric, Prudence, and Moral Pluralism in Machiavelli's *Discourses on Livy*," *History of Political Thought* 17 (1996): 1–29. A different version appears in Robert Hariman, ed., *Prudence: Classical Virtue, Postmodern Practice* (University Park: Pennsylvania State University Press, 2003), 67–98.

CHAPTER FIVE

1. This is *the* understanding of politics in Mulgan, *Aristotle's Political Theory*, 7.

2. "The noble man should either live finely or die finely." *Ajax*, 479–80. See too the story of Dion at *Pol.* V.10.1322a21–39. The relation between excellence and stability as goals reappears in modern arguments about the role of religion in a society, whether religion is either necessary for stability or essential to society because it is true. Religion and the state might be only necessary conditions for living well, or they can be constitutive aspects of the good life.

3. Faction translates *stasis*. Barker translates it as "sedition." His note reads: "*Stasis* is the act of forming (and thence, by an easy transference, the body of persons forming) a combination 'for the attainment of some political end by legal and illegal means'

(Newman). From this point of view, and because it may include illegal as well as legal means, *stasis* may involve revolutionary action, and thus issue in revolution; though it may sometimes stop short of that issue, and only produce non-revolutionary changes, within the four walls of the constitution. Aristotle accordingly connects two different forms of constitutional change with *stasis*." Ernest Barker, *The Politics of Aristotle* (Oxford: Oxford University Press, 1952), 204, n.1. Keyt, quoting *Republic* V.470b4–9, says that "*stasis* is used for hostility in the domestic sphere and *polemos* for hostility in the foreign." Drawing on *Ethics* IX.6, Keyt says that "within a political community *stasis* is opposed to *homonoia*, like-mindedness or concord, which Aristotle identifies with political friendship." David Keyt, trans., *Aristotle: Politics, Books V and VI* (Oxford: Clarendon Press, 1999), 63, 64.

The last three chapters of Book V discuss problems specific to monarchy and tyranny. I won't consider those chapters here. However, the treatment of tyranny is a fitting conclusion to Book V, because the tyrant must choose between two contrasting methods of holding on to power. He can either moderate his ambitions or repress and render impotent anyone who might overthrow him. It is part of the political wisdom that Book V imparts that rulers in constitutions other than tyrannies do not have to make this choice, that acting moderately and acting constitutionally are not at odds as acting moderately and acting tyrannically are.

4. The translation is Lord's, except that I have substituted "constitution" for his "regime" throughout. Carnes Lord, *Aristotle: The Politics* (Chicago: University of Chicago Press, 1984).

5. "The Aristotelian, or the traditional Greek notion of the rule of law lacks of the concept of an agent which could initiate changes in the law, and that consequently, as opposed to its modern counterpart, the Aristotelian rule of the law is not an instrument for initiating changes in the community (that is of positive lawmaking), but rather an instrument for the arrest of change." Moshe Berent, "Sovereignty: Ancient and Modern," *Polis* 17 (2000): 2–34, at 12. In an important sense this asymmetry is unique to Book V. In IV.1, which I will consider in a couple of pages, when Aristotle presents the program that will occupy him in succeeding books (whether IV–VIII or IV–VI, depending on how one orders the books of the *Politics*), he seems to include improving the constitution as well as simply preserving it. In II.8, Aristotle presents arguments in favor of and against changing the constitution, in the context of considering Hippodamus's proposal that political innovations be encouraged and rewarded. After presenting balanced arguments on both sides, Aristotle promises to investigate the issue more fully later, but never does.

6. Not only is there no state of nature, but there is no neutral way of standing outside a conflict. Solon's laws punished people who tried to avoid taking sides. I was reminded of this point by Yack, "The Myth of the Civic Nation," 206.

7. There is a section on refutative enthymemes in *Rhetoric* II.24. Apart from that, there is a book, or a section of the *Topics*, on *sophistical* refutations, but not on refutations in general.

8. Keyt, *Aristotle: Politics, Books V and VI*, 147 (note to V.1013io b31–40): "The word *axia* is a key term in Aristotle's political philosophy and sometimes has a broad and sometimes a narrow sense. In the section before us he uses the word in a narrow sense in which it signifies one specific standard of worth, the aristocratic (see also III.5.1278a19–

20), rather than in the broad sense of his theory of justice where it is a mere place-holder for an unspecified standard of worth (see *NE* V.3.1131a24–29 and the note to 1.1301a25–b4 above)."

9. Even extreme democracy excludes, because defining justice as arithmetic equality denies oligarchic citizenship, denies the claims oligarchs make in the name of proportion to wealth. The wealthy might still be citizens, but not qua wealthy.

10. Michael Davis, "Aristotle's Reflections on Revolution," *Graduate Faculty Philosophy Journal* 11 (1986): 46–63, notices something similar but offers a very different account. Aristotle, he says, "begins Book V with the claim that revolution comes to be as the result of a perceived injustice. But if the truth of the *polis*—of political society—is change, i.e., if Book V really points to the nature of the political, then all regimes come to be as the result of a perceived injustice. Not simply revolution, but all political life as such will be negatively determined. Political regimes are always reactions to a perceived injustice: they are not determined by a notion of justice positively understood."

11. Patrick Coby, "Aristotle's Three Cities and the Problem of Faction," *Journal of Politics* 50 (1988): 896–919, at 912: "He never quite says so, but his account of faction in the early chapters of book 5 seems to rely on the four operative causes outlined in the *Physics* (2.3): efficient, material, formal, and final. For instance, faction has its efficient cause in the beginning points, occasions, and opportunities (1302a21: *archai*) which trigger civil unrest. . . . The material cause of faction is the unsuitability of a regime to its people, a disproportion that occurs at some time in the regime's history or at the moment of its founding (1302b3: *auxēsin tēn para to analogon*; 1302b5: *anomoiotēta*). An increase of the poor in an oligarchic regime or an extreme democracy forced upon an agrarian people are examples (6.1.8). The formal cause (1302a20: *pōs ti echontes*) is the disagreement among citizens about who should rule, those disputes over distributive justice and reciprocal equality. 'Factional conflict,' Aristotle declares, 'is everywhere the result of inequality, at any rate where there is no proportion among those who are unequal' (5.1.11). The last is final cause (1302a21: *tinōn heneken*), or the objectives people pursue when they resort to faction. There are two objectives that Aristotle allows: profit (*kerdos*) and honor (*timē*). The many want profit, while the few seek honor."

12. Josiah Ober, "The Debate over Civil Education in Classical Athens," in *Education in Greek and Roman Antiquity*, ed. Yun Lee Too (Boston: Brill, 2001), 187: "The weaker citizen (especially a poor man, one lacking formal education or powerful friends) was in principle immune from being subjected to unanswerable physical assault or verbal humiliation by his stronger neighbor, whereas all citizens (and especially wealthy citizens) were protected from certain forms of the arbitrary exercise of majority power, especially as regards private property." The danger to the poor from the rich came from the vice associated with honor, hubris. The danger to the rich from the poor came from the vice associated with wealth, confiscation. The first extended political inequality into nonpolitical realms. The second extended political equality into nonpolitical realms.

13. As Belfiore, personal communication, reminded me, this remark of Aristotle's is reminiscent of Thucydides's distinction in I.23 between pretexts and underlying causes. Most commentators on contemporary American politics note two things without trying to make a connection between them. First, the factional divisions between politicians is greater than has been the case in most people's memories. Second, the distance between

politicians' positions on most issues is slighter than ever and certainly less significant than in most other countries. Aristotle here tells us not to be surprised at the lack of correlation between amount of factionalism and the extent of disagreement. Marshall Sahlins, "Structural Work: How Microhistories Become Macrohistories and Vice Versa," *Anthropological Theory* 5 (2005): 5–30, produces helpful examples of small events serving as the impulse for potentially revolutionary action. His example of the Elián González case is particularly telling.

14. Newman, *The Politics of Aristotle*, 4: 306, 318, sees the distinction as lying between the occasions out of which (*ex hōn*) change occurs, as opposed to causes because of which (*di' ha*) they occur.

15. Ronald Polansky, "Aristotle on Political Change," in *A Companion to Aristotle's Politics*, ed. David Keyt and Fred D. Miller, Jr. (Oxford: Blackwell, 1991), 323–45, at 339, n29: "Though Aristotle says the safeguards of constitutions are contraries to the causes of change, it must be appreciated that the causes of *change* usually occur apart from the statesman's contrivance, while the safeguards are the statesman's implementation of modes of *action* that secure a pattern of action in the community."

16. Simpson, *A Philosophical Commentary on the Politics of Aristotle*, 288, n.8: "Some scholars believe that Aristotle's proposals for reforming regimes in the books that follow all involve changing the existing regime into another one, as say into a measured form from an extreme one. . . . But in fact a regime that is made less extreme, or stabilized where it is, is reformed but is still the same regime, for it will still have the same ruling body (which is what defines regimes) save that this ruling body will be less self-destructive in the way it exercises control." But the ruling body does not define regimes; the constitution's end defines it as well. Democracies and polities can have the same ruling body, as can aristocracies and oligarchies, when, as in Book III, the ruling body is defined as one, few, or many. When the end of the constitution changes from life to the good life, from benefiting the rulers to benefiting the whole, the membership of the ruling body need not change. Therefore the ambiguity remains.

17. In *NE* VIII.10, Aristotle does claim that the "smallest and easiest" constitutional changes are from kingship to tyranny, aristocracy to oligarchy, and timocracy to democracy, but nothing like that occurs in the *Politics*.

18. Compare IV.13.1297a6–36, for recommendations on how to use sophisms to deceive the people, even in aristocracies.

19. Note the contrast to the devices tyrants use to stay in power, which do depend on deceptive appearances (e.g., II.11.1314a40, 1314b1, b7, b15, b18, b23–24, b32, b39). Richard Bodéüs wisely distinguishes between deception from the point of view of the ruler and the ruled. "Judged from the point of view of the sovereign, it is clearly hypocrisy, a tyranny that masks itself. But from the point of view of the subject? If the role is well played and the mask convincing, does it matter much that the tyranny isn't sincere when he acts like a king? That the monarch stops terrorizing because he fears to provoke his subjects against him, as the tyrant who takes the trappings of a king, that produces the same effects: no more terror or persecution. To keep power or realize the good, the intention doesn't matter when the same measure procures for the tyrant's subjects the benefits of a king. In these conditions, Aristotle's Machiavellianism is less shocking. If he recommends to the tyrant the trappings of a king, in one sense this is realism; he can't

recommend to him truly to become a king, because that would be contrary to the will of the tyrant. On the other hand, it is also true that, still realistically, he judges that the same effects are produced by a sincere king and someone who affects to be one. In this business, it isn't finally the people who are duped, but the tyrant, condemned to play his role to perfection, under pain of losing his authority and power." Richard Bodéüs, "L'attitude paradoxale d'Aristote envers la tyrannie," *Tijdscrift voor Filosofie* 61 (1999): 556–57.

20. While Aristotle does not tie these remedies to particular causes of instability, Keyt does. Keyt, *Aristotle: Politics, Books V and VI*, 128: "The causes of destruction to which the third way of preserving constitutions is a response are the insolence and greed of those in office (3.1302b5–14); the dishonouring of one man of stature by another (7.1306b31–36); and the division of the governing class of an oligarchy into an inner and an outer circle (6.1305b2–22, 369, 1306a13–19, 31–b5)."

21. Irwin, *Aristotle's First Principles*, 458: "Justice and temperance relative to an oligarchy are not justice and temperance as oligarchs conceive them, but the degree of justice and temperance that are consistent with the preservation of an oligarchy. Aristotle believes that these will actually tend to preserve a fairly reasonable oligarchy (1310a19–22); he implies that an oligarchy that is undermined by the observance of oligarchic justice does not deserve to survive. The virtues of a citizen are not tactics for adaptation to the regime, but the proper way to exercise the genuine virtues in these political systems."

22. Aristotle would agree, then, with Herbert Wechsler's remark that "principles are largely instrumental as they are employed in politics." But he would not see the easy way of a pure and principled intervention into politics that Wechsler and others envision for the Supreme Court: "The main constituent of the judicial process is precisely that it be genuinely principled." Herbert Wechsler, "Toward Neutral Principles of Constitutional Law," *Harvard Law Review* 73 (1959): 1–33, at 14–15. "Seen from the viewpoint of politics, truth has a despotic character," Hannah Arendt, "Truth and Politics," *Between Past and Future* (New York: Viking Press, 1961), 227–64, at 241.

23. I disagree, then, with Polansky, "Aristotle on Political Change," 444–45: "It should . . . be evident that [Aristotle] aims to give virtue as full a place he practically can in political life. A large part of the task of enhancing the role of virtue is to reveal to the prospective statesman, hopefully well along in virtue, the small chance virtue has in dominating the scene." "The class of philosophers is by nature incapable of forming seditious factions or clubs." Kant, "Perpetual Peace," in *Kant's Political Writings*, ed. Hans Reiss (Cambridge: Cambridge University Press, 1991), 115.

24. Such is the thrust of my argument in *Aristotle's Rhetoric: An Art of Character*.

25. See too IV.4.1291b5–6: "All men claim to possess virtue, and think they are worthy to fill most public offices."

26. See too Richard Kraut, *Aristotle: Political Philosophy* (Oxford and New York: Oxford University Press, 2002), 159: "Although doing and suffering injustice are opposites, in that one is the deficiency caused by the other's excess, they are not opposite vices, because only one of them is a vice. Justice, in other words, differs from other virtues because, although it is a mean between two states that should be avoided, it is not intermediate between two vices." One of the morals of the *Phaedrus* is that when art cooperates with nature, that art will differ from an art that conceives itself to be self-sufficient or

a substitute for nature (269d). A practical philosophy such as Aristotle's, which cooperates with *phronēsis*, will be unable to refute the skeptic, and unconcerned with doing so, while a philosophy that sees such refutation as a primary task will be unable to cooperate with the *phronimos*.

27. For example, many of the complications with implementing the school desegregation decisions came from the Supreme Court not being confident in how much it could trust other public officials to carry out its decisions. Its uncertainty made some of its decisions too detailed in instructing other officials, and others too open and vague, merely exhorting them to desegregate with "all deliberate speed." Robin West, "From Choice to Reproductive Justice: De-Constitutionalizing Abortion Rights," *Yale Law Journal* 118 (2009): 1394–1432, at 1421: "The traditional identification and elevation of reasoned discourse with the Court, which is at the heart of rights-oriented constitutionalism, not only pits the principled decisionmaking, of which the Court is so proud, against passion, but also pits itself against compromise. Principle cannot abide compromise, but politics cannot proceed without it. The public discussion of abortion has become as raw as it is, in part, because of that fact. When we battle this issue out in court as a clash of principles, we develop those martial arts of the mind that are necessary to that battle. We lose, though, the arts of political compromise. We lose the ability and willingness to craft deals we can live with, the nimbleness of giving a little and getting a little, the commitment to the project of living with and under the roofs that compromise creates. There is much to worry over, of course, in compromise, but there is also much to applaud: it is neighborly, civil, and inclusive."

28. In chapter 3, I mentioned the trouble Aristotle has in saying whether there is a single polis that undergoes changes in constitutional form, or whether change in constitution creates a new polis. The same problem reemerges here. If each constitution defines by fiat who is a citizen, then *stasis* becomes a fight within the state of nature. So the constitution's definition of who is a citizen somehow does not accomplish all it seems to.

29. For a contemporary example of what is to one faction philosophical necessity, but looks to another party like coercion, see Michael Ignatieff, *Human Rights as Politics and Idolatry* (Princeton: Princeton University Press, 2001), 20: "The idea of rights as trumps implies that when rights are introduced into a political discussion, they serve to resolve the discussion. In fact, the opposite is the case. When political demands are turned into rights claims, there is a real risk that the issue at stake will become irreconcilable, since to call a claim a right is to call it nonnegotiable . . ."

30. I don't mean this as an argument about the order of the books. But it does make the ordering that ends with the ideal state appealing. Equally, if one prefers the other ordering, renaming Books IV–VI as Books VI–VIII, then the *Politics* will move toward practical problems for which the uses of philosophy are increasingly indirect. That ordering has its attractions, too.

CHAPTER SIX

1. To recall the analogies between constitutions and biological species, it makes sense to ask about the best democracy or oligarchy, like the best human or best dog, but makes no sense to ask about the best animal, and, in parallel, the best constitution.

However, these last books of the *Politics* do just that. One precedent is the final chapters of the *Poetics*, in which Aristotle moves from considering the best tragedy to determining that tragedy is the best kind of imitation or work of art altogether. In the *Statesman*, in the age of Chronus all human needs are satisfied, but there is no philosophy. It is the human conflicts of the age of Zeus that give rise to philosophy (272b–d). See Saxonhouse, *Fear of Diversity*.

2. Kraut, *Aristotle: Political Philosophy*, 191: "In Books VII and VIII [and] here, alone, in the *Politics*, he argues for his conception of happiness; having done so, he depicts for his audience the sort of community that can be created for people who have a life that embodies that conception of well-being. (In Books IV–VI, by contrast, it is difficult to discern what role—if any—his conception of happiness is playing."

Because Book VII concerns the relation between the end of the polis and its material, it leaves out the moving causes of the polis. Specifically, the ideal polis of Book VII has no history. This constitution emerges out of ideal material conditions. It does not emerge out of other constitutions. The middle books show how one kind of constitution develops out of another, through either political wisdom or revolution, but the ideal state has no etiology.

3. Yack, *Problems of a Political Animal*, 167: "Although Aristotle does claim genuine knowledge of the human good and does construct a utopian regime in which the human good is best realized, he never suggests that we should measure the justice of laws and public acts by asking how close they come to realizing the states of affairs found in the best regime." Stephen Salkever, "Whose Prayer? The Best Regime of Book 7 and the Lessons of Aristotle's *Politics*," *Political Theory* 35 (2007): 29–46, at 30: Aristotle, "like Plato, seems determined to make it difficult for his readers to appropriate his work as a direct guide to changing or maintaining the world." Miller does think that the ideal is something to be approximated. He quotes the *de Caelo*: "While it is clearly best for any being to attain the real end, yet, if that cannot be, the nearer it is to the best, the better will be its state" (II.2.292b17–19; cf. *Gen. Corr.* II.10.336b25–34). Fred D. Miller, Jr., "Aristotelian Statecraft and Modern Politics," in *Aristotle's Politics Today*, ed. Lenn E. Goodman and Robert B. Tallisse (Albany: State University of New York Press, 2007), 17–18. But Miller also equates such a maxim of approximation with the second sailing (*deuteros plous*) of the *Ethics*: "Since to hit the mean is hard in the extreme, we must as a second best, as people say, take the least of the evils" (*NE* III.9.1109a34–35), and then to a "regulative ideal." Kraut, *Aristotle: Political Philosophy*, 193, too thinks this gives us "a goal that can be approached to some degree." On the other hand, he also says that "one cannot take an oligarchy or a democracy and transform it (even by degrees) into a perfect constitution" (196). Plato's *Statesman* does seem to offer the rule of wisdom as the best constitution, to which others should approximate through imitation. Other constitutions are, in the language of the *Timaeus*, cases of reason persuading necessity (*Statesman* 294c–d).

4. Kraut, *Aristotle: Political Philosophy*, 190: "There is something unsatisfactory about Aristotle's postponement of his discussion of the ideal city to the end of his treatise: he asks his audience to wait a long time before he comes to the destination for which he has been preparing them. It is in Books 7 and 8 that we find Aristotle's fullest and most detailed account of how a city is best organized."

Remembering that the *Politics* is a continuation of the *Ethics* doesn't help. If the *Politics* presupposes the details of the good life articulated in the *Ethics*, no explicit use is made of those details. See Bodéüs, "Le recherche poliqitue d'après le 'programme' de *l'Éthique à Nicomaque* d'Aristote." The particulars of the analysis of the individual virtues, or *akrasia*, or of friendship do not appear in the *Politics*. On the other hand, the claim at the beginning of Book VII that we have to understand the good life before the good constitution does have implications, ambiguous ones, for the ordering of the books of the *Politics*. See Salkever, "Whose Prayer?," 43, n.8: "I would frame the issue thus: if you believe that Aristotle wants to use his discussion of the best life as a ground from which to deduce political principles, then what have been called Books 7 and 8 should then indeed be placed as Books 4 and 5; but if you think as I do that Aristotle wants to teach his students to ask the question of the best life rather than to present them with a doctrine of it, then it makes better sense to leave the books as they are. Much also depends on whether you think that the regime according to prayer is meant to serve as a model for practical reform (with Simpson) or a warning against treating politics as the final and perfect human horizon." I think the *Politics* is neither. I take it as an inquiry into the relation between living the best life and living a common life, living well and living together. There are good and nonconclusive reasons for both possible orderings. I prefer the usual ordering because it allows us to raise the acute questions that organize this final chapter.

5. The translation is Apostle's, the most literal I have found. Hippocrates George Apostle and Lloyd P. Gerson, trans., *Aristotle's Politics* (Grinnell: Peripatetic Press, 1986). C. D. C. Reeve, trans., *Aristotle: Politics* (Indianapolis: Hackett, 1998), has "whether it is the same for an individual as for a community." George Kateb, "Hobbes and the Irrationality of Politics," *Political Theory* 17 (1989): 355–91, eloquently expresses the dangers of talking about states in the language appropriate to individuals. Hobbes, he says, "unhesitatingly transfers to collectivities the vocabulary that is unconfusing only when used about individuals in their attributes, motives, aims and experiences as well as rights. This transference is the most ingrained kind of political irrationality. . . . There is no rational analogy between individuals and nations. It is not merely the case that the analogy is imperfect. Nations are fictions: Their bonds tend to degenerate into kitsch, which favors crime and aggression. . . . The necessities of the collective individual are only imaginary necessities, as imaginary as the collective individual itself, and they get their undeserved legitimacy from the thoughtless conceptual assimilation of the group to the individual."

6. Kraut, *Aristotle: Politics, Books VII and VIII*, 53: "Aristotle then adds a further question 'about whether the life that is most choiceworthy collectively is the same as the one that is most choiceworthy for each separately.' The meaning of this question is not immediately apparent." Kraut, though, thinks that by VII.2 the question becomes unambiguous.

7. There are at least two more passages apart from those that occur in these chapters. At III.6.1278b23–24 he speaks of living well as the end, whether of everyone in common or of each separately (*kai koinē[i] pasi kai chōris*). And VII.15 begins: "Since it is evident that human beings have the same end, both individually and collectively, and since the best man and the best constitution must of necessity have the same aim, it is evident

that the virtues suitable for leisure should be present in both" (*epei de to auto telos einai phainetai kai koinē[i] kai idia[i] tois anthrōpois, kai ton auton horon anagkaion einai tō[i] te aristo[i] andri kai tē[i] aristē[i] politeia[i] . . .*) (1334a11–13). *Rhetoric* I.5, which is about happiness, contains extended discussions of the individual and the common, and in that work the distinction aligns simply with the individual and the state. The chapter begins: "Men, individually and in common (*kai idiai hekastoi kai koinēi*) nearly all have some aim . . . which is happiness." Later in the chapter he defines noble birth "for a nation and a state" (*ethnei kai polei*), and for the individual (*idiai*), and good children for the polis (*toi koinoi*) and for the individual (*idiai*).

8. See too IV.11.1295a40: "The same defining principles (*horoi*) must also hold of the virtue and vice of a polis or a constitution, since a constitution is a sort of life of the polis." And VII.15.1334a11–16: "Since the *telos* is evidently the same for human beings both in common and privately, and there must be the same definition (*horos*) for the best man and the best constitution. it is evident that the virtues directed to leisure should be present." Contrast *NE* I.9.1099b33–1100a2: "We have good reason for not speaking of an ox or horse or any other animal as being happy, because none of these is able to participate in noble activities."

9. For two other places where Aristotle seems untroubled about ascribing moral qualities to poleis, see *Pol.* I.9.1310a19–20 in which poleis as much as people can be akratic, and II.9.1269b14 in which the constitution makes choices (*prohairesis*). Similar problems are examined in Bernard Williams, "The Analogy of City and Soul in Plato's *Republic*," in Williams, *The Sense of the Past: Essays in the History of Philosophy*, ed. and with an intro. by Myles Burnyeat (Princeton: Princeton University Press, 2006), 108–17, reprinted from E. N. Lee, A. P. D. Mourelatos, and R. M. Rorty, eds., *Exegesis and Argument: Studies in Greek Philosophy presented to Gregory Vlastos* (Asen: Van Gorcum, 1973), 196–206. In addition to the problems Williams raises, the different parts of the soul have characteristic desires, and Socrates must postulate analogous desires in the different parts of the state. The different classes in the state have different sizes, since they comprise different numbers of citizens. But it is hard to see what it means for the different parts of the soul to have different sizes. Moreover, not all states have the three classes that Kallipolis does, but all people are supposed to have the three part of the soul.

10. I discuss the lack of psychological depth in the *Ethics* in *Confronting Aristotle's Ethics*, especially chapter 4.

11. In the psychology of the *Republic*, acquisition and domination come from different parts of the soul. On the other hand, *pleonexia* can describe both. See 1.349b8–350c11. The difficulty of separating the two is well expressed in Ryan K. Balot, *Greed and Injustice in Classical Athens* (Princeton: Princeton University Press, 2001), 32: "Aristotle's presentation of greed in the *Ethics* and *Politics* includes both a psychological treatment and consideration of the distributive context within which an agent is judged." Also at 32–33: "It is useful to view greed as operative within two moral 'fields' that overlap but do not entail one another, that of fairness and unfairness, the field of distribution; and that of moderation and excess, the field of acquisition. Although the two 'fields' in which greed participates can be theoretically distinguished, they are often brought together in the psychology and behavior of practical political agents. We are left with a picture of

greed that points in two directions—toward the excessive desires of the individual and toward the ethical context of distributive fairness within which the greedy individual is characteristically evaluated."

12. Arlene W. Saxonhouse, *Athenian Democracy: Modern Mythmakers and Ancient Theorists* (Notre Dame: University of Notre Dame Press, 1996), 121: "Since we cannot rely on nature to give us unambiguous assurances concerning who is superior and who is inferior, the political regime makes those distinctions, but having made them and offering definitions of equality and hierarchies, *para phusin, kata nomon*, these definitions, lacking any grounding in nature, will always be subject to debate; they will always be a source of instability in the regime, a source of conflict as members of the community disagree about the definitions of equality and inequality established by any particular regime. . . . The issue for all political communities is to define who is equal precisely because nature has not given us the skills to recognize equals and those who are not equal. Our powers of observation do not give insight into the souls of individuals such that we can know who is noble and who is base, who is good and who is mad."

13. "The regime of Aristotle's *Politics* VII–VIII is indeed his best regime, and yet it lacks political justice in the strict sense of complete ruling and being ruled in turn." Lockwood, "Polity, Political Justice and Political Mixing," 220.

14. *Republic* 4.423d: "By pursuing the one thing that belongs to him, each will become one and not many, and in that way the city as a whole will grow to be one and not many."

15. The polis is an *energeia* (*NE* I.1.1094a16–18), an action that is its own end (I.2.1094a18–28, *Pol.* I.1.1252a1–3), complete and self-sufficient (1252b27–30, III.9.1280b40–1281a1). None of these things could apply to families or alliances. David Depew, "Politics, Music, and Contemplation in Aristotle's Ideal State," In *A Companion to Aristotle's Politics*, ed. David Keyt and Fred D. Miller, Jr. (Oxford and Cambridge: Blackwell, 1991), 346–80, at 354: "Self-sufficiency does not consist only in the *de facto* achievement of material plenty, but in a condition where the attitudes of political associates are no longer dominated or distorted by a means-oriented mentality—a mentality that, having inevitably arisen in a world of scarcity, can live on even in a world of great abundance, as it does in deviant states."

16. Gerson, "Aristotle's Polis: A Community of the Virtuous," 208: "Puzzlement or reticence in taking Aristotle at his word when he says that the state exists by nature is attributable to the false assumption that in the primary sense of the term, a *polis* is a place or an institution, both of which are more correctly designated as artificial than natural. It is rather the case that by '*polis*' Aristotle means primarily something like a complete human association, in the sense of the actual activity of associating."

17. "In his *Republic*, Plato displays the substance of ethical life in its ideal beauty and truth, but he could only deal with the principle of self-subsistent particularity, which in his day had forced its way into Greek ethical life, by setting up in opposition to it his purely substantive state." G. W. F. Hegel, *Philosophy of Right*, trans. T. M. Knox (Oxford: Clarendon Press, 1942), paragraph 185 (p. 279).

18. For explicit claims that the polis is a substance, see Barker, *The Political Thought*

of *Plato and Aristotle*, 276–77; and Stephen R. L. Clark, *Aristotle's Man: Speculations upon Aristotelian Anthropology* (Oxford: Clarendon Press, 1975), 102–4.

19. Collins, *Aristotle and the Rediscovery of Citizenship*, 111, notes the odd way in which Aristotle seems to answer a question only to raise it again: Aristotle seems satisfied for the moment that the first question—the most choiceworthy life for the individual—is settled and he takes up the second question: whether this life is the same for the city. He offers several prefatory statements: "It may come as a surprise, therefore, that he continues his consideration of the identity of the happiness of a human being and the city, though he asks a slightly different and more limited question: whether 'it is necessary' to assert this identity." And then at 112: "Although he had sought to drop the question of which life is best of the individual simply, or to relegate it to a subordinate place in the inquiry, Aristotle proves unable to do so."

Simpson, *A Philosophical Commentary on the Politics of Aristotle*, 202: "This next paragraph has posed problems for commentators since it looks, first, like needless repetition and, second, like inappropriate arguing, it is needless repetition because this question about the city's happiness has surely just been decided, for it has been shown that the best life for city and individual is a life of virtuous deeds. It is inappropriate arguing because if Aristotle had thought it now necessary to draw in express words this conclusion that the happiness of the city must therefore be the same as the individual, he should simply have appealed back to what he has just proven and not have appealed instead to what people say, including what those people say who deny that the happy life is a life of virtue."

20. Kraut, *Aristotle: Politics, Books VII and VIII*, 60: "Now he adds a new argument to support his affirmative answer. Unlike the argument of VII.1, it does not depend on any specific conception of which life is most choiceworthy." Barker, *The Politics of Aristotle*, 284n2: "Aristotle here appears to glide back into the question of the more desirable life for the individual—a question which . . . he had [just] dismissed as irrelevant. But he only appears to do so. Actually, he is concerned with the more desirable life for the state, and with the form of political constitution which such a life requires; and it is only incidentally that he mentions the individual."

21. The *Ethics* explicitly says that the only practical life that could be happy is a political life: "The *energeia* of the practical virtues is in political and military activity" (X.7. 1177b6–7). Mulgan, *Aristotle's Political Theory*, denies this for the *Politics*, seeing ethical virtue in the household as well. Such an extension is subject to Aristotle's criticism of Plato for failing to distinguish polis from household. Kraut, *Aristotle: Politics, VII and VIII*, 141, notes that "at *NE* X.7.1177b4–5, [Aristotle] claims that political activity is in a certain way unleisurely, but we find no explicit statement of that thesis in the *Politics*."

22. This formulation opens up the possibility that there can be lives fit for philosophers other than the theoretical life. Andrea Wilson Nightingale, *Spectacles of Truth in Classical Greek Philosophy: Theoria in Its Cultural Context* (Cambridge: Cambridge University Press, 2004), 20: "The proponents of the theoretical life, then, use 'freedom' as the marker of the good and happy life; by 'freedom' they mean leisure and detachment from external exigencies and constraints (rather than mere political freedom).

Advocates of the practical life, on the other hand, identify 'action' as the marker of the good life; the theorists, they say, are 'doing nothing' and thus can't be said to live well."

23. Most commentators find the discussion in the *Politics* therefore inferior to that in the *Ethics*, and none, as far as I know, see it as an improvement. Kraut, *Aristotle: Politics, Books VII and VIII*, 62, complains that Aristotle "does not decisively draw a conclusion about which is better." Reeve, *Aristotle, Politics*, xlvi, says that he doesn't "give decisive precedence to either." Miller, *Nature, Justice, and Rights in Aristotle's Politics*, 216, sees it as "somewhat inconclusive." Friedrich Solmsen, "Leisure and Play in Aristotle's Ideal State," *Rheinisches Museum* 107 (1954): 193–220, at 196, sees them as "indicative of a deeper conflict between diverging tendencies and inclinations in his mind." I owe this review of the secondary literature to David Roochnik, "Aristotle's Defense of the Theoretical Life: Comments on *Politics* 7," *Review of Metaphysics* 61 (2008): 713. They prefer the *Ethics* because, as Roochnik puts it, "argues unambiguously in favor of the" theoretical-philosophical life. Since I don't see *NE* X.7–8 that way, I don't buy the terms of comparison.

24. Organizing one's life around philosophy does not disqualify one from citizenship. Such activity is then different from that of music, which can become so specialized that it becomes vulgar, aims at the pleasure of its audience, and so does disqualify the practitioner from citizenship. For a contemporary version of Aristotle's criticism of specialization, consider the following: "Refinement is a form of corruption. Sharpening of the palate may well correspond to deeper deadening. Human organs of sense and experience, cut free from anything but their pleasure, catered to so scrupulously—how can it end in anything other than a spoiled, infantilized, ever-more-demanding state?" Sean Wilsey, review of Phoebe Damrosch, *Service Included*, *New York Times Sunday Book Review*, November 18, 2007, 16.

25. The brief mention of god at VII.3.1325b27–29 is used to confirm, not establish, the conclusion that activity does not necessarily mean activity toward another. Lord, *Education and Culture*, 199: "The citizens of the best regime will also require, with a view to leisure alone, what Aristotle appears to call the 'virtue' of 'philosophy' (1334a16–28). . . . 'Philosophy' can mean one of two things. Either Aristotle is speaking of philosophy—theoretical speculation—in the precise sense, or he is speaking in a looser sense of what would today be called 'culture.' That philosophy in the precise sense can have been intended is, to judge from the argument of the opening chapter of Book VII, extremely unlikely, and Aristotle indicates in Chapter 14 itself that a capacity for speculative thought is not part of the equipment required of the citizens of the best regime."

In chapter 3 I asked if justice was proportion to virtue, it necessarily meant that the virtuous were to be rewarded by being given political office. Here those with unusual intellectual virtue neither have special political privileges nor immunities.

26. Kraut, *Aristotle: Politics, Books VII and VIII*, 63: "The debate between proponents of the philosophical and political lives is familiar from Plato's *Gorgias* 484c–486d, which was written about the time of Aristotle's birth; see too *Theaetetus* 172c–177b. As Plato's references to Euripides *Antiopē* indicate, the conflict between the two lives was a common topic of debate in the late fifth century." See also Amélie Oksenberg Rorty,

"The Place of Contemplation in Aristotle's *Nicomachean Ethics*," *Mind* (1978): 343–58, reprinted in Amélie Rorty, ed., *Essays on Aristotle's Ethics* (University of California Press, 1981), 378: "It is only in a corrupt polity that the contemplative life need be otherworldly, and only in a corrupt polity that the policies promoting the development and exercise of contemplative activity would come into conflict with those establishing requirements for the best practical life."

27. "One should not cultivate virtue as the polis of the Spartans does. For the difference between the Spartans and others is not that they consider different things to be the greatest goods, but that they believe that these goods are obtained by means of a particular virtue. And because they consider these goods and the enjoyment of them to be better than the enjoyment of the virtue, they train themselves only in the virtue that is useful for acquiring them, and ignore the virtue that is exercised in leisure" (VII.15.1334a40–b4). Simpson, *A Philosophical Commentary on the Politics of Aristotle*, 198: "If [goods of the soul] were simply useful then, according to the very idea of the useful, an excess of them, going beyond what they were useful for, would be harmful and useless. . . . They are of course useful with respect to acquiring and preserving the other goods, which is doubtless why he does speak of their usefulness alongside their nobility. For because their usefulness in this respect has no limit, usefulness cannot be the nature or essence of their goodness (as it is, say, in the case of instruments) but must be more like an overflow from what is the essence of their goodness."

28. This passage can be read as an attack on the *Republic*, since the formation of Plato's ideal state depends on cleansing an existing state of everyone over the age of ten.

29. Michael Stocker, "Some Problems with Counter-Examples in Ethics," *Synthese* 72 (1987): 281: "Some think that it is conceptual of the notion of *intrinsic value* that if a value *v* is intrinsic anywhere, it is intrinsic everywhere. Some also think that what is not good everywhere is, therefore, only instrumentally good where it is good. But these are simply confusions of *intrinsic* value with *absolute* or *unconditional* value."

30. The conditions for the best state can be ideal, but cannot be impossible (VII.4.1329b40). It would be "impossible that when a set of men are able to employ force and resist control, these should submit always to be ruled" (VII.9.1329a10–12).

31. For more on this theme, see my *Confronting Aristotle's Ethics*, chapter 5. "The absolutely good is absolutely desirable but what is good for oneself is desirable for oneself; and the two ought to come into agreement. This is effected by virtue; and *the purpose of politics is to bring it about* in cases where it does not yet exist" (*EE* VII.2.1236b38–40). Irwin, *Aristotle's First Principles*, 405: "The comprehensive character of the city gives a virtuous person reason to value it for its own sake, not simply because it is useful to him for other aims he already has. It extends the scope of practical reason and deliberation, as friendships do. Without the city I have to leave many aspects of my life to chance and external circumstances, since they will be out of my rational control."

32. Roochnik, "Aristotle's Defense of the Theoretical Life," 719: "If the practical life were counted as best, then the horizon for human activity would be the city itself. And if this were the case, if there were nothing beyond itself by which a city could be

guided, then its activity would be restricted to the reproduction, extension, or expansion of itself."

33. Salkever, "Whose Prayer?," sees the organization of Book VII somewhat differently. He sees a "double motion, a reconciliation of the quarrel between politics and philosophy on philosophy's terms . . . produced by the implicit dialogue between the prayer of the noble citizen in chapters 4–12 and the quite different voice of the theorist examining the relationship between political life and human virtue(s) in chapters 1–3 and 13–15," 34. See too at 35–36: "One central difference between the horizons of chapters 1–3 and chapters 13–15 on one hand and chapters 4–12 on the other is that the central chapters assert a parity between military and political life (see the end of 7.9, but compare the apparently lower rank of military prowess as compared with the ability to judge well in 7.8, 1328b), a parity explicitly denied by the chapters that bracket the city according to prayer. In the same way, the bracketing chapters are concerned with the virtues of human beings (and the relationship between the good male and the good human being), and the central chapters with the virtues of males (or with the relationship between the good male and the good citizen) only."

34. But see *Republic* II.372b: "For that healthy city is no longer sufficient, but we must proceed to swell out its bulk and fill it up with a multitude of things that exceed the requirements of necessity in states."

35. "It would be absurd if what is despotic and not despotic did not exist by nature" (VII.2.1324b36–37; recall 1267a11–12). One does not become happier by adding something good to an already existing happiness (*NE* I.7.1097b18–21). Herodotus offers an example, albeit a barbarian one, of the person of outstanding virtue becoming a tyrant. Deiokes wanted to rule over the Medes, and did so by acquiring a reputation for justice and righteousness. First they chose him as their judge, but then he said that he couldn't continue to mete our justice, since it was taking too much time away from his own affairs. When he withdrew, anarchy and robbery were rampant, and so the Medes went back to him and asked him to be their tyrant (I.96–100).

36. Roochnik, "Aristotle's Defense of the Theoretical Life," 728, offers another argument on Aristotle's behalf, that "too many people will lead to more poverty, which in turn leads to instability," citing 1265b9–12 and the assumption in 1279b37–38 that "the rich are everywhere few and the poor many."

37. The issue is of practical significance. Athens was so much larger than other Greek poleis that non-Athenians might have seen Athens as too big to be self-sufficient, and so inferred that it must be aiming at hegemony. Aristotle does not note this practical relevance. This issue is also the subject of several of the early numbers of the *Federalist Papers*, which aim at refuting the idea that republican and democratic states must be small. For one instance in which additional resources might make a state less self-sufficient, consider the decision of some countries not to develop or retain nuclear weapons.

Irwin, *Aristotle's First Principles*, 400: "The analogy with natural growth is useful only within limits. We might agree that the mature oak is the natural completion of the acorn and the sapling, because it gets no bigger than its mature, natural size. Aristotle cannot use this argument, since he admits that the city is not the largest community. He might argue that an animal may grow beyond its natural size; if we say it is too big, we have some conception of the proper functions and activities that are the final cause of normal growth and are impeded by excessive growth (1256b31–39, 1326b2–11)."

38. In "The Myth of the Civic Nation," 203, Yack asks, following Finley and others, "why there were no Greek nation-states." Political identity was then distinct from personal identity for the Greeks in a way that it is not today. Yack contrasts the blithe change of loyalties of Themistocles and Alcibaedes to the deep loyalty of Dreyfus. Yack concludes that "modern citizens are more loyal to, and more strongly identified with, their political commitments than their ancient Greek counterparts. . . . For the ancient Greeks, political community referred to the sharing of self-government, not to the identity-shaping cultural community modern citizens experience" (206).

39. Kraut's note seems right here: "When he says that 'in democracies, everyone shares in everything,' he means that in democracies performing one of these tasks (e.g., being a farmer) or failing to perform one (e.g., producing wealth) is no bar to performing any other the others (e.g., being a decision-maker). By contrast, in oligarchies, each task is restricted to those who do not perform certain others (e.g., those who have no property and therefore produce little wealth are not allowed to be decision-makers)." *Aristotle: Politics, Books VII and VIII*, at 130. See too Barker, *The Politics of Aristotle*, 302, n.3: "To understand this passage, we must remember that Plato in the *Republic* had deprived his guardians of property, and had vested property in the farming class. Aristotle would reverse this: he would vest property in the class which corresponds to Plato's guardians (the class concerned with arms and government), and he would make the farming class consist of landless and properytless labororers."

40. Newman and Simpson see the appeal to exoteric discourses here because it is more persuasive to audiences. I see it as showing that there is nothing specifically Aristotelian about the best life needed to establish this point. Newman, *The Politics of Aristotle*, 3: 309; Simpson, *A Philosophical Commentary on the Politics of Aristotle*, 297.

41. In particular, one of the necessary parts of the state in chapter 8 is a ready supply of wealth. In oligarchy, membership in that part of the state qualifies one for political office. In the best constitution, it doesn't disqualify one, as farming or crafts do. Is this a distinction without a difference?

42. "The stress on the necessity of good character for good political action led quite naturally to the politician's life as a whole being open to public scrutiny. For the expert Athenian politician, politics was a full-time occupation." Josiah Ober, *Mass and Elite in Democratic Athens: Rhetoric, Ideology and the Power of the People* (Princeton: Princeton University Press, 1989), 127.

43. Contrast Irwin's criticism of Aristotle here in *Aristotle's First Principles*, 414–16.

44. Irwin, *Aristotle's First Principles*, 413: "While we want rational agency to be exercised in our lives, some types of exercise are preferable to others. We may exercise it even when we decide to make the best of a bad job, and when a less virtuous person would make the same choice. But we prefer the exercise of reason when we are free to do more than adapt ourselves to disagreeable conditions that we would rather avoid. We prefer the exercise of rational agency in conditions that allow its maximum extension and development in forming the character of our lives."

45. In addition to its not being clear whether the extant *Politics* is complete, commentators dispute the genuineness of the final paragraph. For a brief summary of the arguments, see Kraut, *Aristotle: Politics, Books VII and VIII*, 212–13.

46. One exception shows that education and *diagogē* are not identical. The young should be barred from watching comedies, while adult men can enjoy them without being harmed by them (1336b20–23). While Lord rightly says that *mousikē* has a wider scope than our cognate, music, in this section of the *Politics* Aristotle's attention is limited to what we mean by music. Lord, *Education and Culture*, 29.

47. *Pace* Solmsen, "Leisure and Play in Aristotle's Ideal State."

48. Wayne C. Booth, *For the Love of It: Amateuring and Its Rivals* (Chicago: University of Chicago Press, 1999), offers a contemporary analogy. Booth poses as the problem of the amateur the question of why anyone should do something that experts could do much better. One engages in a high form of activity, but is doomed not to do it very well, at least relative to others. Although he doesn't discuss it in these terms, part of the solution may be that there is a different sort of community between performer and audience in the case of amateurs and professionals.

49. Kraut, *Aristotle: Political Philosophy*, 228: "What is remarkable . . . about Aristotle's ideal city is that it is ruled by amateurs: people of ordinary ability who have learnt no abstruse science accessible only to those of rare intellectual talent."

50. Few people seem to have been persuaded by a similar argument made more recently. Robert Maynard Hutchins, *The Higher Learning in America* (New Haven: Yale University Press, 1936), 66: "Education implies teaching. Teaching implies knowledge. Knowledge is truth. Truth is everywhere the same. Hence, education should be everywhere the same."

51. I therefore disagree with Lord's claim that "genuine courage will be taught, it could seem, not by gymnastic of any kind but rather by music—or by a certain kind of music." Lord, *Education and Culture*, 59.

52. Collins, *Aristotle and the Rediscovery of Citizenship*, 160: "Whereas early in his discussion Aristotle largely posits political virtue as the aim of the best regime, he later establishes *diagogē* in leisure as its proper end (*Pol.* 1333a30–b5)."

CONCLUSION

1. My idea of "themes" has some affinities with Stephen Salkever's "questions." Stephen G. Salkever, "Teaching the Questions: Aristotle's Philosophical Pedagogy in the *Nicomachean Ethics* and the *Politics*," *Review of Politics* 69 (2007): 192–214, and Salkever, "Reading Aristotle's *Nicomachean Ethics* and *Politics* as a Single Course of Lectures." For example: "The question of the happiest or most choiceworthy way of life is a question opened anew at a number of places through the *NE* and the *Politics*, as late as the beginning of *Politics* 7. It is, for Aristotle, a permanent question to which there is no permanent universal solution. And it is this question that he wants to teach his audience to ask" (213).

2. Mill, *The Subjection of Women*, chapter 2, p. 95.

3. I argue in chapter 2 that the virtue that is the subject of Book II is liberality, so I don't think that the standard set of four virtues has any place at all in Aristotle's thinking. One place where Aristotle does treat these virtues as canonical is *Politics* VII.1.1323a28–33:

"Nobody would call a man ideally happy that has not got a particle of courage nor of temperance nor of justice nor of wisdom, but is afraid of the flies that flutter by him, cannot refrain from any of the most outrageous actions in order to gratify a desire to eat or to drink, ruins his friends for the sake of a farthing, and similarly in matters of the intellect is also as senseless and mistaken as any child or lunatic."

4. Aristotle's discussions of justice are the ultimate origin for Gallie's notion of "essentially contested concepts," just because understanding justice means understanding the permanent debates about it. W. B. Gallie, "Essentially Contested Concepts," *Proceedings of the Aristotelian Society* 56 (1955–56): 168–98. I earlier discussed this idea in "Essentially Contested Concepts: The Ethics and Tactics of Argument," *Philosophy and Rhetoric* 23 (1990): 251–70, and "Rhetoric and Essentially Contested Arguments," *Philosophy and Rhetoric* 11 (1978): 156–72. For details, see my "Growing Older and Wiser with Aristotle: *Rhetoric* II.12–14," in *Proceedings of the Boston Area Colloquium in Ancient Philosophy*, ed. John Cleary and William Wians, 171–200, Boston Area Colloquium in Ancient Philosophy, 10 (1994) (Lanham, MD: University Press of America, 1996).

5. Bernard Williams, *Shame and Necessity* (Berkeley: University of California Press, 1993), 128–29. See Fleischacker, *A Short History of Distributive Justice*, for an account of how distributive justice came, only relatively recently, to be concerned with distributing property as well as offices.

6. Bernard Williams, "Hylomorphism," in Williams, *The Sense of the Past: Essays in the History of Philosophy*, ed. and with an intro. by Myles Burnyeat (Princeton: Princeton University Press, 2006), 218–229, reprinted from *Oxford Studies in Ancient Philosophy 4: A Festschrift for J. L. Ackrill*, ed. Michael J. Woods (Oxford: Clarendon Press, 1986), 189–199, at 218.

7. What Jonathan Lear says about the *Ethics* seems to me equally true for the *Politics*. Lear, *Aristotle: The Desire to Understand*, 157–58: "The point of the *Nicomachean Ethics* is not to persuade us to be good or to show us how to behave well in various circumstances in life: it is to give people who are already leading a happy, virtuous life insight into the nature of their own souls. The aim of the *Ethics* is to offer its readers self-understanding, not persuasion or advice."

8. See, especially, *The Human Condition*.

9. "The true politician seems to have put more effort into virtue than into anything else, since he wants to make the citizens good and law-abiding" (I.13.1102a7–10). "The principal care of politics is to produce a certain character in the citizens, namely to make them virtuous, and capable of performing noble actions" (I.9.1099b29–32).

WORKS CITED

Apostle, Hippocrates George, and Lloyd P. Gerson, trans. *Aristotle's Politics*. Grinnell, IA: Peripatetic Press, 1986.

Arendt, Hannah. *Between Past and Future*. New York: Viking, 1961. See esp. chap. 7, "Truth and Politics."

———. *Eichmann in Jerusalem*. New York: Viking, 1963.

Balot, Ryan K. *Greed and Injustice in Classical Athens*. Princeton, NJ: Princeton University Press, 2001.

Barker, Ernest. *Greek Political Theory: Plato and His Predecessors*. London: Methuen, 1960.

———. *The Political Thought of Plato and Aristotle*. New York: Dover, 1959.

———. *The Politics of Aristotle*. Oxford: Oxford University Press, 1952.

Belfiore, Elizabeth. "Family Friendship in Aristotle's *Ethics*." *Ancient Philosophy* 21 (2001): 113–32.

Berent, Moshe. "Sovereignty: Ancient and Modern." *Polis* 17 (2000): 2–34.

Berlin, Isaiah. *Against the Current: Essays in the History of Ideas*. Edited by Henry Hardy. New York: Penguin, 1980.

———. "The Originality of Machiavelli." In *Studies on Machiavelli*, edited by Myron P. Gilmore, 147–206. Florence, It.: Sansoni, 1972. Reprinted in *Against the Current: Essays in the History of Ideas*, edited by Henry Hardy, 25–79. New York: Penguin, 1980.

Bodéüs, Richard. "L'attitude paradoxale d'Aristote envers la tyrannie." *Tijdscrift voor Filosofie* 61 (1999): 556–57.

———. "Law and the Regime in Aristotle." In *Essays on the Foundations of Aristotle's Political Science*, edited by Carnes Lord and David K. O'Connor, 234–48. Berkeley: University of California Press, 1991.

———. "The Natural Foundations of Right and Aristotelian Philosophy." In *Action and Contemplation: Studies in the Moral and Political Thought of Aristotle*, edited by Robert C. Bartlett and Susan D. Collins, 69–105. Albany: State University of New York Press, 2000.

———. "Le recherche politique d'après le 'programme' de l'*Éthique à Nicomaque* d'Aristote." *Études classiques* 51 (1983): 23–33.

Booth, Wayne C. *For the Love of It: Amateuring and Its Rivals.* Chicago: University of Chicago Press, 1999.

Boyd, Richard. *Uncivil Society: The Perils of Pluralism and the Making of Modern Liberalism.* Lanham, MD: Lexington Books, 2004.

Bradley, F. H. *Ethical Studies.* Oxford: Oxford University Press, 1927.

Burke, Edmund."On Conciliation with America." In *The Works of Edmund Burke*, 2: 99–186. Boston, 1881.

Burnyeat, Myles F. "Is an Aristotelian Philosophy of Mind Still Credible? A Draft." In *Essays on Aristotle's de Anima*, edited by Martha C. Nussbaum and Amélie Oksenberg Rorty. Oxford: Clarendon Press, 1992.

———. "The Truth of Tripartition." *Proceedings of the Aristotelian Society* 106 (2006): 1–23.

Charles, David. "Perfectionism in Aristotle's Political Theory: Reply to Martha Nussbaum." In supplement, *Oxford Studies in Ancient Philosophy* (1988): 185–206.

Clark, Stephen R. L. *Aristotle's Man: Speculations upon Aristotelian Anthropology.* Oxford: Clarendon Press, 1975.

Coby, Patrick. "Aristotle's Three Cities and the Problem of Faction." *Journal of Politics* 50 (1988): 896–919.

Collins, Susan D. *Aristotle and the Rediscovery of Citizenship.* Cambridge: Cambridge University Press, 2006.

Constant, Benjamin. "The Liberty of the Ancients Compared with That of the Moderns." In *Political Writings*, edited and translated by Biancamaria Fontana, 308–28. Cambridge: Cambridge University Press, 1988.

Cooper, John M. "Political Animals and Civic Friendship." In *Aristoteles' "Politik": Akten des XI. Symposium Aristotelicum*, edited by Gunter Patzig, 221–42. Gottingen, Ger.: Vandenhoeck & Ruprecht, 1990. Revised edition in *Aristotle's Politics: Critical Essays*, edited by Richard Kraut and Steven Skultety, 65–90. Lanham, MD: Rowman & Littlefield, 2005.

Davis, Michael. "Aristotle's Reflections on Revolution." *Graduate Faculty Philosophy Journal* 11 (1986): 46–63.

Depew, David. "Barbarians, Natural Rulers and Natural Slaves: Aristotelian Ethology Meets Aristotelian Psychology." Unpublished manuscript.

———. "Humans and Other Political Animals in Aristotle's *History of Animals*." *Phronesis* 40 (1995): 156–81.

———. "Politics, Music, and Contemplation in Aristotle's Ideal State." In *A Companion to Aristotle's Politics*, edited by David Keyt and Fred D. Miller, Jr., 346–80. Oxford: Blackwell, 1991.

Dewey, John. *Freedom and Culture.* New York: Capricorn Books, 1939.

Ehrenberg, Victor. *The Greek State.* London: Methuen, 1974.

Evrigenis, I. "The Doctrine of the Mean in Aristotle's Ethical and Political Thought." *History of Political Thought* 20 (1999): 410–14.

Farrar, Cynthia. *The Origins of Democratic Thinking: The Invention of Politics in Classical Athens.* Cambridge: Cambridge University Press, 1988.

Finley, M. I. *Authority and Legitimacy in the Classical City-State*. Copenhagen: Munksgaard, 1982.

———. *Politics and the Ancient World*. Cambridge: Cambridge University Press, 1983.

Fleischacker, Samuel. *A Short History of Distributive Justice*. Cambridge, MA: Harvard University Press, 2004.

Frank, Jill. *A Democracy of Distinction: Aristotle and the Work of Politics*. Chicago: University of Chicago Press, 2005.

Funkenstein, Amos. *Theology and the Scientific Imagination from the Middle Ages to the Seventeenth Century*. Princeton, NJ: Princeton University Press, 1986.

Gallie, W. B. "Essentially Contested Concepts." *Proceedings of the Aristotelian Society* 56 (1955–56): 168–98.

Garver, Eugene. "After *Virtù*: Rhetoric, Prudence, and Moral Pluralism in Machiavelli's *Discourses on Livy*." *History of Political Thought* 17 (1996): 1–29. Revised edition in *Prudence: Classical Virtue, Postmodern Practice*, edited by Robert Hariman, 67–98. University Park: Pennsylvania State University Press, 2003.

———. *Aristotle's Rhetoric: An Art of Character*. Chicago: University of Chicago Press, 1994.

———. *Confronting Aristotle's Ethics: Ancient and Modern Morality*. Chicago: University of Chicago Press, 2006.

———. "Essentially Contested Concepts: The Ethics and Tactics of Argument." *Philosophy and Rhetoric* 23 (1990): 251–70.

———. *For the Sake of Argument: Practical Reasoning, Character, and the Ethics of Belief*. Chicago: University of Chicago Press, 2004.

———. "Growing Older and Wiser with Aristotle: *Rhetoric* II.12–14." In *Proceedings of the Boston Area Colloquium in Ancient Philosophy*, edited by John Cleary and William Wians, 10: 171–200. Lanham, MD: University Press of America, 1995.

———. Review of *A Democracy of Distinction: Aristotle and the Work of Politics*, by Jill Frank. *Law, Culture, Humanities* 3 (2007): 493–95.

———. "Rhetoric and Essentially Contested Arguments." *Philosophy and Rhetoric* 11 (1978): 156–72.

Gerson, Lloyd. "Aristotle's Polis: A Community of the Virtuous." In *Proceedings of the Boston Area Colloquium in Ancient Philosophy*, edited by John Cleary, 3: 203–25. Lanham, MD: University Press of America, 1988.

Halper, Edward. "The Substance of Aristotle's Ethics." In *The Crossroads of Norm and Nature: Essays on Aristotle's Ethics and Metaphysics*, edited by May Sim, 3–28. Lanham, MD: Rowman & Littlefield, 1995.

———. "The Unity of the Virtues in Aristotle." *Oxford Studies in Ancient Philosophy* 17 (1999): 115–43.

Hamilton, Alexander, James Madison, and John Jay. *The Federalist Papers: Alexander Hamilton, James Madison, John Jay*. Edited by Ian Shapiro. New Haven, CT: Yale University Press, 2009. Also available at http://www.constitution.org/fed/federa10.htm.

Hansen, Mogens Herman. *Polis and City-State: An Ancient Concept and Its Modern Equivalent*. Copenhagen: Munksgaard, 1998.

———. *The Tradition of Ancient Greek Democracy and Its Importance for Modern Democracy*. Copenhagen: Royal Danish Academy of Sciences and Letters, 2005.

Hegel, G. W. F. *Philosophy of Right*. Translated by T. M. Knox. Oxford: Clarendon Press, 1942.

Herold, J. Christopher, ed. *The Mind of Napoleon*. New York: Columbia University Press, 1955.

Hobbes, Thomas. *Behemoth*. In *The English Works of Thomas Hobbes of Malmesbury*, 6: 161–418. London, 1841.

Hobbs, Angela. *Plato and the Hero: Courage, Manliness and the Impersonal Good*. Cambridge: Cambridge University Press, 2000.

Holmes, Stephen. "Aristippus in and out of Athens." *American Political Science Review* 73 (1979): 113–28.

Hunt, Lynn. *Inventing Human Rights*. New York: Norton, 2007.

Hutchins, Robert Maynard. *The Higher Learning in America*. New Haven, CT: Yale University Press, 1936.

Ignatieff, Michael. *Human Rights as Politics and Idolatry*. Princeton, NJ: Princeton University Press, 2001.

Irwin, Terence H., trans. *Aristotle: Nicomachean Ethics*. Indianapolis, IN: Hackett, 1985.

———. *Aristotle's First Principles*. Oxford: Oxford University Press, 1988.

Isenberg, Arnold. "Natural Pride and Natural Shame." In *Explaining Emotions*, edited by Amélie Oksenberg Rorty, 355–383. Berkeley: University of California Press, 1980.

Johnson, Curtis. *Aristotle's Theory of the State*. New York: St. Martin's Press, 1990.

Kahn, Paul W. *Out of Eden: Adam and Eve and the Problem of Evil*. Princeton, NJ: Princeton University Press, 2007.

———. *Putting Liberalism in Its Place*. Princeton, NJ: Princeton University Press, 2005.

———. *Sacred Violence: Torture, Terror, and Sovereignty*. Ann Arbor: University of Michigan Press, 2008.

———. "Torture and Democratic Violence." *Ratio Juris* 22 (2009): 244–59.

Kammen, Michael G. *A Machine That Would Go of Itself: The Constitution in American Culture*. New York: Knopf, 1986.

Kant, Immanuel. "Perpetual Peace." In *Kant's Political Writings*, edited by Hans Reiss, 93–130. Cambridge: Cambridge University Press, 1991.

Kateb, George. "Hobbes and the Irrationality of Politics." *Political Theory* 17 (1989): 355–91.

Kennedy, George A., trans. *Aristotle: On Rhetoric: A Theory of Civic Discourse*. New York: Oxford University Press, 1991.

Keyt, David, trans. *Aristotle: Politics, Books V and VI*. Oxford: Clarendon Press, 1999.

———. "Aristotle's Theory of Distributive Justice." In *A Companion to Aristotle's Politics*, edited by David Keyt and Fred D. Miller, Jr., 238–78. Oxford: Blackwell, 1991.

———. "Distributive Justice in Aristotle's *Ethics* and *Politics*." *Topoi* 4 (1985): 23–45.

———. "Supplementary Essay." In *Aristotle: Politics, Books III and IV*, edited by David Keyt and translated by Richard Robinson, 125–48. Oxford: Clarendon Press, 1995.

———. "Three Fundamental Theorems in Aristotle's Politics." *Phronesis* 32, no. 1 (1987): 54–79.

Kraut, Richard. *Aristotle: Political Philosophy*. Oxford: Oxford University Press, 2002.

———, trans. *Aristotle: Politics, Books VII and VIII*. Oxford: Clarendon Press, 1997.

Kullmann, Wolfgang. "Man as a Political Animal in Aristotle." In *A Companion to Aristotle's Politics*, edited by David Keyt and Fred D. Miller, Jr., 94–117. Oxford: Blackwell, 1991.

Langbein, John H. "The Legal History of Torture." In *Torture*, edited by Sanford Levinson, 93–104. Oxford: Oxford University Press, 2004.

Larmore, Charles. *The Autonomy of Morality*. Cambridge: Cambridge University Press, 2008.

———. *The Morals of Modernity*. Cambridge: Cambridge University Press, 1996.

Lear, Jonathan. *Aristotle: The Desire to Understand*. Cambridge: Cambridge University Press, 1988.

Lewis, Thomas J. "Acquisition and Anxiety: Aristotle's Case against the Market." *Canadian Journal of Economics* 11 (1978): 69–90.

Lincoln, Abraham. "Fragment on Slavery." In *Collected Works of Abraham Lincoln*, edited by Roy P. Basler, 2: 222–23. New Brunswick, NJ: Rutgers University Press, 1953.

Lockwood, T. C. "Polity, Political Justice and Political Mixing." *History of Political Thought* 27 (2006): 207–22.

Lord, Carnes, trans. *Aristotle: The Politics*. Chicago: University of Chicago Press, 1984.

———. *Education and Culture in the Political Thought of Aristotle*. Ithaca, NY: Cornell University Press, 1982.

Machiavelli, Niccolo. Preface to Book II. In *Discourses on Livy*, translated by Harvey C. Mansfield and Nathan Tarcov, 123–24. Chicago: University of Chicago Press, 1996.

Mansfield, Harvey. "Commentary on [Lloyd] Gerson." In *Proceedings of the Boston Area Colloquium in Ancient Philosophy*, edited by John J. Cleary, 3: 226–229. Lanham, MD: University Press of America, 1988.

Margalit, Avishai. *On Compromise and Rotten Compromise*. Princeton, NJ: Princeton University Press, 2010.

Mathie, William. "Political and Distributive Justice in the Political Science of Aristotle." *Review of Politics* 49 (1987): 59–84.

McKeon, Richard. "Aristotle's Conception of Moral and Political Philosophy." *Ethics* 51 (1941): 253–90.

Meikle, Scott. *Aristotle's Economic Thought*. Oxford: Clarendon Press, 1995.

Mill, John Stuart. *On Liberty*. Indianapolis, IN: Hackett, 1978.

———. "The Subjection of Women." In *Essays on Politics and Society*, edited by J. M. Robson. Toronto: University of Toronto Press, 1977.

Miller, Fred D., Jr. "Aristotelian Statecraft and Modern Politics." In *Aristotle's Politics Today*, edited by Lenn E. Goodman and Robert B. Tallisse, 13–32. Albany: State University of New York Press, 2007.

———. *Nature, Justice, and Rights in Aristotle's Politics*. Oxford: Clarendon Press, 1995.

Morrison, Donald. "Aristotle's Definition of Citizenship: A Problem and Some Solutions." *History of Philosophy Quarterly* 16, no. 22 (1999): 144–46.

Mulgan, R. G. "Aristotle's Doctrine that Man is a Political Animal." *Hermes* 104 (1974): 438–45.

———. *Aristotle's Political Theory: An Introduction for Students of Political Theory*. Oxford: Clarendon Press, 1977.

Murray, Oswyn. "*Polis* and *Politeia* in Aristotle." In *The Ancient Greek City-State*, edited by Mogens Herman Hansen, 197–210. Copenhagen: Royal Danish Academy of Sciences and Letters, 1993.

Newell, W. R. "Superlative Virtue: The Problem of Monarchy in Aristotle's Politics." In *Essays on the Foundations of Aristotelian Political Science*, edited by Carnes Lord and David K. O'Connor, 191–211. Berkeley: University of California Press, 1991.

Newman, W. L., trans. *The Politics of Aristotle*. 4 vols. Oxford, 1887–1902. Reprint, New York: Arno Press, 1973.

Nichols, Mary P. *Citizens and Statesmen: A Study of Aristotle's Politics*. Savage, MD: Rowman & Littlefield, 1992.

Nightingale, Andrea Wilson. *Spectacles of Truth in Classical Greek Philosophy: Theoria in Its Cultural Context*. Cambridge: Cambridge University Press, 2004.

Nussbaum, Martha. "Nature, Function, and Capability: Aristotle on Political Deliberation." In supplement, *Oxford Studies in Ancient Philosophy* (1988): 145–84.

Ober, Josiah. "Aristotle's Natural Democracy." In *Aristotle's Politics*, edited by Richard Kraut and Steven Skultety. Lanham, MD: Rowman & Littlefield, 2008.

——. *The Athenian Revolution: Essays on Ancient Greek Democracy and Political Theory*. Princeton, NJ: Princeton University Press, 1996.

——. "The Debate over Civil Education in Classical Athens." In *Education in Greek and Roman Antiquity*, edited by Yun Lee Too. Boston: Brill, 2001.

——. *Mass and Elite in Democratic Athens: Rhetoric, Ideology and the Power of the People*. Princeton, NJ: Princeton University Press, 1989.

——. *Political Dissent in Democratic Athens*. Princeton, NJ: Princeton University Press, 1998.

O'Connor, David K. "Wilt versus Russell: Excellence on the Hardwood." In *Basketball and Philosophy: Thinking Outside the Paint*, edited by Jerry L. Walls and Gregory Bassham, 116–28. Lexington: University Press of Kentucky, 2007.

Pellegrin, Pierre, trans. *Aristote: Les politiques*. 2nd ed. Paris: GF-Flammarion, 1993.

Polansky, Ronald. "Aristotle on Political Change." In *A Companion to Aristotle's Politics*, edited by David Keyt and Fred D. Miller, Jr., 323–45. Oxford: Blackwell, 1991.

Putnam, Hilary, and Martha Nussbaum. "Changing Aristotle's Mind." In *Words and Life*, edited by James Conant, 22–61. Cambridge, MA: Harvard University Press, 1994.

Rawls, John. *Political Liberalism*. Rev. ed. New York: Columbia University Press, 2005.

——. *A Theory of Justice*. Cambridge, MA: Belknap Press, 1971.

Raz, Joseph. "Disagreement in Politics." *American Journal of Jurisprudence* 43 (1998): 25–52.

Reeve, C. D. C., trans. *Aristotle: Politics*. Indianapolis, IN: Hackett, 1998.

Robinson, Richard, ed. and trans. *Aristotle: Politics, Books III and IV*. Oxford: Clarendon Press, 1962. Revised edition 1995.

Roochnik, David. "Aristotle's Defense of the Theoretical Life: Comments on *Politics* 7." *Review of Metaphysics* 61 (2008): 711–735.

Rorty, Amélie Oksenberg. "The Place of Contemplation in Aristotle's *Nicomachean Ethics*." *Mind* (1978): 343–58. Reprinted in *Essays on Aristotle's Ethics*, edited by Amélie Oksenberg Rorty, 377–94. Berkeley: University of California Press, 1981.

Ross, William David, ed. *Aristotelis Politica*. Oxford: Clarendon Press, 1957.

———. *The Right and the Good*. Oxford: Clarendon Press, 1930.

Rousseau, Jean-Jacques. "Discourse of the Origins of Inequality." In *Basic Political Writings*, translated by Donald A. Cress, 25–110. Indianapolis, IN: Hackett, 1988.

Rui, Zhu. "Equality in Worth as a Pre-Condition for Justice in Greek Thought." *History of Political Thought* 24 (2003): 1–15.

Ryan, Alan. *Property and Political Theory*. Oxford: Blackwell, 1984.

Sahlins, Marshall. "Structural Work: How Microhistories Become Macrohistories and Vice Versa." *Anthropological Theory* 5 (2005): 5–30.

Salkever, Stephen G. "Aristotle's Social Science." *Political Theory* 9 (1981): 479–508.

———. "Reading Aristotle's *Nicomachean Ethics* and *Politics* as a Single Course of Lectures: Rhetoric, Politics, Philosophy." In *The Cambridge Companion to Ancient Greek Political Thought*, edited by Stephen Salkever, 209–42. Cambridge: Cambridge University Press, 2009.

———. "Teaching the Questions: Aristotle's Philosophical Pedagogy in the *Nicomachean Ethics* and the *Politics*." *Review of Politics* 69 (2007): 192–214.

———. "Whose Prayer? The Best Regime of Book 7 and the Lessons of Aristotle's *Politics*." *Political Theory* 35 (2007): 29–46.

Saxonhouse, Arlene W. *Athenian Democracy: Modern Mythmakers and Ancient Theorists*. Notre Dame, IN: University of Notre Dame Press, 1996.

———. *Fear of Diversity: The Birth of Political Science in Ancient Greek Thought*. Chicago: University of Chicago Press, 1992.

Schlaifer, Robert. "Greek Theories of Slavery from Homer to Aristotle." In supplement, *Harvard Studies in Classical Philology* (1941): 451–70. Reprinted in *Slavery in Classical Antiquity*, edited by M. I. Finley, 93–132. Cambridge: Heffer, 1960.

Schofield, Malcolm. "Ideology and Philosophy in Aristotle's Theory of Slavery." In *Aristoteles' "Politik": Akten des XI. Symposium Aristotelicum*, edited by Gunter Patzig, 1–27. Gottingen, Ger.: Vandenhoeck & Ruprecht, 1990.

Shay, Jonathan. *Odysseus in America: Combat Trauma and the Trials of Homecoming*. New York: Scribner, 2002.

Sidgwick, Henry. *The Methods of Ethics*. Indianapolis, IN: Hackett, 2007. First published 1907 by Macmillan.

Simpson, Peter. "Contemporary Virtue Ethics and Aristotle." *Review of Metaphysics* 45 (1992): 503–24.

———. *A Philosophical Commentary on the Politics of Aristotle*. Chapel Hill: University of North Carolina Press, 1998.

Smith, Adam. *An Inquiry into the Nature and Causes of the Wealth of Nations, Vol. I*. Indianapolis: Liberty Fund, 1981. *Reprint of the Glasgow Edition of the Works and Correspondence of Adam Smith, Vol 2a, edited by R. H. Campbell and A. S. Skinner. New York: Oxford University Press, 1976. See esp. chap. 2, "Of the Principle which gives occasion to the Division of Labour."* http://oll.libertyfund.org/title/220/217387.

———. *The Theory of Moral Sentiments*. Edited by D. D. Raphael and A. L. Macfie. Oxford: Clarendon Press, 1976.

Solmsen, Friedrich. "Leisure and Play in Aristotle's Ideal State." *Rheinisches Museum* 107 (1954): 193–220.

Stalley, R. F. "Aristotle's Criticism of Plato's *Republic*." In *A Companion to Aristotle's Politics*, edited by David Keyt and Fred D. Miller, Jr., 182–99. Oxford: Blackwell, 1991.

Stigen, Anfinn. *The Structure of Aristotle's Thought*. Oslo, Nor.: Universitetsforlaget, 1966.

Stocker, Michael. "Some Problems with Counter-Examples in Ethics." *Synthese* 72 (1987): 277–289.

Sunstein, Cass R. "The Law of Group Polarization." In *Debating Deliberative Democracy*, edited by James Fishkin and Peter Laslett, 80–101. Oxford: Blackwell, 2003.

———. *Republic.com*. Princeton, NJ: Princeton University Press, 2001.

Tamanaha, Brian Z. *On the Rule of Law: History, Politics, Theory*. Cambridge: Cambridge University Press, 2005.

Thomson, Judith Jarvis. "The Right and the Good." *Journal of Philosophy* 94, no. 6 (June 1997): 273–98.

Vander Waerdt, P. A. "Kingship and Philosophy in Aristotle's Best Regime." *Phronesis* 30 (1985): 249–73.

———. "The Plan and Intention of Aristotle's Ethical and Political Writings." *Illinois Classical Studies* 16 (1991): 231–51.

———. "The Political Intention of Aristotle's Moral Philosophy." *Ancient Philosophy* 5 (1985): 77–89.

Wade, Nicholas. *Before the Dawn: Recovering the Lost History of Our Ancestors*. New York: Penguin, 2006.

Waldron, Jeremy. "Redressing Historic Injustice." *University of Toronto Law Journal* 52 (2002): 135–60.

———. "What Plato Would Allow." In *Theory and Practice: Nomos 37*, edited by Judith Wagner Decew and Ian Shapiro, 138–79. New York: New York University Press, 1995.

———. "The Wisdom of the Multitude: Some Reflections on Book 3, Chapter 11 of Aristotle's *Politics*." *Political Theory* 23 (1995): 563–84.

Walzer, Michael. "Drawing the Line: Religion and Politics." *Utah Law Review* 1999 (1999): 619–38.

Weber, Max. "Politics as a Vocation." In *From Max Weber*, edited by H. H. Gerth and C. Wright Mills, 77–128. New York: Oxford University Press, 1946.

Wechsler, Herbert. "Toward Neutral Principles of Constitutional Law." *Harvard Law Review* 73 (1959): 1–33.

West, Robin. "From Choice to Reproductive Justice: De-Constitutionalizing Abortion Rights." *Yale Law Journal* 118 (2009): 1394–1432.

Williams, Bernard. *The Sense of the Past: Essays in the History of Philosophy*. Edited by Myles Burnyeat. Princeton, NJ: Princeton University Press, 2006.

———. *Shame and Necessity*. Berkeley: University of California Press, 1993.

Wilsey, Sean. Review of *Service Included*, by Phoebe Damrosch. *New York Times Sunday Book Review*, November 18, 2007.

Wolff, Francis. "L'unité structrelle de livre III." In *Aristote politique: Études sur la Politique d'Aristote*, edited by Pierre Aubenque and Alonso Tordesillas, 289–314. Paris: Presses universitaires de France, 1993.

Wood, Ellen Meiksins, and Neal Wood. *Class Ideology and Ancient Political Theory: Socrates, Plato, and Aristotle in Social Context*. Oxford: Blackwell, 1978.

Yack, Bernard. "Community and Conflict in Aristotle's Political Philosophy." In *Action and Contemplation: Studies in the Moral and Political Thought of Aristotle*, edited by Robert C. Bartlett and Susan D. Collins, 273–92. Albany: State University of New York Press, 2000.

———. "The Myth of the Civic Nation." *Critical Review* 10, no. 2 (1996): 193–211.

———. *Problems of a Political Animal: Community, Justice, and Conflict in Aristotelian Political Thought*. Berkeley: University of California Press, 1993.

———. "A Reinterpretation of Aristotle's Political Teleology." *History of Political Thought* 12 (1991): 15–33.

INDEX OF NAMES